Anticipatory Action in Self-Defence

Kinga Tibori Szabó

Anticipatory Action in Self-Defence

Essence and Limits under International Law

T·M·C·ASSER PRESS

Springer

Dr. Kinga Tibori Szabó
Researcher
Forum for the Law of Armed Conflict and Peace Operations
University of Amsterdam
Amsterdam
The Netherlands

ISBN 978-90-6704-795-1 e-ISBN 978-90-6704-796-8
DOI 10.1007/978-90-6704-796-8

Published by T.M.C. ASSER PRESS, The Hague, The Netherlands www.asserpress.nl
Produced and distributed for T.M.C. ASSER PRESS by Springer-Verlag, Berlin Heidelberg

Cover design: eStudio Calamar, Berlin/Figueres

Printed on acid-free paper

Springer is part of Springer Science+Business Media (www.springer.com)

To my grandparents, János and Margit

Foreword

The concept of self-defence is beyond any doubt one of the most controversial issues in international law. In particular, the question whether the use of force in anticipation of armed action by the other party is permissible as falling within the concept of self-defence is hotly disputed. Some courage therefore is needed to entertain a new analysis of this problem and to offer new solutions to the seemingly elusive issue of the temporal dimension of self-defence. The author of the present book has shown this courage and in my view she has succeeded in offering new vistas.

She presents a thorough analysis of the concept of self-defence as it developed in the Western approach of law throughout the ages, right from the days of Greek and Roman civilisation until the adoption of the Charter of the United Nations which formally recognises the inherent right of self-defence. By focussing on two main research questions (1. is anticipatory action in self-defence part of customary international law? and 2. if so, what are its limits?), she succeeds in an admirable way to keep this analysis of virtually inexhaustible material both succinct and pertinent.

The method of research chosen by the author is lucid and transparent. The codification of the right of self-defence in Article 51 of the United Nations Charter is seen as a key moment. In order to ascertain what the drafters of Article 51 had in mind, it was necessary to examine what the content of the pre-Charter customary right of self-defence was and this is done according to the method of legal-historical research. The material on which this part of the study is based is rich and varied, consisting both of elements of legal doctrine as it developed in the relevant intellectual, political and religious context in its subsequent manifestations, and on various examples of state practice.

This enquiry leads to the conclusion that the customary rule of self-defence always had an intrinsic anticipatory aspect, which was limited by the requirements of necessity and proportionality, and must be sharply distinguished from so-called preventive self-defence.

At the time of the adoption of the Charter, the customary rule of self-defence thus had a clear and intrinsic anticipatory dimension and the second part of the research is therefore focussed on the question whether any new rule affecting the status of anticipatory action has emerged since 1945. This part of the study is based on comparative case studies. In this respect, the author deals with anticipatory action in 'conventional' state-to-state conflicts, in situations where weapons of mass destruction are involved, and in cases of armed action against non-state actors where the 'accumulation of events' theory plays a preponderant role. And again her conclusion is that if a perceived threat of an armed attack creates a present and inevitable need to use force in order to stop the attack from taking place (the requirement of necessity) and if the force used is proportionate, anticipatory action in self-defence may be deemed lawful.

It is not to be expected that all controversies about the anticipatory element of self-defence will be solved on the basis of the findings in this book. But the author's final recommendation, viz. that more attention should be given by judicial and other law-related bodies as well as by legal doctrine to the analysis of the manner in which the three key elements she has identified in her study (conditionality of an armed attack, immediacy and proportionality) and which can be discerned both in pre- and post-Charter customary law, seems strikingly apposite in a world where the risks which endanger society have become ever more disparate and ominous.

April 2011

Pieter H. Kooijmans
Former Judge in the International Court of Justice

Acknowledgments

The present book could have not been written were it not for the generous financial support provided by the Netherlands Organization for International Cooperation in Higher Education—Nuffic, the University of Amsterdam and the T.M.C. Asser Instituut.

I am grateful to Prof. Dr. Terry D. Gill, who continuously encouraged the completion of this book and who offered invaluable advice throughout the writing process.

I owe my innermost gratitude to my family—János, Margit, Zoltán, Emese, Márti, Călin and David – for their relentless and continuously motivating support.

April 2011 Dr. Kinga Tibori Szabó

Content

Abbreviations

Bk.	Book
BMEWS	United States Ballistic Missile Early Warning System
Ch.	Chapter
CIA	United States Central Intelligence Agency
FBI	United States Federal Bureau of Investigation
GA	General Assembly (United Nations)
GA Res.	General Assembly Resolution (United Nations)
GAOR	General Assembly Official Records (United Nations)
IAEA	International Atomic Energy Agency
ICJ	International Court of Justice
ICTY	International Criminal Tribunal for the Former Yugoslavia
ILC	International Law Commission
IRBM	Intermediate-Range Ballistic Missile
ISAF	International Security Assistance Force
MRBM	Medium-Range Ballistic Missile
mtg.	Meeting(s)
NATO	North Atlantic Treaty Organization
OAS	Organization of American States
PLO	Palestine Liberation Organization
PKK	Kurdistan Workers' Party
Recueil de cours	Collected Courses of the Hague Academy of International Law
Repertoire	Repertoire of the Practice of the Security Council
Res.	Resolution
SAM	Surface-to-Air Missile
SC	Security Council (United Nations)
SC Res.	Security Council Resolution (United Nations)
SCOR	Security Council Official Records (United Nations)
Sess.	Session (s)
Supp.	Supplement
TLAM	Tomahawk Land Attack Missile

Vol.	Volume
UN	United Nations
UN Doc.	United Nations Document Series
UK	United Kingdom of Great Britain and Northern Ireland
UNMOVIC	United Nations Monitoring, Verification and Inspection Commission
US	United States of America
USSR	The Union of Soviet Socialist Republics
WMD	Weapons of Mass Destruction

Chapter 1
Introduction

1.1 Anticipatory Action in Self-Defence: A Controversial Concept

On 1 June 2002, at the West Point Military Academy graduation ceremony, the then US President George W. Bush declared that the Cold War doctrines of deterrence and containment were largely obsolete and that it was necessary to "take the battle to the enemy, disrupt his plans, and confront the worst threats before they emerge."[1] Three months later, on 9 September 2002, the then French President Jacques Chirac expressed his concern regarding the new doctrine. In his view, as soon as one nation claimed the right to take preventive action, other countries would naturally do the same.[2] Partially relying on the new doctrine, in March 2003, the United States invaded Iraq.

In April 2004, at the 98th annual meeting of the American Society of International Law, the "pre-emption doctrine" of the Bush administration was discussed by several panellists.[3] Whilst the new doctrine attracted both critical and acquiescing opinions, one of the speakers asserted that contemporary customary law left no room for pre-emptive or anticipatory self-defence *per se* and that such a right had to be viewed as a relic of the past.[4]

A few months later, in December 2004, a high-level UN panel delivered a report on issues of international security and use of force.[5] The panel concluded that "a threatened State, according to long established international law, can take military action as long as the threatened attack is imminent, no other means would

[1] Bush (1 June 2002) Graduation Speech at West Point.

[2] Interview With Jacques Chirac (9 September 2002).

[3] The Bush Administration Preemption Doctrine and the Future of World 2004, pp. 325–337.

[4] Zoller 2004, pp. 334–335.

[5] UN High-Level Panel 2004, para 188, p. 54.

K. Tibori Szabó, *Anticipatory Action in Self-Defence*, DOI: 10.1007/978-90-6704-796-8_1,

deflect it and the action is proportionate".[6] At the same time, the panel stopped short of endorsing unilateral preventive action against potential threats.[7]

In October 2005, a panel of authoritative British international lawyers adopted the *Principles of International Law on the Use of Force by States in Self-Defence*, according to which the view that States had a right to act in self-defence in order to avert the threat of an imminent attack was widely, though not universally, accepted. Hence, it was unrealistic in practice to suppose that self-defence always had to await an actual attack.[8]

In the same year, on 19 December 2005, the International Court of Justice delivered its judgment in the *Armed Activities in Congo* case. The Court declined to discuss the lawfulness of a response to the imminent threat of an armed attack, because the issue had not been raised by the parties, although the evidence adduced by Uganda showed the 'preventative nature' of many of its armed acts.[9]

These are just a few instances illustrating how anticipatory action in self-defence or, generally, the temporality of self-defence can produce considerably differing, if not outright conflicting views.

The legality of pre-emptive strikes is indeed one of the most controversial questions in contemporary international law. At the core of this controversy stands the temporal dimension of self-defence: When and for how long can a state defend itself against an armed attack? Can it resort to armed force before such an attack occurs? How does one define anticipatory action? Is anticipatory action covered by the rules of self-defence or should it be treated as a different concept?

Such questions have generated ample discussion among legal scholars and public officials alike. Claims of self-defence have often been criticised or condemned for transgressing the perceived limits of their temporal dimension. At the beginning of the second decade of the twenty-first century, the temporal boundaries of self-defence are still contentious and hard to pin down.

This book was written on account of the keenness of the author to contribute to the contemporary debate on these temporal limits, in general, and on the legality of anticipatory action, in particular.

The innovative mark of the present research is its comprehensive focus on the temporal dimension and, particularly, the anticipatory aspect of self-defence. By way of conclusion, the definition and limits of anticipatory action in self-defence are incorporated into an accessible formula.

---

[6] Ibid., para 188.

[7] Ibid., paras 190–191. For criticism of the findings of the panel, see Corten 2007, 217–232.

[8] The Chatham House Principles 2006, p. 964.

[9] Armed Activities in Congo 2005, para 143. Some authors maintain, however, that the ICJ has implicitly rejected anticipatory action in self-defence. Détais 2007, pp. 164–166.

1.2 The Temporal Controversy of the Right of Self-Defence

The right of self-defence is widely acknowledged today as one of the two exceptions to the prohibition to use force enshrined in the United Nations Charter (hereafter, 'Charter' or 'UN Charter').[10]

Article 2(4) of the Charter states that all Member States have to refrain in their international relations from the threat or use of force against the territorial integrity or political independence of any state, or in any other manner inconsistent with the purposes of the United Nations.[11] The customary nature of this prohibition was acknowledged by the International Court of Justice (hereafter, ICJ or 'Court') in 1986, in its *Nicaragua* judgment.[12]

Article 51 of the UN Charter consecrated the right of self-defence as an exception to the prohibition to use force. It reads:

> Nothing in the present Charter shall impair the inherent right of individual or collective self-defence if an armed attack occurs against a Member of the United Nations, until the Security Council has taken measures necessary to maintain international peace and security. Measures taken by Members in the exercise of this right of self-defence shall be immediately reported to the Security Council and shall not in any way affect the authority and responsibility of the Security Council under the present Charter to take at any time such action as it deems necessary in order to maintain or restore international peace and security.

The Charter-based content of the right of self-defence thus allows states to undertake military action in case of an armed attack, provided that the endeavour is reported to the Security Council (hereafter, SC or 'Council') and as long as that action does not affect the Council's authority to take measures.

Complementary to the treaty-based description of self-defence is the customary concept of the right that is often used to complement Article 51:

> Article 51 of the Charter is only meaningful on the basis that there is a "natural" or "inherent" right of self-defence, and it is hard to see how this can be other than of a customary nature, even if its present content has been confirmed and influenced by the Charter.[13]

---

[10] See, for instance, Brownlie 1963, p. 265; Dixon 2000, p. 297; Neff 2005, pp. 316–317, Simma 1995, p. 663.

[11] According to Chapter VII of the UN Charter, the other main exception to the general prohibition to use force is the Security Council-controlled collective enforcement action. Also, there is a growing literature discussing humanitarian intervention as a possible third exception to the prohibition. See, for instance, Evans 2008; Lillich 1986; Tesón 2005.

[12] Nicaragua 1986, paras 185–186, 188, 292(4). See *infra* 11.4.4 for main discussion. The major part of the literature agrees with the interpretation of the Court: Dixon 2000, pp. 296–297; Dinstein 2005, p. 92; Gray 2008, p. 30; Schachter 1991, pp. 130–131.

[13] Nicaragua 1986, para 176.

On the basis of this complementary relationship, the vast majority of legal literature acknowledges the customary principles of necessity and proportionality as limits of the right of self-defence.[14]

Notwithstanding the recognition of such common grounds, many controversies arise from the wording of Article 51 and the consequences of its relationship with customary law. The principal disagreements regarding the contemporary understanding of self-defence pertain to the definition of the term 'armed attack', the application of the principles of necessity and proportionality and the temporal dimension of the defensive action.

The lack of a definition of 'armed attack' in Article 51 has led to numerous questions as to what is covered by the term.[15] The relationship between the concepts of 'aggression' and 'armed attack' is still not clarified.[16] Opinions differ as to what the gravity threshold of an armed attack is.[17] Some authors maintain that the term only has an illustrative role and that also other—milder—forms of the use of force can trigger the exercise of self-defence.[18] Other commentators assert that armed attack denotes only the most serious forms of the use of force and that small incidents cannot serve as basis for the exercise of self-defence.[19] Furthermore, there is still legal uncertainty as regards the applicability of the term to armed acts carried out by non-state actors.[20]

Some authors contend that self-defence can only be exercised against states.[21] A significant part of the legal doctrine disagrees with that contention.[22]

Although both the principle of necessity and that of proportionality are acknowledged today as regulating the right of self-defence, their precise application is still disputed.[23] Necessity is constantly—'almost as an

[14] Dixon 2000, p. 300; Gardam 1993, p. 391; Gardam 2004; Malanczuk 1997, pp. 316–317; Simma 1995, p. 677. Some authors have rejected these limitations: Kunz 1947, p. 872.

[15] Bowett 1958, pp. 187–188; Higgins 1963, pp. 204–205; Malanczuk 1987, pp. 243–244; McDougal and Feliciano 1961, pp. 238–240; Alexandrov 1996, pp. 96–101; Lubell 2010, p. 50; Ruys 2010, pp. 53–68.

[16] For instance, the Tokyo Tribunal held that the Netherlands was entitled to defend itself against a Japanese war of aggression (see *infra* 7.5). In the *Nicaragua* case, the ICJ used Article 3 of GA Res. 3314, Definition of Aggression to elucidate on the meaning of 'armed attack'. Nicaragua 1986, para 195. For main discussion see *infra* 11.1. See also: Alexandrov 1996, pp. 105–120; Constantinou 2000, pp. 57–62; Malanczuk 1987, p. 244; Ruys 2010, pp. 127–139.

[17] See, for instance: Constantinou 2000, pp. 63–64, 74–75; Green 2009, pp. 41–42; Lubell 2010, pp. 48–55.

[18] Bowett 1958, pp. 187–188; McDougal 1963, pp. 599–600; Waldock 1962, pp. 233–235.

[19] Cassese 2005, p. 354; Corten 2008, pp. 619–620; Higgins 1963, pp. 204–205; Gray 2008, pp. 147–148; Kunz 1947, p. 878.

[20] See, for instance: Lubell 2010, pp. 30–36; Ruys 2010, pp. 485–489.

[21] Cassese 2001, p. 997. He later changed his opinion: Cassese 2005, p. 355; Kunz 1947, p. 878.

[22] Franck 2002, p. 67; Higgins 1963, pp. 204–205; Kooijmans 2009, p. 465; Lubell 2010, p. 31; Schwebel 1972, p. 482.

[23] Gardam 1993, p. 404; Gardam 2004, pp. 149, 155; Green 2009, p. 75; Higgins 1963, pp. 198–199; Schachter 1992, p. 39; Ruys 2010, pp. 110–116.

incantation'[24]—mentioned in relation to post-Charter self-defence, but its exact content and significance is by no means clear.[25] Proportionality has been discussed both from a more quantitative and a more qualitative perspective. In other words, both the scale and effect of the armed attack suffered (or expected) and the force needed to ward off the danger have played a role in assessing a proportionate action.[26]

The specific meaning attributed to the phrase 'if an armed attack occurs' (*dans le cas où un Membre des Nations Unies est l'objet d'une agression armée*, in the French version) used in Article 51 has produced ample debate as to the temporal dimension of the defensive action. A part of the legal doctrine adopts the view that Article 51, as an exception to the general prohibition to use force, must be interpreted restrictively as forbidding anticipatory action.[27] Relying on the customary basis of self-defence, other authors justify anticipatory action in self-defence against an imminent threat on the basis of the 1841 'Webster-formula'.[28] Another part of the literature promotes the legitimacy of 'preventive self-defence' against a threat that is rather potential than immediate.[29] The wording of Article 51 has also had an impact on remedial action in self-defence. Accordingly, some authors have maintained that self-defence ceases as a right when the armed attack has achieved its purpose and can only be exercised while the attack is still in progress.[30] That view was contested by other commentators as untenable in interstate relations.[31]

The focus of this book is the temporal controversy concerning the right of self-defence and, in particular, the legality and limits of anticipatory action in self-defence. It must be emphasized, though, that a thorough analysis of the contentions relating to the temporal controversy cannot be conducted without taking into consideration the other controversies related to self-defence. Anticipatory action in

---

[24] Gardam 2004, p. 149.

[25] Ibid., pp. 149–153.

[26] Ibid., pp. 156–159; Gray 2004, p. 121; Henkin 1995, p. 121; Higgins 1963, p. 201; McDougal and Feliciano 1961, p. 242; Schachter 1991, pp. 153–155; Waldock 1952, p. 464.

[27] Abi Saab 1987, p. 371; Badr 1980, p. 25; Brownlie 1963, pp. 275–278; Cassese 2005, pp. 361–362 (Cassese offers *de lege ferenda* proposal for a possible future regulation of 'anticipatory self-defence', ibid., pp. 362–363); Constantinou 2000, pp. 120–121; Corten 2008, p. 619; Gray 2004, pp. 98–99; Henkin 1991; Jessup 1948, p. 166; Kolesnik 1989, p. 154; Kunz 1947, p. 878; Ruys 2010, pp. 259–262.

[28] Bowett 1958, pp. 188–189; Fleck 1988, pp. 176–177; Higgins 1963, p. 199; Malanczuk 1987, pp. 247–248; McDougal and Feliciano 1961, pp. 231–236; Schachter 1991, pp. 150–152; Schwebel 1972, p. 481; Waldock 1952, pp. 497–499.

[29] Hill 2004, pp. 329–331; Pierson 2004, pp. 154–155; Taft and Buchwald 2003, pp. 557–563; Wedgwood 2003, pp. 584; Yoo 2003, pp. 571–574.

[30] Badr 1980, p. 25; Badr Myjer and White 2002, p. 7. Abi Saab contends that if the armed attack is instant (such as a bombardment or short incursion), self-defence cannot be exercised after the attack finishes. Self-defence against occupation, however, can be exercised, because that constitutes an attack extended in time. Abi Saab 1987, p. 373.

[31] Gill 2007, pp. 152–154; Schachter 1991, p. 153.

self-defence is intrinsically connected to the content and temporal dimension of the right of self-defence *per se*. The temporal dimension of self-defence is further contingent on what constitutes an armed attack and on how necessity and proportionality are understood. Consequently, where need be, the present work will touch upon the discussions concerning the concept of 'armed attack' and will incorporate the principles of necessity and proportionality in its analysis.

As said above, the temporal controversy revolves around the moment when a state can defend itself against an armed attack. Three main opinion groups can be distinguished in this respect: those rejecting the legality of self-defence before an armed attack occurs, those justifying self-defence against an imminent threat and those advocating the legality of self-defence against potential threats.

The first group adopts the view that Article 51, as an exception to the general prohibition to use force, must be interpreted restrictively as forbidding anticipatory action.[32] Accordingly, it is asserted that self-defence before an armed attack was outlawed by the negotiators of Article 51.[33] Further, it is maintained that, by the time the Charter was adopted, customary law allowed only a narrow right of self-defence.[34] It is also contended that the adoption of the Charter was a crucial step forward for the regulation of the use of force and that many traditional norms were left behind.[35] It has also been asserted that because the actual invocation of the right to 'anticipatory self-defence' is rare in post-Charter state practice, such a legal basis for the use of force can hardly be maintained under customary international law.[36] Consequently, it is argued that even if the drafters of the Charter did not intend to outlaw anticipatory action, subsequent state practice, under the influence of the prohibition to use force, has done so.[37] Most authors belonging to this group distinguish between reactive/remedial self-defence and 'interceptive self-defence'.[38] Accordingly, 'an interceptive strike counters an armed attack which is in progress, even if it still is incipient'.[39] In other words, 'interceptive self-defence' covers the situation where an attack has been launched, but has not

---

[32] Abi Saab 1987, p. 371; Badr 1980, p. 25; Brownlie 1963, pp. 275–278; Cahier 1985, p. 73; Cassese 2005, pp. 361–362; Corten 2008, p. 619; Gray 2004, pp. 98–99; Henkin 1991, pp. 44–46; Jessup 1948, p. 166; Kunz, p. 878; Lachs 1980, pp. 162–164; Ruys 2010, p. 259; Wright 1963, pp. 560–561.

[33] Brownlie 1963, p. 275; Corten 2008, pp. 619–624; Christakis 2005, pp. 208–212; Gray 2004, p. 98; Kunz 1947, pp. 877–878; Ruys 2010, p. 260; Wright 1963, p. 560.

[34] Brownlie 1963, pp. 257–261; Christakis 2005, pp. 201–207; Gray 2004, p. 98.

[35] See *infra* 11.2.1. Summary Record of the 1627th ILC meeting, UN Doc. A/CN.4/SR.1627 (1980) para 3 (comment by Tsuruoka)..

[36] Brownlie 1963, p. 260; Christakis 2005, pp. 215–219; Gazzini 2005, p. 151; Gray 2004, p. 130; Henkin 1995, pp. 121–122.

[37] Brownlie 1963, p. 260; Corten 2008, pp. 630–631; Gray 2004, pp. 98, 130; Zoller 2004, pp. 333–337.

[38] Dinstein 2005, pp. 190–192; Gazzini 2005, pp. 151–153. See also: Abi Saab 1987, p. 371; Christakis 2005, pp. 211–212; Constantinou 2000, pp. 125–126; Corten 2008, pp. 626–627; Kolb 2004, pp. 123–125; Lachs 1980, p. 164; Ruys 2010, p. 266.

[39] Dinstein 2005, p. 191.

yet struck the target.[40] Such authors contend that, as opposed to anticipatory action, an interceptive strike is legal under Article 51, because an armed attack has already begun.[41]

The second group justifies anticipatory action in self-defence against an imminent threat on the basis of the 1837 *'Caroline* incident' which gave birth to the famous 'Webster-formula'.[42] Such authors maintain that the purpose of Article 51 was to preserve the customary understanding of the right, as prescribed by the Caroline criteria.[43] These authors also maintain that the *travaux préparatoires* do not show any intention in defining or restricting self-defence to instances where an armed attack has already occurred.[44] Some writers also point out that the French version of the phrase 'if an armed attack occurs' (*dans un cas où un Membre des Nations Unies est l'objet d'une aggression armée*) is considerably less restrictive.[45] This part of the legal doctrine often makes reference to specific instances of state practice that involved anticipatory action in self-defence and maintains, on their basis, that 'anticipatory self-defence' may still be lawful under strict conditions.[46] It is also contended by this group that modern warfare technology and modern threats make resort to anticipatory action in self-defence necessary.[47] Nonetheless, the meaning of the 'Webster formula', applied to contemporary reality, has given rise to many discussions and a continuous debate about the content of the customary right of 'anticipatory self-defence'.[48]

The third group promotes the legitimacy of 'preventive self-defence' against a threat that is rather potential than immediate.[49] The 2002 US National Security

---

40 Ruys 2010, p. 253.

41 Dinstein 2005, p. 191; Ruys 2010, p. 266.

42 Bowett 1958, pp. 188–189; Fleck 1988, pp. 176–177; Higgins 1963, p. 199; Malanczuk 1987, pp. 247–248; McDougal and Feliciano 1961, pp. 231–236; Schachter 1991, pp. 150–152; Schwebel 1972, p. 481; Waldock 1952, pp. 497–499. In a series of correspondence between the US and Britain, then US Secretary of State, Daniel Webster, called upon the British government to show 'a necessity of self-defence, instant, overwhelming, leaving no choice of means and no moment for deliberation' in order to justify the exercise of self-defence in the Caroline incident of 1837. Webster 1841, p. 1138.

43 Bowett 1958, pp. 188–189; Higgins 1963, p. 199; McDougal and Feliciano 1961, pp. 231–236; Schachter 1991, pp. 150–152; Schwebel 1972, p. 481; Waldock 1952, pp. 497–499.

44 Bowett 1958, p. 188; Dixon 2000, p. 301; McDougal and Feliciano 1961, pp. 234-235; Waldock 1952, p. 497.

45 Higgins 1963, p. 199; Waldock 1952, p. 497.

46 Fleck 1988, pp. 176–177; Franck 2002, pp. 107–108; Higgins 1963, pp. 199–203; Malanczuk 1987, pp. 247–248.

47 Malanczuk 1987, pp. 247–248; McDougal and Feliciano 1961, p. 238; McDougal 1963, p. 601; Schwebel 1972, p. 481.

48 Bowett 1958, pp. 188–189; Gazzini 2005, pp. 149–152; Greenwood 2003, pp. 12–16; Higgins 1963, pp. 199–200; Lubell 2010, pp. 43–44; McDougal and Feliciano 1961, pp. 231–240; Waldock 1952, p. 498; Schachter 1991, pp. 150–152.

49 Hill 2004, pp. 329–331; Pierson 2004, pp. 154–155; Taft and Buchwald 2003, pp. 557–563. Wedgwood 2003, pp. 584; Yoo 2003, pp. 571–574.

Strategy was based on this approach and advocated preventive action against potential threats posed by 'rogue states and terrorists'.[50]

The divisions between the various opinions presented above elucidate on three main lines of contention in the controversy regarding the temporal dimension of self-defence.

First, the manner in which Article 51 is interpreted proves to be at the core of the debate. Those favouring a restrictive approach as to the temporal dimension of self-defence, contend that Article 51 outlaws anticipatory action. In this respect, it is argued that the very wording of the Article excludes anticipatory action, because the conditional 'if an armed attack occurs' qualifies the entire sentence. Conversely, those advocating a permissive approach, contend that the wording of the article cannot be interpreted in isolation and that the intention of the parties also has to be taken in consideration. Those supporting the restrictive approach also submit that, by the time the Charter was adopted, the right of self-defence was narrow enough not to accommodate anticipatory action. On the contrary, the advocates of the permissive approach assert that the Webster-formula was still valid at the time of the adoption of the Charter.

Secondly, the co-existence of treaty law and custom as the dual basis of the right of self-defence is understood in different ways. Those denying the legality of anticipatory action in self-defence contend that even if the drafters of the Charter did not intend to outlaw anticipatory action, subsequent state practice, under the influence of the prohibition to use force, has done so. It is also maintained that the invocation of the right of anticipatory action in self-defence is so rare in post-Charter state practice that it can hardly be maintained as a legal basis for the use of force under customary international law. Conversely, those advocating a permissive approach assert that there are instances of state practice showing that, under strict conditions, anticipatory action could be legal.

Thirdly, the temporal limits of self-defence are differently interpreted by the various groups. Remedial self-defence limits the use of force against an ongoing armed attack or one that had just occurred. 'Interceptive self-defence' allows armed action against an armed attack that has been launched, but has not reached its target. 'Anticipatory self-defence' permits use of force against an imminent threat of an armed attack. 'Preventive self-defence' extends the legality of use of force against potential threats. The different approaches show the controversy surrounding these limits, their legality under contemporary customary international law and the conditions that need to apply for such limits to be respected. For the purpose of this analysis, purely reactive action in self-defence and 'interceptive self-defence' will be treated as remedial self-defence. There are three reasons for this. First, in both cases, an actual armed attack has already been launched. Secondly, in many instances it may be difficult to distinguish between an ongoing armed attack and one that commenced, but has not yet reached its destination. Thirdly, most authors who reject anticipatory action in self-defence acknowledge

50 US National Security Strategy 2002, Part V.

the legality of interceptive self-defence as an extension of the remedial dimension of the right.[51]

All three lines of contention raise important queries as to the legality and limits of anticipatory action in self-defence.

First, the contentions regarding the wording of Article 51 elucidate on two important questions regarding the temporal dimension of self-defence: What was covered by the concept at the time of the adoption of the Charter and what was the intention of the drafters with Article 51? The two questions are closely interrelated. In order to understand the drafters' intention as regards self-defence, one must clarify how the concept was viewed at the time. Accordingly, a legal–historical analysis is needed to explain the evolution of the right of self-defence and the form in which it was accepted as legal at the end of the Second World War. Further, a comprehensive analysis of the drafting process of Article 51 needs to be conducted and the various treaty interpretation approaches have to be applied in order to clarify the intention of the drafters at the conference.

Secondly, the controversy regarding the co-existence of treaty law and custom as the dual basis of the right of self-defence reveals two further questions as to the temporal dimension of the right: what qualifies as relevant post-Charter state practice and how should it be interpreted?

Thirdly, the debate concerning the temporal limits of self-defence elucidates another important question: if anticipatory action in self-defence is legal, can it be exercised against not only an imminent, but also a potential threat?

In order to answer these queries, two main research questions will be used to direct the present research. The controversies depicted above demonstrate that prime reliance on Article 51 of the Charter would not be practical. Since the International Court of Justice acknowledged that self-defence had a strong customary basis, it is self-explanatory that the research will focus on the customary content of the right. With that view in mind, two main research questions are identified:

1. Is anticipatory action in self-defence part of customary international law? (RQ1)
2. If an affirmative answer to the first question is established, what are the limits of anticipatory action in self-defence under customary international law? (RQ2)

The first research question will address the queries regarding the pre-Charter content of the right of self-defence, the intention of the drafters with Article 51 of the Charter and the interpretation of relevant post-Charter state practice. The aim of RQ1 is to elucidate on a pre-Charter concept of self-defence and trace the evolution and transformation of that concept as influenced by the adoption of the Charter and post-Charter state practice. Chapters 2–4 will embark on a legal–historical analysis of the pre-Charter concept of self-defence. Chapter 5 will contrast that concept with the intention of the drafters of Article 51 of the Charter.

---

[51] Dinstein 2005, p. 191; Gazzini 2005, pp. 151–153; Ruys 2010, p. 266.

Chapter 6 will conclude on the temporal dimension of self-defence at the time of the Charter. Chapters 7–11 will look at the evolution of relevant post-Charter state practice and will draw conclusions on its significance. Chapter 12 will outline the temporal dimension of self-defence in post-Charter customary law. Chapter 13 will draw the final conclusions as to the legality of anticipatory action in self-defence.

The second research question will address the controversy regarding imminent and potential threats as bases for the exercise of self-defence. Both the pre-Charter and the post-Charter concepts of self-defence will be examined to understand the evolution of the limits to anticipatory action. Chapter 6 will conclude on such limits regarding pre-Charter self-defence, whereas Chapter 12 will outline the temporal confines of post-Charter self-defence. Chapter 14 will analyse the anatomy of the contemporary limitations of anticipatory action in self-defence.

1.3 Structure and Methods of Research

The previous two sections were aimed at presenting the subject, focal points and main issues addressed in this book. This section will elaborate on the structure and the methods of research used. Apart from the present chapter, this book has three main parts. Part I (Chapters 2–6) will analyse the pre-Charter concept of self-defence. Part II (Chapters 7–12) will examine the post-Charter customary law on self-defence. Part III (Chapters 13–14) will address the two research questions on the basis of the findings of Parts I and II.

1.3.1 Explanation of Central Terms

Before embarking on the methodological aspects of the present research, some preliminary terminological explanations are necessary. First and foremost, the notion of 'self-defence' employed in this book refers to the right of *states* to use *armed* force in their defence. It does not refer to the right of self-defence of private persons under criminal law, unless explicitly specified (as will be done mostly in Part I). Likewise, the notion of self-defence employed in this research does not refer to non-forceful means of defending oneself. Furthermore, it is not identical to the notion of unit self-defence employed in military law.

The terms 'anticipatory' and 'pre-emptive' will be used interchangeably to denote defensive action against so-called imminent threats. 'Remedial' or 'reactive' action in self-defence will pertain to measures taken against an ongoing attack and after an armed attack has occurred. The same term will be used to denote a so-called interceptive strike, unless the resort to the specific term is deemed necessary.[52] 'Preventive self-defence' or preventive use of force will refer

---

[52] See *supra* 1.2.

to those instances where states employ the use of force against so-called potential threats.[53] It is important to note that this author does not consider that anticipatory/pre-emptive action is synonymous with preventive action.

1.3.2 Methods of Research

The research conducted in this book will be organized along the two main research questions identified.

The first research question explores whether anticipatory action in self-defence is part of customary international law. In other words, RQ1 inquires whether anticipatory action is part of the customary right of self-defence. The second research question is very much dependent on the first. Whilst RQ1 explores whether anticipatory action in self-defence is part of contemporary customary international law, RQ2 is put forward on the assumption that an affirmative answer to the former can be established. If that is not the case, RQ2 ceases to be a valid query. Accordingly, the second research question explores the limits of anticipatory action in self-defence under customary international law.

In order to answer the first research question, one has to look at the development of customary international law on self-defence. The right of self-defence within the international society of states has long been acknowledged as the basic, fundamental right of every member.[54] Therefore, contemporary customary law on self-defence is not the result of an instant creation; it is the product of centuries of state practice and doctrine.[55] The present research does not rely on the contention that the passage of a considerable amount of time is always needed for the formation of a customary rule.[56] It is rather maintained that the time needed to form a custom varies 'according to the nature of the case.'[57] The regulation of war (and, implicitly, self-defence) has for long been at the centre of the legal process and some of its aspects are deeply embedded in contemporary principles.[58] For that reason, in order to appreciate the underlying concepts in the current understanding of self-defence, attention has to be given to the development of the relevant customary rules. For the current content of the customary right of self-defence, the adoption of the UN Charter is seen as a key moment. It was then that the right of

---

[53] Hill 2004, pp. 329–331; Pierson 2004, pp. 154–155; Taft and Buchwald 2003, pp. 557–563. Wedgwood 2003, pp. 584; Yoo 2003, pp. 571–574.

[54] Bowett 1958, pp. 3–4; Twiss 1860, p. 11.

[55] For the nature and origins of self-defence, see Bowett 1958, pp. 4–8. See also Schachter for a succinct portrayal of the historical schools of thought regarding self-defence. Schachter 1991, pp. 135–136.

[56] This assertion can be deduced from the materialistic approach to customary law. For criticism of this school of thought, see Koskenniemi 1989, pp. 401–402.

[57] Waldock 1962, p. 44. See also D'Amato 1971, pp. 57–59; Tunkin 1958, pp. 9–10.

[58] Brownlie 1963, pp. 1–2.

self-defence was expressly acknowledged as the only legal exception to the unilateral use of force.[59] At the same time, as shown above, the adoption of the Charter gave rise to several controversies affecting the customary right of self-defence. The content of the right before and at the time of the adoption of the Charter is one such controversy. The intention of the drafters of Article 51 is a further contention. Likewise, the manner in which relevant post-Charter state practice should be interpreted is still open to debate. For these reasons, it proves to be pertinent to trace the evolution of customary law on self-defence in two phases: pre-Charter customary law and post-Charter customary law. For following the development of pre-Charter customary law on self-defence, the method of legal–historical research is the most practicable. For examining the evolution of post-Charter customary rules on self-defence, comparative case studies will be conducted based on different themes. The primary objective of the analysis of pre-Charter customary law is to assess whether anticipatory action was seen as part of the pre-Charter concept of self-defence. The examination of post-Charter customary law is primarily aimed at concluding whether any new customary rule affecting the status of anticipatory action has emerged since 1945. On the basis of these two findings, the answer to the first research question will be put forward: whether anticipatory action in self-defence is part of customary international law.

Since the second research question is dependent on the first, the research methods employed to address the latter are bound to be suitable solutions for the former as well. If it can be established that anticipatory action was seen as part of the pre-Charter customary right of self-defence, it will be necessary to assess its perceived limits. In order to demarcate those limits, the legal–historical research conducted for addressing RQ1 will also be employed to shed light on RQ2. Accordingly, if anticipatory action is found to be part of self-defence in the various, pre-Charter normative frameworks analysed, attention will be given to its acknowledged limits. If a recognizable pattern of such limits can be identified in pre-Charter customary law, then it will become evident how those limits were perceived at the time of the adoption of the Charter. In the case of post-Charter customary law, the comparative case study will continue to trace that recognizable pattern or will shed light on new factors affecting the limits of anticipatory action. On this basis, the answer to the second research question will be put forward: what the limits of anticipatory action in self-defence are under customary international law.

1.3.3 Pre-Charter Customary Law (Part I)

As regards the analysis of pre-Charter customary law, an important question that must be answered is how far back in time should the concept of self-defence be

[59] Ibid., p. 265; Simma 1995, p. 663; Neff 2005, pp. 316–317; Dixon 2000, p. 297.

traced. Examining the state of customary law at the time or just before the adoption of the Charter would not offer a clear picture on the content and temporal dimension of the customary right of self-defence. It is therefore necessary to trace how the relevant customary rules were formed over time and became accepted by sovereign rulers.

Apart from that, the reference made in Article 51 of the Charter to the 'inherent' (*naturel* in the French version) right of self-defence also serves as basis for reaching far back in time with the analysis of pre-Charter customary rules. The International Court of Justice acknowledged, as mentioned above, that the reference to 'inherent' denotes the customary basis of the right.[60] In other words, the right of self-defence referred to in Article 51 is that inherent, natural right that has always been available to the sovereign ruler or, in modern times, to the state. Consequently, in order to fully understand the concept of self-defence referred to in Article 51, one has to go back to its natural law roots and trace its evolution up to the moment of the adoption of the Charter. Only this way can a comprehensive picture be drawn on the content and temporal dimension of the pre-Charter customary right of self-defence. The roots of the natural law of self-defence can be traced back to ancient Greece, Rome and medieval Christianity. For that reason, the starting point of the analysis will be the natural law concept in ancient Greece that will be followed through the centuries until the adoption of the UN Charter.

There are obvious difficulties with mapping out such developments. The most apparent problem is the long time-span that needs to be examined. It is admittedly problematic to map out the myriad of political, religious and intellectual trends that shaped history for more than 2,000 years. Furthermore, it is difficult to make a representative selection of state practice and doctrine relevant to the evolution of the right of self-defence. Similarly, choosing the most authoritative primary sources is also a challenging task. For these reasons, it is paramount to choose the most suitable research method.

Traditional legal–historical writing has so far taken three main forms: epoch-based, principle-based and individual-oriented research.[61] Accordingly, some writers have focused on the succession of 'great historical epochs,' picturing international law as the instrument of state policies.[62] Other authors have examined the application and development of great principles through successive periods.[63] A third group has concentrated on individual persons and their impact on the history of international law.[64] The disadvantages of these approaches were

[60] Nicaragua 1986, para 176.

[61] Classification put forward by Koskenniemi 2001, pp. 61–66. On the state of methodology in the history of international law, see Hueck 2001, pp. 194–217.

[62] Koskenniemi mentions: Grewe 2000; Schmitt 1995; Ziegler 1994. For an appraisal of Ziegler's book, see Roelofsen 1993–1994, pp. 52–58. Roelofsen contends that it would have been desirable that Ziegler's excellent manual devoted more attention to international relations theory. Ibid., pp. 55–56.

[63] See for instance: Redslob 1923.

[64] See for instance: de la Pradelle 1950.

highlighted by Koskenniemi, who maintained that what was needed was a contextualisation of the legal ideologies or concepts within the intellectual, social and political environment in which they have operated.[65] The same need was highlighted by Hueck as well, who asserted that philosophical, theoretical and historical movements can be decisive in the formation of law and therefore history of law has to take them into consideration.[66]

The legal–historical research conducted in Part I will attempt to take into consideration these needs and to place the evolution of the pre-Charter customary law of self-defence in the relevant intellectual, political and religious context. For that purpose, the more general framework of rules in which self-defence developed as a concept must be highlighted. In other words, to understand how self-defence was viewed over time, the general framework in which war and the use of force were regulated must be considered as well.

When analysing the history of war regulation, many authors employ auxiliary concepts such as 'war convention',[67] 'war tradition',[68] 'conceptions of war',[69] 'legitimacy framework'[70] and 'legal framework'.[71] These auxiliary concepts are then employed to identify different phases in the history of war regulation. In this book, the notion of 'normative framework' will be employed to denote all those legal rules, social norms, religious, cultural and political principles as well as common practices that prescribed when, why and how to resort to war or any other use of force. It is important to note that this is not an exclusively legalistic framework—it also encompasses norms of non-juridical character as well as the common practices. Moreover, the normative frameworks identified will be those that had a certain 'international' characteristic. In other words, the elements of the normative frameworks were acknowledged across jurisdictions in the Western tradition.[72]

The normative framework will be used to highlight the main phases in the development of pre-Charter customary law on self-defence. First, the historical era and any key events or important intellectual, political, cultural or religious trends that had an impact on the interpretation given to war will be identified. Secondly, the main tenets of the normative framework will be described: how war was defined, how its nature was perceived and what its legitimate causes were. For that purpose, the writings of contemporaneous authors and, if available, the statements of public authority will be referred to. Thirdly, the concept of self-defence will be

---

[65] Koskenniemi 2001, p. 65.

[66] Hueck 2001, pp. 198–199.

[67] Walzer 2006, pp. 44 et seq.

[68] Bellamy 2006, pp. 2 et seq.

[69] Neff 2005, pp. 2 et seq.

[70] Bellamy 2006, pp. 8 et seq.

[71] Neff 2005, pp. 3 et seq.

[72] For different historical phases of 'international law', see Steiger 2001, pp. 180–193. For another classification, see Neff 2005, pp. 3–5.

given attention. The content and temporal dimension of the right will be examined in order to elucidate on the justifiability and limits of anticipatory action. The notion of normative framework will also aid the legal-historical research in identifying which elements of self-defence have been taken over from one phase to another and in what form.

Three main normative frameworks in the development of pre-Charter customary law of self-defence will be identified. Accordingly, Chapter 2 will examine self-defence as a natural law concept (from ancient Greece to the seventeenth century). Chapter 3 will look at self-defence as a measure short of war (seventeenth to nineteenth centuries). Chapter 4 will discuss self-defence as an exception to the prohibition of war (nineteenth century and early twentieth century). Chapter 5 will analyse the way the customary concept of self-defence was enshrined in the United Nations Charter.

Part I heavily relies on the writings of jurists, historians and other publicists. Preference is, however, given to contemporaneous writings (primary sources). There are few instances of state practice discussed in Chapters 2–4. First, it is admittedly difficult to select representative instances of state practice over a considerable period of time. Secondly, preference was given to those instances where exercise of self-defence was coupled with official statements on behalf of the parties to the conflict defining or characterizing self-defence. For that reason, the legal–historical research of Chapters 2–4 should be seen as an account of authoritative and representative writings (doctrine) supplemented by those instances of state practice that left explicit qualifications of the right of self-defence behind. Chapter 5 mainly uses as sources the travaux préparatoires of the 1945 United Nations conference at San Francisco.

On the basis of this legal–historical research, a comprehensive representation of the pre-Charter concept of self-defence, its content and temporal dimension will be offered. If it is established that anticipatory action was part of that concept of self-defence, a recognizable pattern of the limits of such action will be demarcated. The thus identified understanding of self-defence will be seen as the one taken into consideration by the drafters of the UN Charter in their negotiations on Article 51. The pre-Charter concept of self-defence will be further tested against the influence of post-Charter developments in Part II of this research.

1.3.4 Post-Charter Customary Law (Part II)

After establishing a pre-Charter content and temporal dimension of the right of self-defence, further analysis will be conducted to assess if and how that content altered under the influence of the UN Charter. For this purpose, several themes that characterized the post-World War II use of force will be used as the basis for comparison. Accordingly, besides the classic state-to-state conflicts, the novel security threats will be considered. The role of nuclear, chemical and biological weapons as well as the impact of non-state actors on the law governing the use of force will serve as specific themes on the basis of which state practice and doctrine will be interpreted. Likewise, the work of various UN organs connected to the right of self-defence will also be treated as a separate, influencing theme of the twentieth- and twenty-first-century laws on the use of force.

As a result, post-Charter customary law will be analysed on the basis of different, old and new themes of the twentieth and twenty-first centuries: state-to-state conflicts, weapons of mass destruction, non-state actors and UN work. Within these themes, several instances of state practice related to self-defence will be examined and compared. The analysis of these instances of state practice will be complemented with the contemporaneous doctrine and, if relevant, judicial decisions.

The list of selected instances of state practice of Part II is not exhaustive. The main consideration in selecting the cases was to offer a representative illustration of the circumstances in which claims of self-defence were contemplated or used. The common element in all cases examined is that a claim of self-defence (anticipatory, remedial or 'preventive') was at least contemplated by the government of the target state. The cases greatly differ in their outcome: acceptance, criticism or condemnation as apparent in the '(general) reaction'[73] of states and organizations. This outcome will be dependent on the variables of each case. Certainly, the factual circumstances of the individual cases will vary greatly. For the sake of comparison, however, a fixed set of juridical variables will be identified to test and explain the outcome of each case. These variables will be deduced from the limits of the concept of self-defence as identified in the conclusions of Part I. The use of these variables and the conduct of the comparative case study will be further elaborated in the introductory remarks of Part II. At this point, it is sufficient to note that each case will be analysed on the basis of these variables and each theme-chapter will draw the conclusions on their role. Furthermore, each theme-chapter will draw the conclusions on the content and temporal dimension of self-defence, as well as the status and limits of anticipatory action.

To prepare the analysis of post-Charter customary law on self-defence, Chapter 7 will depict the understanding given to self-defence and the prohibition to use force by the Nuremberg and Tokyo Tribunals. Chapter 8 will examine the state-to-state conflicts in which claims of self-defence were contemplated or used. Chapter 9 will look at the impact of weapons of mass destruction on the development of post-Charter self-defence. Chapter 10 will analyse the role played by non-state actors in shaping the content and temporal dimension of self-defence. Chapter 11 will examine the work of various UN organs (the General Assembly, the International Law Commission and the International Court of Justice) that affected in some way the post-Charter concept of self-defence. Chapter 12 of Part II will compare the findings of the previous chapters and will draw the conclusions on the temporal dimension of self-defence.

[73] See *infra* 1.4 for details on the understanding given to the term.

Part II will rely on the use of official documents (diplomatic correspondence, public statements, UN records and reports as well as other documents) and legal literature. In reproducing the reaction of states to a certain claim of self-defence, the discussions before the Security Council will be given particular attention. For that purpose, records of the Security Council meetings as well as annual repertoires of the Security Council practice will be used as the primary sources.

The aim of Part II is to assess whether the pre-Charter status and limits of anticipatory action have been altered in the post-Charter understanding of the temporal dimension of self-defence. Accordingly, Part II will examine whether any new customary rule affecting the content of self-defence has emerged since 1945 and will conclude on the state of the current debate on the temporal dimension of self-defence. On that basis, Part II will discern whether the status and limits of anticipatory action have been affected by the post-Charter developments.

1.3.5 Rationale of Part III

Part III will outline the findings of Parts I and II on the basis of the two research questions.

Regarding the first research question, Part III will look at the findings on the content and temporal dimension of self-defence and, in particular, the status of anticipatory action before the adoption of the Charter and will conclude whether that status has been changed after the adoption of the Charter. In relation to the second research question, Part III will examine if and how the recognizable pattern of limits of anticipatory action demarcated in the pre-Charter customary law have been altered in the post-Charter developments. Based on this analysis, Part III will conclude whether anticipatory action in self-defence is still part of customary international law, and if yes, what are its limits.

1.3.6 Tracing the Evolution of Customary Law

This book examines the place of the anticipatory action in self-defence in customary law. Accordingly, the development and functioning of customary law is a main theme of the present research. In order to trace the development and examine the functioning of customary law, there has to be a clear understanding of what a customary rule is made of. It is not the purpose of this research to dwell into the controversies surrounding custom-formation and the various methods of analysing and tracing the development of customary rules. A brief review of these divergences is nevertheless necessary in order to explain the approach adopted by the present author.

1.3.6.1 Main Controversies Regarding Custom-Formation

Although most international jurists agree that international custom has two elements—state practice and *opinio juris*—, there is ample disagreement on the definition of and the relationship between the two elements.[74] The main controversies of the customary process relate to the character and continuity of state practice and the determination of *opinio juris*.[75]

The ambiguity in what forms of behaviour constitute state practice has given rise to different groups of opinion.[76] Some authors have contended that only acts and not statements constitute state practice.[77] Others have adopted a more inclusive view and maintained that state practice covers not only acts, but also statements or even omissions.[78] Some authors went as far as to suggest that state practice was the only element that could be truly identified in the development of a custom (materialistic approach).[79]

Another difficulty relates to the continuity of state practice. The materialistic view suggested the need for a uniform state practice in order to discern the existence of a certain rule.[80] Other writers have adopted a different view.[81] Tunkin contended that discontinuity could not be decisive in destroying a rule of law.[82] As he observed, 'not one norm of international law has appeared as a result of international practice that had no interruption.'[83] To support his statement, Tunkin analysed the state practice related to the principle of non-intervention and found that, although it had been forced at times to retreat under the pressure of reactionary forces (he mentioned, in particular, the many interventions of the nineteenth century), non-intervention had gradually become a generally recognized principle of international law.[84] A similar opinion was expressed by D'Amato, who contended that each deviation from a customary rule may contain the seeds of a new rule depending on a number of factors. Accordingly, the number of acts of the original rule, the number of the 'discontinuatory acts', their remoteness in time, the legal

---

74 For elaboration on the difficulties and controversies surrounding customary international law, see Byers 1999, pp. 129–146; D'Amato 1971, pp. 47–72; Koskenniemi 1989, pp. 342–410.

75 Byers 1999, pp. 130–142.

76 Ibid., pp. 133–136.

77 D'Amato 1971, pp. 88; Wolfke 1993, pp. 41–44.

78 Akehurst 1976, pp. 2–3; Brownlie 1986, p. 156. Brownlie warned against what he called 'Rambo positivism': the view that it is only actual action or reaction that constitutes state practice; Villiger 1997, pp. 16–17.

79 Kelsen 1939, pp. 264–265; Kelsen 1966, pp. 450–451. For criticism of this approach, see Koskenniemi 1989, pp. 401–402.

80 For instance, Kelsen 1939, p. 262.

81 D'Amato 1971, pp. 97–98; Koskenniemi 1989, p. 403; Tunkin 1958, p. 10; Tunkin 1961, pp. 420–421.

82 Tunkin 1958, p. 10.

83 Tunkin 1961, p. 420.

84 Ibid.

authoritativeness of the participating states and the frequency of articulations of the valid rule were the factors that decided whether the original rule was confirmed or a new rule was developing.[85] Koskenniemi took this reasoning one step further and contended that a fundamental change of circumstances that had taken place outside the law could make the old custom obsolete and the new one justified.[86]

Perhaps the most important difficulty of the customary process is the determination of *opinio juris*. If both acts and statements constitute state practice, it is very problematic to determine what constitutes *opinio juris*.[87] Some authors have sought to diminish the importance of practice by maintaining that there was no need for continuous and consequent usage to create a custom, the acceptance of the rule was enough (psychological approach).[88] According to this approach, the creation of 'instant' customary law was also possible by a common stipulation of states of a new rule.[89]

The difficulties in determining what *opinio juris* is, lead to a circularity of the argument about custom.[90] As Koskenniemi observed, in attempting to identify the presence of the psychological element (*opinio juris*), inferences are drawn on the basis of the material element (state practice). Likewise, to ascertain which acts of state practice are relevant for custom-formation, references are made to *opinio juris*. The two elements are defined by each other.[91]

After this succinct presentation of the main controversies regarding custom formation, the approach adopted in this research will be explained.

1.3.6.2 Approach Adopted Regarding Custom-Formation

It is beyond the purpose of this research to offer general solutions to the problems of custom-formation outlined above. It is not the ambition of this project to formulate universally valid definitions for state practice and *opinio juris*. This section will merely explain how the concepts of state practice and *opinio juris* will be interpreted for analysing pre-Charter and post-Charter customary laws on self-defence. In explaining the interpretation of this concept, the author relies on the relevant doctrine and some of the assertions of the International Court of Justice in the *Nicaragua* case.[92]

---

[85] D'Amato 1971, pp. 97–98.

[86] Koskenniemi 1989, p. 403.

[87] Byers 1999, pp. 136–141; Koskenniemi 1989, pp. 362–363.

[88] Anzilotti 1928, pp. 73–76; Strupp 1934, p. 263. For criticism of this approach, see Koskenniemi 1989, pp. 401–402.

[89] See, for instance, Cheng 1965, pp. 35–36.

[90] Byers 1999, pp. 136–140; Koskenniemi 1989, pp. 362–363.

[91] Koskenniemi 1989, p. 363.

[92] The *Nicaragua* case offered, *inter alia*, an elaborate analysis of the theory of customary international law. It discussed the relationship between treaty and custom, as well as the elements of a customary rule. For the purpose of this section, only the assertion regarding the elements of customary law will be discussed. Nicaragua 1986, paras 183–186. See *infra* 11.4.4, for the discussion regarding the relationship between treaty and customary law as well as self-defence.

For the purpose of the present research, the more inclusive view on state practice will be adopted.[93] Accordingly, state practice will be understood as encompassing acts and statements as well as omissions. For instance, for the examination of pre-Charter customary law, the way sovereign rulers conducted and justified their wars will be considered state practice. Likewise, diplomatic correspondence, the conclusion of bilateral or multilateral treaties will also be understood to reflect state practice. The practice of the Council of the League of Nations will have the same status. For the analysis of post-Charter customary law, not only the various instances of the exercise of self-defence will be considered state practice, but also the statements made by states before the Security Council or General Assembly (hereafter, 'GA'). Similarly, UN Security Council and General Assembly resolutions will generally be considered as state practice.

Regarding continuity in state practice, this author upholds the view that perfect uniformity is not a *sine qua non* condition.[94] On this topic, the ICJ also stated that it was not necessary for state practice to be perfectly uniform.[95] It was sufficient if the conduct of states was, in general, consistent with the relevant rule. Instances of state conduct inconsistent with a given rule still confirmed that rule, if they had been treated as breaches of it and not as indications of the recognition of a new rule.[96] Accordingly, 'if a State acts in a way *prima facie* incompatible with a recognized rule, but defends its conduct by appealing to exceptions or justifications contained within the rule itself, then whether or not the State's conduct is in fact justifiable on that basis, the significance of that attitude is to confirm rather than to weaken the rule.'[97]

Consequently, the present research will also take into consideration instances of state practice inconsistent with a certain rule in order to assess whether they weaken or confirm that rule.

For the purpose of this research, *opinio juris* will be discerned by corroboration.[98] By way of example, the repetition of certain acts and statements on the part of states (state practice) coupled with a specific reaction from the legal literature and a possible substantiation by judicial bodies will be understood to reflect *opinio juris*. If some acts or statements go against that perceived rule, the reaction by other states as well as by legal doctrine (or, if it is the case, judicial bodies) will be considered to assess whether those instances of behaviour weakened or confirmed the rule. Furthermore, certain multilateral treaties as well as specific UN Security

---

93 Akehurst 1976, pp. 2–3; Brownlie 1986, p. 156; Tunkin 1961, pp. 421–422; Villiger 1997, pp. 16–17.

94 D'Amato 1971, pp. 97–98; Koskenniemi 1989, p. 40; Tunkin 1961, pp. 420–421.

95 Nicaragua 1986, para 186.

96 Ibid.

97 Ibid.

98 Schachter 1989, pp. 730–734. Schachter discusses the various sources from which *opinio juris* can be inferred, such as UN General Assembly resolutions, records of discussions, expert opinions as well as decisions of the ICJ and some treaty provisions can all contribute, under certain conditions, to infer *opinio juris*.

Council or General Assembly resolutions will be interpreted as reflecting *opinio juris*. Such an approach was adopted by the ICJ as well in considering the effect of consent to the General Assembly Resolution 2625 (The Friendly Relations Declaration)[99] as an acceptance of the validity of the rule or set of rules declared by the resolution itself.[100]

1.4 Notes on Terminology

Certain notions used in Part I need clarification. Accordingly, many times reference will be made to the 'Western tradition', 'Western war tradition' or Western (European) philosophy, history or politics in general. The use of these phrases stems from the Eurocentric perspective employed by the present research. Although analysis of non-European or non-Western normative frameworks would have certainly enriched the present legal–historical study, such additional perspectives would have considerably complicated and lengthened the conduct of this research and the timely accomplishment of this project. Accordingly, the reference to 'Western' traditions, etc., will denote the various developments in the European and (North) American space.

Furthermore, in Chapters 2 and 3 use will be made of the concepts of 'just war' and 'just cause' to describe those circumstances and conditions under which Christian philosophers approved wars on the basis of natural law and divine law. Accordingly, a 'just war' will be understood as one sanctioned by the law of nature and a 'just cause' will be seen as a combination of circumstances that allowed war to be waged.[101]

Part I will also examine the work of 'Christian legalists'. The authors discussed under this notion will be those late scholastics and reformer writers who devoted special attention to normative thinking about war between nations.[102]

Certain notions used in Part II need clarification. The term '(general) reaction' will be often used to describe the various approaches taken as regards a specific instance of state practice. The use of the term will be based on the following sources: statements made by several states (both those affected and those neutral to the conflict) before the Security Council or the General Assembly and legal doctrine. If available, official (UN) reports on the legality of certain instances of state practice will also be used.

---

[99] GA Res. 2625, Friendly Relations Declaration.

[100] Nicaragua 1986, para 188.

[101] For a thorough analysis of the 'just war' tradition and the significance of 'just causes', see Vanderpol 1919; Bellamy 2006, pp. 5–8, 15–29, 39–40, 126–134; Christopher 2004; Neff 2005, pp. 29–30, 49–57.

[102] Reichberg et al. 2006, pp. 288, 339–340, 371–372, 385–386.

1.5 Disclaimers

Certain specifications are important to be made before embarking on the analysis of the customary law of self-defence. Part I will frequently refer to the natural law paradigm that was dominant over centuries in Europe. Nonetheless, it is not the aim of this book to offer a comprehensive portrayal of natural law theories and their evolution. It merely puts the subject of self-defence within that context to shed light on its evolution within the main intellectual and legal paradigm of the period analysed in Chapter 2. Likewise, it is not the purpose of this research to offer an exhaustive portrayal of the origin and evolution of the Christian just war tradition. Consequently, there will be no detailed analysis of the conditions under which a war could be deemed 'just' under that tradition; what will be examined is the place and meaning of self-defence within that context.

Furthermore, this book does not aim to offer a comprehensive portrayal of realism and legal positivist approaches from the seventeenth and the nineteenth centuries. It merely illustrates the main tenets of these currents in order to place the subject of self-defence within their context.

Part II of the research will refer to many juridical controversies directly or indirectly connected to self-defence. Although care will be taken to offer an objective view of these issues, it is beyond the scope of this book to elaborate on all the intervening questions. Accordingly, this research does not aim to offer an extensive elaboration on the controversies surrounding the notion of 'armed attack' and its relationship with other forms of the use of force. Likewise, there will be minimal analysis on the connection between the principle of proportionality and the rules of armed conflict. Furthermore, in examining the arguments regarding self-defence against non-state actors, there will be no comprehensive representation of the contentions concerning the responsibility of sending, sponsoring or harbouring states. Collective self-defence will receive some attention in the context of certain instances of state practice, but no elaborate analysis of the concept will be done. Likewise, protection of nationals will not be treated as a separate theme, although some relevant cases will be discussed as part of various chapters. Although many of these issues are interconnected, the aim of the research is to focus on the temporal dimension of self-defence. For that reason, many interesting and undoubtedly significant issues will only receive peripheral attention. Finally, this research takes into consideration and analyses relevant events up to 1 June 2010.

1.6 Contribution

This book aims to participate in the current debate on the temporal dimension of self-defence and, in particular, in the discussion regarding the legality of anticipatory action.

There are several ways in which this research attempts to contribute to this debate. Part I of this book was written in the hope that the legal–historical research conducted will serve as basis for those interested in the pre-Charter legal history of self-defence. Likewise, Part II aims to complement those studies that focus on how state practice 'in word, vote and deed'[103] has shaped the understanding of self-defence since the adoption of the Charter. This research attempts to offer a pragmatic and fact-specific analysis of the current controversies surrounding anticipatory action in self-defence. Rather than focusing on a literalistic analysis of legal texts, the arguments put forward in this book rely on a corroborated understanding of state and UN practice as well as legal doctrine on the concept of self-defence. Most importantly, perhaps, this research attempts to highlight the need for a more inclusive perspective for the analysis of the right of self-defence. The controversies surrounding the content and temporal dimension of self-defence are interconnected. Focusing on an isolated number of instances of state practice in order to shed light on one or more of these controversies does not suffice for a comprehensive portrayal of the underlying questions. This research attempts to offer a wider focus in which the interplay of various factors affecting the content and temporal dimension of self-defence can be more visibly discerned.

Self-defence has always been a popular topic in international legal literature. The relationship between custom and practice has been discussed many times in the last seven decades. Specific questions, relating to the concepts of 'armed attack', necessity and proportionality, have long preoccupied legal publicists around the world. The attacks of 9/11 have prompted a surge in the legal literature analysing the applicability of self-defence against non-state actors as well as the legality of pre-emptive and preventive actions. The last few years have also seen the emergence of more comprehensive publications on the right of self-defence, focusing not only on specific aspects, but also on general content, application and legality of defensive actions.[104] This book aims to contribute to this trend by offering a fact-specific legal analysis of the controversies surrounding the temporal dimension of self-defence, in general, and anticipatory action, in particular. A comprehensive analysis that focuses on both the legal arguments put forward and the underlying circumstances can help to understand the way in which the centuries-old concept of self-defence has been shaped over time.

References

Abi Saab G (1987) Cours general du droit public. Recueil des Cours 207(1987-VII):9–463

Akehurst M (1976) Custom as a source of international law. British Year b Int Law 47:1–53

Alexandrov S (1996) Self-defense against the use of force in international law. Kluwer Law International, The Hague

[103] Franck 2002, p. 52.

[104] See, for instance: Green 2009; Lubell 2010; Ruys 2010.

Anzilotti D (1928) Corso di diritto internationale. Atheneum, Roma
Armed activities on the territory of the Congo (Democratic Republic of the Congo v. Uganda), Judgment of 19 December 2005, ICJ Rep. (2005)
Badr GM (1980) The exculpatory effect of self-defence in state responsibility. Ga J Int Comp Law 10:1–28
Bellamy AJ (2006) Just wars: from Cicero to Iraq. Polity Press, Cambridge
Bowett DW (1958) Self-defense in international law. Manchester University Press, Manchester
Brownlie I (1963) International law and the use of force by states. Clarendon Press, Oxford
Brownlie I (1986) Comparative approaches to the theory of international law: remarks. Am Soc Int Law Proc 80:154–157
Bush GW (1 June 2002) Graduation Speech at West Point. http://georgewbush-whitehouse.archives.gov/news/releases/2002/06/20020601-3.html. Accessed 21 January 2010
Byers M (1999) Custom, power and the power of rules: international relations and customary international law. Cambridge University Press, Cambridge
Cahier P (1985) Changements et continuité du droit international: cours général de droit international public. Recueil des Cours 195(1985-VI):9–374
Cassese A (2001) Terrorism is also disrupting some crucial legal categories of international law. Eur J Int Law 12:993–1001
Cassese A (2005) International Law. Oxford University Press, Oxford
Cheng B (1965) United Nations resolutions on outer space: 'instant' international customary law? Indian J Int Law 5:23–48
Christakis T (2005) Existe-t-il un droit de légitime défense en cas de simple "menace"?: une réponse au "groupe des personnalités de haut niveau" de l'ONU. In: Société française pour le droit international, Les métamorphoses de la sécurité collective: droit, pratique et enjeux stratégiques. Pedone, Paris, pp 197–222
Christopher P (2004) The ethics of war and peace: an introduction to legal and moral issues. Pearson/Prentice Hall, Upper Saddle River
Constantinou A (2000) The right of self-defence under customary international law and Article 51 of the United Nations Charter. Sakkoulas, Athens
Corten O (2007) Le débat sur la légitime défense préventive à l'occasion des 60 ans de l'ONU: nouvelles revendications, oppositions persistantes. In: Kherad R (ed) Légitimes défenses: colloque international organisé par le Laboratoire Angevin de Recherches sur les Actes Juridiques en collab. avec le Centre d'Études sur la Coopération Juridique International. LGDJ, Paris, pp 217–232
Corten O (2008) Le droit contre la guerre: l'interdiction du recours à la force en droit international contemporain. Pedone, Paris
D'Amato AA (1971) The concept of custom in international law. Cornell University Press, Ithaca
Détais J (2007) Les critéres du droit de légitime défense dans la jurisprudence de la Cour Internationalde de Justice. In: Kherad R (ed) Légitimes défenses: colloque international organisé par le Laboratoire Angevin de Recherches sur les Actes Juridiques en collab. avec le Centre d'Études sur la Coopération Juridique International. LGDJ, Paris, pp 149–171
Dinstein Y (2005) War, aggression and self-defence. Cambridge University Press, Cambridge
Dixon M (2000) Textbook on international law. Blackstone Press, London
Evans GJ (2008) The responsibility to protect: ending mass atrocity crimes once and for all. Brookings Institution Press, Washington, D.C.
Fleck D (1988) Rules of engagement for maritime forces and the limitation of the use of force under the UN Charter. Ger Yearb Int Law 31:165–186
Franck T ((2002)) Recourse to force: state action against threats and armed attacks. Cambridge University Press, Cambridge
GA Res. 2625: General Assembly Resolution 2625 (1970) Friendly Relations Declaration
Gardam JG (1993) Proportionality and force in international law. Am J Int Law 87:391–413
Gardam JG (2004) Necessity, proportionality and the use of force by states. Cambridge University Press, Cambridge

Gazzini T (2005) The changing rules on the use of force in international law. Manchester University Press, Manchester

Gill TD (2007) The temporal dimension of self-defence. In: Schmitt M, Pejic J (eds) International law and armed conflict: exploring the faultlines. Essays in honour of Yoram Dinstein. Martinus Nijhoff, Leiden, pp 113–155

Gray C (2004) International law and the use of force. Oxford University Press, Oxford

Gray C (2008) International law and the use of force. Oxford University Press, Oxford

Green JA (2009) The International Court of Justice and self-defence in international law. Hart, Oxford

Greenwood C (2003) International law and the pre-emptive use of force: Afghanistan, Al-Qaida and Iraq. San Diego Int Law J 4:7–38

Grewe WG (2000) The epochs of international law (trans: Byers M). De Gruyter, Berlin

Henkin L (1991) The use of force: law and US policy. In: Henkin et al (eds) Right v. Might. international law and the use of force. Council on Foreign Relations Press, New York, pp 37–69

Henkin L (1995) International law: politics and values. Martinus Nijhoff, Dordrecht

Higgins R (1963) The development of international law through the political organs of the United Nations. Oxford University Press, London

Hill C (2004) The Bush Administration preemption doctrine and the future of world order: remark. Am Soc Int Law Proc 98:329–331

Hueck IJ (2001) The discipline of the history of international law: new trends and methods on the history of international law. J Hist Int Law 3:194–217

Interview with Jacques Chirac (9 September 2002), New York Times. http://www.nytimes.com/2002/09/09/international/europe/09CTEX.html. Accessed 26 January 2011

Jessup PC (1948) A modern law of nations: an introduction. Macmillan, New York

Kelsen H (1939) Théorie du droit international coutumier. Revue international de la theorie du droit (New Series) 1:25–57

Kelsen H (1966) Principles of international law. Holt Rinehart and Winston, New York

Kolb R (2004) Self-defense and preventive war at the beginning of the millennium. Zeitschrift für öffentliches recht 59(2):111–134

Kolesnik DN (1989) The development of the right to self-defence. In: Butler WE (ed) The non-use of force in international law. Nijhoff, Dordrecht, pp 153–159

Kooijmans PH (2009) The legality of the use of force in the recent case law of the International Court of Justice. In: Yee S, Morin JY (eds) Multiculturalism and international law—essays in honour of Edward McWhinney. Martinus Nijhoff, Leiden, pp 455–466

Koskenniemi M (1989) From apology to utopia: the structure of international legal argument. Lakimiesliiton Kustannus, Helsinki

Koskenniemi M (2001) Why history of international law today? Rechtsgeschichte 4:61–66

Kunz J (1947) Individual and collective self-defence in Article 51 of the Charter of the UN. Am J Int Law 41:872–879

Lachs M (1980) The development and general trends of international law in our time. Recueil des Cours 169(1980-IV):9–377

Lillich RB (ed) (1986) Humanitarian intervention and the United Nations. University Press of Virginia, Charlottesville

Lubell N (2010) Extraterritorial use of force against non-state actors. Oxford University Press, Oxford

Malanczuk P (1987) Countermeasures and self-defence as circumstances precluding wrongfulness in the International Law Commission's Draft Articles on States Responsibility. In: Spinedi M, Simma B (eds) United Nations codification of state responsibility. Oceana, New York, pp 197–286

Malanczuk P (1997) Akehurst's modern introduction to international law. Routledge, London

McDougal MS (1963) The Soviet-Cuban quarantine and self-defense. Am J Int Law 57:597–604

McDougal MS, Feliciano FP (1961) Law and minimum world public order: the legal regulation of international coercion. Yale University Press, New Haven

Myjer PJ, White ND (2002) The twin towers attack: an unlimited right to self-defence? J Confl Secur Law 7:5–17
Neff SC (2005) War and the law of nations: general history. Cambridge University Press, Cambridge
Nicaragua 1986: Military and paramilitary activities in and against Nicaragua (Nicaragua v. USA), Judgment of 27 June 1986, ICJ Rep. (1986)
Pierson C (2004) Preemptive self-defence in an age of weapons of mass destruction: Operation Iraqi Freedom. Denver J Int Law Policy 33:150–178
de la Pradelle AG (1950) Maîtres et doctrines du droit des gens. Editions internationales, Paris
Redslob R (1923) Histoire des grands principes du droit des gens depuis l'antiquité jusqu'à la veille de la grande guerre. Rousseau, Paris
Reichberg GM, Syse H. Begby E (eds) (2006) The ethics of war: classic and contemporary readings. Blackwell, Malden
Roelofsen CG (1993–1994) History of the law of nations. A few remarks apropos some recent and not so recent publications. Grotiana 13–14:52–58
Ruys T (2010) 'Armed attack' and Article 51 of the UN Charter. Evolutions in customary law and practice. Cambridge University Press, Cambridge
Schachter O (1989) Entangled treaty and custom. In: Dinstein Y (ed) International law at a time of perplexity. Essays in honour of Shabtai Rosenne. Martinus Nijhoff, Dordrecht, pp 717–738
Schachter O (1991) International law in theory and practice. Martinus Nijhoff, Dordrecht
Schachter O (1992) Implementing limitations on the use of force: the doctrine of proportionality and necessity. Am Soc Int Law Proc 86:39–40
Schmitt C (1995) Staat, Grossraum, Nomos. Arbeiten aus den Jahren 1916–1969, Maschke G (ed), Duncker & Humblot, Berlin
Schwebel SM (1972) Aggression, intervention and self-defence in modern international law. Recueil des Cours 136(1972-II): 411–497
Simma B (ed) (1995) The Charter of the United Nations, A commentary. Oxford University Press, Oxford
Steiger H (2001) From the international law of Christianity to the international law of the world citizen: reflections on the formation of epochs of the history of international law. J Hist Int Law 3:180–193
Strupp K (1934) Les règles générales du droit de la paix. Récueil des Cours 47:259–595
Taft WH, Buchwald TF (2003) Preemption, Iraq, and international law. Am J Int Law 97:557–563
Tesón FR (2005) Humanitarian intervention: an inquiry into law and morality. Transnational Ardsley, NY
The Bush Administration preemption doctrine and the future of world order (2004) Am Soc Int Law Proc 98:325–337
The Chatham House principles of international law on the use of force in self-defence (2006) Int Comp Law Q 55: 963–972
Tunkin GI (1958) Co-existence and international law. Recueil des Cours 95:1–81
Tunkin GI (1961) Remarks on the juridical nature of customary norms of international law. Calif Law Rev 49:419–430
Twiss T (1860) Law of nations considered as independent political communities, vol. 1. Oxford University Press, Oxford
UN high level panel: Report of the High-Level Panel on Threats, Challenges and Change (2004). United Nations. http://www.un.org/secureworld/report2.pdf. Accessed 1 February 2011
US National Security Strategy (2002) The White House (2002) The National Security Strategy of the United States of America Part V. Washington, D.C.
Vanderpol A (1919) La doctrine scolastique du droit de guerre. Pedone, Paris
Villiger ME (1997) Customary international law and treaties. Kluwer, The Hague
Waldock CHM (1952) The regulation of the use of force by individual states in international law. Recueil Des Cours 81(1952-II):451–517
Waldock CHM (1962) General course on public international law. Recueil des Cours 106:1–251

Walzer M (2006) Just and unjust wars. Basic Books, New York
Webster 1841: Letter from Daniel Webster, US Secretary of State, to Henry Fox, British Minister in Washington, 24 April 1841, in British and Foreign State Papers, 1840–1841, Vol. 29 (1857). James Ridgway and Sons, London, pp. 1129–1139
Wedgwood R (2003) The fall of Saddam Hussein: Security Council mandates and preemptive self-defense. Am J Int Law 97:576–585
Wolfke K (1993) Custom in present international law. Martinus Nijhoff, Dordrecht
Wright Q (1963) The Cuban quarantine. Am J Int Law 57:546–565
Ziegler KH (1994) Völkerrechtsgeschichte: ein Studienbuch. Beck, Munich
Yoo J (2003) International law and the war in Iraq. Am J Int Law 97:563–576
Zoller E (2004) The law applicable to the preemption doctrine. Am Soc Int Law Proc 98:333–337

Part I
Pre-Charter Customary Law on Self-Defence

We have to consider whether the injustice is, practically speaking, simply about to take place, or whether it has already done so, and redress is sought through war. In this second case, the war is aggressive. In the former case, war has the character of self-defence, provided that it is waged with a moderation of defence which is blameless.

Francisco Suárez

The objective of Part I is to trace the evolution of pre-Charter customary law on self-defence from its ancient Greek natural-law roots to the time of the adoption of the UN Charter. This legal-historical research is needed to understand how the content and temporal dimension of self-defence was viewed in the first decades of the twentieth century. On that basis, Part I will conclude whether anticipatory action was part of self-defence at that time and, if yes, under what conditions.

The need to return to the natural-law roots of self-defence was explained in Sect. 1.3.2. It is important to reiterate here that the terms 'inherent' and '*naturel*' employed in Article 51 of the UN Charter to characterise self-defence evoke an understanding of that right that had existed for centuries before the adoption of the Charter. It remains to be seen whether that understanding had survived the test of time and if yes, in what form was it acknowledged at the end of the Second World War.

Part I seeks therefore to show the changes through which the natural law concept of self-defence went through over three main 'normative frameworks': the natural law-dominated (Christian), the positivist and the incipient international law frameworks. Accordingly, Chapter 2 will offer a brief review of self-defence as part of the ancient Greek as well as early and medieval Christian conceptions of natural law (ca. 500 BC up to the seventeenth century CE). Chapter 3 will look at self-defence as a measure short of war and will assess whether its natural-law content remained unaltered (seventeenth–nineteenth centuries). Chapter 4 will discuss self-defence as an exception to the prohibition of war and will analyse its evolution in the midst of the emerging modern international law of the late nineteenth century and the early twentieth century. Chapter 5 will analyse the way the natural-law concept of self-defence was enshrined in the United Nations Charter.

On the basis of this legal-historical research, a comprehensive representation of the pre-Charter concept of self-defence, its content and temporal dimension will be offered (Chapter 6). If it is established that anticipatory action was part of that concept of self-defence, a recognizable pattern of the limits of such action will be demarcated. The thus identified understanding of self-defence will be seen as the one taken in consideration by the drafters of the UN Charter in their negotiations on Article 51. The pre-Charter concept of self-defence will be further tested against the influence of post-Charter developments in Part II of this book.

Chapter 2
Self-Defence in Ancient and Medieval Natural-Law

The aim of this chapter is to offer a brief review of how self-defence was viewed in the ancient Greek as well as the early and medieval Christian conceptions of natural law. It is important to reiterate at this point that this chapter does not aim to offer a comprehensive portrayal of natural-law theories and their evolution.[1] It merely puts the subject of self-defence within the context of natural law. This contextualisation is needed given the fact that natural law had been the predominant intellectual foundation of legal order for much of the historical phase examined in this chapter.[2]

The concept of natural law has evolved over the centuries. In the Western tradition, the idea began with the ancient Greeks' conception of a universe governed by an eternal law on the basis of which one could distinguish between what was just or unjust by nature.[3] Christian philosophers took over the natural-law theory and equated eternal law with that of God. Later, the Renaissance and the Reformation process brought about a gradual secularization of society in which positive law and judicial processes gained more important roles. Against this background, natural-law theory also became more secular and gradually shifted its emphasis from divine order to human reason. Starting with the seventeenth to eighteenth centuries, however, natural-law theory was confined to the realms of ethics and morality in the face of the positivist and jurisprudential trends of the time.[4]

After a succinct portrayal of the importance of self-defence in the ancient Greek and Roman conceptions of natural law, this chapter will examine the early, medieval and reformer Christian theory of natural law up to the end of the Thirty Years' War and the conclusion of the Peace of Westphalia. Attention will

---

[1] Also stated *supra* 1.5.

[2] Neff 2005, p. 10; Reichberg et al. 2006, p. 37.

[3] For an elaborated analysis on how law was viewed in ancient Greece, see Phillipson 1911, vol. 1, pp. 53–65.

[4] Bellamy 2006, pp. 120–121.

K. Tibori Szabó, *Anticipatory Action in Self-Defence*, DOI: 10.1007/978-90-6704-796-8_2,

be given to the way war and warfare were understood in this natural-law conception in order to map out the framework in which the right of self-defence was acknowledged.

As explained in Sect. 1.3.3, because of the long time-span reviewed in this chapter, the legal–historical research will mainly rely on authoritative and representative writings of the different time periods analysed within it. This chapter will thus concentrate on the way self-defence was defined, justified and limited by contemporaneous publicists. The concluding remarks of this section will assess whether anticipatory action was part of the natural-law understanding of self-defence, and if yes, under what conditions.

Before embarking on the analysis, the clarification of certain terms needs to be reiterated.[5] Use will be made of the concepts of 'just war' and 'just cause' to describe those circumstances and conditions in which Christian philosophers approved wars on the basis of natural law and God. Accordingly, a just war was one sanctioned by the law of nature and a 'just cause' was a combination of circumstances that allowed war to be waged. Since it is not the purpose of this research to offer an exhaustive portrayal of the Christian just war tradition, there will be no detailed analysis of the conditions under which a war could be deemed 'just'.[6] Furthermore, distinction will be made between '(early and) medieval Christian' thinking, on one hand, and 'Christian legalist' approach, on the other. The first category will examine the work of Christian theologians and canonists in the first fifteen centuries of the Common Era. The second category will look at the writings of late scholastics and reformer writers who devoted special attention to normative thinking about war between nations.[7]

2.1 War in Ancient Greece and Rome

While it is considerably laborious to offer an elaborate exposition of how ancient civilizations viewed and regulated war, a short incursion into ancient war-related traditions is useful, because many of their elements have survived and are part of contemporary frameworks. This short portrayal will only focus on ancient Greek and Roman rules, because in many ways, they served as basis for the development of Western war traditions.[8]

Both the ancient Greeks and Romans recognized several causes for legitimate war. In the absence of these causes, to engage in warfare was forbidden by law and

---

5 Also stated *supra* 1.4.

6 For a thorough analysis of the 'just war' tradition and the significance of 'just causes', see Bellamy 2006, pp. 5–8, 15–29, 39–40, 126–134; Christopher 2004; Neff 2005, pp. 29–30, 49–57.

7 Reichberg et al. 2006, pp. 288, 339–340, 371–372, 385–386.

8 In case of Greece, the time frames under review are the Classical (500–336 BC) and the Hellenistic (336–146 BC) periods. For ancient Rome, the period of the Republic (510–23 BC) and of the Early Empire (23 BC–96 AD) are relevant.

religion alike.[9] In ancient Greece, warfare was certified by both natural law and conventional law (customs). The concept of natural law stemmed from a general idea of just and unjust in accordance with nature, which all human beings understood, even if there was 'neither communication nor agreement between them.'[10] Apart from natural law, ancient Greeks also recognized conventional law. Accordingly, rules stemming from natural law were seen as possessing the same validity everywhere regardless of being deliberately adopted or not.[11] Conversely, conventional law was viewed as acquiring existence and importance only after it had been laid down. As part of conventional law, customs were given great importance, because they were seen as having intrinsically more force than written laws.[12] Such customs were considered in both ancient Greece and Rome to be applicable to all sovereign, properly organized states or communities, but not to those seen as barbarians, robbers or pirates.[13]

No war was commenced in either Greece or Rome before allegations of legitimacy (*justum bellum*, for Romans) were made. Phillipson identified as 'the most usual grounds' for resorting to war violation of a treaty, withdrawal from an alliance, offence committed against the state or an ally, breach of neutrality, offence against envoys and so on.[14]

The Roman *ius fetiale*[15] gave a formal legality to matters of war. Commencement of hostilities was considered "just" only when it was carried out in conformity with this set of religious laws. The adherence to the rules was assured and overseen by the *fetiales,* a college of priests who had special responsibility for maintaining peaceful relations among the Latin. They had to oversee, *inter alia*, the making of treaties and declarations of war.[16] The fetials, although required to discuss only the mere formalities of war, often analysed the legitimacy of the reasons invoked.[17] Although the *ius fetiale* had a prominent religious character, the actual proceedings possessed also a political and a judicial nature, because the fetials could act as ambassadors or judges and not only as guardians of religion.[18] As Watson explained, Roman declarations of war were cast in the form of a lawsuit, if they were preceded by a verdict of the fetials that proclaimed the war to be legitimate.[19]

---

[9] Phillipson 1911, vol. 2, p. 167.

[10] Aristotle 1959, Book I, Chap. 13, Section 2, p. 139.

[11] Aristotle 1968, Book V, Chap. 7, Section 1, p. 295; Phillipson 1911, vol. 1, p. 54.

[12] Phillipson 1911, vol. 1, pp. 54–55.

[13] Phillipson 1911, vol. 2, p. 195.

[14] Phillipson 1911, vol. 2, p. 182.

[15] Fetial law was a set of religious norms related to the commencement and conduct of war by Romans. It was developed during the regal period in the seventh century BC and it lasted until the first century AD. 60. Phillipson 1911, vol. 2, pp. 315–316; Reichberg et al. 2006, p. 47.

[16] Reichberg et al. 2006, p. 47.

[17] Brownlie 1963, p. 4.

[18] Phillipson 1911, vol. 2, pp. 181, 325–329.

[19] Watson 1993, p. 13.

The romans dispatched envoys to the potential enemy to present the formal demand of the Roman government. According to Cicero, wars had to be formally declared and limits were imposed on what the state might do to its enemies in the form of retribution or punishment.[20]

An important aspect of the natural-law conception of the ancient Greeks was their perception of the city–state or the commonwealth. Aristotle saw the state as a 'wider self',[21] the conclusion of a process of human development, in which each step was necessary and natural.[22] Therefore, the city–state was itself natural.[23] The same view was later adopted by the Roman orator Cicero, who believed that Nature prompted human beings to form public assemblies and take part in them themselves.[24]

Since the state was natural, ensuring its survival and prosperity was also seen as natural. Accordingly, both ancient Greek and Roman philosophers accepted that defending the state from its enemies was also natural. Aristotle believed that a city had to be ready to 'avoid becoming enslaved to others.'[25] Likewise, Cicero asserted that the main justification for going to war was that 'we may live in peace unharmed.'[26] Besides this narrow understanding of defence, both Aristotle and Cicero added a broader ground for war as well. Accordingly, the state could also 'hold despotic power over those who deserved to be slaves' (Aristotle) and fight for supremacy and glory (Cicero).[27]

The Peloponnesian War[28] was a good illustration of how the expansionist ideals of a state could raise the suspicion and fear of its neighbours without their survival being endangered. One of the reasons for the outbreak of the Peloponnesian War was the help that Athens had given to Corcyra against Corinth, a Spartan friend and ally, in pursuance of its expansionist plans.

According to Thucydides, the Corinthians encouraged the Spartans to attack Athens to prevent plans for further Athenian expansion and dominance in the Peloponnesus:

> Spartans, you still delay and fail to see that peace stays longest with those who are not more careful to use their power justly than to show their determination not to submit to injustice [...]. Here, at least, let your procrastination end. For the present, assist your allies and Potidaea in particular, as you promised, by a speedy invasion of Attica, and do not

---

[20] Cicero 1968, Book I, Chaps. 11–12, Sections 36–38, pp. 39–41.

[21] Barker 1959, p. 269.

[22] Barker 1959, pp. 269–270; Everson 1997, p. 294.

[23] Aristotle 1967, Book I, Chap. 1, Sections 8–9, p. 9.

[24] Cicero 1968, Book I, Chap. 4, Section 12, pp. 13–15.

[25] Aristotle 1967, Book VII, Chap. 13, Section 14–15, p. 611.

[26] Cicero 1968, Book I, Chap. 11, Section 35, p. 37.

[27] Aristotle 1967, Book VII, Chap. 13, Sections 14–15, p. 611; Cicero 1968, Book I, Chap. 11, Section 38, p. 41.

[28] The Peloponnesian War (431–404 BC) was fought between the city–state of Athena and the Peloponnesian League, led by Sparta.

> sacrifice friends and kindred to their bitterest enemies, and drive the rest of us in despair to some other alliance.[29]

The justification for the Spartan military action not only bore the characteristics of war for supremacy (in Cicero's words), but was also a very strong argument for preventive war. Cicero, however, cautioned that such wars had to be waged with less brutality than those for survival, because one was not fighting against a deadly enemy, but rather against a worthy rival.[30]

Early and medieval Christian thinkers adopted the ancient Greek and Roman theory of natural law and saw it as stemming from the law of God.[31] Within this concept, both individuals and the state had the natural right to defend themselves.[32]

2.2 Early Christian Views on War and Self-Defence

The first three centuries of Christianity were characterized by an isolationist and pacifist approach to all social matters, including military action. Pacifism was propagated by the Early Christian Fathers, such as Tertullian of Carthage (circa 160–circa 225). Although early Christianity mixed elements of Greek culture (still dominant in the Roman Empire) and Jewish religion (from the Old Testament), participating in warfare proved to be a difficult question, because the teachings of the New Testament endorsed a 'turn the other cheek' approach to violence. Consequently, the Early Church Fathers believed that the New Testament demanded them to avoid violence.[33]

The general prohibition of war in the early pacifist philosophy had the merit of persuading later theologians to grant great importance to thorough justifications of military actions. Accordingly, starting with the fourth century, the main characteristic of the Christian normative framework was the requirement to demonstrate the existence of a justifying ground to make the resort to war acceptable to both divine and earthly authority.

Although pacifists propagated avoiding service in the army, the first accounts of Christian soldiers began to appear by the end of the third century.[34] During the reign of Constantine (306–337 AD), there were already many Christians serving in

---

[29] Thucydides, The Peloponnesian War, Book I, Chap. 71, reprinted in Reichberg et al. 2006, pp. 4–5.

[30] Cicero 1968, Book I, Chap. 12, Section 38, p. 41. Cicero also advocated the granting of protection for those who laid down their arms and for those who did not participate in the hostilities. Ibid., Book I, Chap. 12, Section 35, p. 37.

[31] For instance, the influence of Aristotelian natural-law theory on Thomas Aquinas was thoroughly discussed in Lisska 1996. The same book also makes reference to the work of other early and medieval Christian thinkers who borrowed ideas from the ancient Greek conception of natural-law.

[32] Mattox 2006, pp. 73–74.

[33] See, for instance, Tertullian, On Idolatry, Chap. 19, in Swift 1983, pp. 41–42.

[34] Brownlie 1963, p. 5; Bellamy 2006, p. 21.

the military and taking up important public positions. Once Christianity was proclaimed the official (state) religion of the Roman Empire, it became necessary to have a more comprehensive approach towards military service and warfare. In this way, the isolationist pacifist attitude was replaced by a more pragmatic perspective on the issue and the main question to be answered referred to the conditions under which a Christian could participate in warfare.[35]

These changes were also mirrored in contemporaneous religious writings. One of the most important thinkers of early Christianity was Augustine,[36] who built his observations on Cicero's writings and on the Roman concept of *justum bellum*. Although his work did not contain significantly new ideas, but rather a refinement and synthesis of earlier writings, Augustine's merit was to give expression to an early Christian understanding of just wars.[37] As said by Mattox, Augustine's criteria for 'just cause' constituted a synthesis of the theories embraced by Cicero and early Christian predecessors.[38] Accordingly, war had to be fought to obey a divine command, to defend the safety or the honour of the state, to avenge injuries, to punish a nation for failure to take corrective action for wrongs committed by its citizens and to come to the defence of one's allies.[39] Augustine also asserted that wars could not be fought for territorial expansion and had to be authorized by the appropriate public authority.[40]

In *The Problem of Free Choice*, Augustine explained that when an individual killed in self-defence, he killed to protect earthly things and such conduct was only justifiable by temporal law (as opposed to eternal), because one should love only that which cannot be taken against one's own will. Killing for defending one's own life or property was a sign of loving transitory, earthly goods; hence such conduct could not be justified before God. Although Augustine rejected the idea of killing in one's self-defence, he discussed two situations in which the necessity of self-defence might arise: against an attacking enemy (*hostis inruens*) and against an assassin lying in ambush (*insidiator sicarius*).[41] He treated both situations as equally life-threatening and the reasons why he rejected such defence were not related to the timing of the defence, but to the nature of the goods and values protected. Augustine, however, admitted that when individuals used force to defend others, public order or the common good, their act was justified by both temporal and eternal laws. Soldiers could be exonerated of sins on this basis, because 'self-defence' in this case meant fighting for the sake of others or for the

---

[35] Bellamy 2006, pp. 23–25; Neff 2005, pp. 46–48.

[36] Aurelius Augustinus also known as Augustine of Hippo or Saint Augustine (354–430) was one of the most important figures in the development of Christianity in Europe. His most important works are On Christian Doctrine (397–426), Confessions (397–398) and City of God (?413–426).

[37] Bellamy 2006, p. 25.

[38] Mattox 2006, p. 74.

[39] Ibid.

[40] Augustine, City of God, Book XIX, Chap. 7, reprinted in Fortin et al. 1994, p. 149.

[41] Augustine 1955, Book I, 5.12, pp. 44–45. See also Smith 2007, p. 147.

city in which they resided, provided that they acted according to the commission lawfully given to them.[42]

What is interesting to note in Augustine's view on self-defence, is that he first discussed individual self-defence and then inferred his conclusions on the defence of the community. This was in line with the practice of the ancient Greek and Roman philosophers, who regarded the community as the completion of the self and derived their findings from the latter to the former.[43] Further, he treated self-defence separately from any retaliatory measures and understood it as a situation in which the soldier had to fight against an on-going attack.[44] Additionally, Augustine discussed the hypothesis of defence against an enemy lying in ambush, and thus the necessity to act pre-emptively.[45] The redressal of injuries and the punishment of the guilty were seen as separate causes.[46]

2.3 Medieval Christian Views on War and Self-Defence

From the fifth century onwards, the Catholic Church assumed a more prominent role in European affairs. After the fall of the Roman Empire, several smaller kingdoms and provinces were established and the Catholic Church acquired ever greater responsibility. Early medieval popes often had to act as political rulers to keep a frail public order. Between the fourth and the eighth centuries, the so-called barbarian invasions took place, which forced the Church and the European rulers to adopt a more realistic view on issues of military action.[47] During this period, the doctrinal tradition of Augustine was maintained by authors such as Gregory of Tours (538–594) and Isidore of Seville (560–636).[48]

Beginning with the tenth century, the secular functions of the Catholic Church became as important as its divine functions. In its secular function, the Church took up the tasks of a sovereign. Hence, towards the end of the first millennium, the Church began to engage in military affairs. For instance, Pope Leo IV ordered the restoration and fortification of the walls of the City of Rome and the building of a battle fleet which inflicted a defeat on Muslim forces in the Battle of Ostia in

[42] Excerpts from Augustine, Letter 47, Section 5, in Mattox 2006, p. 108.

[43] Barker 1959, pp. 269–270; Cicero 1968, Book I, Chap. 4, Section 12, pp. 13–15; Everson 1997, p. 294.

[44] Mattox 2006, p. 74.

[45] Smith 2007, pp. 146–147.

[46] Mattox 2006, p. 74.

[47] Nussbaum 1947, pp. 23–27.

[48] Gregory of Tours was a historian and a bishop and through his work he aimed to popularize Christian faith. Saint Isidore, Archbishop of Seville, not only took further the teachings of Augustine, but also the ideas of Aristotle and other ancient Greek philosophers. Fontane 2000; Mitchell and Wood 2002.

849.[49] In 1095, Pope Urban II called upon the first crusade, against the Muslims and the Jews in the Holy Land.[50] Approximately one hundred years later, Pope Innocent IV asserted that it was licit for the pope, 'by persuading the faithful and granting indulgences, to defend the Holy Land and all the faithful inhabiting it.'[51]

In the twelth and thirteenth centuries, eight other crusades took place, most of them for the (re-)conquest of the Holy Land. In this period, the Church took up the role of a true sovereign and did not shy away from commanding several invasions under the auspices of the Christian cross.

A comprehensive description of how war was understood in the time of the crusades was given by the *Decretum*, attributed to Gratian, a twelfth-century canon lawyer from Bologna. The *Decretum* was a monumental collection of canon law compiled and written in the form of a legal textbook. The collection was continuously annotated by canonists (Decretists, later coined Decretalists) in the second half of the twelfth century.[52]

The *Decretum* had three main parts, the second of which was a compilation of cases coined *causae*. In the *causae* Gratian raised a number of legal questions. *Causa 23* was dedicated to the conditions under which Christians could resort to war (private or public) and it was a reliable characterization of the contemporaneous beliefs held by the Church on the topic:

> That war is just which is waged by an edict in order to regain what has been stolen or to repel the attack of enemies.[53]

Accordingly, the *Decretum* justified war to punish wrongdoings and to resist injury. In line with its predecessors, Gratian also specified that defending the *patria* from the barbarian invasions was a 'just cause'.[54] Moreover, Gratian asserted that if someone failed to ward off an injury from an associate, if he could do so, he was as blameable as the one who inflicted it.[55] Likewise, Gratian acknowledged holy war as a 'just cause' and asserted that those who died 'in the fight against the infidels' should not be seen as murderers, but as soldiers worthy of the kingdom of heaven.[56]

---

[49] Neff 2005, p. 48; Llewellyn 1970, pp. 263–264.

[50] Pope Urban II's speech at Clermont, 27 November 1095, as reported by Robert the Monk, in Laffan 1929, pp. 54–56. The term 'Holy Land' usually refers to the historic geographical region comprising ancient Palestine (Concise Oxford Dictionary, 1995).

[51] Pope Innocent IV, On Vows and the Fulfilling of Vows, decretal Quod superbis, reprinted in Reichberg et al. 2006, p. 152.

[52] More on the legacy of the Decretists and the Decretalists in Reichberg et al. 2006, p. 104; Bellamy 2006, pp. 34–36.

[53] Gratian, Decretum, Part II: Decreti Pars Secunda, causa 23, question II, canon 1, reprinted in Reichberg et al. 2006, p. 113.

[54] Ibid., question III, canon 5, in Reichberg et al. 2006, p. 114.

[55] Ibid., canon 7, in Reichberg et al. 2006, pp. 114–115.

[56] Ibid., question V, canon 46, in Reichberg et al. 2006, p. 119.

Despite the permissive rights of the Church and the sovereign to wage holy wars, the *Decretum* also discussed a more *stricto sensu* self-defence from the perspective of an individual. Individuals—be they lords, property owners, soldiers, merchants or peasants—could wage 'particular wars'[57] in self-defence against their attacker. 'Blameless defence' did not need the special authority of the church or of the prince, because it was allowed by natural law.[58] They could defend themselves against an ongoing attack or against an enemy in ambush. Self-defence thus referred to the time immediately before and during the attack. Action after the attack was seen as a reprisal or revenge of injuries which was seen more as a prerogative of the sovereign. The only case in which one could defend himself after an attack was if the attacker was preparing to strike again.[59]

A good illustration of this distinction is served by the Decretists' glosses, which appeared alongside the *Decretum* from the thirteenth century onwards:

> Let us see who may resist violence, and how it may be resisted [...]. If it is directed at persons, then force may be resisted before it strikes. But certain people have contended that no one ought to resist force before it strikes, yet it is permitted to kill an ambusher and anyone who tries to kill you [...]. If, however, someone returns violence, this should be done with the assumption that it is for defence, rather than for revenge [...], and only if the first attacker intends to strike once more; otherwise, if the attacker does not intend to strike once more and the other person still returns force, this should be seen as revenge rather than resistance to force. And this is what I understand when it is said that force may be resisted "on the spot" (*incontinenti).* It is therefore required that a return blow be in defence, not in revenge [...], and that self-defence be exercised in moderation (*cum moderamine*).[60]

Another important document that, *inter alia*, confirmed the distinction was Raymond of Peňafort's *Summa de casibus poenitentiae,* written from 1224 to 1226, revised between 1234 and 1245 and annotated by William of Rennes in the thirteenth century. The Summa relied extensively on the *Decretum* and Peňafort argued that self-defence had to aim solely at repelling an attack that was already in progress or about to commence. In this way, Peňafort put defence in sharp contrast with reprisals, because he saw the former as concerning the present and the near future, whereas the latter imposed sanctions for acts already done.[61] This view reinforced the opinions held by Augustine (thus the *Decretum* as well) on the separation between defence (against imminent or on-going attacks) and retaliation (punishment of wrongs or response to attacks that already occurred). William of Rennes, however, in his annotations argued that a defender could be justified in

---

57 According to Neff, in the fourteenth century, Giovanni da Legnano, professor of civil law at the University of Bologna, characterized self-defence as a species of 'particular war', in other words, a 'war' waged by one person on his own behalf, as opposed to a 'universal war' waged by the prince and involving the entire community. Neff 2005, p. 60 n. 67.

58 Raymond of Peňafort, Summa de casibus poenitentiae, Part II, Section 18, reprinted in Reichberg et al. 2006, pp. 138–139.

59 Gratian, question I, in Reichberg et al. 2006, p. 110.

60 Ibid., in Reichberg et al. 2006, pp. 109–110.

61 Peňafort, Section 18, in Reichberg et al. 2006, pp. 133, 140.

delaying his armed response for a significantly longer time, provided it was for defensive and not retaliatory purposes.[62]

There are thus three important points to be made regarding the understanding given to self-defence by the above-mentioned works. First, exercising self-defence (by an individual or a sovereign) was a natural right that needed no special authority. Secondly, self-defence was distinguished from punishment on a temporal basis. Accordingly, the former pertained to the time before or during the attack, whereas the latter related to the time after the attack. Thirdly, 'blameless' self-defence had to be exercised with moderation.

At the time when the *Decretum* was compiled, a new approach on combining ancient philosophy with Christian theology emerged under the name of scholasticism.[63] Thomas Aquinas (ca. 1225–1274) was a prominent scholastic author and his best-known work was the *Summa Theologiae*, written between 1265 and 1274, which compiled all of the main theological teachings of the time. The *Summa Theologiae* was based on a clear theory of natural law, which was seen by Aquinas as the way through which the human being participated in eternal law. As in the ancient Greek conception, natural law was binding on the whole universe and on its basis one could distinguish right from wrong in the interest of the greatest good.[64] From the sixteenth century onwards, this work served as a textbook in theology and many professors in Western Europe organized their teachings on its basis.[65]

In *Question 40—On War*, Aquinas discussed whether any war was legitimate or otherwise. In his answer, he named three conditions for a war to be 'just': the war had to be ordered by a public authority, it had to have a 'just cause' and it had to be fought with the right intention. As to the 'just cause' of the war, Aquinas cited Augustine and agreed that war should be fought to avenge wrongs and to punish a nation for failure to take corrective action for wrongs committed by its citizens.[66]

Although Aquinas held that wars could be waged in defence of the faith, he also believed that faith depended on the will and that unbelievers could not be compelled to take up Christ, as long as they did not endanger the faith or they had not promised to accept it.[67] Thus Aquinas was more in favour of limiting the

[62] William of Rennes, Apparatus ad Summam Raymundi, Section 18, reprinted in Reichberg et al. 2006, pp. 133, 143.

[63] This method of teaching was earlier used by Muslim scholastics of Al-Andalus (today Andalusia). The scholastic method was based on the critical analysis of the main work (or works) of a renowned scholar (auctor) and in this way, the students learned to understand and appreciate the theories of the author. Three periods of scholasticism can be distinguished: early scholasticism (eleventh–twelfth century), high scholasticism (thirteenth century) and late scholasticism (fourteenth and early fifteenth century).

[64] Thomas Aquinas, Summa Theologiae, Secunda Secundae, question 91, Articles 1 and 2, and question 94, Articles 2 and 4, in Lisska 1996, pp. 263–266, 272–278.

[65] Reichberg et al. 2006, p. 169.

[66] Thomas Aquinas, Summa Theologiae, Part II–II, question 40, Article 1, in Reichberg et al. 2006, pp. 176–177.

[67] Ibid., question 10, Article 8, in Reichberg et al. 2006, pp. 192–193.

prerogative of the sovereign to wage war only in defence of the country rather than religious expansion.

Aquinas had a restrictive view on the so-called particular wars or private wars. When discussing 'strife', which he defined as 'a kind of private war (*bellum particulare*),' Aquinas claimed that:

> [O]nly him who defends himself, it may be without sin [...]. For if his sole intention be to repel the injury done to him, and he defend himself with due moderation, it is no sin, and one cannot say properly that there is strife on his part.[68]

Accordingly, Aquinas was of the opinion that individuals could wage wars only in self-defence and not to avenge injuries. In other words, Aquinas denounced private reprisals as unjust. His view was taken over by some of the subsequent authorities, but many continued to permit private reprisals.[69]

The differentiation between self-defence and the revenge of injuries made by Aquinas, upheld the temporal distinction that the *Decretum* and the Decretalists had made.[70] He also reiterated the requirement to exercise self-defence with due moderation.[71]

The enthusiasm for crusades subsided towards the end of the thirteenth century, as both statesmen and theologians departed from the concept of religious wars for the defence of the Holy Land. The justification of crusades served the Church and the sovereign with a much broader right of defence than that articulated by the early Christians. Accordingly, a sovereign could wage defensive war not only against an invader, but also against a religious enemy that endangered Christianity or peace. The existence of a *justa causa* ('just cause') only required that 'the war be fought out of necessity, so that peace is achieved by the fighting.'[72] Accordingly, many objectives of a war could qualify as 'necessity' and such objectives were usually combined. As Neff observed, just wars had the purpose of preventing evil from overcoming good and even if they had a punitive objective, they were waged to prevent a recurrence of the wrongdoing.[73] For instance, crusades were seen as defensive wars against the 'infidels', but they also purported a strong expansionist, punitive or preventive character.

---

[68] Ibid., question 41, Article 1, in Reichberg et al. 2006, pp. 182–183.

[69] Such an author was Bartolus de Sassoferrato (ca.1313–1357), who considered private reprisals for the recovery of property legal if there was no judge available to protect the person. Bartolus de Sassoferrato, Secunda super Digesto novo, ad Dig., 49, 15, 24, n. 9 in Reichberg et al. 2006, p. 207. For details on the law of reprisals in the Middle Ages and Bartolus' work, see Grewe 2000, pp. 116–118. Another author who extensively dealt with the issue of reprisals was Giovanni da Legnano (ca. 1320–1383) in his Tractatus de Bello, de Represaliis et de Duello (1360). See: Legnano 1917, Chaps. cxxii–clxvii, pp. 307–331.

[70] Gratian, question I, in Reichberg et al. 2006, pp. 109–110; Peňafort, in Reichberg et al. 2006, pp. 131–133.

[71] Aquinas, question 41, Article 1, in Reichberg et al. 2006, p. 183.

[72] Peňafort, Section 17, in Reichberg et al. 2006, p. 134.

[73] Neff 2005, p. 59.

Nonetheless, self-defence in its strict sense was distinguished by Christian thinkers when analysing the natural right of the individual. Accordingly, individual self-defence was believed to stem from natural law, thus no special authority was needed for its exercise. Furthermore, self-defence allowed action against an imminent or an ongoing attack. It did not allow punitive action after the attack occurred, unless a new attack was in preparation. Likewise, the strict interpretation of self-defence did not justify preventive action against a potential enemy. Furthermore, self-defence had to be exercised with moderation.

The distinction between individuals' self-defence and public defensive wars was taken further by authors of chivalric codes (created for the purpose of offering a code of conduct to crusaders). In the age of medieval chivalry, thinking about war had its emphasis on the righteous conduct in battle. Since knighthood was the symbol of loyalty and generosity, the limits on the conduct of hostilities gained importance.[74]

Writings such as the *Ordene de chevalerie* (written before 1250), the *Book of the Order of Chivalry* of Ramon Lull (?1232–1315) and the *Book of Chivalry* by Geoffrey de Charny (?1300–1356), are just a few worth mentioning.

Christine de Pisan's *Book of Deeds of Arms and of Chivalry*, written around 1410 discussed many questions related to righteous conduct in war. One of the questions (addressed to an imaginary 'master') reads as follows: 'A man has injured another, and soon after striking the blow, he flees as far as he can. But the injured party goes after him, overtakes him and injures him. I ask you whether the pursuer should be punished. From what you have said, it would seem not, in view of the fact that he did not exceed the limits of justice. As he was the first one to be assaulted, he has the right of self-defence and should be excused, even if he has killed his adversary. Also he did not wait, for if he had waited until another day, I would not say this, for that would be vengeance.'[75] The imaginary master replied that it was illegal to pursue the attacker. Self-defence had to be instant. Accordingly, 'if he had killed the other when the other struck the first blow, and it can be proved that said other struck first' it could be seen as legitimate self-defence.[76] But if the first attacked pursued the assailant, then the attacked had to be punished.[77]

This passage identified similar conditions as to the individual's right to defend himself as did earlier works. First, self-defence concerned imminent and ongoing attacks, not wrongs already committed. Secondly, the 'limits of justice' had to be observed when exercising self-defence, that is to say that any counteraction had to be moderate. Thirdly, pursuing an attacker was seen as vengeance, rather than self-defence, in line with the defensive–offensive dichotomy recognized by Augustine, Gratian's *Decretum* and Raymond of Peňafort's *Summa.*

---

[74] Many rules of righteous conduct in battle were recorded by Legnano in his Tractatus: Legnano 1917, Chaps. xvii–lviii, pp. 235–268. See also: Keen 1965, pp. 19–22.

[75] Pisan, The Book of Deeds of Arms and of Chivalry, Part III, Chap. 12, in Reichberg et al. 2006, p. 219.

[76] Ibid.

[77] Ibid.

The works cited in this section have long been acknowledged as representative of the early and medieval (theological) approach to war.[78] All works allow individuals to defend themselves against an imminent or an ongoing attack and to resort to moderate action for that purpose. The defensive right of the sovereign was broader than that of the individual: it allowed preventive wars against potential conquerors and religious enemies.

2.4 Christian Legalist Views on War and Self-Defence

The tenets of the early and medieval Christian approaches to war were partly retained by the authors of the fifteenth to seventeenth centuries. Nevertheless, some aspects had undergone definite changes, as a result of certain key events of that period. The year of 1453 saw both the end of the Hundred Years' War between France's main crown contenders and the fall of Constantinople marking the beginning of the Ottoman Empire. At the same time, the fifteenth century gave birth to the ideas of Italian Renaissance as well as to early French humanism. The sixteenth century was torn by the conflict between the Catholic Church and the Protestant reformers and saw the boundaries of Europe being endangered by the Ottoman threat. The discovery of new territories brought on fresh expansionist plans in Spain and brought forward the question of the justice of forcing European rule upon peoples outside the European continent.[79] Against this background, the fifteenth- and sixteenth century Christian ideas about just war combined both the more traditional theological teachings and the new humanist thought, while engaging in the discussion of topics that had not been previously addressed.[80] Additionally, the first incipient forms of rejection of the principles of just war appeared.

Two distinct trends could be distinguished in this period: Christian legalism (as a continuation of early and medieval Christian thought) and early realism (as the first clear-cut rejections of the Christian just war doctrine).

2.4.1 Probabilistic Arguments and the First Rejections of the Just War Theory

Beginning with the fourteenth century the idea that war was just if it was public and if it was declared by public authority (regardless of the ethical aspects of a 'just cause') started to gain territory.[81] By analysing Roman texts on war, Italian commentator, Raphael Fulgosius (1367–1427), advanced the idea that war could

---

[78] Reichberg et al. 2006, p. 9.

[79] Nussbaum 1947, pp. 53, 58–59.

[80] Bellamy 2006, pp. 49–50; Nussbaum 1947, p. 57.

[81] Fulgosius, In primam pandectarum partem comentaría, reprinted in Reichberg et al. 2006, pp. 228–229.

be just on both sides and that no distinction should be made in public war as to which side was right and which side was wrong.[82] This argument was later coined the bilateralist or probabilistic theory.[83]

Fulgosius' ideas were slowly taken up, in part or in whole, by subsequent thinkers. Spanish scholastics (fifteenth–sixteenth centuries) accepted the probabilistic view, but only under certain conditions.[84] Later, Protestant theologians (sixteenth–seventeenth centuries) took over the concept, but did not completely renounce the just war tradition. Other authors, such as Balthazar Ayala (1548–1584), assumed the bilateralist argument and used it to shift the focus from just wars to lawful wars. In his treatise, published in 1582, Ayala asserted that 'just causes' of war rather dealt with considerations of fairness and goodness, and not with the character of the legal result which was produced. If war was waged by a sovereign prince who had no superior, then the discussion of the equity and fairness of the cause was superfluous. Accordingly, nothing was needed other than that the war was waged by parties which considered themselves enemies and who had the right to wage war. In such a case, Ayala argued, the opinion of Fulgosius had to be accepted.[85]

Spanish scholastics of the sixteenth century and Protestant jurists of the seventeenth century were not the only ones who took up the bilateralist argument. For those who sought the rejection of the just war tradition, Fulgosius' opinion was just a small part of the equation.

For Niccolò Machiavelli (1469–1527), the relative nature of what was 'just' in war was obvious, when he quoted an ancient Roman saying that 'war is just to whom it is necessary and arms are pious when there is no hope but in arms.'[86] His rejection of the just war tradition was obvious. In his opinion, war was a necessary tool to secure one's principality and to enlarge one's possessions. Moreover, Machiavelli believed that when it came to the safety of one's country, no attention had to be paid 'either to justice or injustice, kindness or cruelty, or to its being praiseworthy or ignominious' and the alternative adopted had to be the one that 'will save the life and will preserve the freedom of one's country.'[87] Machiavelli thus put aside concerns of morality and ethics and did not engage in the analysis of 'just causes' stemming from natural law. For him, political power was a value in itself and the prince was vested with omnipotent power—unrestrained by morality—to preserve the freedom of the state.[88]

---

[82] Fulgosius, In primam pandectarum partem comentaría, reprinted in Reichberg et al. 2006, pp. 228–229.

[83] Brownlie 1963, pp. 10–11.

[84] Vitoria 1991b, p. 313.

[85] Brownlie 1963, p. 10 (quoting Balthasar Ayala, De jure et officiis bellicis et disciplina militari libri (On the Law and Duties of War and Military Discipline) Book I, Chap. 2).

[86] Machiavelli 2004, Chap. 26, p. 130.

[87] Machiavelli 1970, p. 515.

[88] Reichberg et al. 2006, pp. 251–253; Russell 2009, p. 468.

Although at the time his works were published Machiavelli's views did not directly lead to the general rejection of the just war theory (Spanish scholasticism was still to follow the early and medieval Christian doctrine), his contribution to the development of realist thinking was of great significance. Similar opinions were expressed by the Italian jurist Alciatus (1492–1550) in *Paradoxa* and by the French jurist and political philosopher Jean Bodin (1529/30–1596) in *De republica*.[89]

2.4.2 Spanish Scholastics and their View on Self-Defence

Despite the incipient realist trends, the Christian just war tradition was continued by both Catholic and reformer thinkers. Late Spanish scholasticism was the first that combined early and medieval Christian theology with humanist thought.

The first philosopher to write an independent treatise on the problem of war between nations was Francisco de Vitoria (ca. 1492–1546), a Spanish scholastic and Renaissance theologian, founder of the tradition in philosophy known as the School of Salamanca. He delivered two lectures (*De Indis and De iure belli*) in 1539, which were first published in 1557.[90] Both lectures thoroughly discussed recourse to war and were subsequently used as essential points of reference by authors. Because of them, Vitoria is still acknowledged as a significant contributor to the Christian doctrine of just war and the origins of international law.

In *De Indis*, Vitoria discussed illegitimate and legitimate titles of conquest in relation to Spain's claim to dominion in the New World. He asserted that military conquest and claims of domination could not be made on the basis of the Catholic Church's acclaimed secular jurisdiction over the non-Christian world.[91] Vitoria also refuted the claim that a refusal to accept the faith of Christ was in itself reason enough to conquer the so-called barbarians.[92] Vitoria therefore followed Aquinas' lead in rejecting war and conquest for the mere difference of religion or for the rejection of the Christian faith. He did, however, defend the right of proselytising Christianity by engaging in trade and commerce with the non-believers.[93]

In *De jure belli* Vitoria discussed the conditions for the recourse to war and the righteous conduct of hostilities. In this lecture, he rejected the enlargement of an empire as a legitimate cause for waging war, as well as the personal glory or convenience of the prince as a justification.[94] Vitoria distinguished between

[89] Brownlie 1963, p. 11.
[90] Vitoria 1991a, pp. 233, 293.
[91] Ibid., pp. 250–252.
[92] Ibid., pp. 269–270.
[93] Ibid., pp. 285–286.
[94] Vitoria 1991b, pp. 302–303.

offensive and defensive wars.[95] Concerning the former, he asserted that 'offensive war is for the avenging of injuries and the admonishment of enemies' and that 'there can be no vengeance where there has not first been a culpable offence.'[96] Regarding defensive wars, Vitoria believed that they were justified by both natural and divine law, inasmuch as it was lawful 'to resist force with force.' In his findings, he relied on the teachings of Augustine and Thomas Aquinas to prove that there was no doubt about the natural justifiability of defensive wars.[97]

Vitoria cautioned against waging war to inflict cruel punishment for all crimes indiscriminately. He believed that it was unlawful to persecute those responsible for trivial offences by waging war upon them. In his opinion, only the most serious offences justified recourse to war.[98] In other words, war had to be contemplated as the last resort, only to be adopted when it was truly necessary. Moreover, he advised that once the war had been fought and victory won, the victor ought to show moderation and Christian humility.[99]

Regarding conduct of warfare, Vitoria reiterated his predecessors' view on moderation and offered the first attempt to organize rules pertaining to that principle. Accordingly, he devoted a separate section in his *De jure belli* lecture on the limits to be observed in a just war.[100]

Vitoria reiterated his predecessors' view on self-defence as a precept of natural law. Accordingly, 'any person, even a private citizen, may declare and wage defensive war' to defend himself, others or his property, because such action was allowed by the natural-law principle of 'force may be resisted by force.'[101] For such action, no authority was needed, because it was permitted by natural law.

Vitoria also acknowledged the prerogative of any commonwealth to declare and wage war.[102] Here again, he reiterated earlier views on the rights of the sovereign. Accordingly, Vitoria recognized defence of the homeland as one of the most important 'just causes' for waging war together with offensive war for avenging injuries.[103]

In his opinion, the difference between the right of a private person to wage war and that of the commonwealth was that the former only had the right to defend himself and his property. A private person did not have the right to avenge injury, to seize back property and to 'teach its enemies a lesson' as the sovereign had.[104]

---

95 Ibid., p. 300.

96 Ibid., p. 303.

97 Ibid., p. 297.

98 Ibid., p. 304.

99 Ibid., p. 327. At the same time, Vitoria also asserted that 'even after the victory had been won and property restored to its rightful owners, and peace and security were established, it was lawful to avenge the injury done by the enemy and to teach the enemy a lesson by punishing them for the damage they have done.' Ibid., p. 305.

100 Ibid., pp. 314–326.

101 Ibid., p. 299.

102 Ibid., p. 300.

103 Ibid., p. 300.

104 Ibid., pp. 299–301.

The tradition of Vitoria was taken further by several sixteenth-century scholastics, of which one of the most important was the Jesuit theologian Francisco Suárez (1548–1617). His most famous work was the *Metaphysical Disputations*, written in 1597, which also analysed the question of war (chapter *De bello*). Besides being a follower of Vitoria, Suárez adhered to the teachings of Aquinas and to some extent, to those of Augustine. Similar to Vitoria, Suárez distinguished between defensive and offensive wars and rendered a war justifiable if it was fought by a sovereign ruler with the purpose of redressing an injury or for the purposes of defence.[105] He also confirmed Vitoria's opinion that no cause whatsoever was sufficient to justify war, but only causes that were very serious and proportionate to the ravages of war, 'for it would be contrary to reason to inflict the most serious damage because of a slight injury.'[106] Suárez also believed that since war was the severest punishment of all, it had to be inflicted with the utmost restraint.[107]

The attempt to restrict aggressive wars to the realm of sovereign rights was also apparent with Suárez. In his opinion, aggressive war could only be waged by 'the possessor of sovereign power.'[108] He saw offensive war 'to repel injuries' and 'to hold enemies in check' as 'right and necessary' in accordance with 'the custom of the Church' and the opinion of 'the Fathers and the popes.'[109]

When it came to self-defence, Suárez believed that such a right was 'natural and necessary' and defence of others (on an individual level) or defence of the homeland (on a commonwealth level) was prescribed or could be rendered an official duty.[110] Suárez also made a distinction between defensive and offensive wars.

> We have to consider whether the injustice is, practically speaking, simply about to take place, or whether it has already done so, and redress is sought through war. In this second case, the war is aggressive. In the former case, war has the character of self-defence, provided that it is waged with a moderation of defence which is blameless.[111]

Since Suárez was against offensive private wars, it is clear that the above-quoted passage referred to public wars—defensive and offensive.

Both Vitoria and Suárez acknowledged that the main difference between the right of a private person to wage war and that of a sovereign is that the latter has the privilege to resort to punitive actions (offensive wars). What is apparent in both opinions is a tendency to restrict the right of the individual to wage offensive wars and, in parallel, to limit the defensive right of the sovereign to actual threats. Vitoria believed that self-defence was resistance of force by force, while Suárez

---

105 Suárez 1944, Disputation XIII, Section 2, pp. 802–804, 815–816.

106 Ibid., Section 4, pp. 815–817.

107 Ibid., Section 7, pp. 845–846, 850–851.

108 Ibid., Section 2 (1), p. 805.

109 Ibid., Section 1 (5), p. 804.

110 Ibid., Section 1 (4), pp. 802–803.

111 Ibid., Section 1 (6), p. 804.

asserted that defensive wars were against injustices 'simply about to take place'.[112] That shows a discernable inclination to exclude preventive wars (against religious enemies, for instance) from the list of a sovereign's prerogatives. This tendency was to resurface in Grotius' approach to self-defence, although other authors, such as Gentili, would support the right of the sovereign to wage preventive wars.

2.4.3 Protestant Legalist Views on War: Gentili and Grotius

While Spanish scholastics were criticizing war against non-believers, the European sovereigns were dragged into their own holy war: the conflict between the Catholic Church and the Protestant Reformation movement. The roots of this movement went back to the fourteenth and fifteenth centuries, but open and organized dissent manifested itself only from 1517 onwards, with the protests of Martin Luther, a Roman Catholic monk and academic. The Reformation process and the firm opposition from the Catholic Church led Europe into its own holy war period, in spite of the fact that both jurists and theologians attempted to depart from the concept of religious wars. After many fifteenth- and sixteenth-century commentators renounced war for differences of religion (like Vitoria and Suárez), political arguments in favour of war for the faith were dominant during the first half of the seventeenth century, when the Thirty Years' War[113] engaged virtually all European powers in conflict.

During this time, the tradition of Spanish scholastics was taken further by Protestant jurists, who brought new insights into the normative framework. Both Alberico Gentili and Hugo Grotius continued to discuss 'just causes' for waging war in line with Vitoria and Suárez. Nonetheless, they also dismissed many arguments that were held by theologians such as Augustine or Aquinas.

Alberico Gentili is most famous for his *De jure belli libri tres*, first published in 1588–1589.[114] Gentili affirmed that war was a 'just and public contest of arms' between sovereign equals and that only 'supreme princes', who had no superior, could resort to war. Gentili also cautioned that war had to be the last resort: 'whereas there are two modes of contention, one by argument and the other one by force, one should not resort to the latter if it is possible to use the former.'[115] Gentili rejected the justification of war for religious motives, explicitly breaking away from the doctrine of holy war and from the idea of obeying a divine command to go to war.[116]

---

[112] Vitoria 1991b, p. 299; Suarez 1944, Disputation XIII, Section 2 (1), p. 804.

[113] The Thirty Years' War (1618–1648) began as a religious conflict between Catholics and reformer Protestants, but ended up involving many other issues, such as territorial annexations and consolidation of power.

[114] Nussbaum 1947, p. 94.

[115] Gentili 1933, Book I, Chap. 3, p. 15.

[116] Ibid., Chap. 9, pp. 38–39.

Hugo Grotius also believed that war had to be considered only as a last resort: 'where judicial means (*iudicia*) fail, war begins.'[117] His *De jure belli ac pacis libri tres* (On the Laws of War and Peace), published in 1625, marked the beginning of a more modern conception of the law of nations, which served as the basis for the development of modern international law, 'valid apart from religious sanction, suprasectarian and human in spirit and still embodying the tradition of Christian piety and morality.'[118]

Grotius distinguished between private wars and public wars. According to him, public war was waged by one who had jurisdiction (the sovereign), whereas private war was waged by one who had no such authority, but was nevertheless allowed to resort to war to ward off an injury.[119]

Both private and public wars were permitted by the law of nature, if certain conditions applied. Grotius defined the law of nature as a 'dictate of right reason' that pointed out which acts were in conformity with rational nature and thus 'enjoined by the author of nature, God.'[120] Regarding public wars, Grotius named four 'just causes'. Regarding the first three, he acknowledged that they were accepted by the majority of authors: defence, recovery of property, and punishment. He added a fourth, 'the obtaining of what is owed to us,' in other words, pursuing an obligation not fulfilled by the other.[121] Grotius reiterated the view of the Spanish scholastics and outlawed wars for religious motives.[122] When it came to private wars, Grotius asserted that the law of nature allowed individuals to wage war in cases where 'public tribunals' could not help.[123] This argument will be given thorough attention below.

Like his predecessors, Grotius also employed the offensive–defensive dichotomy. Punishment and the recovery of property was to be exercised after the wrong was done. Punishment had to be exercised only in cases when the recovery of the property or the undoing of the wrong was no longer possible.[124] Defence, on the other hand, had to do with 'an injury not yet inflicted *(iniuria nondum facta)*, which menaces either one's body or one's property.'[125]

Grotius took further Vitoria's attempt to discuss the limits of warfare as a separate matter and devoted an entire Book to this topic. Accordingly, in Book III of his *De jure belli*, Grotius extensively discussed righteous and moderate conduct

---

117 Grotius 1964, Book II, Chap. 1 (ii), p. 171.

118 Nussbaum 1947, p. 2. For Grotius' importance for international relations theory, see Roelofsen 1990, pp. 96–131. For a succinct summary of his life, see: Holk 1983, pp. 32–39.

119 Grotius 1964, Book I, Chap. 3 (i), p. 91. He also named a third category, mixed wars, which were partly public, partly private.

120 Ibid., Chap. 1 (x), pp. 38–39.

121 Ibid., Book II, Chap. 1 (ii), pp. 171–172.

122 Ibid., Chap. 20 (xlviii), pp. 516–517.

123 Ibid., Chap. 3 (i–ii), pp. 91–92. See also: Haggenmacher 1997, pp. 368–369.

124 Ibid., Chap. 20 (i), p. 462.

125 Ibid., Chap. 1 (ii), p. 172.

in war as permitted by the law of nature and established by the law of nations.[126] Owing to his detailed emphasis on the conduct of warfare, subsequent authors began to discuss the topic as a separate one, distinct from the causes of war.[127]

2.4.4 *Self-Defence: As Seen by Gentili and by Grotius*

Both Gentili and Grotius understood self-defence as pertaining to the time before and during the attack. Gentili referred to 'necessary defence' to describe an imminent or an ongoing attack:

> One who is attacked by an armed enemy makes a necessary defence, and his action is that of necessary defence, and so also does one against whom an enemy has been making preparations.[128]

The 'necessary defence' was sanctioned by the law of nature and was a right of both an individual and a sovereign.[129] The individual could not go beyond the limits of such a right, because for him reparation could be secured through the authority of a magistrate.

> For if a private citizen commits some offence against a fellow citizen, reparation may be secured through the authority of a magistrate. But what a sovereign has done to a sovereign, no one will make good.[130]

Gentili thus took further the restriction both Vitoria and Suárez endorsed and according to which private individuals were only allowed to defend themselves and their property through private war; the redress of an injury was insured by the public authority.

This view was also adopted by Grotius. War was permissible 'if an attack by violence is made on one's person, endangering life, and no other way of escape is open.'[131] 'This right of self-defence,' Grotius asserted, 'has its origin directly and chiefly in the fact that nature commits to each his own protection, not in the injustice or crime of the aggressor.'[132] On the basis of this right, both private and public wars were allowed, but under different conditions.

In Grotius' view, private war was allowed only to ward off an injury. Moreover, killing the assailant in self-defence could not be the primary intent, but 'the only

---

[126] Ibid., Book III, Chap. 1 (i), p. 599. For an appraisal of Grotius' Book III, see Draper 1990, pp. 197–199.

[127] Roberts 2008, p. 938.

[128] Gentili 1933, Book I, Chap. 13, p. 58.

[129] Ibid., p. 59.

[130] Ibid., Chap. 14, p. 62.

[131] Grotius 1964, Book II, Chap. 1 (iii), p. 172.

[132] Ibid. Because of this, self-defence was permitted also against a blameless assailant, because the protection of one's life is more important than the absence of guilt of the attacker.

resource available at the time.'[133] In other words, 'the person who is attacked ought to prefer to do anything possible to frighten away or weaken the assailant, rather than cause death.'[134] In case of private wars, the danger of an attack had to be 'immediate and imminent in point of time.'[135] If the danger could in any other way be avoided or if it was not altogether certain that the danger could not be otherwise avoided, killing in self-defence—thus private war—was not permissible.[136] Moreover, private war was not permissible if 'judicial procedure' was readily available. Grotius thus defended private wars in self-defence only if judicial remedy was temporarily or continuously unavailable.[137]

Matters were different when it came to public wars. Grotius asserted that the arguments pertaining to private self-defence could also be applied to public wars, 'if the difference in conditions be taken into account.'[138] Since public wars arose only where there were no courts or where courts ceased to function, such wars were prolonged and were 'continually augmented by the increment of fresh losses and injuries.'[139] For that reason:

> Public powers have not only the right of self-defence, but also the right to exact punishment. Hence for them it is permissible to forestall an act of violence which is not immediate, but which is seen to be threatening from a distance.[140]

Grotius thus saw the forestalling of an immediate act of violence as defence and the forestalling of an act of violence threatening from a distance as a form of punishment. This view is somewhat confusing given the fact that elsewhere he maintained the defensive–offensive dichotomy based on temporal considerations.[141] Nonetheless, he gave an eloquent explanation of what he meant by acts of violence threatening from a distance: 'a wrong action commenced but not yet carried through.'[142] In other words, Grotius believed that sovereigns were entitled to forestall not only an immediate attack, but also one that was commenced, but not carried out (thus imminent or in preparation). He further believed that this right of the sovereign stemmed from the same foundation as the right of individuals to defend themselves.[143] For the same reasons, Gentili believed that in case of a war 'undertaken for the purpose of necessary defence,' a declaration of war was not required.[144]

---

133 Ibid., Chap. 1 (iv), p. 173.

134 Ibid.

135 Ibid., Chap. 1 (v), p. 173.

136 Ibid., pp. 174–175.

137 Ibid., Book I, Chap. 3 (ii), p. 92. Haggenmacher asserts that Grotius also saw private wars to vindicate one's right as legal if no legal remedy was available. Haggenmacher 1997, p. 368.

138 Grotius 1964, Book II, Chap. 1 (xvi), p. 184.

139 Ibid.

140 Ibid.

141 Ibid., Chap. 1 (ii), p. 172.

142 Ibid., Chap. 1 (xvi), p. 184.

143 Ibid.

144 Gentili 1933, Book II, Chap. 2, p. 136.

From this point onwards though, the views of Gentili and Grotius part. According to Gentili, sovereigns also had a right to 'defence dictated by expediency':

> I call it defence dictated by expediency when we make war through fear that we may ourselves be attacked. No one is more quickly laid low than one who has no fear, and a sense of security is the most common cause of disaster.[145]

In Gentili's view, a watchful sovereign would not waste the opportunity to 'strike at the root of the growing plant and check the attempts of an adversary who is meditating evil.'[146] Although he insisted that '[a] just cause for fear is demanded; suspicion is not enough,'[147] Gentili claimed that 'defence is just which anticipates dangers that are already meditated and prepared, and also those which are not meditated, but are probable and possible.'[148] In other words:

> No one ought to expose himself to danger. No one ought to wait to be struck, unless he is a fool. One ought to provide not only against an offence which is being committed, but also against one which may possibly be committed.[149]

Moreover, he advised to 'oppose powerful and ambitious chiefs, for they are content with no bounds, and end by attacking the fortunes of all.'[150] He cautioned, however, that the existence of 'probable and possible dangers' should not be interpreted as allowing a state 'to resort to a war [...] as soon as anyone becomes too powerful.'[151] Despite such restrictions, Gentili's definition of 'defence dictated by expediency' pertained to a veritable preventive war. Unlike necessary defence, war dictated by expediency had to be declared.[152] The causes that Gentili named as justifying such expediency were very similar to those that started the Peloponnesian War. This is not to say that Gentili revived the ancient Greek concept of preventive war. That concept had survived the ancient times and was acknowledged as part of the sovereign's broader right to wage war. Nonetheless, Gentili made a far more elaborate exposé of this prerogative than his predecessors. His ideas were taken further by positivist jurists of the seventeenth and eighteenth centuries.

Grotius did not share Gentili's view on preventive wars. Although he agreed that public wars could be waged in face of a danger 'threatening from a distance,'[153] Grotius characterized Gentili's view as plainly 'untenable'.[154] In his opinion, such reasoning could prove to be far-sighted to undertake the war.

---

[145] Ibid., Book I, Chap. 14, p. 61.
[146] Ibid.
[147] Ibid., p. 62.
[148] Ibid., p. 66.
[149] Ibid., p. 62.
[150] Ibid., p. 64.
[151] Ibid., p. 66.
[152] Ibid., Book II, Chap. 2, p. 136.
[153] Grotius 1964, Book II, Chap. 1 (xvi), p. 184.
[154] Ibid., Chap. 1 (xvii), p. 184.

> That the possibility of being attacked confers the right to attack is abhorrent to every principle of equity.[155]

It may be concluded that Grotius' arguments were similar to Gentili's in as much as both concurred that private wars could be waged against an ongoing or imminent attack. They also agreed on the permissibility of public wars in the face of an immediate attack, as well as one that was imminent or in preparation. Nevertheless, they differed on the permissibility of preventive wars. Grotius adopted a more restrictive view, in which simple fear of being attacked was not enough to allow self-defence, whereas Gentili upheld the right of the sovereign to defend the state against possible dangers.

There are three lines of reasoning on the content of self-defence that can be contoured in the combined opinions of Gentili and Grotius. First, there is a *stricto sensu* understanding of self-defence that applies to individuals and which is only allowed in the face of an imminent or ongoing attack. This is the same understanding that was given to individual self-defence by Augustine, the *Decretum*, Aquinas and chivalric codes.[156] This will be referred to as the concept of individual or private self-defence.

Secondly, there is an intermediate understanding of self-defence according to which states or sovereigns could exercise self-defence against a danger which 'is not immediate, but which is seen to be threatening from a distance.'[157] By this contention, Grotius was differentiating between the right of self-defence of individuals (which was very much a form of on-the-spot action) and that of states (where an invasion could be imminent or prepared without being about to happen in the sense of an attack from one person to another). The phrase 'threatening from the distance' did not refer to action against a potential threat, because, as shown above, Grotius distanced himself from justifying such use of force.[158] Moreover, Grotius actually explained what he meant by a danger threatening from a distance: a wrong action that was commenced, but not carried through.[159] In other words, an attack that was in process of being prepared or launched against the target state. The intermediate understanding of self-defence referred thus to states and allowed defensive action against an ongoing attack or one that was imminent, in a somewhat more reasonable understanding meant to correspond to the realities of public warfare. The limiting tendency observed in the writings of Vitoria and Suarez as to defensive public wars can be related to Grotius' views on the concept. Although Grotius referred to defence in full-fledged public wars when he put forward his arguments, the understanding he gave to this form of forestalling

155 Ibid.

156 Gratian, question I, in Reichberg et al. 2006, pp. 109–110; Aquinas, question 41, Article 1, in Reichberg et al. 2006, pp. 182–183; Pisan, Part III, Chap. 12, in Reichberg et al. 2006, p. 219.

157 Grotius 1964, Book II, Chap. 1 (xvi), p. 184.

158 Ibid., Chap. 1 (xvii), p. 184.

159 Ibid., Book II, Chap. 1 (xvi), p. 184.

assaults would resurface in subsequent justifications for 'imperfect' wars in self-defence. This Grotian understanding of self-defence was thus the result of applying *stricto sensu*, private self-defence to the realities of public warfare.

Thirdly, the argument of defence against 'probable and possible'[160] dangers was put forward by Gentili. This is the broadest understanding of self-defence within the three lines of reasoning. On the basis of this conception, self-defence should also permit preventive wars against potential threats. Grotius disagreed with this argument and characterized it as simply untenable for the purposes of self-defence.[161] Nonetheless, this conception was adopted by subsequent authors and treated as part of the sovereign's right to wage 'perfect wars'. Therefore, this understanding will not be referred to as self-defence, but rather 'preventive war' or 'preventive use of force'.

2.5 The Christian Normative Framework and Self-Defence

The aim of this chapter was to elucidate the understanding given to the right of self-defence in the early and medieval Christian as well as Christian legalist conceptions of natural law. Early Christian theologians borrowed natural-law concepts from ancient Greek and Roman philosophers and adjusted them to the requirements of the new religion. Medieval Christian thinkers further amended the natural-law theory to fit the realities of the Catholic Church and its worldly functions. Scholastics and reformer jurists enriched these tenets with renaissance and humanist thought. Although some differences could be observed between, on one hand, the early and medieval Christian framework and, on the other, the legalist Christian framework, the main legal paradigm of the fourth to the seventeenth centuries was Christianity and its natural-law conception. It is therefore reasonable to view this historical phase under one normative framework, dominated by the Christian religion.[162]

In this normative framework, self-defence was viewed as a natural right of both the private person and the sovereign. It was thus accepted as one of the 'just causes' for waging private wars as well as public wars. Self-defence was clearly distinguished from avenging injuries and punishment for wrongdoings.

It is important to note at this point that because of the 'international' characteristic of the Christian natural-law framework,[163] the natural-law conception of self-defence also had an 'international' quality. Simply put, its meaning was generally accepted across the Western tradition and did not pertain only to a

160 Gentili 1933, Book I, Chap. 14, p. 66.

161 Grotius 1964, Book II, Chap. 1 (xvii), p. 184.

162 Steiger 2001, pp. 184–187.

163 Christianity being the intellectual–religious basis in the Western tradition, its norms affected not only the personal lives of individuals, but also every type of rulership in the European space. Steiger 2001, pp. 184–185.

specific jurisdiction. Even if it could not be regarded as an international customary rule in the modern sense of the word, it definitely had a certain 'international' character on the basis of the general acceptance of natural law.[164] It is also essential to note that the work of Grotius marked the advent of a more modern conception of the 'law of nations' that served as the basis for the developments in subsequent centuries.[165]

There are two essential characteristics of the Christian natural-law concept of self-defence that need emphasis. First, there was *no need for public authority* to allow the exercise of this natural right in the face of danger. Secondly, the natural right of self-defence was relevant in the face of an injury *not yet received.* Augustine referred to 'an enemy lying in ambush,' Gratian allowed resistance to force 'before it strikes,' Suárez permitted defensive war against an injury 'simply about to take place', Gentili saw defence as necessary against an enemy preparing to attack and Grotius asserted that defence had to do with 'an injury not yet committed.' Consequently, the natural right of self-defence was, by nature, anticipatory. There was no strict differentiation made between 'self-defence' and 'anticipatory self-defence', because the right *as such* had an anticipatory meaning. Consistent differentiation was made between defensive and offensive wars, where the former always referred to an injury not yet inflicted or to an attack not yet occurred and the latter pertained to revenge and punishment of past injuries. This defensive–offensive dichotomy was already present in the writings of Gratian and Aquinas and later clarified by Vitoria, Suárez, Gentili and Grotius.[166]

While medieval reprisals were a prerogative of both the individual and the sovereign, starting with scholasticism, the idea that private wars could only be waged in self-defence began to gain ground. This restriction was strengthened by both Gentili and Grotius: private wars were only allowed to ward off an injury when public tribunals could not offer assistance.

The sovereign also had the right to ward off an injury without officially declaring war.[167] The right of the sovereign to defend the state stemmed from the same natural-law understanding as did private self-defence. Nonetheless, as it became clear from the arguments put forward by Grotius, when applying the concept of private self-defence to public warfare, its limits had to be interpreted more permissively, given the realities of inter-state conflicts. Given the fact that individuals could resort to the central authority for protection, their right of

---

[164] Ibid. Nussbaum explains that the term 'law of nations' is more adequate to describe the interrelations of human groups over the centuries before the more modern 'international law' system emerged. Nussbaum 1947, pp. 1–2. For the difference between the 'law of nations' and present international law, see: Haggenmacher 1997, pp. 369–370.

[165] Nussbaum 1947, p. 2.

[166] Gratian, question II, canon 1, in Reichberg et al. 2006, p. 113; Aquinas, question 40, in Reichberg et al. 2006, pp. 176–178; Vitoria 1991b, pp. 297, 303; Suárez 1944, Disputation XIII, Section 1 (6), p. 804; Grotius 1964, Book II, Chap. 1 (ii), p. 172, and Chap. 20 (i), p. 462.

[167] Gentili 1933, Book II, Chap. 2, p. 172.

Table 2.1 Self-defence, a right of the individual and the sovereign, as interpreted in the Christian normative framework

Self-Defence	Augustine, Decretum, Aquinas, Pisan	Vitoria, Suarez	Grotius	Gentili
Individuals	Attacking enemy or enemy lying in ambush	Force may be resisted by force when life and property is attacked	To ward off an injury	Attacking enemy or enemy making preparations
Sovereigns	Defence against invasion, defence against religious enemies (preventive)	Injuries just about to take place	Immediate attacks and attacks threatening from a distance	Necessary defence and defence dictated by expediency (preventive)

self-defence was understandably more *stricto sensu* than that of states. Nevertheless, according to Grotius, public defensive wars could only be waged against immediate (ongoing) threats and dangers that were imminent.

Preventive war in self-defence was advocated by Gentili, but rejected by Grotius. Defence against potential threats went well beyond the confines of the natural-law concept of self-defence, which only justified defensive action in the *stricto sensu* (for individuals) and in the Grotian understanding (for states).

The various views adopted by authors in the Christian normative framework are illustrated in Table 2.1. It should nevertheless be borne in mind that all the mentioned authors believed that the sovereign also had an extensive right to wage punitive, offensive wars.

Three elements of self-defence could be identified in the Christian conception of natural-law. First, there always had to be an ongoing or imminent attack. Secondly, the danger posed by that attack had to give rise to an immediate need for response. In case of individuals, the immediacy referred to on-the-spot reaction. For sovereigns, it also allowed action against threats that were not necessarily about to happen, but still gave rise to an immediate need to act. Thirdly, self-defence had to be exercised with moderation. Only by observing the limits of this principle could one 'blamelessly' defend himself.

Consequently, anticipatory action was an intrinsic part of the natural law of self-defence. Therefore, the elements of self-defence (existence of an attack, immediate need to respond and moderation) were also applicable to anticipatory action, as inherently part of self-defence. Since these elements limited the exercise of self-defence, they also limited anticipatory action. It is therefore pertinent to conclude at this point, that the limits of anticipatory action—as understood in the Christian natural-law concept of self-defence—are the imminence of an attack, the immediate need for a response and moderation. The following chapters will examine whether these limits were reiterated by subsequent doctrine and state practice.

References

Aristotle (1959) The 'Art' of Rhetoric (trans: Freese JH). William Heinemann, London
Aristotle (1967) Politics (trans: Rackham H). William Heinemann, London
Aristotle (1968) XIX The Nicomachean ethics (trans: Rackham H). William Heinemann, London
Augustine (1955) The problem of free choice (De libero arbitrio) (trans: Pontifex M). Newman Press, Westminster
Augustine (1994) City of God, reprinted in Fortin EL et al (eds) Political Writings/Augustine, Hackett, Indianapolis, Ind
Barker E (1959) The political thought of Plato and Aristotle. Dover Publications, New York
Bellamy AJ (2006) Just wars: from Cicero to Iraq. Polity Press, Cambridge
Brownlie I (1963) International law and the use of force by states. Clarendon Press, Oxford
Christopher P (2004) The ethics of war and peace. An introduction to legal and moral issues. Pearson/Prentice Hall, Upper Saddle River
Cicero, MT (1968) De Officiis (trans: Miller W). Heinemann, London
Draper GIAD (1990) Grotius' place in the development of legal ideas about war. In: Bull H, Kingsbury B, Roberts A (eds) Hugo Grotius and international relations. Clarendon Press, Oxford, pp 177–207
Everson S (1997) Aristotle on the foundations of the state. In: Dunn J, Harris I (eds) Aristotle, vol 2. Edward Elgar, Cheltenham, pp 292–304
Fontane J (2000) Isidore de Seville: genese et originalite de la culture hispanique au temps des Visigoths. Brepols, Turnhout
Gentili A (1933) De jure belli libri tres (trans: Rolfe JC). Clarendon Press, Oxford
Grewe WG (2000) The epochs of international law (trans: Byers M. De Gruyter, Berlin
Grotius H (1964) De jure belli ac pacis libri tres (trans: Kelsey FW. Oceana, New York
Haggenmacher P (1997) On assessing the Grotian heritage. In: Dunn J, Harris I (eds) Grotius, vol 2. Edward Elgar, Cheltenham, pp 365–375
van Holk LE (1983) Hugo Grotius, 1583–1645: a biographical sketch. In: van Holk LE, Roelofsen CG (eds) Grotius reader: a reader for students of international law and legal history. T.M.C. Asser Instituut, The Hague, pp 23–44
Keen MH (1965) The laws of war in the late Middle Ages. Routledge and Kegan Paul, London
Laffan RGD (ed) (1929) Select documents of European history: 800–1492. Henry Holt, New York
Legnano G da (1917) Tractatus de Bello, de Represaliis et de Duello, ed. by Holland TE. Oxford University Press, Oxford
Lisska AJ (1996) Aquinas' theory of natural law. An analytic reconstruction. Clarendon Press, Oxford
Llewellyn P (1970) Rome in the dark ages. Faber and Faber, London
Machiavelli N (1970) Discourses on the first decade of Livy. Reprinted in: Crick B, Walker LJ (eds), Niccolo Machiavelli: The Discourses. Penguin, London
Machiavelli N (2004) The Prince and the art of war. Collector's Library, London
Mattox JM (2006) Saint Augustine and the theory of just war. Continuum, London
Mitchell K, Wood I (2002) The world of Gregory de Tours. Brill, Leiden
Neff SC (2005) War and the law of nations: general history. Cambridge University Press, Cambrdige
Nussbaum A (1947) A concise history of the law of nations. Macmillan, New York
Phillipson C (1911) The international law and custom of ancient Greece and Rome, vol. 1–2. MacMillan, London
Reichberg GM, Syse H, Begby E (eds) (2006) The ethics of war: classic and contemporary readings. Blackwell, Malden
Roberts A (2008) The equal application of the laws of war: a principle under pressure. Int. Rev. Red Cross 90(872):931–962

Roelofsen CG (1990) Grotius and the international politics of the seventeenth century. In: Bull H, Kingsbury B, Roberts A (eds) Hugo Grotius and international relations. Clarendon, Oxford, pp 96–131
Russell B (2009) History of western philosophy. Routledge, London
Smith WS (2007) Augustine and the limits of preemptive and preventive war. J. Relig. Stud. 35:141–162
Steiger H (2001) From the international law of Christianity to the international law of the world citizen: reflections on the formation of epochs of the history of international law. J. Hist. Int. Law 3:180–193
Suárez F (1944) The three theological virtues: on charity. Reprinted in: Brown Scott J (ed), Selections from three works of Francisco Suárez, S.J. (trans: Williams GL et al). Clarendon Press, Oxford, pp. 799–865
Swift LJ (1983) The early fathers on war and military service. Michael Glazier, Wilmington
Vitoria F de (1991a) De Indis. Reprinted in: Pagden A, Lawrance J (eds) Vitoria: political writings. Cambridge University Press, Cambridge
Vitoria F de (1991b) De jure belli. Reprinted in: Pagden A, Lawrance J (eds) Vitoria: political writings. Cambridge University Press, Cambridge
Watson A (1993) International law in Archaic Rome: war and religion. John Hopkins University Press, Baltimore

Chapter 3
Self-Defence as a Measure Short of War

The aim of this chapter is to analyse the views adopted during the seventeenth to nineteenth centuries regarding the natural-law concept of self-defence and to assess whether the status and limits of anticipatory action were altered during that period. As concluded in the previous chapter, the natural right of self-defence was intrinsically anticipatory; its temporal dimension pertained to the time before and during an attack. Furthermore, the elements that limited the exercise of self-defence (existence of an attack, immediate need to respond and moderation) automatically served as the limits of anticipatory action. It remains to be seen whether the positivist influence on the legal thinking of the seventeenth to nineteenth centuries changed that perception.

Starting with the seventeenth century, the doctrine of just war and the old Christian conception of natural law were gradually confined to the realm of ethics, while realist and positivist considerations gave voluntary (positive) law a dominant role in state affairs. From the middle of the seventeenth century onwards, the sovereign became the sole authority entitled to resort to war and the limits of this right concerned the formalities of force rather than its underlying motives.

In the following paragraphs, attention will be given to the way war was understood by the realist–positivist approach in order to map out the normative framework in which the right of self-defence was acknowledged. Apart from relying on authoritative and representative writings, this chapter will also discuss a few instances of state practice relevant for self-defence. Nonetheless, the extensive state practice of privateering, pacific blockades and special reprisals of the seventeenth–nineteenth centuries will not be discussed as they do not aid in understanding how self-defence was viewed by the parties to a conflict. The chapter will focus on the way the content and temporal dimension of self-defence were understood during this period. The concluding remarks of this section will assess whether the status and limits of anticipatory action were altered during this period.

It is important to note at this point that this chapter does not aim to offer a comprehensive portrayal of realism and legal positivist approaches. It merely puts the subject of self-defence within the context of these developments that shaped the legal paradigm of the age.

K. Tibori Szabó, *Anticipatory Action in Self-Defence*, DOI: 10.1007/978-90-6704-796-8_3,

3.1 The Rise of Positive Law

From the middle of the seventeenth century onwards, realist thinking quickly developed to characterize the national and foreign policy in Europe. Jurists gradually left behind the Christian just war doctrine and adopted a more positivist view in their legal writings about war. Although natural law still featured in the works of certain prominent thinkers of the seventeenth and eighteenth centuries, its Christian understanding was either challenged or reinterpreted to accommodate realist views.

The move to realism brought new ideas regarding the status of states and the rights of the sovereign. These ideas influenced the approach to war as well. The Peace of Westphalia (1648) reconfigured contested boundaries as well as recognized—in some cases the already factual—independence of numerous states (such as the Dutch Republic and Switzerland). According to Baylis and Smith, the Peace of Westphalia was based on three principles. The first was '*rex est imperator in regno suo*,' in other words 'the king is emperor in his own realms,' This meant that sovereigns were recognized as not being subject to any higher authority. From this principle stemmed the idea of sovereign equality. The second principle was the *cuius regio, eius religio*, according to which the sovereign chose the religion of his country. The function of the third principle was to prevent any hegemon from arising and dominating other states and later it became known as the 'balance of power'.[1]

These concepts have changed over time and their scope has widened much beyond the aims of those present at Westphalia. Nonetheless, they were the initial form of the ideas that later shaped Western European politics and were often reiterated by the Concert of Europe until 1914.[2]

In this framework, war was seen as an absolute prerogative of the sovereign, who had no other legal superior and who could decide on efficient action when the state's vital interests were at stake. This position came to be known as *raison d'état* (reason of state, national interest), which put the survival and interests of states before any other consideration of foreign policy. According to Baylis and Smith, *raison d'état* was seen as a set of maxims that leaders had to follow on how to conduct their foreign affairs so as to ensure the security of state.[3]

---

[1] Baylis and Smith 2001, p. 43. Realist, neo-liberal and nationalist theories view the Peace of Westphalia as the foundation of the modern European state system. For such an opinion and for addressing the criticisms brought to the model, see Krasner 1995–1996, p. 115. Recently, some international relations scholars expressed the view that the Westphalian sovereignty principle and state-system model is the result of a laborious mythification process brought about by nineteenth- and twentieth-century nationalist historians. See Osiander 2001, pp. 264–265. See also Beaulac 2000, pp. 148–177.

[2] The Concert of Europe (the 'Congress System') was a series of meetings between the old great powers of Europe between 1815 and 1914. Its founding members were Britain, Austria, Russia and Prussia.

[3] Baylis and Smith 2001, p. 142.

As mentioned above, this approach 'downgraded' old Christian natural law arguments about 'just causes' of war to the sphere of morality and ethics. As shown below, some clearly challenged the tenets of Christian natural law, while others tried to reinterpret it to fit the realist paradigm.

3.1.1 The Departure from the Christian Concept of Natural Law

Until about the middle of the seventeenth century, the Christian just war framework dominated legal writing in Western Europe. The concept of just war was intrinsically linked to the law of nature, according to which the state of nature was fundamentally peaceful and war was an unfortunate necessity through which natural justice was sought.[4] The seventeenth century brought important challenges to this perspective. Thomas Hobbes challenged the very definition of the state of nature.[5] Other writers, such as Pufendorf and Wolff, while confirming the classic state of nature, believed that natural law was suspended during war and only voluntary law applied.[6]

In his most famous work, *Leviathan* (published in 1651), Thomas Hobbes (1588–1679) portrayed his idea on the structure of society. Hobbes believed that the 'state of nature' was one of constant war, in which the principle of self-preservation—stemming from natural law—was the most important. Since there was no international supreme ruler, who could adjudicate disputes among nations, it was natural that states were also in a constant state of conflict.[7] The 'state of nature' Hobbes was referring to clearly departed from the one formulated by Christian theologians; it was one based on self-preservation and voluntary contracts, by which human beings decided what was the best way to survive and what could bring about their enemies' destruction.[8] Hobbes' arguments were similar to those of Machiavelli, as both concurred that when it came to survival, moral concerns would only have a prudential character.

Although Hobbes promoted a new understanding of the state of nature, some jurists of the time still followed Gentili's and Grotius' ideas and tried to accommodate their views with the realist approach. One such author was Samuel von Pufendorf (1632–1694), German jurist and statesman. In accordance with the Christian approach, Pufendorf believed that natural law stemmed from God and commanded humans to be sociable and friendly to each other, by obeying certain natural duties. In his treatise published in 1673, *On the Duty of Man and Citizen*, he asserted that nature had created a kind kinship among people. Humans were

[4] See Aquinas' definition of natural law in Lisska 1996, pp. 263–266, 272–278.

[5] Reichberg et al. 2006, pp. 441–442.

[6] Neff 2005, pp. 132, 138.

[7] Hobbes, Leviathan 1991, Chap. 13 (12), in May et al. 2006, p. 82.

[8] Ibid., pp. 80–83.

capable of imposing such kinship on themselves and the emerging state system was able to preserve such sociability between citizens.[9] Pufendorf departed from natural law precepts inasmuch as he saw war as exclusively regulated by voluntary (positive) law.[10]

In line with his predecessors, Pufendorf divided wars into defensive and offensive ones:

> The just causes of engaging in war come down to the preservation and protection of our lives and property against unjust attack, or the collection of what is due to us from others but has been denied, or the procurement of reparations for wrong inflicted and of assurance of the future. Wars waged for the first of these causes are said to be defensive, for the other cases, offensive.[11]

Nonetheless, his views were strongly influenced by the contemporaneous balance-of-power ideas. He saw the right to wage war as the prerogative of the sovereign and a powerful tool to preserve the state and its interests. In other words, 'that country is considered happy which even in peace contemplates war.'[12] Such a view was very much the product of Pufendorf's age, when states not only had to be prepared to go to war, but, perhaps more importantly, they had to be *seen* as capable of going to war. Pufendorf thus inserted in his work beliefs that were widely accepted by statesmen at that time and which bore the symbols of realist thought. This was true also regarding his views on moderation in war. He believed that it was not always unjust:

> [T]o return a greater evil for a less, for the objection made by some that retribution should be rendered in proportion to the injury, is true only of civil tribunals, where punishments are meted out by superiors. But the evils inflicted by right of war have properly no relation to punishments. Since they neither proceed from a superior as such, nor have as their direct object the reform of the guilty party or others, but the defence and assertion of my safety, my property and my rights.[13]

After this exposé against a quantitative interpretation of proportionality, Pufendorf nonetheless advised that 'so far as it is possible, and as our defence and future security allow, we suit the evils inflicted upon an enemy to the process usually observed by a civil court' and he made reference to Grotius' discussion of moderation.[14] Consequently, Pufendorf endorsed the absolute prerogative of states to use force whenever it was deemed necessary for safety and future security, but he recommended humane behaviour during the hostilities and after victory.

A successor of Pufendorf in the natural law school was Christian von Wolff (1679–1754), who did not depart from the precepts of his precursor, except where

---

[9] Pufendorf 1991, Book II, Chap. 1 (11), pp. 118–119.

[10] Pufendorf 1934, Book VIII, Chap. 6 (7), p. 1325.

[11] Pufendorf 1991, Book II, Chap. 16 (2), p. 168.

[12] Ibid., Book II, Chap. 1 (11), p. 119.

[13] Pufendorf 1934, Book VIII, Chap. 6 (7), p. 1298.

[14] Ibid., Book VIII, Chap. 6 (7), p. 1298 (referring to Chaps. 11–16 of Book III of Grotius' De jure belli treatise).

the issues of moderation in war were concerned. Accordingly, Wolff held that 'so much is allowable in a just war against the person of the enemy as is sufficient to ward from us and our property the force used by him.'[15]

These challenges made the weaknesses of the natural law theory apparent as regards the realities of the seventeenth-century Europe. Although subsequent legal writers acknowledged natural law as the moral standard to which voluntary law should relate, they began to focus more on customs and treaties in their analysis of inter-state relations.

3.1.2 Positive Law and War in Due Form

Although natural law was still regarded as the primordial source of many duties and rights, from the eighteenth century onwards, positive law was viewed as a more usable basis for law enforcement. Many contemporary lawyers considered that the law of nations was predominantly voluntary in character, although certain rights stemmed from natural law.

The Swiss diplomat Emerich de Vattel (1714–1767) was one of such lawyers. His most famous work, *Le Droit de Gens*, published in 1758, is acknowledged as being at the crossroads of the centuries' old tradition of just war and the emergent international law of the eighteenth century.[16] *Le Droit de Gens* was widely circulated after its publication and was used as a handbook by statesmen and diplomats until the beginning of the First World War.[17]

Vattel did not denounce natural law as such. He rather asserted that natural law 'recommends for the common advantage of Nations the observance of the voluntary law of nations.'[18] In other words, in order to see the aims of the law of nature achieved, positive law was necessary to regulate the affairs of states. Accordingly, a sovereign, when deliberating upon the steps to take to fulfil his duty, could never 'lose sight' of the necessary (natural) law, which was always 'binding in conscience'.[19] Nonetheless, when it was a question of determining what he could demand from other states, he had to take into consideration the voluntary (positive) law of nations and 'restrict even his just claims within the bounds of a law whose principles are consecrated to the safety and welfare of the universal society of Nations.'[20] Consequently:

> [L]et us […] leave to the conscience of the sovereigns the observance of the natural and necessary law in all its strictness […]. But as regards the external effects of that law in

[15] Wolff 1934, Section 791.

[16] Reichberg et al. 2006, p. 504.

[17] Vattel 1964, pp. xxix–xlii.

[18] Ibid., Book III, Chap. 12, Section 189, pp. 304–305.

[19] Ibid., p. 305.

[20] Ibid.

> human society, we must necessarily have recourse to certain rules of more certain and easy application, and this in the interest of the safety and welfare of the great society of the human race.[21]

As many thinkers before him, Vattel also distinguished between defensive and offensive wars. Defensive war stemmed from the right of resisting by force any attack upon a state or its rights. Offensive war was based upon the right to use force to obtain justice, if it could not otherwise be secured, or to follow up one's rights by the force of arms.[22]

The preservation of the state, in Vattel's view, was the obligation of the sovereign bestowed on him by natural law and therefore, any action that was necessary for its survival was allowed, including the use of force, as long as war was conducted in due form.[23]

The requirement to conduct war in due form applied to both sides, regardless of the justice of the cause.[24] Vattel believed that:

> [T]he rights founded on the state of war [...] in no way depend on the justice of the cause. They depend rather on the legitimacy of the means, [...] on the presence of the elements constituting a war in due form.[25]

Vattel took thus further the tradition started by Vitoria and developed by Grotius to treat the rules concerning conduct of war separately from the principles relating to the right to make war. His approach greatly contributed to the two major innovations of the era: the even-handed treatment of both belligerents, regardless of the justice of the cause, and the establishment of a fixed set of rules governing conduct of war.[26] Vattel's approach was adopted by subsequent authors and currently forms part of the principle of equal application of the laws of war in international humanitarian law.[27]

3.1.3 'Perfect' Wars

In the seventeenth and eighteenth centuries, waging a full-fledged war was the exclusive prerogative of the sovereign. Although just war explanations were still used in deciding when a state could go to war, the emphasis was much more on the formalities surrounding it, rather than on the justice of the cause.

---

21 Ibid., p. 304.

22 Ibid., Book II, Chap. 5, Sections 67–68, p. 135, and Book III, Chap. 1, Section 5, p. 236.

23 Ibid., Book I, Chap. 2, Sections 16 and 18, pp. 13–14.

24 Ibid., Book III, Chap. 11, Section 187, p. 303, and Chap. 12, Sections 191–192, pp. 305–306.

25 Ibid., Chap. 12, Section 190, p. 305.

26 Neff 2005, pp. 111–115.

27 Roberts 2008, p. 938.

Wars were still divided into public and private, defensive and offensive. Public wars had to be ordered by the public authority, be initiated after a formal declaration and carried out in accordance with the voluntary rules of war.[28] If all conditions applied, a 'state of war' was instituted and the war was a 'perfect' one.[29] Perfect wars offered the sovereign the full panoply of right to commence an offensive or a defensive armed action.[30]

In case of defensive 'perfect' wars the limits extended to preventive action as understood by Gentili.[31] Hobbes maintained that preventive war was the best way to prepare against one's foes. Either by force or by wiles, one had to master his own enemies, until he saw 'no other power great enough to endanger him.' Hobbes believed that if one attacked preventively, the enemy could not both defend itself and pursue its invasion plans. For that reason, Hobbes stated that preventive wars were the best defence a state could have.[32] In *De jure naturae et gentium libri octo*, Pufendorf also defended preventive war:

> [N]ot only may I use force against an enemy until I have warded off the peril with which he threatened me, or have received or extorted from him what he had unjustly robbed me of, or refused to furnish, but I can also proceed so far as to secure guarantees for the future.[33]

For the preservation of the state, Vattel also supported preventive war. While he agreed that a nation must have received an injury or be threatened with one to use force as the last resort, he asked the following questions:

> Must we await the danger? Must we let the storm gather strength when it might be scattered at its rising? Must we suffer a neighbouring State to grow to power and await quietly until it is ready to enslave us? Will it be time to defend ourselves when we are no longer able to?[34]

In answering these questions, Vattel first noted that:

> [I]t is a sacred rule of the Law of Nations that the aggrandizement of a State cannot alone and of itself give any one the right to take up arms to resist it.[35]

By distinguishing between sheer power and the will to injure, Vattel emphasized that the two are not inseparable and a state had to notice that its neighbour had

---

[28] Vattel 1964, Book III, Chap. 4, pp. 254–258.

[29] One famous case in which the formalities concerning the declaration of war and the commencement of hostilities were not observed was the Japanese surprise attack on Port Arthur in February 1904 opening the Russo-Japanese War of 1904–1905. For more details, see: Neff 2005, pp. 182–183.

[30] Ibid., Chap. 2, pp. 237–242, especially Section 6, p. 237.

[31] Gentili 1933, Book I, Chap. 14, p. 62.

[32] Hobbes 1991, Chap. 13, p. 88.

[33] Pufendorf 1934, Book VIII, Chap. 6 (7), p. 1298.

[34] Vattel 1964, Book III, Chap. 3, Section 42, p. 248.

[35] Ibid.

non-peaceful intentions and only then could it contemplate war. The non-peaceful intentions, however, received a considerably permissive definition:

> As soon as a state has given evidence of injustice, greed, pride, ambition, or desire of domineering over its neighbours, it becomes an object of suspicion which they must guard against. They may hold it up at the moment it is about to receive a formidable addition to its power, and demand securities of it; and if it hesitates to give these, they may impede its designs by force of arms.[36]

Besides this, Vattel also emphasized the importance of alliances 'to counterbalance the sovereign who excites their alarm.'[37] Without a doubt, Vattel was placing his arguments on preventive war in the wider context of European politics, dominated by the balance of power concept.

Natural law thinkers and positivist lawyers not only took further the Gentilian definition of preventive war, but also strengthened it and acknowledged it as part of the balance-of-power system.

3.1.4 'Imperfect' Wars

When a declaration of war was missing, the war was deemed irregular or imperfect. These wars came to be excluded from the overall category of wars and treated as something different. The right (or even duty) of self-preservation was seen by Vattel as 'imposed by nature' and giving rise to both a right of resistance and a right to obtain redress, none of which were necessarily linked to perfect wars.[38] These irregular or 'imperfect wars'—based on the duty to preserve the state—did not give the sovereign the full panoply of belligerent rights that a 'perfect' war would entail.[39]

Although Vattel denounced wars launched without observing these formal requirements, the seventeenth and eighteenth centuries saw a myriad of armed conflicts undertaken without an official 'state of war' being instituted.[40]

Contemporary state practice was abundant in armed actions connected to privateering. Such a conflict was the 1798–1801 naval conflict between the United States and revolutionary France. France was eager to take punitive measures against the United States, for conferring certain privileges to Great Britain which France had previously enjoyed. Although French soldiers and privateers committed numerous depredations on American vessels, and American citizens on board were beaten and imprisoned, the French and the US governments never

[36] Ibid., Section 44, p. 249.
[37] Ibid., Section 46, p. 250.
[38] Ibid., Book II, Chap. 4, Section 49, p. 130.
[39] Neff 2005, p. 156.
[40] Vattel 1964, Book III, Chap. 4, Section 67, p. 257. See also: Grewe 2000, pp. 525–530.

considered that a state of war existed between them. It was viewed as an 'imperfect war' or a 'limited' or 'partial' war.[41]

Special reprisals—permitted under the right to obtain redress as a corollary of the duty of self-preservation—were also very frequent in seventeenth- and eighteenth-century state practice.[42] General reprisals came to be equated with perfect wars, so they were treated under a different heading.[43]

The right of self-preservation could also permit an 'imperfect war' in self-defence. Without a state of war instituted by an official declaration, the belligerent right of the sovereign was restricted in the instance of such imperfect, irregular conflicts.[44] It was necessary to provide a legal justification on which an armed action—outside a state of war—could be based.

For that reason, an 'imperfect' war in self-defence was closest in its meaning to the *stricto sensu* self-defence applicable to individuals. Nonetheless, in this transfer of meaning, a slight change was applied to the limits of *stricto sensu* self-defence, dictated by the realities of inter-state conflict.[45] This alteration was already explained by Grotius, who limited public defensive wars to armed action against immediate dangers as well as imminent attacks.[46]

The availability of *stricto sensu* self-defence to private persons was further restricted during the seventeenth to nineteenth centuries. Hobbes' view was that war waged by individuals should become obsolete and the creation of a social contract should offer enough security to private persons so that in case of injury, they would be protected or compensated by the public authority.[47] As a result, although individuals retained the right of self-defence, such a right flowed from, and was limited by, positive law and it was the incipient form of the present-day right to self-defence, permitted by criminal law. Vattel expressed a similar opinion, although he still allowed for private war in self-defence 'if the police force was lacking,' because such a right was given to individuals by nature.[48]

Although quite blurry in the seventeenth and eighteenth centuries, the 'imperfect' form of self-defence was to survive under the auspices of the right to self-preservation and be known in the nineteenth century as a measure short of war. The

---

[41] Brownlie 1963, p. 30.

[42] Vattel 1964, Book II, Chap. 18, Sections 343–347, pp. 228–229. See also: Grewe 2000, pp. 525–527.

[43] Consult for difference between special and general reprisals: Neff 2005, pp. 122–126; Twiss 1863, pp. 30–31.

[44] Neff 2005, p. 156.

[45] Vattel also draws a parallel between the right of individuals and nations to resist attack and asserts that the content of that right stems from the same source. Vattel 1964, Book II, Chap. IV, Section. 49, p. 130.

[46] Grotius 1964, Book II, Chap. 2 (xvi), p. 184.

[47] Hobbes, Leviathan1991, Chap. 13 (8), Chap. 14 (3), (6)–(7), and Chap. 15 (5), in May et al. 2006, pp. 81–87.

[48] Vattel 1964, Book III, Chap. 15, Section 223, p. 318.

Gentilian preventive wars would become part of the absolute rights of the sovereign to wage official war.

3.2 War as an Instrument of Policy

Early positivist approaches were further developed by subsequent state practice in the eighteenth and nineteenth centuries further increasing the gap between the old Christian thinking about war and the new 'balance-of-power' approach.

The French Revolutionary Wars and the Napoleonic Wars (between 1792–1802 and 1805–1815, respectively) saw the enrolment of huge masses of people into the army as opposed to the relatively small sized forces employed in wars prior. This innovation made a new method of waging war possible: the devastating defeat of the enemy army with a single blow, a method which, according to Neff, became the hallmark of the Napoleonic Wars.[49] These developments were coupled with the system of 'total war', which referred to the French and British practice of large-scale blockading and the manipulation of neutral commerce.[50] As Neff observed, the Napoleonic Wars did not bring any revolutionary changes to international law, thus the nineteenth century was still dominated by the same positivist and realist concepts of the unrestricted right to war, although modest moves towards restriction of this right were made.[51] Consequently, Vattel's statement that the right to resort to war was a question of morality outside the sphere of law was widely reiterated by public officials and state practice throughout the nineteenth century.

3.2.1 Positive Law and War as a Legal Institution

The nineteenth-century realist approach produced one of the most famous military strategy treatises of all times: Carl von Clausewitz's *Vom Kriege* (On War). In his treatise, Clausewitz defined war as 'an act of force to compel our enemy to do our will.' Force, he stated, was the means of war, whereas to impose one's will on the enemy was the object of war.[52] As regards the means of warfare, Clausewitz believed that 'the maximum use of force is in no way incompatible with the simultaneous use of the intellect.' Kindness could lead to grave mistakes in war, so war had to be accepted as it was, distressful and brutal.[53]

The most famous assertion of Clausewitz, the one that characterized, if not directly affected, the foreign policy of many European governments, was that:

---

[49] Neff 2005, pp. 92–93.

[50] Ibid. See also Nussbaum's definition of total war Nussbaum 1947, p. 246.

[51] Neff 2005, p. 93.

[52] Clausewitz 1976, Book I, Chap. 1, Section 2, pp. 75–76.

[53] Ibid., Section 3, pp. 75–76.

> [W]ar is not merely an act of policy but a true political instrument, a continuation of political intercourse, carried on with other means [...]. The political objective is the goal, war is the means of reaching it, and means can never be considered in isolation from their purpose.[54]

Thus war was nothing more than an exercise of will on the part of the state based on rational and strict calculations of strategic advantages and disadvantages. Consequently, nineteenth-century state practice employed a subjective notion of 'war' and an equally interpretable concept of 'measures short of war'. States were entitled to judge on their own whether they found themselves in a state of war or not. Certainly, as Brownlie observed, most of the governments could find substantial reasons of policy to avoid a state war, while still being able to exert coercion, if necessary. Each declaration of war had to be preceded by ample preparation on a military, financial and society level, which necessitated great efforts from the executive of every country.[55] Therefore, resorting to small-scale coercive measures ('imperfect wars'), proved to be a less costly, less iniquitous and more time-efficient choice. These measures came in all shapes and sizes: blockades, naval demonstrations, armed interventions, defensive measures and reprisals—all were seen as justified by the interest of the state and all had their own particular place within nineteenth-century state practice.

3.2.2 State Practice and 'Measures Short of War'

Measures short of war were those small-scale conflicts—'imperfect wars' of the seventeenth and eighteenth centuries—that were justified on the basis of the principle of self-preservation. Legal authors of the nineteenth century all gave the principle of self-preservation a privileged place in the system of the law of nations. Phillimore, English judge and politician, saw the principle of self-preservation as an exception to territorial inviolability that allowed both the preclusion and the repelling of an attack.[56] Twiss, English lawyer, called self-preservation 'the primary duty of national life'—implying in this way its natural law origins.[57] Another English jurist, Hall asserted that 'almost the whole of the duties of states are subordinated to the right of self-preservation.'[58]

Under the aegis of the right or duty of self-preservation, a whole range of armed actions qualified as 'interferences', 'interventions' or 'measures short of war'.[59]

---

[54] Ibid., Section 24, p. 87.

[55] Brownlie 1963, pp. 45–47.

[56] Phillimore 1854, p. 225.

[57] Twiss 1863, p. 3.

[58] Hall 1880, p. 226.

[59] Ibid., pp. 240-250, 306–314; Phillimore 1854, pp. 225–235; Phillimore 1857, pp. 1–35; Twiss 1863, pp. 1–42.

Accordingly, contemporaneous authors identified a category of 'interferences' or 'interventions' that were directly connected to the principle of self-preservation: self-defence, securing obligations of treaty stipulations, intervention on humanitarian grounds, intervention to preserve the balance of power, invitation of contending parties in a civil war.[60] Not all of these measures were equally sustained. Securing obligations of treaty stipulations, participation in civil wars and interventions to preserve the balance of power were gradually renounced as obsolete or giving rise to dangerous situations and by the beginning of the twentieth century they were seen as illegal.[61]

A separate category of armed action was that of retortion, retaliation and reprisal. These were characterized as 'amicable' or 'compulsive' methods of dispute settlement which did not amount to war and were treated separately from 'measures short of war'.[62] Reprisals were permitted when justice had been plainly denied or most unreasonably delayed.[63] These measures were still accepted at the beginning of the twentieth century. Moreover, Oppenheim asserted that reprisals were allowed 'in every case of an international delinquency for which the injured state cannot get reparation through negotiation.'[64]

Two measures belonging to the 'interventions' category survived into the twentieth century under different forms: armed interventions on humanitarian grounds and self-defence.

Armed interventions on humanity grounds or for community interests was a category that was favourably viewed by lawyers and statesmen alike, although concerns over its abuse were often expressed.[65] The collective intervention in China in 1900–1901 serves as example. The measure was undertaken to stop the Boxer Rebellion, an anti-imperialist uprising that targeted Christian missionaries and foreigners. Between 1900 and 1901, several armed interventions took place, involving forces from American, French, German, British and Russian war vessels amongst others. The international forces were put under a single command and, until April 1901, the force made several incursions into North China in order to rescue European nationals from insurgent action and to suppress the Boxers. Again, the governments concerned did not admit the existence of a state of war; rather they viewed it as an *armed intervention*, meant to eradicate the local militia which targeted foreigners.[66]

---

60 Phillimore 1854, p. 434; Halleck 1861, p. 83; Hall 1880, pp. 242–250; Oppenheim 1905, pp. 181–183.

61 Halleck 1861, pp. 83–84; Hall 1880, pp. 242–250; Oppenheim 1905, pp. 181–183.

62 Phillimore 1857, pp. 10–13; Halleck 1861, p. 297; Hall 1880, p. 306; Twiss 1863, pp. 18–20; Oppenheim 1906, pp. 34–35.

63 Halleck 1861, p. 297; Hall 1880, p. 308.

64 Oppenheim 1906, pp. 34–35.

65 Phillimore 1857, p. 434; Hall 1880, p. 245.

66 Brownlie 1963, pp. 33–34.

Measures of self-defence were seen as 'a primary right of Nations'[67] that could be exercised against serious and immediate dangers.[68] Primary rights were seen as stemming from natural law, thus self-defence continued to be viewed as a natural prerequisite of the state.[69]

During this period, other, necessity-related measures were also linked to self-preservation, such as hot pursuit, punitive expeditions or rescue of nationals.[70] A good illustration of hot pursuit and punitive expeditions is the 1916–1917 Pershing Expedition in pursuit of Francisco 'Pancho' Villa, one of the main leaders of the 1910–1921 Mexican Revolution. Between November 1915 and March 1916, Villa ordered his Mexican raiders to carry out several cross-border attacks against American settlements, culminating in the raid on Columbus (New Mexico) on 9 March 1916.[71] The raids were organized as a reaction to the US government's official recognition of the opponent regime in Mexico. In the Columbus attack, the raiders attacked a detachment of the US Cavalry, killed 17 US citizens and torched buildings in the town.[72] Despite the standing order prohibiting commanders from sending troops across the international boundary, a cavalry detachment pursued the raiders into Mexican territory and killed between 75 and 100 Mexicans. Although the incursion was unauthorized, US senior army officials quickly deemed it as 'hot pursuit'. The same attitude was adopted by the US President Woodrow Wilson.[73]

Plans were set in motion for a larger expedition to pursue Villa's raiders. Before launching the operation, the US and the Mexican governments agreed to a protocol providing for reciprocal crossing in pursuit of bandits. Nevertheless, the US expedition ignored several aspects of this protocol, which resulted in the Mexican government annulling the agreement.[74] The first elements of the expedition nevertheless crossed the border a week after the Columbus raid. The Mexican government, although in conflict with Pancho Villa, refrained from offering any assistance to the US force.[75] Tensions between the Pershing expedition and the Mexican government and army increased throughout the following weeks, with the prospect of capturing Villa becoming more and more improbable. Negotiations

---

67 Twiss 1860, p. 11.

68 Hall 1880, pp. 227–232.

69 Phillimore 1857, p. 225; Twiss 1860, p. 11.

70 Phillimore 1857, pp. 225–231; Twiss 1860, pp. 143–145.

71 Hall and Coerver 1990. pp. 35–36,

72 Ibid., p. 60.

73 Ibid., pp. 60–61.

74 Ibid., p. 62. The protocol provided that crossing would be permitted only if another raid took place, pursuant to the principle of 'hot pursuit'. Consequently, the Mexican government did not agree in the protocol to admit the crossing of a force clearly bigger than small detachments six days after an incident took place. A division composed of more than five thousand men with plans to venture deep inside Mexican territory launched well after the raid took place went well beyond the characteristics of 'hot pursuit'.

75 Hall and Coerver 1990, pp. 61–64.

concerning the withdrawal of the expedition started as early as May 1916 and went on for several months. Finally, between November 1916 and February 1917, the Pershing Expedition was withdrawn, without Pancho Villa being found.

Hot pursuit differed thus from the natural-law concept of self-defence inasmuch as it concerned action in the immediate aftermath of the attack rather than in the face of it. The attacked had the right to pursue the attacker in the territory of another state, without its action being considered as a hostile act against that state as long as it was made to address a great and immediate danger and was not excessive.[76] As the example of the Pershing expedition shows, punitive expeditions required more preparation, thus more time elapsed between the initial attack and the response.

Self-defence, hot pursuit, punitive expeditions and rescue of nationals were all measures short of war under the wider umbrella of the principle of self-preservation. The demarcation line between these measures was often blurred in nineteenth-century state practice and the notions of self-defence and self-preservation were often used interchangeably.[77] Nonetheless, defensive action as a measure short of war—regardless of its denomination—was made conditional upon the existence of a danger 'serious and imminent'.[78] Moreover, armed action could not go beyond what was necessary to ward off the danger.[79]

Known today as the incident that triggered the formulation of the customary law standard for 'anticipatory self-defence', the *Caroline* incident is worth being thoroughly analysed, because it prompted an essential legalistic discussion about the limits of self-defence.

3.2.2.1 The *Caroline* Incident (1837)

During the insurrection in Canada in 1837, small, sympathetic disturbances occurred at various places in the United States, especially along the Canadian border. The Government of the United States adopted active measures for the enforcement of the neutrality laws, but the difficulty of the situation was increased by the insurgents, who, when defeated, sought refuge in the United States, where they resumed recruiting their forces. The *Caroline*, a Great Lakes steam vessel, was owned by some American sympathizers of the insurgents and was used for transporting aid supplies for the rebel forces. To put an end to this practice, on 29 December 1837, British forces crossed into American territory, without the consent of the American government, took possession of the *Caroline* and sent it over the Niagara Falls, with some loss of life in the process.[80] The case was settled in

---

76 Hall 1880, pp. 227–229.

77 Jennings 1938, p. 82.

78 Hall 1880, p. 232.

79 Ibid., pp. 229–232.

80 Jennings 1938, pp. 82–84.

1842 and friendly relations were not interrupted, although the incident was seen as prone to 'justify reprisals or even general war.'[81]

The *Caroline* incident bears importance because of the correspondence that ensued between the parties. The first complaint of the destruction of the vessel was the Note of 5 January 1838 addressed by John Forsyth, the American Secretary of State, to Henry Fox, British Minister at Washington. In this note, Forsyth asserted that the lamentable incident was to be made the subject of a demand for redress. The British Minister replied a month later and invoked, *inter alia*, the principles of self-defence and self-preservation as justifying the action of the British forces.[82] One year later, in an official report, the Law Officers of the Crown confirmed that justification and characterized the action of the British forces as 'absolutely necessary as a measure of precaution for the future and not as a measure of retaliation for the past.'[83]

After another two years, the discussion was renewed as a result of the arrest of British citizen Alexander McLeod by the American authorities. McLeod claimed that he took part in the destruction of the *Caroline* and was consequently arrested and charged with murder. On 24 April 1841, the new American Secretary of State, Daniel Webster addressed a letter to Henry Fox, in which he took up both the issues of *Caroline* and McLeod's arrest. Webster discussed each and every point of justification that was brought up by the British government in early January 1838. On the issue of self-defence, Webster asserted that:

> A just right of self-defence attaches always to nations as well as to individuals, and is equally necessary for the preservation of both. But the extent of this right is a question to be judged of by the circumstances of each particular case, and when its alleged exercise has led to the commission of hostile acts within the territory of a Power at peace, nothing less than a clear and absolute necessity can afford ground for justification.[84]

With a formula which has become famous, Webster further defined absolute necessity as a 'necessity of self-defence, instant, overwhelming, leaving no choice of means, and no moment for deliberation.'[85] On this basis, Webster looked in detail at the circumstances of the *Caroline* incident in order to demonstrate that there was no absolute necessity to justify the destruction of the vessel. Accordingly, Webster called upon the British government to show that the legal authorities of Canada 'did nothing unreasonable and excessive'[86] and that a seizure of the vessel during daylight was impossible, that detaining the vessel as opposed to destroying it was not enough and that attacking the crew on board, killing some and injuring others 'was a necessity, present and inevitable.'[87]

---

[81] Webster 1841, p. 1140.

[82] Jennings 1938, p. 85 nn. 8 and 9.

[83] Ibid., p. 87 n. 14 (Law Officers' Report of 25 March 1839).

[84] Webster 1841, pp. 1132–1133.

[85] Ibid., p. 1138.

[86] Ibid.

[87] Ibid.

Webster's discussion of the *Caroline* incident was a true legal analysis conducted in order to examine whether the requirements of absolute necessity really applied. This formula was adopted by many subsequent commentators and statesmen as the classic customary standard for 'anticipatory self-defence'.[88]

Four important notes need to be made. First of all, Webster's analysis had no immediate effect on contemporaneous state practice. Many commentators still discussed *Caroline* as a case of 'self-preservation'. Phillimore, for instance, characterized the British justification as a 'sufficient answer and a complete vindication' of the incident under the right of self-preservation.[89] Similarly, Hall was of the opinion that there was no difficulty for the British to satisfy the requirements of Webster, because the act was indeed within the limits of necessity of self-preservation.[90] Although the British–American correspondence referred to the limits of self-defence, the overall discussion was still dominated by the principle of self-preservation as the overarching concept.

Secondly, the British–American correspondence confirmed the contemporary requirement of providing legal justification for armed actions outside a state of war. As with 'imperfect wars', measures short of war needed to be justified on the basis of a legal norm or principle.[91] States did not have a *carte blanche* to engage in such an armed action without providing a legal justification.

Thirdly, there is nothing in Webster's analysis that would suggest that the action of the British forces was seen as 'anticipatory self-defence'. As a matter of fact, Webster defined absolute necessity as a trigger of the right of self-defence *as such*—he did not emphasize on any special anticipatory aspect. The fact that the destruction of the *Caroline* was a 'measure of precaution for the future'[92] was not challenged by anybody. It was evident that self-defence *per se* justified such an action. The controversy surrounded the specific circumstances of the act and the lack of justification for destroying the vessel. Consequently, the existence of a *necessity of self-defence, instant, overwhelming, leaving no choice of means, and no moment for deliberation* was the condition under which self-defence could be invoked. The fact that this had an anticipatory aspect was seen as obvious. This understanding of self-defence was the same that the early and medieval Christian thinkers, the Spanish scholastics and Grotius saw as the natural right to wage wars to ward off injuries. The concept is best traced if one looks at the circumstances allowing private war in self-defence. From Augustine and Aquinas all the way to Gentili and Grotius, just war theorists allowed individuals to defend themselves in the face of a present or imminent attack. A slightly more permissive interpretation

---

88 Bowett 1958, pp. 188–189; Fleck 1988, pp. 176–177; Higgins 1963, p. 199; Malanczuk 1987, pp. 247–248; McDougal and Feliciano 1961, pp. 231–236; Schachter 1991, pp. 150–152; Schwebel 1972, p. 481; Waldock (1952, pp. 497–499).

89 Phillimore 1857, p. 228.

90 Hall 1880, pp. 227–229.

91 Neff 2005, p. 156.

92 Jennings 1938, p. 87 n. 14 (Law Officers' Report of 25 March 1839).

of this *stricto sensu* self-defence—best described by Grotius[93]—was transferred to 'imperfect wars' waged by sovereigns without officially declaring war between each other. As a measure short of war, self-defence retained the same characteristics: it was an armed action undertaken in the face of an immediate attack or an imminent threat. It was not 'anticipatory self-defence'. It was self-defence with an intrinsic anticipatory aspect. That is what the Webster-formula also confirms.

Fourthly, the arguments of Webster highlight the same three elements of self-defence that could be discerned in the natural-law concept of self-defence. First of all, there had to be an attack, present or imminent. It is essential to note here that there was no discussion of the authorship of the attack; it was accepted by both sides that self-defence could be invoked against insurgents and rebels who did not belong to the regular forces of a state. Secondly, the danger posed by that attack had to create an immediate need for action. As Webster put it, there had to be 'a necessity, present and inevitable'[94] for self-defence to be exercised. Thirdly, the use of self-defence could not include anything 'unreasonable or excessive',[95] thus it had to be exercised with moderation.

The Webster-formula thus vindicated the centuries' old understanding of the natural-law concept of self-defence. Anticipatory action was not only part of this concept, but pertained to its basic understanding. Accordingly, the elements that limited the exercise of self-defence also served as limits of anticipatory action.

Unfortunately, not all nineteenth-century state practices that invoked the right of self-defence ended in such a ground-breaking juridical differentiation between self-defence and self-preservation. Another case that concerned the limits of self-defence was the *Virginius* affair involving the United States and Spain (then proprietor of Cuba). This incident is a good illustration of how the concept of self-defence was employed to justify actions that went well beyond its limits and how the principle of self-preservation was used as a corollary.

3.2.2.2 The *Virginius* Affair (1873)

The *Virginius* was an ex-Confederate blockade runner that was used by Cuban rebels (and their American sympathizers) during the Ten Years' War between Cuban insurgents and Spain (1868–1879).[96] From 1870 to 1872, the *Virginius* was used to transport arms and men to aid the insurgency. Spain became aware of the mission of the steamer and regarded it as a pirate ship. After several narrow escapes, the *Virginius* was finally captured on 31 October 1873 by the Spanish

---

93 See *supra* 2.4.4. Grotius 1964, Book II, Chap. 1 (xvii), p. 184.

94 Webster 1841, p. 1138.

95 Ibid.

96 The Ten Years' War (1868–1878) was the first of three wars that Cuba fought against Spain for its independence. The second occurred between 1879 and 1880, whereas the third between 1895 and 1898, the last three months of which are known as the Spanish–American War.

man-of-war *Tornado* and hauled with its crew to internment at Santiago.[97] A few days later, three dozen of the crew members were executed after swift military trials. Spain first justified its action by claiming that the expedition or voyage undertaken by the *Virginius* from the port of New York 'was not of purely commercial nature [...], but that in view of the articles which she carried, her character was an essentially military one.' Hence, the Spanish government claimed that, according to the law of nations, the acts pertained to the crime of piracy.[98] During the long diplomatic correspondence between the two sides, Spain further characterized the acts as 'a breach of international law to the injury of Spain,' which permitted self-defence:

> Neither natural law, nor the law of nations, can authorize [...] that the enemies of a sovereign state can, with impunity, navigate the high seas, carrying soldiers and resources to the hosts of an enemy without the country menaced by such an invasion having the privilege of disturbing them.[99]

An unconditional and absolute prohibition to act in such circumstances 'would restrict, if not completely annul, the right of self-preservation and of self-defence, which is a right with respect to other countries, and one of the most solemn and sacred of the duties of any state with relation to its citizens.'[100] The US did not accept this justification. Even before Spain resorted to invoking self-defence, both the US and the British governments considered that such defensive action would have entailed the capture of the vessel and the detention of the crew, but not the execution of the crew members. The same opinion was expressed by contemporary lawyers such as Hall, who was of the opinion that an imminent necessity under the principle of self-preservation did exist, but it only justified the capturing of the vessel and not the execution of its crew.[101] The summary executions were viewed as a massacre 'which shocked the public sense of Europe as well as of America.'[102]

The *Virginius* affair illustrates the growing tendency in the nineteenth-century state practice to view self-defence not only as a measure to fend off attacks, but also as a method for securing the non-repetition of such acts (after an attack had occurred).

In this case, both the pre-emptive and the remedial side of self-defence were recognized. The remedial aspect of self-defence was acknowledged by medieval Christian publicists, but only for the purpose of precluding the repetition of attacks.[103] No time of preparation was allowed between the attack suffered and the

---

97 Virginius Correspondence p. 3 (No. 165 (Fifty fourth Cong., first Sess. 1896).

98 Ibid., p. 21 (No. 18, Admiral Polo de Bernabé to Mr. Fish, Washington, 30 December 1873). For details on the way piracy was defined at that time, see: Rubin 1988, pp. 238–245.

99 Virginius Correspondence pp. 108–109 (No. 46, Mr. Cushing to Mr. Fish, Madrid, 5 December 1874).

100 Ibid.

101 Hall 1880, pp. 232–234.

102 Virginius Correspondence p. 90 (No. 31, Mr. Cushing to Mr. Fish, Madrid, 22 July 1874).

103 See, for instance, Gratian, question I, in Reichberg et al. 2006, p. 110; Pisan, Part III, Chap. 12, in Reichberg et al. 2006, p. 219.

defensive action, because that would have qualified as revenge.[104] These restrictions were applied to the *stricto sensu* self-defence, which was the natural right of the individual to defend himself. During nineteenth-century state practice, the remedial aspect of self-defence acquired more importance due to the myriad of measures short of war justified by self-preservation. As the *Virginius* affair shows, remedial action was meant to ward off the repetition of injuries. Preparation for and resort to such an action was allowed as long as it was confined 'within the narrowest limits consistent with obtaining the required end.'[105] The reason why the self-defence claim of Spain could not be maintained was not because of the partly remedial nature of their action, but because of the excessiveness thereof. The execution of the *Virginius* crew went well beyond the necessary precaution that moderation in self-defence allowed.

The nineteenth-century state practice thus carried on the narrow understanding of self-defence (with the alterations dictated by the realities of public warfare) in the form of measures short of war. The temporal dimension of that understanding traditionally pertained to the time before and during the attack and increasingly related also to the time after the attack. Self-defence, whether in its anticipatory or remedial form, was limited by three elements: the occurrence or threat of an attack, the immediate need to take action and moderation.

3.3 The Positivist Normative Framework and Self-Defence

The aim of this chapter was to analyse the views adopted during the seventeenth to nineteenth centuries regarding the natural-law concept of self-defence and to assess whether the status and limits of anticipatory action were altered during that period. Due to the realist and positivist influences, starting with the middle of the seventeenth century, the issue of war was seen as outside religious and moral considerations. Instead of a substantive analysis of 'just causes', positivist jurists and realist philosophers across the European space focused more on the procedural aspects of recourse to war (preparations, declaration, conduct during hostilities). Against this background, the old Christian conception of natural law lost its dominant position and the just war doctrine was gradually replaced by balance-of-power ideas. Thus war was seen as the absolute prerogative of the sovereign, who could alone decide when it was necessary, for the sake of the state. Moreover, with the famous work of Clausewitz, war became 'an instrument of policy' that had to be used when state interests commanded it.

The body of law that received more attention than before was the one concerning conduct of hostilities. Lawful conduct of war was viewed as an autonomous category regardless of the justice of the cause.

---

[104] See *supra* 2.2, 2.3 and 2.5.

[105] Hall 1880, p. 229.

Needless to say, the positivist normative framework was also 'international' in character, even more so than its Christian natural-law predecessor. Interrelations of states in the Western tradition made the tenets of this normative framework known and accepted across jurisdictions. Moreover, building on the work of Grotius, several positivist lawyers (with Vattel deserving special attention) laid the basis of a more modern conception of the law of nations in which treaty law was increasingly dominant.

Public war had to follow all the formalities prescribed by voluntary law in order to be lawful and 'perfect'. As regards the rights to make war, the sovereign had the full prerogatives to resort to offensive or defensive armed action. Defensive 'perfect' war also allowed preventive action against possible dangers and was thus close in its *rationale* to preventive war as described by Gentili.

During this period, state practice was abundant in special reprisals, pacific blockades and privateering.[106] Further, a full array of measures short of war—the descendants of 'imperfect wars'—was permitted under the principle of self-preservation. This principle was viewed as imposed on society by nature and self-defence was seen as a 'primary' right incidental to it. In this form, self-defence was indeed still seen as a right given to all by nature.

In nineteenth-century Western-hemisphere state practice, self-defence as a measure short of war was acknowledged across jurisdictions as a customary rule.[107] That rule did not allow preventive action.[108] Self-defence as a measure short of war was a concept inherited from medieval scholars and just war theorists and originated from the *stricto sensu* self-defence for individuals, although it had slightly more permissive limits accommodated to the realities of inter-state conflicts. Accordingly, it allowed action against an imminent threat or an ongoing attack. It also allowed a strike after an attack, if the purpose was to fend off ensuing attacks. The *Caroline* incident confirmed these limits and later served as a basis for clarifying the differences between self-defence and self-preservation. The arguments put forward by Daniel Webster also shed light on the three elements of self-defence: existence of an attack, immediate need to respond and moderation. The importance of the Webster-formula became more obvious in the beginning of the twentieth century, when the international trend to restrict war started to gain ground (Table 3.1).

It is important to conclude at this point that the natural-law concept of self-defence surfaced in seventeenth- to nineteenth-century state practice as 'imperfect war' and later, as a 'measure short of war'. The temporal dimension of this concept pertained to the time before and during the attack. Due to the myriad of measures short of war justified by self-preservation, self-defence increasingly related to the time after the attack. The anticipatory nature of this concept of self-defence has

---

[106] Grewe 2000, pp. 525–530.

[107] According to Webster, the law of nations acknowlegded a right of self-defence for the preservations of nations and individuals alike. Webster 1841, pp. 1132–1133.

[108] Hall 1880, pp. 227–233. Nonetheless, Twiss continued Gentili's and Vattel's tradition and acknowledged self-defence as a right that could be exercised not only against immediate assault, but also 'threatened aggression' which was not necessarily imminent. Twiss 1860, pp. 11–12.

Table 3.1 Self-defence, as understood in the seventeenth–nineteenth centuries, in and outside a state of war

Self-defence	Seventeenth–eighteenth centuries	Eighteenth–nineteenth centuries
Sovereigns	'Perfect war' Declared by public authority All formalities observed Allowed for preventive wars (Hobbes, Vattel, Pufendorf) 'Imperfect war' A state of war did not exist Justification based on a legal principle had to be put forward Allowed for self-defence against ongoing attacks and imminent threats (similar to individual self-defence)	'Declared war' Declared by public authority All formalities observed Allowed for preventive wars (Clausewitz, Twiss) 'Measures short of war' A state of war did not exist Justification based on a legal principle had to be put forward Overarching concept of self-preservation Allowed for self-defence against ongoing attacks, imminent threat and after an attack had occurred (Hall, *Caroline*, *Virginius*)
Individuals	Allowed for use of force against ongoing attacks or imminent threats Increasingly viewed as restricted by positive law in the face of existing law enforcement remedies	Increasingly viewed as restricted by positive law in the face of existing law enforcement remedies

stood its ground against the test of time, and so did its limits (occurrence or threat of an attack, immediate need for action and moderation). This concept of self-defence did not allow preventive action. That was a prerogative that could be used only in a 'perfect' war that respected all the formalities required to institute an official state of war.

References

Baylis J, Smith S (eds) (2001) The globalisation of world politics. Oxford University Press, New York
Beaulac S (2000) The Westphalian legal orthodoxy: myth or reality? J Hist Int Law 2:148–177
Bowett DW (1958) Self-defense in international law. Manchester University Press, Manchester
Brownlie I (1963) International law and the use of force by states. Clarendon Press, Oxford
von Clausewitz C (1976) On war. Princeton University Press, Princeton
Fleck D (1988) Rules of engagement for maritime forces and the limitation of the use of force under the UN Charter. Ger Yearbk Int Law 31:165–186
Gentili A (1933) De jure belli libri tres (trans: Rolfe JC). Clarendon Press, Oxford
Grewe WG (2000) The epochs of international law (trans: Byers M). De Gruyter, Berlin
Grotius H (1964) De jure belli ac pacis libri tres (trans: Kelsey FW). Oceana, New York
Hall LB, Coerver DM (1990) Revolution on the border: The United States and Mexico 1910–1920. University of New Mexico Press, Albuquerque
Hall WE (1880) International law. Clarendon Press, Oxford
Halleck HW (1861) International law or rules regulating the intercourse of states in peace and war. H.H. Bancroft, San Francisco

Higgins R (1963) The development of international law through the political organs of the United Nations. Oxford University Press, London
Hobbes T (1991) Leviathan. Cambridge University Press, Cambridge
Jennings RY (1938) The Caroline and McLeod cases. Am J Int Law 32:82–99
Krasner SD (1995–1996) Compromising Westphalia. Int Secur 20(3):115–151
Lisska AJ (1996) Aquinas's theory of natural law. An analytic reconstruction. Clarendon Press, Oxford
Malanczuk P (1987) Countermeasures and self-defence as circumstances precluding wrongfulness in the International Law Commision's Draft Articles on States Responsibility. In: Spinedi M, Simma B (eds) United Nations codification of state responsibility. Oceana, New York, pp 197–286
May L et al (2006) The morality of war: classical and contemporary readings. Pearson Prentice Hall, Upper Saddle River
McDougal MS, Feliciano FP (1961) Law and minimum world public order: the legal regulation of international coercion. Yale University Press, New Haven
Neff SC (2005) War and the law of nations: general history. Cambridge University Press, Cambrdige
Nussbaum A (1947) A concise history of the law of nations. Macmillan, New York
Oppenheim L (1905) International law: a treatise, vol 1. Longmans, Green and Co, New York
Oppenheim L (1906) International law: a treatise, vol 2. Longmans, Green and Co, New York
Osiander A (2001) Sovereignty, international relations and the Westphalian myth. Int Org 55:251–287
Phillimore R (1854) Commentaries upon international law, vol 1. W. Benning, London
Phillimore R (1857) Commentaries upon international law, vol 3. W. Benning, London
von Pufendorf S (1934) De jure naturae et gentium libri octo, vol 2. Clarendon Press, Oxford
von Pufendorf S (1991) On the duty of man and citizen according to natural law. Cambridge University Press, Cambridge
Reichberg GM, Syse H, Begby E (eds) (2006) The ethics of war: classic and contemporary readings. Blackwell, Malden
Roberts A (2008) The equal application of the laws of war: a principle under pressure. Int Rev Red Cr 90(872):931–962
Rubin AP (1988) The law of piracy. Naval War College Press, Newport
Schachter O (1991) International law in theory and practice. Martinus Nijhoff, Dordrecht
Schwebel SM (1972) Aggression, intervention and self-defence in modern international law. Recueil des Cours 136(1972-II):411–497
Twiss T (1860) Law of nations considered as independent political communities, vol 1. Oxford University Press, Oxford
Twiss T (1863) Law of nations considered as independent political communities, vol 2. Oxford University Press, Oxford
de Vattel E (1964) The law of nations or the principles of natural law: applied to the conduct and to the affairs of nations and of sovereigns. Oceana, New York
Virginius Correspondence: Message from the President of the United States, Transmitting, in answer to the resolution of the Senate of the 12th instant. A report from the Secretary of State, with accompanying Correspondence, with regard to the claim of indemnity from Spain for the Execution at Santiago de Cuba of persons who were on board the Virginius, US Senate Doc. No. 165 (54th Congress, 1st Session 1896)
Waldock CHM (1952) The regulation of the use of force by individual states in international law. Recueil Des Cours 81(1952-II):451–517
Webster 1841: Letter from Daniel Webster, US Secretary of State, to Henry Fox, British Minister in Washington, 24 April 1841, in British and Foreign State Papers, 1840–1841, vol 29 (1857). James Ridgway and Sons, London, pp 1129–1139
Wolff C (1934) Jus gentium methodo scientifica pertractatum. Clarendon Press, Oxford

Chapter 4
Self-Defence as an Exception to the Prohibition of War

The purpose of this chapter is to follow the evolution of the right of self-defence within the emerging system of modern international law of the late nineteenth and early twentieth centuries. Starting with the late nineteenth century, the major change in the approach to war was an ever-growing trend to restrict it. In this process, many forms of war and measures short of war began to be criticized and characterized as illegal. Moreover, this period saw the emergence of modern international law as we understand it today.[1]

In the early twentieth century, several multilateral agreements were concluded, which, in general terms, aimed to restrict or to prohibit recourse to war. Apart from that, the state practice connected to the League of Nations arbitration system was also very important, because it showed how specific forms of force (especially the so-called measures short of war) came under sharp criticism by the members of the League.

This chapter will make reference to representative and authoritative writings of the period as well as important instances of state practice relevant for self-defence. In the following paragraphs, emphasis will be put on the way self-defence was understood during this period and whether its narrow, natural-law understanding was still accepted. Both in the Christian natural-law and in the positivist conception, the temporal dimension of self-defence pertained to the time before, during and (increasingly in the nineteenth century) after an attack. In both frameworks, this understanding of self-defence was differentiated from the broader sense, which allowed the preventive use of force. Moreover, both normative frameworks identified the same elements of self-defence (whether anticipatory or remedial): the existence of an attack, the immediate need to respond and moderation. This chapter will assess whether the temporal dimension and elements of self-defence were altered during the examined period. On that basis, it will be deduced whether anticipatory action was still part of the contemporaneous understanding of self-defence, and if so, under what conditions.

---

[1] Hueck 2001, p. 198; Nussbaum 1947, pp. 191–199; Steiger 2001, pp. 190–192.

K. Tibori Szabó, *Anticipatory Action in Self-Defence*, DOI: 10.1007/978-90-6704-796-8_4,

4.1 Pacifist Trends of the Late Nineteenth and Early Twentieth Centuries

In the second part of the nineteenth century, the concept of war as a 'last resort' started to gain momentum. The view that war was a means of last resort was also strengthened by the increasing attention given to peaceful means of settling disputes. But apart from those who promoted peaceful means of dispute settlement, realist thinkers also had to admit that the creation of an organized system of peaceful dispute settlement was indeed needed.[2]

As a consequence of the growing tendency to favour peaceful dispute settlement, the principle of self-preservation started to lose its dominant position. At the beginning of the new century, international lawyers began to denounce it as a dangerous concept. Oppenheim, for instance, explicitly called for the restriction of the principle:

> It is frequently maintained that every violation is excused as long as it was caused by the motive of self-preservation, but it becomes more and more recognized that violations of other states in the interest of self-preservation are excused in case of necessity only.[3]

At the same time, the first signs of an 'International Civil Society' appeared with the regular organization of the Universal Peace Congresses, starting with 1889, which had the cessation of the arms race as one of their objectives.[4] The foundation of the International Committee for Relief to the Wounded (later to be known as the International Committee of the Red Cross) in 1863, through the work of Henry Dunant, also contributed to the development of a transnational civil society focused on matters of war and peace.[5]

The end of the nineteenth century and the beginning of the twentieth century saw the conclusion of the first international conventions regulating recourse to war and the conduct of hostilities. Moreover, the first international organization was created, which, *inter alia*, had the objective of restricting military action among its members. The Hague Conventions and the League of Nations initiated a process in which the seventeenth- and eighteenth-century normative framework changed substantively and moved towards the restriction of war. These initial moves were taken further by a series of bilateral agreements (such as the Bryan treaties)

---

[2] For the increasing importance of arbitration in the nineteenth century, see Nussbaum 1947, pp. 212–218.

[3] Oppenheim 1905, p. 178.

[4] These congresses are seen today as the primary fora for the pre-First World War peace movement. The first Universal Peace Congress was held in Paris in June 1889, and meetings followed almost every year until 1913. The outbreak of the First World War postponed further congresses until 1921, when they recommenced and were held during the inter-war years. The last inter-war congress met at Zurich in August 1939, concluding their meeting four days before Nazi Germany invaded Poland.

[5] For a succinct presentation of the peace movement, see Nussbaum 1947, pp. 221–222.

restricting recourse to war and, in 1928, by the Kellogg-Briand Pact.[6] The lessons learned in this transition period bore great importance to the drafting of the Charter of the United Nations.

The two Hague Peace Conferences were seen as the first truly international, intergovernmental summits. Although both conferences tacitly accepted the right of states to wage war, they set out certain principles which states were obliged to follow before resorting to war.

The initiation of the first Hague Peace Conference of 1899 was made by Russia in August 1898.[7] At the invitation of the Dutch Queen Wilhelmina, the participating states decided to hold the conference in The Hague.[8] Because most participants feared that the conference might result in the diminishing of their prerogatives to defend themselves and in revision or recognition of some political situation with which they were not satisfied, the Russian statesmen had to repeatedly ensure the incumbents that the conference would avoid any sensitive political question which would touch the susceptibility of any power, and that it would be more technical, than political.[9]

The main success of the first Hague conference was the creation of a procedure for arbitration of disputes between members. In the end, the Permanent Court of Arbitration was created, but resort to arbitration was declared voluntary.

A second Hague peace conference was convened in 1907 with the aim of including states not represented in 1899, developing the arbitration procedure and further developing the laws of war.

Self-defence was not addressed during the two Hague conferences, because there was no discussion regarding the restriction of the right to wage war.

That question was, nevertheless, taken up by the legal literature at the time. Along with the calls for restricting the principle of self-preservation, the authors also moved towards designating self-defence as the only measure that can be excused as self-preservation. On this topic, Oppenheim asserted:

> Such acts of violence in the interest of self-preservation are exclusively excused as are necessary in self-defence, because otherwise the acting state would have to suffer or have to continue to suffer a violation against itself. If *an imminent violation or the continuation of an already commenced violation* can be prevented and redressed otherwise than by a violation of another state on the part of the endangered state, this latter violation is not necessary, and therefore not excused and justified.[10]

---

[6] For an analysis of the Bryan treaties, see The Bryan Peace Treaties 1913, pp. 823–829.

[7] For a detailed account on genesis of the idea of a peace conference, see Ford 1936, pp. 354–382. For a different view on the same matter, see Morrill 1974, pp. 296–313.

[8] Participating countries: Germany, The United States of America, Austria–Hungary, Belgium, China, Denmark, Spain, France, Great Britain and Ireland, Greece, Italy, Japan, Luxembourg, Mexico, Montenegro, The Netherlands, Persia, Portugal, Romania, Russia, Serbia, Siam, Sweden and Norway, Switzerland, Turkey and Bulgaria.

[9] Ford 1936, p. 378.

[10] Oppenheim 1905, p. 178 (emphasis added).

Accordingly, if a state was informed that on a neighbouring territory a body of armed men was being organised for the purpose of a raid into its own territory and the danger could be removed through an appeal to the authorities of that country, there was no need to act in self-defence. Conversely, if such an appeal proved to be fruitless or impossible, or if there was even more danger in delaying defence, the threatened state was justified to resort to self-defence.[11]

Oppenheim's description of self-defence bears importance for several reasons. First of all, it demonstrates that the close link between the principle of self-preservation and the right of self-defence was still acknowledged in the early twentieth century. Secondly, the example used by Oppenheim shows that the right of self-defence was seen as a measure short of war. Thirdly, there was need for a legal explanation pertaining to self-defence in order to justify a measure short of war. Fourthly, the above-quoted passage describes self-defence as a right against 'an imminent violation or the continuation of an already commenced violation,' thus acknowledging the urgency element of the narrow understanding of the right. Fourthly, the requirement of an irremovable danger echoes the inevitability element of the narrow understanding of self-defence.

4.2 War in the Regulatory System of the Covenant of the League of Nations

Despite moves towards the regulation of warfare, the dominant view in foreign policy was still influenced by the Clausewitzian interpretation of war. The result of this approach was the first global war that brought profound changes to society and morality, as well as to the legal interpretation of war.

The aftermath of the war led to the more powerful resurgence of pacifist voices demanding the imposition of legal restrictions on resort to war.[12] Many argued that the war had been the product of the balance-of power system, so the main purpose was to construct a legal and institutional structure that would prevent wars in the future. It was thus believed that the main purpose of the creation of a League of Nations was to make member states accept and maintain the obligation to never wilfully resort to war. Moreover, on the basis of the Covenant of the League, states were supposed to recognize the necessity to control the arms race and reduce national armaments to the level of meeting the basic national safety requirements.[13]

The Covenant of the League of Nations was adopted by the Paris Peace Conference in April 1919. It entered into force on 10 January 1920. Although its President at the time greatly contributed to the idea of a League of Nations, the

[11] Ibid., pp. 178–179.

[12] Benes 1932, p. 66; Neff 2005, p. 285.

[13] Benes 1932, p. 67.

United States never became a member of the League.[14] Another 'great absent' at the founding negotiations was Germany, which accepted membership only in 1926, but withdrew after seven years. Similarly, the USSR was a League member only between 1934 and 1939. Out of the 42 founding members, only 24 remained members of the League until the end.[15] Many other states (such as Italy, Japan, Denmark, Czechoslovakia and Romania) withdrew at the beginning of the Second World War. Spain withdrew in 1939 as a result of the Spanish Civil War.

Perhaps the most revolutionary element of the Covenant was Article 10, according to which the members of the League undertook 'to respect and preserve as against external aggression the territorial integrity and existing political independence of all Members of the League.' It was seen as a revolutionary provision for mainly two reasons. First of all, it was the firm formulation of a collective security system on an international level, in which Member States had to show respect towards and preservation of each other's territorial integrity and political independence in the face of an external aggression. Secondly, it was the first express prohibition of aggression in an international treaty. As Benes observed, this clause was seen as having the ability to change the traditional foreign policy of all countries from 'egoistic and self-centred' to acknowledging 'certain moral and material interests common to all nations.'[16]

Although it did not go as far as to restrict or prohibit the use of force itself, Article 10 was often mentioned by members of the League as a general principle to which appeal could be made whenever a serious threat to the territorial integrity or the political independence of a state was alleged. China, for instance, submitted its dispute with Japan over Manchuria under Articles 10, 11 and 15, and consequently, in 1932, members of the Council addressed an appeal to the Japanese government calling attention to Article 10.[17]

The Covenant also elaborated a dispute settlement procedure for the League members. Article 12 provided that if a dispute arose between the members that was likely to lead to a rupture, they would submit the matter 'either to arbitration or judicial settlement or to enquiry by the Council' and they agreed 'in no case to resort to war until three months after the award by the arbitrators or the judicial decision, or the report by the Council.' Similarly, Article 13(4) stated that members of the League had to carry out 'in full good faith any award or decision that may be rendered' and they had to refrain from resorting to 'war against a Member of the League which complies therewith.'

Article 15(1) stated that 'if there should arise between Members of the League any dispute likely to lead to a rupture, which is not submitted to arbitration or

[14] For a detailed account of Woodrow Wilson's role and the main forces behind the rejection of the ratification, see Walters 1965, pp. 68–72.

[15] The 24 members included the Free French Government during the German occupation of France.

[16] Benes 1932, p. 68.

[17] Brownlie 1963, p. 64.

judicial settlement in accordance with Article 13, the Members of the League agreed that they will submit the matter to the Council.' Nonetheless, if the Council could not reach a decision, paragraph 7 of the same Article allowed Member States to 'reserve to themselves the right to take such action as they shall consider necessary for the maintenance of right and justice.' In support of this provision, Article 16 stated that if a member of the League resorted to war in disregard of Articles 12, 13 or 15, it was deemed to have committed an act of war against all other members of the League, which were required to subject the aggressor to various sanctions.

In the 1920s, the League proved to be successful in many dispute settlement cases, although it also registered a few failures, which, however, did not prove to be fatal. One of the successes of the League dispute settlement system was the resolution of the Åland Islands crisis.[18]

A less successful dispute resolution of the League was the tackling of the 1923 Corfu incident involving the occupation of the Greek island of Corfu by Italian forces under Mussolini.[19] The outcome of the dispute resolution showed that the outlawry of 'coercive measures' was still not generally acknowledged in the first decades of the twentieth century.[20] Despite this, many members of the League shared the view that forceful reprisals were incompatible with the Covenant. After the Corfu incident, these types of reprisals gradually disappeared from state practice in the period before the Second World War.[21]

With armed reprisals increasingly perceived as illegal, state practice was slowly moving towards rendering self-defence as the only valid exception to the prohibition to wage war.[22]

4.3 Self-Defence in the League System

The right of self-defence was not explicitly stated in the Covenant. Nonetheless, by requiring Member States to help each other when faced with an external aggression, the Covenant implicitly recognized the right to individual and collective defensive action. We can infer from the wording of Articles 10, 12 and 15 that Member States were allowed to exercise self-defence (individually or collectively) only when faced with an actual external aggression. The system of dispute settlement envisaged by the Covenant purported in itself the objective of avoiding, if possible, preventive or punitive wars. Thus it could be inferred that the

[18] For a brief description, see Walters 1965, pp. 103–105.

[19] For a brief description, see Walters 1965, pp. 244–246.

[20] For the opinion expressed by an appointed Committee of Jurists as regards reprisals, see League Council meeting of 13 March 1924, p. 524.

[21] Brownlie 1963, p. 222; Kalshoven 2005, p. 4.

[22] Wehberg 1931, pp. 49, 92.

self-defence the drafters had in mind was not necessarily the broad privilege of sovereigns to wage wars for the interest of the state.[23]

According to Bowett, the reason why no specific reservation of the right of self-defence appeared in the Covenant, was that such specification was regarded as superfluous.[24] The legality of self-defence as an exception to the prohibition stipulated in the Covenant was, nevertheless, confirmed by one of the preliminary reports on the Geneva Protocol on the Pacific Settlement of International Disputes:

> The prohibition affects only aggressive war. It does not, of course, extend to defensive war. The right of legitimate self-defence continues, as it must, to be respected. The State attacked retains complete liberty to resist by all means in its power any acts of aggression of which it might be the victim.[25]

Self-defence was explicitly recognized as an exception to the restriction of war in the Locarno Treaties, agreements negotiated between several European states in 1925.[26] Although the agreements were concluded outside the League system, they were based on the principles laid down in the Covenant. Accordingly, in the Treaty of Mutual Guarantee between Germany, Belgium, France, Great Britain and Italy, the parties undertook not to invade or attack each other as well as not to resort to war against each other. Three exceptions were stipulated to this undertaking: the right to self-defence, action in pursuance of Article 16 of the Covenant and action resulting from a decision taken by the Assembly or by the Council of the League of Nations or in pursuance of Article 15(7) of the Covenant, provided that in this last event the action was directed against a State which was the first to attack.

The treaty defined self-defence as 'resistance to a violation of the undertaking' not to attack, invade or resort to war against each other or resistance to a 'flagrant breach' of the demilitarization provisions of the Treaty of Versailles (Articles 42 and 43), 'if such breach constitutes an unprovoked act of aggression and by reason of the assembly of armed forces in the demilitarised zone immediate action is necessary.'[27]

---

[23] Wehberg 1931, pp. 10, 100–103.

[24] Bowett 1958, p. 124.

[25] Benes and Politis 1924, p. 483. The draft Protocol (1924) proposed sanctions against an aggressor state and provided a mechanism for the peaceful settlement of disputes. States had to agree to submit all disputes to the Permanent Court of International Justice, and any state refusing arbitration was to be deemed the aggressor. The protocol was rejected.

[26] The Locarno Treaties were seven agreements negotiated at Locarno (Switzerland) in October 1925 and signed in London in December 1925 between Germany, France, Belgium, Britain, Italy, Poland and Czechoslovakia. The particular agreement referred to in this section is the Treaty of Mutual Guarantee between Germany, Belgium, France, Great Britain and Italy, 16 October 1925 (hereafter, Locarno Pact 1925).

[27] Art. 2 Locarno Pact 1925.

4.4 The Kellogg-Briand Pact and the Right of Self-Defence

The Kellogg-Briand Pact was born out of France's post-war system of alliances, negotiated to maintain the peace of Europe.[28] France saw its security and implicitly, the security of Europe, greatly endangered by its former enemy, Germany. Consequently, it sought to obtain reassurances from the other Powers that they would stand together in case of another belligerent move by its neighbour. Between 1920 and 1927, the French government managed to secure alliances with all important states neighbouring Germany (Belgium, Poland and Czechoslovakia) as well as with the Balkans (Romania and Yugoslavia).[29] After securing the amiability of all major neighbours of Germany and of the progressively unfriendly Italy, France attempted to open negotiations with the US. The greatest role in this initiative was played by the foreign minister of France, Aristide Briand, who was a prominent politician and diplomat, an important French political figure of the interwar period.[30]

On 6 April 1927, in a statement issued through the Associated Press, Briand proposed to the US government to enter into an agreement never to use war as an instrument of national policy against each other.[31] This suggestion was made official in June that year and it took the form of a draft agreement, the first Article of which was to serve as the basis for the final version of the Pact.

The American reply came in December 1927, from Frank B. Kellogg, the American Secretary of State, who suggested obtaining 'the adherence of all the principal powers of the world to a declaration renouncing war as an instrument of national policy.'[32] The French replied on 5 January the following year by changing the wording of the proposal. Briand's formula—condemning war and renouncing it as an instrument of national policy—was altered to a more permissive phrase: 'to renounce all wars of aggression.' This suggestion, however, was abandoned as a result of subsequent negotiations and the original wording was kept.[33]

Although the right of self-defence was not explicitly recognised in the Pact, it was discussed during the pre-Pact negotiations. In the official note of 30 March 1928 sent to the US, the French government made three reservations regarding the content of the would-be treaty. One of them referred to self-defence and stipulated that the renunciation of war would not deprive the signatories of the right to legitimate defence.[34]

---

[28] Ferrell 1952, p. 51.

[29] Ferrell 1952, pp. 63–64.

[30] On various theories on how Briand got to the idea of proposing an agreement to the US for the renunciation of war, see Butler 1939–1940, pp. 202–203.

[31] Watkins 1932, p. 16.

[32] Watkins 1932, p. 18.

[33] Miller 1928, pp. 20–21, 45.

[34] Watkins 1932, pp. 18–19.

These reservations were answered by Kellogg in his final note of 23 June 1928, after several other powers (Germany, Japan, Italy and Great Britain) received proposals to adhere and copies of the French-American diplomatic correspondence. All powers reacted favourably to the proposal.[35] Kellogg's final note was sent to all would-be signatories and took the form of an interpretative reply to all the comments, reservations and concerns expressed by the French and the other governments.[36]

Kellogg discussed several issues in his note, including self-defence. Although his response was meant to explain why there was no stipulation of such right in the draft, Kellogg managed to give a strong characterization of the right, which made the other states believe that it was obvious to consider self-defence as the unnamed, but natural exception to the Pact.

Kellogg started his interpretation by stating that there was nothing in the draft that restricted or impaired in any way the right of self-defence. He went on to say:

> That right is inherent in every sovereign state and is implicit in every treaty. Every nation is free at all times and regardless of treaty provisions to defend its territory from attack or invasion and it alone is competent to decide whether circumstances require recourse to war in self-defence. If it has a good case, the world will applaud and not condemn its action.[37]

The American Secretary of State further explained that it was not in the interest of peace that a treaty would stipulate a 'juristic conception' of 'the natural right of self-defence', since it was 'far too easy for the unscrupulous to mould events to accord with an agreed definition' and because no specific reference to self-defence as an inalienable attribute of sovereignty was necessary or desirable.[38]

What Kellogg coined as the inherent right of the state was the same concept that the drafters of the Covenant and the Locarno Treaties had in their mind: a right of self-defence that could be exercised when a state was faced with an invasion or an attack. This right did not allow defence against dangerously powerful neighbours, suspicious aggrandizement plans of sovereigns or other potential dangers.

Kellogg's phrase 'to defend their territory from attack or invasion' did not purport any temporal restriction as to the time before or after the attack. It rather evoked the understanding according to which self-defence was allowed when an immediate need for action was present Table 4.1.[39]

The Pact was signed by 15 states on 27 August 1928.[40] The Pact consisted of three articles: two substantive and one procedural. In Article I the contracting

---

[35] Ibid., p. 19. As a result of Great Britain's *proviso*, invitations were sent to Canada, The Irish Free State, Australia, New Zealand, South Africa and India.

[36] Ibid., p. 20.

[37] June 23 Note, in Miller 1928, pp. 213–214.

[38] Ibid., pp. 214, 216.

[39] Webster 1841, p. 1138.

[40] The initial signatories were France, US, Germany, Great Britain, Canada, Australia, New Zealand, South Africa, Irish Free State, India, Belgium, Japan, Poland, Czechoslovakia and Italy. By August 1932 47 other states signed the Pact, raising the number of parties to a total of 62. At the outbreak of the Second World War, however, the number of the parties to the Pact dropped considerably.

Table 4.1 Self-defence as an exception in the emerging international legal framework

Self-Defence	Explicit provisions	Implicit understanding
League of Nations system		Deduced from the draft Geneva Protocol Resist aggression No expressed temporal limits Also instructive Oppenheim's view (an imminent violation or the continuation of an already commenced violation)
Locarno Treaties	Immediate action necessary No expressed temporal limits	
Kellogg-Briand Pact		Deduced from Kellogg's 23 June 1928 Note Defence from attack or invasion No expressed temporal limits

parties condemned recourse to war for the solution of international controversies, and renounced it, as an instrument of national policy in their relations with one another. Article II referred to the settlement of disputes and stipulated that the parties agreed that the solution of 'all disputes or conflicts of whatever nature or of whatever origin,' which might arise among them, would never be sought except by pacific means. Article III concerned the procedure of further signatures and ratification. There was no explicit mention of compatibility with the Covenant or other treaties, the violation of the treaty or self-defence. For that reason, the final note of Frank Kellogg served as an official basis for the interpretation of the Pact.

The immediate reaction to the Pact was enthusiastic. Contemporary analysts saw it as a strong pledge for the renunciation of war. According to Watkins, the Pact was a 'direct blow at the institution of war' also because it allowed only pacific means of settling disputes.[41]

The Pact also had its weaknesses. Most significantly, perhaps, the Pact shared the weakness of the Covenant of being too narrowly targeted and only renouncing resort to *war* and not the use of armed force in general.[42] On the positive side, the Kellogg-Briand Pact was the first clear sign of the break-away of legalism from the tenets of the realist balance-of-power system. The fact that the Pact pledged the renunciation of war as an instrument of national policy, a Clausewitzian phrase cherished by realism, was the sign that the first firm grounds for a new framework were being laid down.

Although the concept of self-defence was not expressly included in the Pact (as it was not addressed in the Hague conventions or the Covenant), the common understanding given to the right echoed the narrow, natural-law understanding of

[41] Watkins 1932, pp. 32–33.

[42] Neff 2005, p. 285.

self-defence, applied to the realities of public warfare, according to which 'immediate action was necessary'[43] 'to defend [...] from attack or invasion.'[44]

4.5 State Practice in the 1930s and the Collapse of the League of Nations

Although the Kellogg-Briand Pact was received with enthusiasm and was seen as an additional consolidation of the League of Nations, state practice in the 1930s demonstrated the fatal weaknesses of the League system.

Apart from the rise of fascism in Italy and Germany, the political and military weakness of the most active members of the League (France and Britain), rendered its functioning more than difficult. The fact that the US never became a member and that Germany and the USSR shifted to be enemies of the League, rendered the survival chances of the organization minimal. With such weak pillars for a collective security system, the cumbersome decision-making procedure in the League Council turned into an invincible obstacle. The determination of whether a particular use of force constituted an act of aggression or the formulation of a resolution for a dispute had to be the result of a unanimous decision of the League Council. The membership in the League Council changed over time, but it was continuously based on the permanent/non-permanent divide, having the great European powers as its permanent members. With such a structure, unanimity in the difficult cases was impossible to achieve.

The collapse of the League was facilitated by the Council's inability to tackle three major conflicts: the Japanese invasion of Manchuria (1931–1932), the conflict between Bolivia and Paraguay (1932–1933) and the Italian invasion of Abyssinia in 1935. All three conflicts have been explained and interpreted (by parties and commentators) in terms of aggression and response to aggression.

The conflict between Bolivia and Paraguay involved the Gran Chaco, a vast area separating the two countries. Both governments claimed the whole area and each was in effective control of a small part near its own territory.[45] Although early skirmishes in the 1920s were anesthetized by the League, in 1932 the two parties launched hostilities against each other.[46] In 1933, the League agreed to dispatch a commission of its own to solve the conflict. After several failures to secure agreement between the two parties, in 1934, the commission returned to

---

[43] Article 2 Locarno Pact 1925. See *supra* 4.3.2.

[44] June 23 Note, in Miller 1928, pp. 213–214.

[45] As a result of the 1879–1884 war between Bolivia, Peru and Chile, Bolivia lost its narrow strip of coast and became landlocked. The Gran Chaco remained the only route which permitted Bolivia to reach the Atlantic coast through the Río de La Plata estuary. Bolivia and Paraguay several times attempted to agree on a frontier without success. By the late 1920s, both countries maintained several military posts in the disputed region. Farcau 1996, p. 8.

[46] Walters 1965, pp. 527, 531–532.

Geneva.[47] Reaching a state of mutual stalemate, the two belligerents finally agreed on a truce in June 1935 and the war was declared over in November the same year. A peace treaty was finally signed in Buenos Aires in July 1938, but the League was no longer formally associated with the proceedings.

Although the concept of self-defence was not invoked by either of the parties, this crisis clearly showed that the members of the League still did not see self-defence as the sole exception to the prohibition of war.

The invasions of Manchuria and that of Ethiopia were specifically linked to the concept of self-defence by one or the other party. Nonetheless, in both cases, the self-defence invoked lacked the elements of the right understood in its narrow (natural-law) sense.

4.5.1 The Invasion of Manchuria by Japan (1931–1932)

According to Walters, the Japanese occupation of Manchuria was a turning point in the history of the League and of the world.[48]

On the night of 18 September 1931, the Japanese Quantung Army, which was policing the South Manchurian Railway, alleged that a small group of Chinese soldiers blew up a few metres of the railway track near Mukden (a city in the south of Manchuria, now Shenyang) and used the event as an excuse to seize the arsenal of the city and occupy it by morning the following day.[49]

After the incident of 18 September, some attempts were made to reach an agreement between China and Japan regarding Manchuria. However, national sentiments ran high on both sides and the talks subsequently failed. China referred the matter to the League Council pursuant to Articles 10, 11 and 15 of the Covenant.[50] Japan continued its campaign and in the remainder of 1931 occupied the entire region of Manchuria. In 1932 Chinese regulars and guerrillas strengthened their resistance, causing the spread of the conflict beyond the region, to Shanghai (January–March 1932) and to Jehol (March 1933) as well as the other areas of China. In May 1933 an armistice agreement was concluded.[51]

Before the League, Japan declared that there was no military occupation and that there were no warlike intentions. Indeed, neither China nor Japan declared the existence of a state of war between 1931 and 1933. Moreover, Japan justified its action as, *inter alia*, 'defence of rights and interests on which her very existence depends.'[52]

---

[47] Ibid., pp. 532–533.

[48] Ibid., p. 465.

[49] Shotwell and Salvin 1949, p. 81; Brownlie 1963, p. 385.

[50] Walters 1965, pp. 468–469; Brownlie 1963, p. 386.

[51] Brownlie 1963, pp. 385–386.

[52] League Council meeting, 25 January 1932, p. 332.

Japan stipulated that it had no territorial desires and that most of the troops had already been withdrawn, while the rest would be evacuated as soon as Japanese citizens and property in Manchuria were no longer endangered. But as the situation in Manchuria grew worse, the Council started to doubt the assurances given by Japan. Faced with criticism for its actions, the Japanese government put forward another explanation, according to which China breached the Kellogg-Briand Pact by boycotting Japanese goods throughout its territory and thus Japan was entitled to take forcible counteraction.[53]

Negotiations overseen by the Council and the United States started in October 1931, but failed to reach an agreement. The military situation grew worse with the Japanese army marching further into Chinese territory on the pretext of rescuing its own nationals in Tientsin, south to Manchuria.[54]

The Council was wary in accepting such justifications and it repeatedly stated that the Covenant did not authorize states to seek redress by other than peaceful means. Eventually, the Council rejected the pretext of self-defence or rescuing nationals and deemed Japanese military action illegal. But this verdict came too late to prevent the invasion and occupation of a considerable part of China.[55]

The now famous report of the Lytton Commission was published in September 1932 and it served as an authoritative record of facts. As a verdict, the Lytton Report was a substantial endorsement of the Chinese case. The report clearly stated that the actions of the Japanese army after the Mukden incident could not be viewed as legitimate self-defence and hinted that the Japanese military campaign was planned beforehand.[56] Moreover, the report concluded that the newly formed state was not the result of a genuine independence movement and therefore the re-establishment of Chinese sovereignty over Manchuria was recommended.[57]

As a response, Japan reiterated its argument of self-defence against a disorganized and civil war-torn China and rejected the recommendations of the Lytton Report. Following a statement adopted by the Assembly of the League in February 1933, which endorsed the findings and recommendations of the Lytton Report, on 27 March, Japan announced its withdrawal from the League.[58] Despite the resounding appraisal of the Lytton Report, the prestige of the League suffered a great deal because of the Manchurian incident and its aftermath.

The claim of self-defence invoked by Japan was far from meeting the requirements of the narrow, natural-law concept. Japan failed to demonstrate the existence of an immediate need for action against an imminent attack, let alone an attack in progress. The disturbances caused by the Chinese soldiers in Manchuria could have never amounted to a danger that created an immediate need for action.

---

53 Walters 1965, pp. 473–475.

54 Ibid., pp. 475, 479–480.

55 Brownlie 1963, pp. 294–295.

56 Walters 1965, p. 491; Brownlie 1963, p. 294; Shotwell and Salvin 1949, p. 88.

57 Walters 1965, p. 492; Shotwell and Salvin 1949, p. 88.

58 Walters 1965, p. 495.

Moreover, the full-scale invasion of Manchuria could not be seen as a moderate response to the turbulence. Although the Lytton Report eventually condemned the actions of Japan, the illegality of its actions had been visible from the beginning.

4.5.2 The Italian Invasion of Ethiopia (1935–1936)

Admitted to the League in 1923 and under the rule of Hailie Selassie from 1928, Ethiopia was bordered on the north and south by Italian colonies. The ancient kingdom had made considerable progress under the rule of Hailie Selassie, but still lacked full control over its territory, especially regarding tribes in frontier regions.[59]

According to the memoirs of his General, Emilio de Bono, Italian dictator Mussolini began planning an attack on the country as early as 1933, but a pretext was needed to launch hostilities.[60] Such an excuse finally presented itself on 5 December 1934, in the form of clashes in the disputed area between Italian Somaliland and the Ogaden province inhabited by Ethiopian tribes. The direct clash between the armed forces of the two states was of insignificant proportions, but Mussolini saw it as a unique chance to put his plan into action. The Italian government promptly reacted to the clashes, claiming that it was forced by Ethiopian hostility to exercise legitimate self-defence and, simultaneously, to spread civilization among the Ethiopians.[61]

Hailie Selassie duly referred the matter to the Council of the League, submitting it for arbitration and pledging to accept whatever outcome of it. Action on behalf of the Council was delayed because France and Britain hoped to solve the matter with Italy alone.[62] Meanwhile, Italian preparations for the invasion of Ethiopia continued, although the official discourse was excluding any military intervention. This attitude changed in the spring of 1935 and Italy started to refer to it as a 'colonial war' in defence of its territories, a war that was manifestly distinguished from any form of aggression. The proposals of the League for peaceful solutions were quickly discarded by none other than France and Britain, who wished to solve the conflict through secret negotiations with Italy.[63]

By June 1935 it became clear that Italy was massively arming itself. The League Council met again in September 1935 and drafted a plan of international assistance to Ethiopia which was, however, rejected by Italy.[64] The Italian

59 Shotwell and Salvin 1949, p. 92.

60 Bono 1937, pp. 13–14.

61 Walters 1965, p. 625.

62 The reason of French and British reluctance to refer the matter to the Council was their fear to upset Mussolini, who was believed to be willing to hold back rising Nazi aggressiveness. Walters 1965, pp. 627–629.

63 Ibid., pp. 634–635, 638–639.

64 Shotwell and Salvin 1949, p. 95.

government claimed that Ethiopia failed to respect its obligations under various treaties, that it had committed a long series of outrages against Italian diplomats and that, in fact, it was incapable of being a true member of the League, because Ethiopia was not an organized state at all and because it did not succeed in abolishing slavery as promised at its entry to the League. On this basis, Italy once again reiterated its right to defend its own colonies and claimed that it was defending the prestige and good name of the League of Nations.[65]

With the Council not being able to stop the unfolding of the events, the Italian offensive began on 3 October 1935. Although the League imposed sanctions against Italy, the French Prime Minister Pierre Laval and the British Chancellor Sir Samuel Hoare secretly decided not to employ such sanctions, allowing in this way Mussolini to carry out his plans in Eastern Africa. This infamous accord was to be known as the Hoare-Laval Plan and although it never came into force, the two dignitaries had to resign when information leaked to the media.[66]

Addis Ababa was captured in May 1936 and the Abyssinian emperor was forced to flee. Although the League condemned the action of Italy as unlawful aggression and although it denied its right to attack Ethiopia on the basis of legitimate defence, the Council's paralysis—as a consequence of the attitudes of France and Britain—permanently damaged the reputation and functioning of the organization.

As with the Japanese invasion of Manchuria, the Italian claim of self-defence against Ethiopia was far from meeting the requirements of the narrow, natural-law concept of self-defence. There was no evidence of an attack, imminent or in preparation. The clashes that occurred in the disputed area were far from qualifying as an attack that created an immediate need for action or, in Webster's words, 'a necessity, present and inevitable.'[67] Moreover, the full-scale invasion of Ethiopia and the use of chemical weapons could hardly be justified as a moderate use of self-defence.

It is important to conclude at this point that the narrow, natural-law concept of self-defence maintained its validity in the League system of prohibition of war. Both public officials and legal publicists characterized self-defence as the only exception to the prohibition of war. State practice was slower in accepting this restriction. As the Corfu incident and the Chaco War showed, other forms of the use of force, remnants of the nineteenth-century measures short of war, were still employed by states. Nonetheless, there were other instances of state practice which showed that the use of force was condemned for not meeting the requirement of self-defence. Accordingly, both the Japanese invasion of Manchuria and the Italian invasion of Ethiopia were condemned for not meeting the requirements of a moderate exercise of self-defence to ward off an attack in a situation of 'present and inevitable' necessity. These instances of state practice can be corroborated with statements of officials (such as the informative note of Kellogg), certain multilateral agreements

[65] Walters 1965, pp. 642–644.

[66] Shotwell and Salvin 1949, p. 100.

[67] Webster 1841, p. 1138.

(such as the Treaty of Mutual Guarantee between Germany, Belgium, France, Great Britain and Italy) and the legal literature that made explicit reference to self-defence and which are reflecting of *opinio juris* of that time.[68]

4.6 Operation Catapult (1940)

With Hitler remilitarizing the Rhineland and Mussolini rallying to the German dictator's side, the days of the League were numbered and the Second World War was looming over Europe. With the German invasion of Poland in 1939, the second global war of the twentieth century started and was to last for 6 years.

An instance of wartime state practice that deserves attention at this point is the British attack on the French naval fleet in July 1940. *Operation Catapult*—as it was named—was an attempt to ensure that the German forces would not make use of French war vessels.[69]

In June 1940, Great Britain found herself in a precarious strategic position. France was steps away from an armistice, while Italy had just announced its participation in the war alongside Germany. Britain had suddenly found herself standing alone against the Third Reich.[70]

The terms of the German–French Armistice Agreement caused serious concerns to the British. In particular, Article 8 of the Agreement stipulated that all French vessels outside territorial waters were to immediately return to France. Britain was worried that the French vessels stationed in the Mediterranean could in this way very easily come within the grasp of the German forces.[71]

British Prime Minister Winston Churchill ordered substantial reinforcements to the British fleet stationed in the Mediterranean, but this manoeuvre could not entirely solve the problem. At that time, the French fleet was acknowledged as the world's fourth largest navy. If Germany and Italy were allowed to make use of the fleet in addition to their existing naval force, Britain would be faced with an overwhelming threat that was impossible to meet.[72] Not only would Britain be isolated from the vital Atlantic supply routes and from its empire, but also the waters around it would become an open avenue for a German invasion force.[73]

Churchill resorted to diplomacy at first, but the French government refused to order its ships to sail to British ports. Negotiations failed and Churchill decided that a

---

[68] June 23 Note, in Miller 1928, pp. 213–214; Art. 2 Locarno Pact 1925. See *supra* 4.3. Oppenheim 1905, pp. 178–179.

[69] For a review of Anglo-French relations between 1940 and 1942 and *Operation Catapult*, see Tute 1989.

[70] Lasterle 2003, pp. 837–838.

[71] Brown 1997; Lasterle 2003, p. 837.

[72] Brown 1997.

[73] Ibid.

pre-emptive use of force was needed to protect Britain from the danger that Axis possession of the French vessels threatened. This danger had to be overcome as soon as possible in order for the British warships shadowing the French to be released for operations elsewhere. Churchill set 3 July as the day on which all French naval warships within Britain's grasp would either be seized or destroyed.[74]

In choosing primary targets, the planners were not concerned with the French ships that had taken refuge in home ports, such as those stationed at Casablanca, Dakar or Alexandria. The real concern of the British War Cabinet was Mers-el-Kebir, near Oran in Algeria, where the strongest concentration of French ships was anchored. The force included two older battleships (*Bretagne* and *Provence*), six destroyers, one seaplane carrier and two modern battle cruisers, (*Dunkerque* and *Strasbourg*). The War Cabinet was especially worried about the latter two; these battle cruisers were two of the most modern ships afloat at that time, both more powerful than the German battle cruisers and faster than the British (except the battle cruiser Hood).[75]

On 3 July 1940, the British first seized the French naval vessels in the British ports. This operation also confirmed the necessity of the take-over, because the same seizure could have been accomplished by the Germans as well.[76] The same course of action was followed with the French vessels located in Alexandria and the West Indies. When it came to the French fleet at Mers-el-Kebir, the operation took another turn. The British offered an ultimatum to the French naval commander, Admiral Gensoul, which included four alternatives: have the French fleet join the British Royal Navy, take the fleet to British ports, take the fleet to a French West Indian or a US port or sink the fleet in the harbour. If none of these options were accepted within three hours, the British admiral on the scene would be instructed to sink the French fleet by naval gunfire.[77] Tense negotiations followed throughout the day, with the British naval commander, Vice Admiral Somerville trying to secure a peaceful resolution of the situation. Admiral Gensoul, however, refused to accept the ultimatum.[78] At 5:30 in the afternoon, the British naval force opened fire on the French fleet. Most of the vessels were either destroyed or sank, while a small group managed to escape and harbour at Toulon. Some 1,300 French sailors died and another 340 were wounded in the attack.[79]

Although there was no conclusive evidence of a clear German intention to take control of the French fleet, once returned to their French ports, the vessels could have been boarded and seized by German forces at any time and the British could have done nothing about it.[80] In Lasterle's words, if that scenario took place,

[74] Battle Summary No. 1, 3–6 July 1940.

[75] Brown 1997; Battle Summary No. 1, 3–6 July 1940.

[76] Gill 2007, p. 132.

[77] Brown 1997; Battle Summary No. 1, 3–6 July 1940; Lasterle 2003, p. 836.

[78] Lasterle 2003, pp. 840–843.

[79] Gill 2007, p. 132; Lasterle 2003, p. 843.

[80] Gill 2007, p. 134; Lasterle 2003, p. 838.

Britain would have been 'doomed'.[81] The present and inevitable necessity perceived by Churchill's War Cabinet was thus based on an inference, made in good faith, that the only way such a disaster could be avoided was to either place the French fleet under British control or destroy it. Although sinking the French ships was the last resort option of the operation, the unsuccessful negotiations between Somerville and Gensoul led to the destruction of the French fleet stationed at Mers-el-Kebir.[82]

4.7 The Emerging International Legal Framework and Self-Defence

The aim of this chapter was to assess whether the temporal dimension and elements of self-defence acknowledged in the Christian natural-law and the positivist normative frameworks were altered during the emerging system of modern international law of the late nineteenth and early twentieth centuries. Such an assessment was intended to deduce whether anticipatory action was still part of the contemporaneous understanding of self-defence, and if so, under what conditions.

The end of the nineteenth and the beginning of the twentieth centuries saw the emergence of a new normative framework that moved towards the prohibition of aggressive war. Notwithstanding the ambiguities surrounding the specific object of this prohibition, there was a clear trend towards invalidating the absolute right of war that dominated the seventeenth- to nineteenth century Western tradition. Within this framework, self-defence was given a privileged place: it was to be viewed as the only exception to war as an instrument of national policy. Most of the ground-breaking treaties, however, shied away from stipulating (let alone defining) self-defence as an explicit exception. In order to discern what the content and temporal dimension of this right was, the legal-historical analysis of this chapter corroborated information from diplomatic notes, regional treaties, reactions to instances of state practice and the legal literature.[83]

On the basis of this corroborating exercise, it is the conclusion of this chapter that the concept of self-defence, accepted as a customary rule in the emerging international law framework, retained its narrow, natural-law understanding (applied to the realities of interstate conflict) which was apparent in the previous two normative frameworks identified. Accordingly, self-defence was seen as giving rise to an immediate need for armed action to defend the state from an

[81] Lasterle 2003, p. 838.

[82] Gill 2007, p. 132. *Per a contrario*, Lasterle asserts that 'the die was already cast' on the morning of 3 July 1940, when Churchill decided that the French fleet at Mers-el-Kebir had to be destroyed. Lasterle 2003, p. 844.

[83] June 23 Note, in Miller 1928, pp. 213–214; Art. 2 Locarno Pact 1925. See *supra* 4.3. Benes and Politis 1924, p. 483; Oppenheim 1905, pp. 178–179.

attack or invasion. Expressions such as 'to resist by all means in its power any acts of aggression of which it *might* be the victim.',[84] 'to defend its territory *from* attack or invasion'[85] did not purport a temporal limitation. They rather echoed Oppenheim's interpretation of self-defence, as armed action against 'an imminent violation or the continuation of an already commenced violation',[86] view that reiterated the present and inevitable necessity that the Webster-formula rendered as a primary condition for the exercise of self-defence. Moreover, the relevant texts of the draft Geneva Protocol, Locarno Treaties and also Kellogg's June 23 Note expressly guaranteed the continuity of the right of self-defence. The reason for that was the reluctance of potential contracting parties to adopt the new instruments in the absence of some assurance that their customary right of self-defence was safeguarded.

Consequently, it is hard to discern any apparent trend of restricting the temporal dimension of self-defence to after an attack. The visible limiting tendency rather targeted expansionist ambitions portrayed as preventive action in self-defence. Accordingly, the negative reaction to the Japanese and Italian invasions of Manchuria and Ethiopia, respectively, showed that the traditional preventive war arguments were being widely rejected. The reaction to the scale of these invasions also showed that moderation was still viewed as a limit of any purportedly defensive action.

Consequently, the requirements of present and inevitable necessity and due moderation (proportionality) can be viewed as the elements that limited the exercise of self-defence at the beginning of the twentieth century, regardless of the anticipatory or remedial nature of the defensive action. Chapter 5 will examine whether this understanding was the one taken into consideration during the adoption of the UN Charter.

References

Battle Summary No. 1: Operations against the French fleet at Mers-el-Kebir, 3–6 July 1940. HMS Hood Reference Materials, Doc. AIR 234/317. http:\\www.hmshood.org.uk/reference/official/adm234/adm234–317.htm. Accessed 5 June 2009

Benes E (1932) The League of Nations: successes and failures. Foreign Aff 11:66–80

Benes E, Politis N (1924) Report on the Protocol, submitted to the Fifth Assembly. League of Nations Official Journal (Special Supp. No. 23) 483

de Bono E (1937) Anno XIIII. The conquest of an empire. Cresset Press, London

Bowett DW (1958) Self-defence in international law. Manchester University Press, Manchester

Brown RJ (1997) Operation Catapult: Naval destruction at Mers-el-Kebir. World War II. http:\\www.historynet.com/operation-catapult-naval-destruction-at-mers-el-kebir.htm. Accessed 5 June 2009

---

[84] Benes and Politis 1924, p. 483 (draft Geneva Protocol, emphasis added).

[85] June 23 Note, in Miller 1928, pp. 213–214 (emphasis added).

[86] Oppenheim 1905, p. 178 (emphasis added).

Brownlie I (1963) International law and the use of force by states. Clarendon Press, Oxford
Butler NM (1939–1940) Across the busy years: recollections and reflections. Scribner, New York
Farcau BW (1996) The Chaco war: Bolivia and Paraguay, 1932–1935. Praeger, Westport, Conn
Ferrell RH (1952) Peace in their time: the origins of the Kellogg-Briand Pact. Yale University Press, New Haven
Ford TK (1936) The genesis of the first Hague Peace Conference. Polit Sci Q 51:354–382
Gill TD (2007) The temporal dimension of self-defence. In: Schmitt M, Pejic J (eds) International law and armed conflict: exploring the faultlines. Essays in honour of Yoram Dinstein. Martinus Nijhoff, Leiden, pp 113–155
Hueck IJ (2001) The discipline of the history of international law: new trends and methods on the history of international law. J Hist Int Law 3:194–217
Kalshoven F (2005) Belligerent reprisals. Martinus Nijhoff, Leiden
Lasterle P (2003) Could Admiral Gensoul have averted the tragedy of Mers el-Kébir? J Military Hist 67:835–844
League Council meeting of 13 March 1924 (1924) League Nations Off. J. 5:523–529
League Council meeting of 25 January 1932 (1932) League Nations Off. J. 13:326–333
Miller DH (1928) The Peace Pact of Paris: a study of the Briand-Kellogg Treaty. G.P. Putnam's Sons, New York
Morrill DL (1974) Nicholas II and the call for the First Hague Conference. J Mod Hist 46:296–313
Neff SC (2005) War and the law of nations: general history. Cambridge University Press, Cambridge
Nussbaum A (1947) A concise history of the law of nations. Macmillan, New York
Oppenheim L (1905) International law: a treatise, vol 1. Longmans Green and Co., New York
Shotwell JT, Salvin M (1949) Lessons on security and disarmament. From the history of the League of Nations. King's Crown Press, New York
Steiger H (2001) From the international law of Christianity to the international law of the world citizen: reflections on the formation of epochs of the history of international law. J Hist Int Law 3:180–193
The Bryan Peace Treaties—Editorial Comment (1913) American Journal of International Law 7: 823–829
Tute W (1989) The reluctant enemies: the story of the last war between Britain and France, 1940–1942. Collins, London
Walters FP (1965) A history of the League of Nations. Oxford University Press, London
Watkins AC (1932) The Paris Pact. a textbook for schools and colleges. Harcourt, Brace and Company, New York
Webster 1841: Letter from Daniel Webster, US Secretary of State, to Henry Fox, British Minister in Washington, 24 April 1841. In: British and Foreign State Papers, 1840–1841, vol 29 (1857). James Ridgway and Sons, London, pp 1129–1139
Wehberg H (1931) The outlawry of war. Carnegie Endowment for International Peace, Washington

Chapter 5
The Right of Self-Defence and the Drafting of the UN Charter

5.1 Preliminaries and the Dumbarton Oaks Proposals

The end of the Second World War brought back the pacifist aspirations stronger than ever before. Even before the war ended, several meetings took place between the Allied states to adopt common positions regarding international peace and security. In June 1941, at St. James' Palace in London, the Allied states and several governments in exile signed a declaration in which they stipulated their intention to work together for the furtherance of peace.[1] Two months later, in August 1941, US President Franklin D. Roosevelt and UK Prime Minister Winston Churchill signed the Atlantic Charter which declared that 'all of the nations of the world, for realistic as well as spiritual reasons, must come to the abandonment of the use of force.' The bilateral agreement also stipulated that 'no future peace can be maintained if land, sea or air armaments continue to be employed by nations which threaten, or may threaten, aggression outside of their frontiers' and for that reason the disarmament of such states was essential 'pending the establishment of a wider and permanent system of general security.' The Atlantic Charter was followed by the UN Declaration of 1 January 1942 signed initially by President Roosevelt, Prime Minister Churchill, Maxim Litvinov, of the USSR, and T.V. Soong, of China. The following day the representatives of 22 other nations added their signatures. The list of agreements signed during the war was complemented with the Moscow Declaration (October 1943) and the Teheran Declaration (December 1943). The Moscow and Teheran Declarations were furthered in October 1944 by the four-power (China, Great Britain, the USSR and the US) conversations at Dumbarton Oaks, Washington, D.C.

[1] The Declaration at St. James' Palace in London, 12 June 1941. The participants were: Great Britain, Canada, Australia, New Zealand and the Union of South Africa and the exiled Governments of Belgium, Czechoslovakia, Greece, Luxembourg, the Netherlands, Norway, Poland, Yugoslavia and General de Gaulle of France.

K. Tibori Szabó, *Anticipatory Action in Self-Defence*, DOI: 10.1007/978-90-6704-796-8_5,

The discussions were completed on 7 October 1944, and a proposal regarding the principles and the structure of the new world organization was submitted to all the signatories of the United Nations Declaration.

During the Dumbarton Oaks conversations, the issue of self-defence was brought up by China. The Chinese delegation wanted to know whether, under the proposal, member or non-member states could use force unilaterally under the claim that such action was not inconsistent with the purposes of the organization. The US representative ensured the Chinese delegation that 'except in cases of self-defence, no unilateral use of force could be undertaken without the approval of the Council.' The Chinese delegate seemed satisfied with such a clarification, but desired 'explicit assurance that use of force in self-defence would not be regarded as inconsistent with the purposes of the organization.'[2]

In spite of the Chinese demand for such explicit assurance, the issue of self-defence was not addressed in any of the provisions of the Dumbarton Oaks Proposals.

What the proposals did address, was the general prohibition to use force. Accordingly, paragraph 4 of Chapter II stated:

> All members of the Organization shall refrain in their international relations from the threat or use of force in any manner inconsistent with the purposes of the Organization.

The only exception expressly provided for in the Proposals was that in paragraph 4 of Section B of Chapter VIII, which permitted the Security Council to take forceful measures if diplomatic, economic or other non-forceful alternatives failed.

The matter was to resurface, however, in connection with Section C of Chapter VIII of the Dumbarton Oaks Proposals. The first paragraph of Section C was meant to safeguard the autonomy of regional arrangements:

> 1. Nothing in the Charter should preclude the existence of regional arrangements or agencies for dealing with such matters relating to the maintenance of international peace and security as are appropriate for regional action, provided such arrangements or agencies and their activities are consistent with the purposes and principles of the Organization. The Security Council should encourage settlement of local disputes through such regional arrangements or by such regional agencies, either on the initiative of the states concerned or by reference from the Security Council.

The second paragraph contained, nevertheless, a restriction to this autonomy:

> 2. The Security Council should, where appropriate, utilize such arrangements or agencies for enforcement action under its authority, but no enforcement action should be taken under regional arrangements or by regional agencies without the authorization of the Security Council.

Further, the third paragraph was meant to ensure that the Security Council was regularly informed about the development of such regional arrangements:

---

[2] Memorandum of the Under Secretary of State (Stettinius) to the Secretary of State, Washington, 2 October 1944. In foreign Relations of the US 1944, vol. 1, p. 862.

> 3. The Security Council should at all times be kept fully informed of activities undertaken or in contemplation under regional arrangements or by regional agencies for the maintenance of international peace and security.

As will be shown below, the second paragraph raised a difficult question during the negotiations at the San Francisco Conference. The matter was finally solved by including an explicit assurance regarding the right of self-defence, just as the Chinese delegate had requested.

5.2 The Drafting of the UN Charter at the San Francisco Conference

5.2.1 Proposals Ahead of the Conference

The Dumbarton Oaks Proposals were sent to all United Nations Governments for review and for proposing amendments ahead of the San Francisco Conference.

The issue of self-defence was first raised by the French Government on 21 March 1945. In its submission, the French Government affirmed that it was 'incompatible with the conditions of security of some states, which may demand immediate action, to defer, until such time as the Council has reached a decision, emergency measures for which provision is made, in the case of contingencies, by treaties of assistance, concluded between Members of the Organization and filed with the Security Council.'[3]

The French Government was trying to safeguard the Allied regional assistance agreements concluded against the Axis. According to its proposal, the second paragraph of Section C was to be supplemented:

> Nevertheless, an exception is made to this rule in the case of the application of measures of an urgent nature provided for in treaties of assistance concluded between members of the Organization and of which the Security Council has been advised. In any event, the signatory states of such treaties should report to it, with the least possible delay, the measures which they may have been led to take in execution of their provisions.[4]

A similar position was adopted by the Turkish Government. According to the Turkish submission, in cases of emergency, the immediate action that may be initiated through the application of regional arrangements should not be deferred pending the decision of the Security Council, because any procedure-related delay would be detrimental to the endangered country.[5]

---

[3] Proposal of the French Government, 21 March 1945. In UN Charter travaux préparatoires, vol. 3, p. 379.

[4] Ibid., p. 387.

[5] Suggestions of the Turkish Government concerning the proposals for the maintenance of peace and security agreed at the Four-Power Conference at Dumbarton Oaks, 1 May 1945. In UN Charter travaux préparatoires, vol. 3, p. 483.

Both submissions signalled the beginning of a major debate regarding the relationship between pre-existing regional assistance treaties and the principle of the prohibition to use force of the new world organization. The proposals of the French and Turkish Governments were taken up at the plenary and committee sessions of the San Francisco Conference.

5.2.2 *The Plenary Discussions of the San Francisco Conference*

On 25 April 1945 the San Francisco Conference started. One day later, on 26 April, at one of the meetings of the delegation of the US the matter of self-defence was brought up. The majority view of the delegates was that if—in spite of its willingness to resort to peaceful measures for dispute settlement—a state was attacked by military force, clearly then such a state had the right to defend itself. Although such an interpretation was viewed as mirroring common sense, several representatives considered it necessary to have 'an authoritative explanation' in the final text of the Charter.[6]

On the basis of such an explanation, the test would be whether the action was taken in accordance with the purpose of the Organization. Accordingly, as explained by the US delegate Durward Sandifer, 'a state might have the right to act in an emergency, and, if there was an allegation that this action was contrary to the purpose of the Organization, the Security Council might review it.'[7] Moreover, the view was expressed that if such explanation was not included in the Charter, the Senate of the US would definitely make a reservation.[8]

A few days later, at the preliminary plenary sessions of 1 May 1945, both France and Turkey reiterated their opinions. France justified its position by reminding the delegates that it was 'geographically placed in the immediate vicinity of one of the most dangerous zones', referring in this way to Germany and Italy. Further, the French delegate emphasized that France knows to its own cost that in order to discourage any future attempt of aggression the gap between 'the lightning rapidity of aggression and the inevitable slowness of consultation' must be bridged.[9]

Turkey reiterated its opinion as well, but ascertained that such 'automatically functioning arrangements' should only be allowed for the exclusive purposes of self-defence. It also asked for the inclusion of an explicit clause on the issue of legitimate defence.[10]

---

6 Minutes of the eighteenth meeting of the US delegation, held at San Francisco, 26 April 1945. In Foreign Relations of the US 1945, vol. 1, p. 427.

7 Ibid., pp. 428–429.

8 Ibid., p. 428.

9 Plenary Sess., 1 May 1945: Discussion. In UN Charter travaux préparatoires, vol. 1, p. 437.

10 Ibid., p. 453.

The question concerning regional arrangements and emergency situations was thoroughly addressed by Technical Committee 4 (on regional arrangements) of Commission III (on the Security Council).

5.2.3 The Work of Technical Committee 4 (Committee III/4)

The task of the members of Committee III/4 was to prepare draft provisions on regional arrangements. The most difficult problem that arose in the committee was the relationship between regional agreements or arrangements and the control exercised by the Security Council of the new organization. In Bowett's words, the members feared that 'by the exercise of the veto a single permanent member might prevent the regional organization from taking any action.'[11]

The French and Turkish concerns were also shared by Czechoslovakia. In the view of the Czechoslovak delegation, authorization of the Security Council was to be given 'in advance and as a general rule for cases of immediate danger,' because the suspension of any coercive action until the intervention of the Security Council could cause 'irremediable delays'.[12]

The question of autonomy of regional arrangements went beyond the concerns of the Allied states and was especially taken up by the American states who sought to safeguard their mutual assistance system and the Act of Chapultepec.[13] According to the Inter-American system (affirmed at Chapultepec), an attack against an American state was to be viewed as an attack against all American states. Moreover, the Act allowed action to be taken not only after such aggression occurred, but also if there were 'reasons to believe that an aggression is being prepared' (Section 4 of the Act). Since the US was party to the Act of Chapultepec, the matter of regional autonomy in emergency situations was repeatedly discussed by the US representatives at several of their delegation meetings. The question was asked what the US could do if Germany sent a fleet into the waters of Argentina.

> Would it be illegal if we shot across the German bows when they attempted to land in Argentina? Mr. Pasvolsky [Leo Pasvolsky, US delegate, KTSz] said that we would act, and that the Security Council would then be in a position to review our action, asking us what we were trying to do.[14]

---

[11] Bowett 1958, p. 183.

[12] Terms of Reference of Committee III/4, Chapter VIII, Section C of the Dumbarton Oaks Proposals with Pertinent Excerpts from Comments and Draft Amendments submitted by Delegations, 14 May 1945. In UN Charter travaux préparatoires, Vol. 12, p. 773.

[13] The Act of Chapultepec was an agreement adopted at Chapultepec Castle (Mexico City) by The Inter-American Conference on the Problems of War and Peace a few weeks before the San Francisco Conference (21 February–8 March 1945). The Chapultepec Conference was attended by all the nations of North and South America except Argentina. The signatories agreed to a policy of mutual defense during Second World War against aggression towards any one of them.

[14] Minutes of the Twenty-Ninth Meeting of the US Delegation, Held at San Francisco, Friday, 4 May 1945, In Foreign Relations of the US 1945, Vol. 1, p. 592.

The first amalgamation proposal was jointly submitted by the US, the UK, the Soviet Union and China and it took as point of departure the submission of France and Turkey. Accordingly, the amendment aimed to solve the question of security regarding the ex-enemy states of the war. The four states proposed to complement paragraph 2 of Section C, by adding the phrase 'with the exception of measures against enemy states in this war provided for pursuant to Chapter XII, paragraph 2,[15] or, in regional arrangements directed against renewal of aggressive policy on the part of such states' until the Organization can take over the measure.[16]

The purpose of this amendment was to ensure that the European states were protected against a potential rearming of the Axis. However, this did not solve the concerns of the American states, because the two exceptions did not provide any autonomy to non-European regional arrangements. Thus, they were left without a similar freedom of action under the Act of Chapultepec.

For remedying this shortcoming, the idea was to extend this proposal in such a way as to apply for the Latin American States as well. Senator Vandenberg, delegate of the US at the conference, proposed to apply a 'limited extension of the European exemption' to the benefit of the American states.[17]

Nevertheless, this extension was criticized on the basis that it 'would gut the international power by emphasizing regional authority.'[18] Moreover, the regional question speedily developed into a problem of concern of all. Apart from the South American delegates trying to protect the Act of Chapultepec and the Arabian bloc concerned about its impact on Palestine, the Australians were also anxious about their regional autonomy. The Australian delegation proposed an amendment that allowed 'self-defensive action, regional or otherwise [...] after failure of the Security Council to authorize such action or to take action itself.'[19] Vandenberg's amendment was thus rejected by the members of the committee and the regional question seemed to become 'the crux of the Conference.'[20]

---

[15] Paragraph 2 of Chapter XII of the Dumbarton Oaks Proposals stated: 'No provision of the Charter should preclude action taken or authorized in relation to enemy states as a result of the present war by the Governments having responsibility for such action.'

[16] Terms of Reference of Committee III/4, Chapter VIII, Section C of the Dumbarton Oaks Proposals with Pertinent Excerpts from Comments and Draft Amendments submitted by Delegations, 14 May 1945. In UN Charter travaux préparatoires, Vol. 12, p. 765.

[17] Vandenberg 1952, pp. 187–188.

[18] Ibid., p. 188.

[19] Interim Report to Committee III/4 on the work of Sub-Committee III/4/A, submitted by the Rapporteur Dr. V. K. Wellington Koo (China), 15 May 1945. In UN Charter travaux préparatoires, Vol. 12, p. 837.

[20] Vandenberg 1952, pp. 190–191. Among the South American states, Bolivia adopted a fundamentally opposite position. It submitted an amendment on the basis of which paragraph 2 of Section C was to be complemented with the sentence: 'In no case should such regional systems, arrangements, or agencies be able to adopt measures of sanction, whether economic or military, without the expressed authority of the Security Council.' Interim Report to Committee III/4 on the work of Sub-Committee III/4/A, submitted by the Rapporteur Dr. V. K. Wellington Koo (China). In UN Charter travaux préparatoires, Vol. 12, p. 836.

In a renewed effort to find a solution to the regional problem, the amendment was subjected to revision. The wording was changed in such a way as to clarify that regional arrangements could be autonomous for the sole purpose of self-defence. Accordingly, the revised draft read as follows:

> Should the Security Council not succeed in preventing aggression, and should aggression occur by any state against any member state, such member state possesses the inherent right to take necessary measures for self-defence. The right to take such measures for self-defence against armed attack shall also apply to understandings or arrangements like those embodied in the Act of Chapultepec, under which all members of a group of states agree to consider an attack against any one of them as an attack against all of them. The taking of such measures shall be immediately reported to the Security Council and shall not in any way affect the authority and responsibility of the Security Council under this Charter to take at any time such action as it may deem necessary in order to maintain or restore international peace and security.[21]

This proposal was met with strong dislike on the part of the UK delegation. According to the opinion of the UK delegate Anthony Eden, the draft could result 'in regionalism of the worst kind.' Eden also emphasized that 'no one had been able to define aggression for thirty years' and thus the wording would lead to confusion.[22] Other drafts were also discussed during several five-power informal consultation meetings, but consensus seemed impossible to reach.[23]

Finally, the five powers concurred in adopting an amendment with a more general language that would make no specific reference to the Act of Chapultepec or any other regional arrangement. Additionally, the delegates agreed with the opinion of the UK delegate Eden that any attempt to specify in the Charter conditions under which self-defence measures could be taken would raise many difficult issues.[24]

Finally, the proposal drafted by the UK delegate Jebb seemed to bring the delegates closer to an agreement:

> 'Nothing in this Charter should invalidate the right of self-defence against armed attack, either individual or collective, in the event of the Security Council failing to take the necessary measures to maintain or restore international peace and security. Measures taken in the exercise of this right shall be immediately reported to the Security Council and shall not in any way affect the authority and responsibility of the Security Council under this Charter to take at any time such action as it may deem necessary in order to maintain or restore international peace and security.'[25]

---

[21] Minutes of the Thirty-Seventh Meeting of the US Delegation, held at San Francisco, 12 May 1945. In Foreign Relations of the US 1945, Vol. 1, pp. 685–686.

[22] Minutes of the Third five-Power Informal Consultation Meeting on Proposed Amendments (Part 1), held at San Francisco, 12 May 1945. In Foreign Relations of the US 1945, Vol. 1, p. 692.

[23] Foreign Relations of the US 1945, Vol. 1, pp. 691–706.

[24] Memorandum by Mr. Robert W. Hartley of the US Delegation of a Conversation held at San Francisco, 12 May 1945. In Foreign Relations of the US 1945, vol. 1, p. 703.

[25] Ibid., p. 704.

After consultation between the UK and US delegates, the first part of this amendment was revised and read:

> Nothing in this Charter impairs the inherent right of self-defence, whether individual or collective, in the event that the Security Council has failed to maintain international peace and security and armed attack against a member state has occurred.[26]

In order to ensure general agreement with the proposal, the US delegation invited the South American delegations to a private meeting in which they presented the new proposal. The new wording, as Senator Vandenberg explained, would reserve the right of self-defence 'including regional self-defence if and when the Security Council fails to act' and would guarantee the resort to regional facilities 'among the peaceful mechanisms to be embraced.' Although the new wording did not encounter any staunch opposition, the Latin American states expressed their concern that such general phrasing might jeopardize the Inter-American system and that a public statement was necessary to clarify the purpose of such provision.[27]

To meet such concerns, the US delegates proposed to include a separate provision that would clarify and strengthen the role of regional agencies and arrangements in the peaceful settlement of disputes.[28] In this way, the acquiescence of the Latin American states was ensured.[29]

On the same day (15 May), the US delegation announced that it was elaborating an amendment 'intended to reconcile the global organization of the collective security system and the continued operation of the Inter-American system.'[30]

The promised proposal was finally put forward on 21 May, having as sponsoring states the UK, China, Russia, the US, France and the Latin American countries. The text of the proposal read:

> Nothing in the Charter impairs the inherent right of individual or collective self-defence if an armed attack occurs against a member state, until the Security Council has taken the measures necessary to maintain international peace and security. Measures taken in the exercise of this right of self-defence shall be immediately reported to the Security Council and shall not in any way affect the authority and responsibility of the Security Council

---

[26] Minutes of Informal Drafting session, by Mr. Robert W. Hartley, 12 May 1945. In Foreign Relations of the US 1945, vol. 1, p. 705.

[27] Note on Second Informal Consultative Meeting with Chairmen of Delegations of Certain American Republics, held at San Francisco, 15 May 1945. In Foreign Relations of the US 1945, Vol. 1, pp. 730–736.

[28] Minutes of the Fourth Five-Power Informal Consultation Meeting on Proposed Amendments, held at San Francisco, 15 May 1945. In Foreign Relations of the US 1945, vol. 1, p. 737. The proposal for a separate provision on regional arrangements in the peaceful settlement of disputes became Art. 33 of the UN Charter.

[29] Vandenberg 1952, pp. 192–193.

[30] Interim Report to Committee III/4 on the Work of Sub-Committee III/4/A, submitted by the Rapporteur Dr. V.K. Wellington Koo (China). In UN Charter travaux prĕparatoires, Vol. 12, p. 834.

> under this Charter to take at any time such action as it may deem necessary in order to maintain or restore international peace and security.[31]

On 23 May 1945, at the fourth meeting of Committee III/4, the proposal was unanimously adopted. Senator Vandenberg wrote on that day: 'The subject itself was difficult—how to save legitimate regionalism (like Pan-Am) and yet not destroy the essential overall authority of the International Organization. By hammering it out vis-à-vis, *we have found an answer which satisfies practically everybody*.'[32]

5.3 The Final Provision on Self-Defence: Interpretation

The proposal unanimously adopted on 23 May 1945 suffered some minor wording changes before it was adopted by the San Francisco Conference as Article 51 of the UN Charter. The delegates involved in the drafting of the provision viewed it as a successful compromise that satisfied the wants of all concerned. Moreover, Article 51 was viewed as an explicit assurance of the legality of self-defensive action.

In order to interpret the provision in Article 51, the ordinary meaning of its terms has to be elucidated in the context in which they were negotiated and in the light of the provision's object and purpose.[33] Based on this rule, some authors have maintained that Article 51 outlaws anticipatory action in self-defence, because the phrase "if an armed attack occurs" acts as a conditional for the entire provision.[34] If the textual meaning of Article 51 is analysed in isolation from its context and the object and purpose of the article, indeed it seems to qualify the exercise of self-defence to the time after an armed attack has occurred.[35] Nonetheless, in interpreting a treaty provision, equal weight should be given to all particular factors, such as the text, the supposed intention of the parties as well as the object or purpose of the treaty.[36] Consequently, if one takes into consideration the context

---

[31] Proposal for the Amalgamation of Amendments offered to Chapter VIII, Section C, prepared by the Delegation of the US in Consultation with the Other Sponsoring Governments and France, 21 May 1945. In UN Charter travaux préparatoires, Vol. 3, p. 635.

[32] Vandenberg (1952), p. 198 (emphasis added).

[33] Article 31(1) of the Vienna Convention on the Law of Treaties 1969 states: 'A treaty shall be interpreted in good faith in accordance with the ordinary meaning to be given to the terms of the treaty in their context and in the light of its object and purpose.'

[34] See, for instance: Brownlie 1963, p. 275; Jessup 1948, pp. 165–166; Ruys 2010, p. 259. See also *supra* 1.2.

[35] The argument advanced by some authors that "if an armed attack occurs" does not mean that "if and only if, an armed attack occurs" is not the best way to approach the problem. Indeed, in terms of logic "if A, then B" is equivalent with the statement that "if not B, then not A", which, *in casu*, purports that the literal meaning of Article 51 does not permit self-defence if there is no armed attack. For the mentioned argument, see McDougal and Feliciano 1961, p. 237.

[36] Aust 2007, p. 231. Draft Articles on the Convention of the Law of Treaties with Commentaries 1966, Vol. 2, p. 220.

and purpose of Article 51, a different conclusion can be reached. The context in which Article 51 was negotiated pertained to regional arrangements and the legality of the unilateral use of force. Whilst the object and purpose of the Charter was the creation of a world organization based on international peace and security, the specific purpose of Article 51 was to clarify that regional arrangements could be autonomous for the sole purpose of self-defence and thus to reach a compromise between such arrangements and the envisaged prohibition to use force. Hence the concern of the Latin American states that the new prohibition would invalidate their mutual assistance system.

Accordingly, an interpretation of Article 51 in accordance with the ordinary meaning of the terms in their context and in the light of its object and purpose leads to an inconsistency. Whilst the text seems to restrict self-defence to remedial measures, its context and purpose aims to ensure its compatibility with a mutual assistance system that permits pre-emptive action.

Resort to the *travaux préparatoires*, as a supplementary tool of interpretation, does not solve the puzzle.[37] Indeed, the content and limits of self-defence were addressed by neither the Dumbarton Oaks Proposals nor the San Francisco negotiations.[38] Some viewed the right as implicit and subject to common sense; others considered it too difficult to define. For instance, during the discussions in Commission I (dealing with general provisions), it was affirmed that 'the use of arms in legitimate defence remains admitted and unimpaired' and that no specific reservation was needed to safeguard such right.[39] On the other hand, UK delegate Eden repeatedly emphasized that self-defence (and aggression) was very difficult to define and that it was better to avoid interpretive formulations.[40]

Discussions regarding the limitation of self-defence to those instances where an armed attack had already occurred took place within the US delegation.[41] Some of the delegates have indeed expressed their intention to limit self-defence to the time after an armed attack had occurred.[42] The proposal was, however, questioned by other US delegates who saw it as 'greatly qualifying the right of self-defence.'[43]

---

[37] Article 32(a) of the Vienna Convention on the Law of the Treaties (1969) states: 'Recourse may be had to supplementary means of interpretation, including the preparatory work of the treaty and the circumstances of its conclusion, in order to confirm the meaning resulting from the application of Article 31, or to determine the meaning when the interpretation according to Article 31(a) leaves the meaning ambiguous or obscure.'.

[38] See also: Ciobanu 1970, pp. 327–330.

[39] Report of the Rapporteur of Committee 1 to Commission I, 13 June 1945. In UN Charter travaux préparatoires, Vol. 6, p. 459.

[40] Memorandum by Mr. Robert W. Hartley of the US delegation of a conversation held at San Francisco, 12 May 1945. In Foreign Relations of the US 1945, Vol. 1, p. 703.

[41] Franck 2002, p. 50.

[42] Minutes of the Forty-Eighth Meeting (Executive Session) of the US Delegation, held at San Francisco, 20 May 1945. In Foreign Relations of the US 1945, Vol. 1, p. 818.

[43] Ibid.; Minutes of the Thirty-Eighth Meeting of the US Delegation, held at San Francisco, 14 May 1945. In Foreign Relations of the US 1945, Vol. 1, pp. 707–709.

This exchange was interpreted by Franck as showing 'beyond dispute that the negotiators deliberately closed the door on any claim of anticipatory self-defence.'[44] This view overlooks the fact that only a few of the delegates of the US expressed such restricting intentions at the meetings of the US delegation. These proposals were not discussed in the plenum of Technical Committee 4, in order to discern the opinion of the delegates from other countries. Even if some of the US delegates had such implicit agendas regarding Article 51, it is reasonable to assume that Latin American delegates would have interpreted such restrictions as impairing the mutual assistance system under the Act of Chapultepec. Hence, the issue was never brought up in the plenum of Technical Committee 4 and such restrictive intentions cannot be viewed as reflecting the general intention of the drafters.

Consequently, the preparatory negotiations of the Charter cannot shed light on whether self-defence was exclusively seen as an anticipatory or a remedial forcible measure. No clear conclusion can be drawn from the records as to the temporal dimension attributed to self-defence. Accordingly, the argument put forward by some authors that Article 51 settled the issue of anticipatory action in self-defence by rejecting it, cannot be maintained.[45]

Although the temporal dimension of self-defence did not come up during the negotiations, the wording used by delegates in their submissions does not show any tendency to restrict that dimension to a post-attack time. The delegates referred to 'measures of urgent nature' (France),[46] 'cases of emergency' (Turkey)[47] or 'immediate danger' (Czechoslovakia),[48] all circumstances that needed immediate action without temporally limiting self-defence to the time before or after an attack.

Both the US and the other American states viewed the new provision as a successful compromise and as a safeguard of the Inter-American system. Although Section 4 of the Act of Chapultepec did not make express reference to self-defence (it only allowed for action against aggression or when aggression was prepared), the Latin American states viewed Article 51 as the confirmation of the legitimacy of their right to take steps according to the Act. The Director General of the

---

[44] Franck 2002, p. 50. See also Corten 2008, pp. 628–629; Ruys 2010, p. 260. Franck himself regards the restrictive proposal of the US delegates as 'logically indefensible'. Franck 2002, p. 50.

[45] Brownlie 1963, p. 275; Corten 2008, pp. 619–624; Christakis 2005, pp. 208–212; Gray 2004, p. 98; Kunz 1947, pp. 877–878; Ruys 2010, p. 260; Wright 1963, p. 560.

[46] The attitude of France was interpreted differently by Olivier Corten, who referred to a statement made by a French delegate at San Francisco who asserted that precluding an armed attack was the function of the Security Council. Corten 2008, pp. 628–629.

[47] Suggestions of the Turkish Government concerning the Proposals for the Maintenance of Peace and Security agreed at the Four-Power Conference at Dumbarton Oaks, 1 May 1945. In UN Charter travaux préparatoires, Vol. 3, p. 483.

[48] Terms of reference of Committee III/4, Chapter VIII, Section C of the Dumbarton Oaks Proposals with Pertinent Excerpts from Comments and Draft Amendments Submitted by Delegations, 14 May 1945. In UN Charter travaux préparatoires, Vol. 12, p. 773.

Pan-American Union in a report submitted to the Governing Board of the Union on the action of the San Francisco Conference with regard to regional arrangements drew the following conclusion:

> 'The right of any group of nations to enter into agreements for self-defence is recognized. Consequently, the Act of Chapultepec, or the treaty that may be concluded to convert this wartime measure into a peacetime agreement, is entirely in harmony with the World Charter.'[49]

Section 4 of the Act of Chapultepec read:

> [I]n case acts of aggression occur or there may be reasons to believe that an aggression is being prepared by any other State against the integrity and inviolability of the territory, or against the sovereignty or political independence of an American State, the States signatory to this Act will consult among themselves in order to agree upon the measures it may be advisable to take.

Prima facie, the provision seems to establish a system of collective security much broader than the concept of self-defence. Nonetheless, its compatibility with the UN Charter system was solved by addressing two issues: regional arrangements (that allowed Latin American states to take non-military action in the face of aggression) and self-defence (which permitted the parties of the Act of Chapultepec to take military action in face of aggression). Accordingly, Section 4 of the Act—in as much as it refers to military action—has to be viewed as compatible with Article 51 of the UN Charter.

It is reasonable to assert that the understanding that was given to self-defence at the time of the drafting of the Charter was the same that Kellogg used and that Webster formulated on the basis of centuries of consequent interpretation.[50] Obviously, this understanding did not allow preventive action in face of a possible danger. Thus the argument put forward by some authors that by the time of the Charter customary law allowed only a narrow right of self-defence is accurate, with the *proviso* that such a narrow sense permitted anticipatory action against imminent threats.[51] Preventive unilateral action was indeed prohibited by the UN Charter as an element of the absolute right to wage war that sovereigns had enjoyed over many centuries. Under the Charter system, preventive action in face of potential dangers could only be exercised on express authorization of the Security Council as part of the new system of collective security. Accordingly, if the Security Council deemed a conflict a threat to or a breach of international peace and security under Chapter VII, it could also call for collective measures involving the use of force to prevent the escalation of the conflict.[52]

---

[49] Canyes 1945, p. 508 (quoting the report submitted to the Governing Board of the Pan-American Union by the Director General, Congress and Conference Series, No. 48).

[50] See *supra* 3.3 and 4.7. Bowett 1958, pp. 188–189.

[51] Brownlie 1963, pp. 257–261.

[52] Gill 1989, pp. 58–60.

Unilateral defensive wars, on the other hand, could no longer be preventive and could not be employed in cases of more or less serious suspicions regarding another state's plans. One of the major effects of the UN Charter was, indeed, to prohibit unilateral preventive war. The narrow conception of self-defence was implicitly accepted by the drafters and was embedded in Article 51. The temporal dimension of this narrow understanding of self-defence was not restricted to pre-attack or post-attack time. It was rather based on the existence of a 'present and inevitable'[53] necessity of resorting to moderate (proportionate) armed action in the face of an attack or invasion.[54]

5.4 Concluding Remarks

With the first steps towards the restriction of war, the absolute right of the sovereign to decide when and why to wage war started to weaken. As a result of a surge in bilateral and multilateral agreements restricting or prohibiting war, the right to wage punitive and preventive wars as well as to resort to reprisals or other, smaller armed interventions was beginning to be challenged. The adoption of the UN Charter was the culmination of this cascade of law-creation. The corroborated purpose of Article 2(4) and Article 51 excluded both punitive and preventive wars as well as other measures short of war from the list of rights that individual states enjoyed. The broad right of states to wage preventive wars was transferred to the Security Council. Accordingly, Article 24 and Chapter VII enabled the Security Council to take collective enforcement measures against a situation that endangered international peace and security.

The only prerogative of states that survived the movement to restrict and prohibit war was the natural-law conception of self-defence. This narrow, natural-law understanding of the right was increasingly viewed as the only lawful exception to the prohibition of war.[55] Self-defence thus understood had been accepted as a customary rule across jurisdictions in the three normative frameworks identified. It is reasonable to conclude at this point that, by the time of the adoption of the Charter, that customary rule was international in the modern sense of the word and not only in the traditional 'law of nations' connotation.[56]

The drafters of the UN Charter saw Article 51 as a compromise that both prohibited illegal use of force and guaranteed the right of self-defence against such use of force. The wording of the article cannot be analysed in an isolated manner,

---

[53] Webster 1841, p. 1138.

[54] June 23 Note, in Miller 1928, pp. 213–214; Benes and Politis 1924, p. 483; Oppenheim 1905, Vol. 1, pp. 178–179.

[55] See *supra* 4.7 and 5.4.

[56] Nussbaum 1947, pp. 1–2. For the 'international' characteristic of self-defence as a customary norm in earlier frameworks, see *supra* 2.5 and 3.3.

but has to be read in conjunction with the drafting negotiations and with the interpretation given to self-defence at that time.

It is the conclusion of this chapter that the narrow, natural-law conception of self-defence was the one accepted as customary law at the time the UN Charter was drafted. This understanding of self-defence was taken into consideration when the compromise of Article 51 was reached.

References

Aust A (2007) Modern treaty law and practice. Cambridge University Press, Cambridge
Benes E, Politis N (1924) Report on the Protocol submitted to the Fifth Assembly. League Nations Off J (Special Supp No 23) 483
Bowett DW (1958) Self-defence in international law. Manchester University Press, Manchester
Brownlie I (1963) International law and the use of force by states. Clarendon Press, Oxford
Canyes MS (1945) The Inter-American system and the Conference of Chapultepec. Am J Int Law 39:504–517
Christakis T (2005) Existe-t-il un droit de légitime défense en cas de simple "menace"?: une réponse au "groupe des personnalités de haut niveau" de l'ONU. In: Société française pour le droit international, Les métamorphoses de la sécurité collective: droit, pratique et enjeux stratégiques. Pedone, Paris, pp 197–222
Ciobanu D (1970) The contribution of the Advisory Committee of Jurists to the drafting of the UN Charter. Rivista di Diritto Internazionale 53:300–333
Corten O (2008) Le droit contre la guerre: l'interdiction du recours à la force en droit international contemporain. Pedone, Paris
Draft Articles on the Convention of the Law of Treaties with Commentaries (1966) In: Yearbook of the International Law Commission, vol 2
Foreign Relations of the US: Diplomatic Papers 1944 (1966) vol 1. US Government Printing Office, Washington, D.C.
Foreign Relations of the US: Diplomatic Papers 1945 (1967) vol 1.: General US Government Printing Office, Washington, D.C.
Franck T (2002) Recourse to force: state action against threats and armed attacks. Cambridge University Press, Cambridge
Gill TD (1989) The second Gulf crisis and the relation between collective security and collective self-defence. Grotiana 10:47–76
Gray C (2004) International law and the use of force. Oxford University Press, Oxford
Jessup PC (1948) A modern law of nations: an introduction. Macmillan, New York
Kunz J (1947) Individual and collective self-defence in Article 51 of the Charter of the United Nations. Am J Int Law 41:872–879
McDougal MS, Feliciano FP (1961) Law and minimum world public order: the legal regulation of international coercion. Yale University Press, New Haven
Miller DH (1928) The Peace Pact of Paris: a study of the Briand–Kellogg Treaty. GP Putnam's Sons, New York
Nussbaum A (1947) A concise history of the law of nations. Macmillan, New York
Oppenheim L (1905) International law: a treatise, vol 1. Longmans, Green and Co, New York
Ruys T (2010) 'Armed attack' and Article 51 of the UN Charter. Evolutions in customary law and practice. Cambridge University Press, Cambridge
UN Charter travaux préparatoires: documents of the UN conference on international organization, San Francisco, 1945 (1945–1955), vols 1, 3, 6 and 12. UN Information Organizations, London

Webster 1841: Letter from Daniel Webster, US Secretary of State, to Henry Fox, British Minister in Washington, 24 April 1841. In: British and Foreign State Papers, 1840–1841, vol 29 (1857). James Ridgway and Sons, London, pp 1129–1139
Vandenberg AH Jr (1952) The private papers of Senator Vandenberg. Houghton Mifflin, Boston
Wright Q (1963) The Cuban quarantine. Am J Int Law 57:546–565

Chapter 6
The Temporal Dimension of Self-Defence at the Time of the Charter

The objective of Part 1 was to trace the evolution of pre-Charter customary law on self-defence from its ancient Greek natural law roots to the time of the adoption of the UN Charter. In order to understand the drafters' intention as regards self-defence, it was necessary to understand how the content and temporal dimension of self-defence was viewed in 1945. Accordingly, a legal–historical analysis was needed to explain the evolution of the right of self-defence and the form in which it was accepted as legal at the end of the Second World War. Further, a comprehensive analysis of the drafting process of Article 51 was conducted and the various treaty interpretation approaches applied in order to clarify the intention of the drafters at the conference. On that basis, Part 1 assessed whether anticipatory action was part of self-defence at that time and, if so, under what conditions.

The concept of self-defence was traced through different historical phases and three succeeding frameworks that regulated war: the Christian natural law, the positivist and the emerging international law frameworks. In each of these frameworks, the concept of self-defence was identified and explained on the basis of available works and relevant state practice. In this process, the forms, the temporal dimensions and the limits of self-defence were addressed. Moreover, the analysis aimed at identifying those traits of the concept that had been transferred from one framework to another.

The findings of Part 1 will be employed as the basis for the analysis of post-Charter state practice regarding self-defence. In order to do that, the most important conclusions will be herewith summarized.

6.1 Forms and Content of Self-Defence in the Three Identified Frameworks

From the ancient Greek conception of natural law onwards, self-defence was viewed as a right given by nature. Accordingly, each human being had the right to preserve his or her own life and had the moral duty to defend others from

K. Tibori Szabó, *Anticipatory Action in Self-Defence*, DOI: 10.1007/978-90-6704-796-8_6,

wrong.[1] Although the early Christians (such as Augustine) believed that an individual was not allowed to defend himself (because that showed dependence on earthly things), starting with Aquinas, theologians and philosophers asserted that self-defence was every human being's natural right.[2] On this basis, not only did individuals had the right to self-defence, but also sovereigns were entitled (if not obliged) to defend the homeland.[3]

On the basis of this right, individuals were allowed to wage 'particular wars' or 'private wars' in defence of themselves and their property.[4] Such defence did not necessitate the permission of a public authority, because the right itself was viewed as natural. In the Christian natural law framework, the right of self-defence was one of the causes permitting private war. In the positivist normative framework, the natural right of self-defence was still recognized as a legal basis for private wars, although their justifiability was decreasing. From the nineteenth century onwards, the legality of 'private wars' (in self-defence or otherwise) started to decline given the availability of law enforcement measures. Nonetheless, the content of self-defence as a right of the individual to wage war is instructive in order to understand the corresponding right of the sovereign.

When it came to public wars, self-defence was viewed as the inherent right of the sovereign to defend the homeland. Nonetheless, this right was much broader than that of the individual. In the Christian natural law framework, self-defence was one of the 'just causes' of war and permitted not only strict defence, but also preventive action against religious enemies and potential conquerors. In the positivist framework, the sovereign had an absolute right to wage 'perfect wars' and as long as they were declared and all formalities were respected there was no need to refer to clear justifications. Defensive wars had thus a prominent preventive character and the concept of defence was viewed as a tool to stop the aggrandizement of potentially hostile neighbours. The justifiability of such wars was based on the constructed interests and priorities of the king, emperor or leader. For that reason, this prerogative is more accurately described as preventive war and not as 'self-defence'. According to such an understanding of defence, war could be waged against expansionist neighbours (Peloponnesian War), against enemies of the religion (crusades, holy wars) and against any country that jeopardised the vital interests of the state (Gentili, Vattel and Clausewitz).[5]

---

[1] See *supra* 2.1. Cicero 1968, Book I, Chap. 11, Section 35, p. 37.

[2] Augustine 1955, Book I, 5.12, pp. 44–45; Peñafort, Section 18, in Reichberg et al. 2006, pp. 138–139; Aquinas, question 40, Article 1, in Reichberg et al. 2006, pp. 179–180; Vitoria 1991, p. 299; Gentili 1933, Book I, Chap. 13, p. 59; Grotius 1964, Book II, Chap. 1 (iii), p. 172.

[3] Aquinas, question 40, Article 1, in Reichberg et al. 2006, p. 177; Vitoria 1991b, p. 300; Suárez 1944 Disputation XIII, Section 1 (4), pp. 802–803; Grotius 1964, Book II, Chap. 2 (xvi), p. 184.

[4] Aquinas, question 40, Article 1, and question 41, Article 1, in Reichberg et al. 2006, p. 177 and pp. 182–183, respectively.

[5] Thucydides, The Peloponnesian War, Book I, Chap. 71, reprinted in Reichberg et al. 2006, pp. 4–5; Gratian, question V, canon 46, in Reichberg et al. 2006, p. 119; Gentili 1933, Book I, Chap. 14, p. 62; Pufendorf 1934, Book VIII, Chap. 6 (7), p. 1298; Vattel 1964, Book. III, Chap. 3, Section 42, p. 248; Twiss 1860, pp. 11–12.

In the emerging international law framework such permissive interpretations of the right to defend the state subsided and a clear move towards the prohibition of war began. This trend culminated in the adoption of the UN Charter, which declared the right of self-defence as the only exception to the prohibition to use force. This right, however, was not the broad privilege that sovereigns enjoyed as part of their right to wage 'perfect wars'. The narrow understanding of self-defence, applicable to individuals, transcended to public wars in the form of 'imperfect wars' and, later, 'measures short of war'. Self-defence in this form was similar to that granted to individuals with the realities of public warfare taken into consideration. As Jessup explained:

> When an individual is set upon by an armed thug who threatens his life, instantaneous action is clearly requisite and it can be said that there is 'no moment for deliberation'. When a state anticipates a threatened injury from another state or from a lawless band, there is usually opportunity for deliberation in a chancellery or war office, and an officer on the spot does not act until he has received instructions from a higher command. Telegraphic or radio communication between the officer and his superiors can be taken as a counterpart of the impulses in the nervous system of the individual whose brain instructs his arm to strike.[6]

Although its status changed throughout these frameworks, the concept of self-defence regarded legal at the time of the adoption of the Charter was the narrow understanding of the natural right which permitted private wars, 'imperfect wars' or measures short of war in self-defence.

6.2 The Temporal Dimension of the Narrow Concept of Self-Defence

In the temporal sense, the natural right of 'blameless defence' pertained to three moments: before, during and after the attack. Individuals could exercise self-defence against an ongoing or an imminent attack. They could also defend themselves after an attack took place, but only if the purpose of such action was to fend off a future attack.[7]

The temporal dimension of self-defence was thus often used to differentiate it from reprisals.[8] Reprisals had as their objective redress of injuries, the punishment of the enemy and the requisition of lost property. They were used only after the specific injury had been inflicted, so they had an inherently reactive nature. Self-defence, on the other hand, always had an intrinsic anticipatory aspect.

---

[6] Jessup 1948, p. 164.

[7] Gratian, question I, in Reichberg et al. 2006, p. 110; Pisan, Part 3, Chap. 12, in Reichberg et al. 2006, p. 219.

[8] Peñafort, § 18, in Reichberg et al. 2006, p. 133; Vitoria 1991, pp. 297–303; Suárez 1944, Disputation XIII, Section 1 (6), p. 804; Grotius 1964, Book II, Chap. 1 (ii), p. 172.

When this narrow understanding of self-defence was transferred to 'imperfect wars' and 'measures short of war', the temporal limits were interpreted slightly more permissibly to correspond to the realities of public warfare. Accordingly, whereas self-defence of individuals was always an on-the-spot action, self-defence of states also allowed the preparation needed for organizing the armed forces.[9] Nonetheless, even with the more permissive interpretation, the self-defence states could exercise as measures short of war only allowed action against ongoing or imminent attacks and after an attack had already occurred.[10]

6.3 The Temporal Dimension of Preventive Wars

'Perfect'—officially declared—wars waged by sovereigns for defensive purposes had a much broader scope than the defensive action allowed for 'imperfect wars' or 'measures short of war'. A 'just cause' that allowed full-fledged military action could be punitive or defensive. Punitive war was waged for the punishment of the enemy, the redress of injury or for other reasons. Defensive war could also be waged for many reasons, including the prevention of 'probable and possible dangers.'[11] The threat that justified preventive war only had to be possible, but not necessarily meditated or prepared (Gentili).[12] This view was specifically upheld in the period when sovereigns enjoyed an absolute right to wage war. The suspicious aggrandizement of a state or the arguably non-peaceful intentions of a neighbour could be interpreted as possible dangers that justified preventive war.

The broader understanding of defensive wars was gradually deemed unlawful in the emerging international law framework of the late nineteenth and early twentieth centuries. In contrast, the narrow understanding of self-defence survived as a customary rule and was increasingly viewed as the only lawful exception to the prohibition of war in that period.

6.4 Limits of the Narrow Concept of Self-Defence

In all the three normative frameworks the same recognizable pattern of elements of self-defence could be contoured (See Table 6.1).

---

[9] See the differentiation made by Grotius regarding private and public defensive wars. Grotius 1964, Book II, Chap. 2 (xvi), p. 184. See also Jessup 1948, p. 164.

[10] Grotius 1964, Book II, Chap. 2 (xvi), p. 184; Hall 1880, pp. 229–232. See also *supra* 3.3.

[11] Gentili 1933, Book I, Chap. 14, p. 66; Vattel 1964, Book III, Chap. 3, Section 42, p. 248; Pufendorf 1934, Book VIII, Chap. 6 (7), p. 1298.

[12] Gentili 1933, Book I, Chap. 14, p. 62.

Table 6.1 Elements of the narrow concept of self-defence

Narrow concept of self-defence	Elements	Limits
Necessity	Attack	Occurrence or expectation (conditionality)
	Immediacy	Immediate need to take action
Proportionality	Moderation	Force required to ward off an attack

First, self-defence always entailed the existence (occurrence or expectation) of an *attack*. Secondly, this attack (its occurrence or its imminence) had to give rise to an *immediate need to take action*. Thirdly, the exercise of self-defence had to be *moderate*. The first two elements are intrinsically linked to each other and can be treated under the general heading of 'necessity'. The third condition pertains to the modality of the exercise of self-defence and can be treated under the heading of 'moderation' or 'proportionality'.

6.4.1 Necessity

None of the three normative frameworks identified entailed a precise definition of what sort of attack could justify self-defence. In case of individuals it was accepted that both the life and property of private persons could be defended.[13] In case of sovereigns, reference was usually made to an 'attack',[14] 'danger'[15] or 'invasion'[16] without laying down the specific conditions. Nonetheless, it was generally understood that for the narrow understanding of self-defence such an attack had to involve the use of armed force.[17] Since the narrow understanding of self-defence was relevant for 'imperfect wars' and measures short of war, it was generally accepted that also small-scale uses of force could trigger self-defence. Neither the *Caroline* incident nor the *Virginius* affair entailed large-scale uses of force.[18] The very rationale of measures short of war was to tackle conflicts that did not necessitate the launching of a full-scale war.[19] Consequently, there was no common understanding of what such an attack had to endanger; the territory, the independence, the government of the state as well as its nationals could all be the

[13] Vitoria 1991, p. 299; Grotius 1964, Book II, Chap. 1 (xi), p. 179.

[14] Gratian, question II, canon 1, in Reichberg et al. 2006, p. 113; Grotius 1964, Book II, Chap. 1 (iii), p. 172 (attack by violence) and Chap. 2 (xvi), p. 184 (act of violence); June 23 Note, in Miller 1928, pp. 213–214.

[15] Gentili 1933. Book I, Chap. 14, p. 62.

[16] June 23 Note, in Miller 1928, pp. 213–214.

[17] Gentili 1933, Book I, Chap. 13, p. 58; Grotius 1964, Book II, Chap. 1 (iii), p. 172; Webster 1841, p. 1138; June 23 Note, in Miller 1928, pp. 213–214.

[18] See *supra* 3.2.2.1 and 3.2.2.2.

[19] For instance, see Hall's treatment of such measures: Hall 1880, pp. 306–314.

objects of such an attack.[20] Moreover, self-defence could be invoked against forces other than official, such as private armed groups or rebels. In both the Christian natural law and the positivist normative frameworks, individuals were allowed to defend themselves against any attacker and that liberty was also given to the state. The *Caroline* incident is an illustrative example in this respect.[21] Article 51 of the Charter employed the term 'armed attack' to describe this condition. Nonetheless, no definition of the term was provided by the drafters.

It was nevertheless clear that the occurrence or imminence of such an attack had to create an immediate need for action. In Webster's words, this necessity had to be present and inevitable.[22] The immediacy element of necessity was reiterated by public officials and publicists of the late nineteenth and early twentieth centuries and was mentioned—in various forms—by the delegates at the San Francisco Conference.[23]

6.4.2 Proportionality

Medieval Christian doctrine recognized the principle of '*moderatio*', according to which one was supposed to act only for fending off the attack and was not allowed to exceed the limits of 'blameless defence' (Decretists, Aquinas).[24] The principle of moderation was acknowledged by Grotius as well.[25] With the dawn of the absolute right of war of sovereigns, the focus shifted from the causes to wage war to the modality of warfare. Hence, the principle of moderation (proportionality) received more attention and was connected not only to the right of self-defence, but also to other forms of military action.[26] Nonetheless, its importance for the right of self-defence could be discerned in all the three normative frameworks. Stemming from its meaning relevant for private self-defence, proportionality in public defensive actions limited the use of force to what was required to ward off an attack.[27]

---

[20] The *Caroline* incident and the *Virginius* affair involved private citizens and property (see *supra* 3.2.2.1 and 3.2.2.2). The Japanese invasion of Manchuria and the Italian invasion of Ethiopia endangered the territorial integrity and political independence of the occupied states (see *supra* 4.5.1 and 4.5.2).

[21] See *supra* 3.2.2.1.

[22] Webster 1841, p. 1138.

[23] June 23 Note, in Miller 1928, pp. 213–214; Art. 2 Locarno Pact 1925; Oppenheim 1905, pp. 178–179. See also *supra* 5.3.

[24] Peñafort, Section 18, in Reichberg et al. 2006, pp. 138–139; Aquinas, question 41, Article 1, in Reichberg et al. 2006.

[25] See *supra* 2.4.3, pp. 182–183.

[26] See the different sections on moderation in Grotius 1964, Book III, Chap. 11, pp. 722–744, Chap. 12, pp. 745–756, Chap. 13, pp. 757–760, Chap. 14, pp. 761–769, Chap. 15, pp. 770–777. See also *supra* 2.4.3. Vattel 1964, Book III, Chaps. 8–13, pp. 279–312; Twiss 1863, pp. 17–18. See also Roberts 2008, pp. 938–939.

[27] See also Gardam 1993, pp. 394–397.

6.5 The Status and Limits of Anticipatory Action in Self-Defence

Three layers of focus have been employed in Part I. First, the temporal dimension of self-defence was examined. Secondly, the status of anticipatory action within that spectrum was given attention. Thirdly, a recognizable pattern of limits of anticipatory action was demarcated.

Regarding the temporal dimension of self-defence, it was shown that it always pertained to the time before and during the attack and, under certain conditions, to the time after the attack. There was no separate right of 'anticipatory self-defence'. Self-defence always had an intrinsic anticipatory aspect. Consequently, the elements of self-defence *per se* were automatically limiting the exercise of anticipatory action. These limits have been identified as: the occurrence or expectation of an attack, the immediate need for action and moderation. This pattern of limitation could be recognized through all the three normative frameworks discussed. As all the three frameworks had a certain international characteristic, with the emergence of modern international law in the late nineteenth century, these limits were accepted as customary rules among states.[28]

With the broader understanding of 'defensive' wars gradually restricted, the only understanding of self-defence that could play a role in the minds of the Charter negotiators was the customary rule of the natural law self-defence described above. This natural law understanding of the right always had an anticipatory aspect and it was limited by the requirements of necessity (attack and immediate need for action) and proportionality (moderation).

Part II will examine whether post-Charter state practice has altered the centuries old understanding given to the natural right of self-defence. In order to do that, the analysis in Part II will have to assess whether post-Charter developments have brought about the emergence of a new customary rule on self-defence that has affected the pre-Charter understanding of that right. On that basis, it will be examined whether the status and limits of anticipatory action have been altered by the new developments.

References

Augustine (1955) The problem of free choice (De libero arbitrio) (trans: Pontifex M). Newman Press, Westminster Maryland
Cicero MT (1968) De Officiis (trans: Miller W). Heinemann, London
Gardam JG (1993) Proportionality and force in international law. Am J Int Law 87:391–413
Gentili A (1933) De jure belli libri tres (trans: Rolfe JC). Clarendon Press, Oxford
Grotius H (1964) De jure belli ac pacis libri tres (trans: Kelsey FW). Oceana, New York

[28] For an elaboration on the 'international' characteristics of the normative frameworks, see *supra* 2.5, 3.3 and 4.7.

Hall WE (1880) International law. Clarendon Press, Oxford
Jessup PC (1948) A modern law of nations: an introduction. Macmillan, New York
Miller DH (1928) The Peace Pact of Paris: a study of the Briand–Kellogg Treaty. G.P. Putnam's Sons, New York
Oppenheim L (1905) International law: a treatise, vol 1. Longmans, Green and Co, New York
von Pufendorf S (1934) De jure naturae et gentium libri octo, vol 2. Clarendon Press, Oxford
Reichberg GM, Syse H, Begby E (eds) (2006) The ethics of war: classic and contemporary readings. Blackwell, Malden
Roberts A (2008) The equal application of the laws of war: a principle under pressure. Int Rev Red Cr 90(872):931–962
Suárez F (1944) The three theological virtues: on charity. Reprinted in: Brown Scott J (ed) Selections from three works of Francisco Suárez SJ (trans: Williams GL et al). Clarendon Press, Oxford, pp 799–865
Twiss T (1860) Law of nations considered as independent political communities, vol 1. Oxford University Press, Oxford
Twiss T (1863) Law of nations considered as independent political communities, vol 2. Oxford University Press, Oxford
de Vattel E (1964) The law of nations or the principles of natural law: applied to the conduct and to the affairs of nations and of sovereigns. Oceana, New York
de Vitoria F (1991) De jure belli. Reprinted in: Pagden A, Lawrance J (eds) Vitoria: political writings. Cambridge University Press, Cambridge
Webster 1841: Letter from Daniel Webster, US Secretary of State, to Henry Fox, British Minister in Washington, 24 April 1841, in British and Foreign State Papers, 1840–1841, vol 29. James Ridgway and Sons, London, pp 1129–1139

Part II
Post-Charter Customary Law on Self-Defence

[s]self-defence is (...) action whereby "defensive" use of force is opposed to an "offensive" use of comparable force, with the object —and this is the core of the matter—of preventing another's wrongful action from proceeding, succeeding and achieving its purpose.

Roberto Ago

The aim of Part II is to analyse the development of post-Charter customary law on self-defence. It was the conclusion of Part I that the pre-Charter, narrow concept of self-defence always had an anticipatory aspect and it was limited by the requirements of necessity (attack and immediate need for action) and proportionality (moderation).[1] Against this background, Part II will have to assess whether post-Charter developments have effectuated the emergence of a new customary rule on self-defence that has affected the pre-Charter understanding of that right.

It is essential to note at this point that the aim of Part II is not to ascertain the existence of a clear customary rule justifying anticipatory action in self-defence. This objective was reached in Part I by concluding that there existed such a customary rule before and at the time of the adoption of the UN Charter. Therefore, what Part II needs to assess is whether a *new* customary rule *prohibiting* anticipatory action has emerged since the adoption of the Charter.

On that basis, it will be examined whether the right of self-defence has retained its intrinsically anticipatory aspect and whether its limits (as outlined above) are still automatically applicable to anticipatory action.

Post-Charter developments in the regulation of war and the use of force will be treated as the progression of the third normative framework identified in Part I (the emerging international law framework of the nineteenth and early twentieth centuries). To analyse the post-1945 evolution of this normative framework,

---

[1] See *supra* 6.4.

several themes will be identified in order to depict the main challenges of the twentieth and twenty-first centuries. As outlined in Chapter 1, the following themes will be given attention: state-to-state conflicts, conflicts involving weapons of mass destruction, conflicts involving non-state actors and the relevant work of UN organs. Within these themes, several instances of state practice will be analysed and compared.

To prepare the analysis of post-Charter customary law on self-defence, Chapter 7 will depict the understanding given to self-defence by the Nuremberg and Tokyo Tribunals in the immediate aftermath of the adoption of the Charter. Chapter 8 will examine state-to-state conflicts in which claims of self-defence were contemplated or used. Chapter 9 will look at the impact of weapons of mass destruction on the development of post-Charter self-defence. Chapter 10 will analyse the role played by non-state actors in shaping the content and temporal dimension of self-defence. Chapter 11 will examine the work of various UN organs (the General Assembly, the International Law Commission and the International Court of Justice) that influenced in some way the post-Charter understanding of self-defence. Chapter 12 will compare the findings of the previous chapters and will draw conclusions on the temporal dimension of the post-Charter customary rule of self-defence.

Post-Charter customary law on self-defence will be analysed in a very different way from its pre-Charter equivalent. A comparative case study is best suited to trace the influence of the various themes of the twentieth and twenty-first centuries mentioned above on the development of self-defence. For that reason, Part II will rely on state practice considerably more than the legal-historical research of Part I.

In selecting the instances of state practice for the comparative study, the main consideration was to offer a representative illustration of the circumstances in which claims of self-defence were contemplated or used. It is important to note at this point that Part II will give equal attention to anticipatory and remedial claims of self-defence. The reason for that can be deduced from the findings of Part I. The pre-Charter, narrow concept of self-defence was found to have both an anticipatory and remedial dimension, limited by the same elements (see Table 6.1). In order to trace the evolution of the temporal limits after the adoption of the Charter, analysis of both dimensions is necessary. Only this way can the post-Charter evolution of the identified elements (conditionality of an armed attack, immediate need for action and proportionality) be understood and the temporal dimension be delimited.

The common element in all cases examined is that a claim of self-defence (anticipatory, remedial or 'preventive') was at least contemplated by the government of the target state. The instances of state practice will greatly differ in their outcome: acceptance, criticism or condemnation.[2] This outcome will

[2] The outcome of the various instances of state practice will be assessed on the basis of a 'general reaction', which will be understood as the opinion of a majority of the members of the Security Council (and, where relevant, the General Assembly) as well as the views expressed by a significant part of the legal doctrine. See *supra* 1.4.

be dependent on the factual circumstances and the juridical variables of the case. The juridical variables applied to each case will be the three elements identified as the content of the pre-Charter customary rule of self-defence: conditionality of an attack, immediate need for action and moderation.[3] Although no precise definition of these limits existed in pre-Charter customary law, their resurfacing in all three of the normative frameworks analysed shows that they were considered as forming part of the customary rule of self-defence.[4] Starting with nineteenth century legal doctrine and especially as a result of the Webster formula, these elements were grouped under the general headings of necessity and proportionality.[5] Accordingly, these variables will be analysed in Part II as:

1. Necessity ('conditionality of an armed attack' and 'immediacy').
2. Proportionality (what was generally understood as moderation).

Each case will be analysed on the basis of these variables and each theme-chapter will draw conclusions on their role. Furthermore, each theme-chapter will draw conclusions on the temporal dimension of self-defence to assess whether it has retained its intrinsically anticipatory aspect and whether its limits (as outlined above) are still automatically applicable to anticipatory action.

In all chapters, reference will be made to instances of state practice, relevant Security Council or other UN-related work, judicial decisions (if applicable) and legal literature.

---

[3] See *supra* 6.4.

[4] See *supra* 2.5, 3.3 and 4.7.

[5] For the rationale of this grouping, see *supra* 6.4 and 6.5.

Chapter 7
The Right of Self-Defence in the Judgments of the Nuremberg and Tokyo Tribunals

7.1 Introduction

This chapter will shed light on how the new prohibition to use force and the right of self-defence were perceived by two judicial bodies in the immediate aftermath of the adoption of the Charter. The judgments delivered by the Nuremberg and Tokyo Tribunals show how the relevant law was interpreted and applied at that time. On that basis, it will be concluded how the content of self-defence was viewed by these judicial organs in the immediate aftermath of the adoption of Article 51 of the UN Charter.

Although they were created outside the United Nations system, the International Military Tribunals of Nuremberg and Tokyo were the first fora in which self-defence was discussed after the adoption of the Charter.

The Nuremberg trials were conducted under the auspices of two courts: the International Military Tribunal (1945–1946) and the US Nuremberg Tribunals (conducted under Control Council Law No. 10). The International Military Tribunal of Nuremberg conducted the famous 'Major War Criminals Trial', while the US Military Tribunals tried other prominent figures of Nazi Germany. Much like the International Tribunal at Nuremberg, the International Military Tribunal for the Far East (Tokyo Tribunal) was set up with the purpose to bring Japanese political and military authorities to justice. The Charter of the Tokyo Tribunal was approved on 19 January 1945 and the Tribunal was first convened on 3 May 1946.

The Nuremberg Tribunal discussed self-defence in relation to the German invasion of Norway, whereas the Tokyo Tribunal addressed the same concept in connection with the Japanese invasion of the Dutch East Indies.

K. Tibori Szabó, *Anticipatory Action in Self-Defence*, DOI: 10.1007/978-90-6704-796-8_7,

7.2 The 'Major War Criminals' Trial' (Nuremberg, 1945–1946)

The need to punish the crimes committed by the Nazis was recognized as early as January 1942 at an Allied meeting in London and reiterated in 1943 in the Moscow Declaration.[1] By the beginning of 1945, a trial plan was put together by the Roosevelt administration. After the death of Roosevelt on 12 April 1945, President Harry Truman continued the policy accepted by his predecessor.[2]

The establishment of the new Tribunal also implied the drafting and adoption of a charter that would serve as the basis for the jurisdiction and competence of the judicial institution. A series of negotiations between the representatives of the US, the Provisional Government of the French Republic, the UK and the USSR started in 1945 and culminated in the London Conference on Military Trials of July 1945.[3] During the negotiations, the question of holding Nazi officials responsible for attacking and invading other countries came up.[4] Accordingly, the final version of Article 6 of the new (Nuremberg) Charter provided that, *inter alia*, '(a) crimes against peace: namely, planning, preparation, initiation or waging of a war of aggression, or a war in violation of international treaties, agreements or assurances, or participation in a common plan or conspiracy for the accomplishment of any of the foregoing' ought to be punished by the Tribunal.

The concept of self-defence was explicitly mentioned in one of the earlier drafts of Article 6. In suggesting a definition for aggression and aggressive war, the American delegation submitted a draft proposal that included the following statement:

> No political, military, economic or other considerations shall serve as an excuse or justification for such actions [i.e., aggressive war]; but the exercise of the right to legitimate self-defence, that is to say, resistance to an act of aggression, or action to assist a state which has been subjected to aggression, shall not constitute a war of aggression.[5]

Although this draft proposal was subsequently changed and the explicit reference to self-defence was dropped, it shows that the right of self-defence was viewed as the only exception to the prohibition to wage war. It is also evident that the content of this draft article was very similar in its meaning to the understanding given to Article 51 of the UN Charter at the San Francisco Conference, which had been

---

[1] Marrus 1997, pp. 18–19.

[2] Ibid., pp. 26–27, 32–33.

[3] For the records of the negotiations, see Jackson 1949.

[4] For discussions involving the concept of aggressive war, see Minutes of Conference Session of 19 July 1945. In Jackson 1949.

[5] Ibid., definition of 'aggression', suggested by the American delegation as the basis of discussion.

adopted a few weeks before the London negotiations. The lack of explicit mentioning of the right of self-defence in the Nuremberg Charter was not a hindrance for the Tribunal to apply it in the Major War Criminals Trial.

The Charter of the Nuremberg International Military Tribunal was adopted at the London Conference of July 1945 and it was incorporated in the London Agreement of 8 August 1945.

Twenty-one of the highest Nazi officials ('the major war criminals') were indicted on 6 October 1945 and the Nuremberg trial began on 20 November 1945. Counts I and II dealt with the issue of aggressive war. Count I was described as 'the formulation or execution of a common plan or conspiracy to commit, or which involved the commission of, crimes against peace, war crimes, and crimes against humanity.' Count II referred to the participation 'in the planning, preparation, initiation and waging of wars of aggression, which were also wars in violation of international treaties, agreements, and assurances.' Count III dealt with war crimes and Count IV with crimes against humanity.

The defendants were indicted under all or some of these four counts. The judgment was delivered on 30 September and 1 October 1946 and sentenced 12 of the defendants to death by hanging. Three defendants were sentenced to imprisonment for life and the remaining accused received milder prison sentences.[6] Twelve accused, including Hermann Göring, Rudolf Hess, Alfred Jodl and Joachin von Ribbentrop, were all found guilty under Count II (crimes against peace) for the planning, preparation, initiation, and waging of wars of aggression.[7] Moreover, the judgment held the entire Nazi government and thus, the German Nazi state, responsible for the planning and waging of aggressive wars: 'the evidence has made it plain that this war of aggression [...] was pre-meditated and carefully prepared, and was not undertaken until the moment was thought opportune for it to be carried through as a definite part of the pre-ordained scheme and plan.'[8] For that purpose, 'war was seen to be inevitable, or at the very least, highly probable, if these purposes were to be accomplished.'[9] The judgment dealt separately with the invasion of each Allied country and found them all to be aggressive wars.

7.3 Self-Defence and the 'Major War Criminals' Trial'

The issue of self-defence came up in connection with the April 1940 invasion of Norway by Germany. After invading Poland in September 1939, the German government assured Norway that it would not launch an invasion against it as long

---

[6] Nazi Conspiracy and Aggression 1947, pp. 189–190.

[7] The other accused found guilty under Count II were: Wilhelm Keitel, Konstantin von Neurath, Erich Räder, Alfred Rosenberg, Karl Dönitz, Wilhelm Frick, Walter Funk and Arthur Seyss-Inquart. Nazi Conspiracy and Aggression 1947, pp. 189–190.

[8] Ibid., p. 17.

[9] Ibid.

as unimpeachable neutrality towards the Reich was observed.[10] Notwithstanding such an assurance, in seven months' time, Norway was invaded by Germany. As the UK Chief Prosecutor Sir Hartley Shawcross described the events before the judges, 'in the early hours of the 9 April [1940], 7 cruisers and 14 destroyers and a number of torpedo boats and other small craft carried advance elements of six divisions, totalling about 10,000 men, forced an entry and landed troops in the outer Oslo Fjord, Kristiansand, Stavanger, Bergen, Trondheim and Narvik.'[11] Apart from some smaller units that landed on the southern Norwegian coast, airborne troops and aircraft were landed near Oslo and Stavanger.[12]

The prosecution saw the specific details of the German invasion of Norway as an unquestionable proof that the attack was a premeditated, thoroughly planned military action.[13] On the contrary, the defence contended that the invasion of Norway was a measure of prevention, as Britain and France were contemplating to occupy the country and use it as a basis for further military operations.[14]

The prosecution asserted that the Nazi attack 'had been planned long before any question of breach of neutrality or occupation of Norway by England could ever have occurred.'[15] Further, the prosecution claimed that the German assurances were made for no other purposes than to lull suspicion and to prevent Norway from preparing to resist the attack.[16] In order to sustain that argument, the prosecution exposed all the strategic and military preparations made by the German officials to invade Norway, such as the disguise of the German warships as British craft, the deceptive names, codes and messages that the crew had to use or send if intercepted by enemy vessels. All the preparations were made in order to secure a surprise-landing of troops in Norway.[17]

In contrast, the defence asserted that the invasion of Norway was a preventive measure of self-defence. In the direct examination of defence witness Admiral Schulte-Mönting by defence counsel for Erich Räder, the assertion was made that there were numerous reports about the Allies' intentions to occupy Norway.[18]

Accordingly, Admiral Schulte-Mönting claimed that 'the rumours were increasing that the Allies intended to drag Scandinavia into the war in order to

---

[10] Ibid., p. 34.

[11] Exposé of UK Chief Prosecutor, 4 December 1945. In Trial of the Major War Criminals, vol. 3.

[12] Ibid.

[13] Ibid.

[14] Examination of Defence Witness Admiral Schulte-Mönting, 22 May 1946. In Trial of the Major War Criminals, vol. 14.

[15] Exposé of UK Chief Prosecutor, 4 December 1945. In Trial of the Major War Criminals, vol. 3.

[16] Ibid.

[17] Exposé of UK Junior Prosecution Counsel, 7 December 1945. In Trial of the Major War Criminals, vol. 3.

[18] Examination of defence witness Admiral Schulte-Mönting, 22 May 1946. In Trial of the major war criminals, vol. 14.

prevent, if possible, the iron ore imports from Sweden to Germany'.[19] Schulte-Mönting defended the credibility of such rumours by referring to the 'documentary evidence from the last world war' according to which Winston Churchill had seriously considered the occupation of Norway.[20] Moreover, according to the same defence witness, there were reports concerning the presence of British air crews allegedly posing as civilians in Oslo and of Allied officers making surveys of Norwegian bridges, viaducts and tunnels. These reports were taken as indication that 'the transportation of heavy material and equipment was planned.'[21] In his direct examination of the witness, the defence counsel for Erich Räder put the emphasis on the dangers that arose for Germany on account of such reports. The witness stated that, in the opinion of the German government, with Norway occupied, operations in the North Sea would have become almost impossible. Furthermore, the ore imports would have been stopped and the danger of airborne attacks would have become grave for the north of Germany and the eastern territories. In Schulte-Mönting's opinion, 'in the long run, the North Sea and the Baltic would have been blocked completely, and this would eventually have led to the total loss of the war'.[22]

The defence also tried to show that such reports had become available as early as the autumn of 1939 and that Germany did not rush into invading Norway, but rather took cautious steps in monitoring the situation. According to Schulte-Mönting, the actual drafting of the military operation took place in February 1940 and by that time, the invasion of Norway became a 'compelling necessity'.[23]

The judges were not convinced by this argument. In their view, the invasion of Norway was a strategic move to secure a significant military advantage. The judgment recalled the fact that the memorandum for 'gaining bases in Norway' was drafted in October 1939 and there was no mention of any danger arising from a potential Allied invasion. On the contrary, the plan aimed at improving the German strategic and operational position and addressed the question whether bases could be gained by military force against Norway's will and whether such bases could be acquired without fighting.[24] While the plan was being forwarded to the Fuehrer, Norway was receiving repeated assurances of neutrality on the part of Germany.[25] According to the judges, although the disadvantages of a British occupation of Norway were eventually reported to Hitler, the issue was discussed from a military and strategic point of view, rather than as a defensive measure.[26] The judgment also quoted the directive issued by Hitler on 1 March 1940:

---

[19] Ibid.

[20] Ibid.

[21] Ibid.

[22] Ibid.

[23] Ibid.

[24] Nazi Conspiracy and Aggression 1947, p. 35.

[25] Ibid.

[26] Ibid., pp. 35–36.

> The development of the situation in Scandinavia requires the making of all preparations for the occupation of Denmark and Norway by a part of the German armed forces. This operation should prevent British encroachment on Scandinavia and the Baltic; further, it should guarantee our ore base in Sweden and give our navy and air force a wider start line against Britain [...]. It is most important that the Scandinavian states as well as the western opponents should be taken by surprise by our measures.[27]

In the opinion of the judges, the directive and the entire narrative of the preparations for invasion showed no compelling circumstances that would have justified a pre-emptive attack. The judgment referred to the *Caroline* incident and affirmed that 'preventive action in foreign territory' was only justified in case of 'an instant and overwhelming necessity for self-defence, leaving no choice of means and no moment of deliberation.'[28] On the basis of the available evidence, the judges found that when the plans for an attack on Norway were being made, they were not made for the purpose of forestalling an imminent Allied landing, but, 'at the most', that they were aimed at preventing an Allied occupation at some future date.[29] The use of the term 'preventive' in the judgment gives rise to some confusion. On the one hand, the judges analyse 'preventive action' on the basis of the Webster formula and allow it only in the face of an imminent threat. On the other hand, they refer to prevention in the face of a possible, future attack. It is nevertheless clear that the 'preventive action' the judges found *admissible* was only that against an imminent threat, on the basis of the Webster formula.

The judgment admitted that there were indeed Allied plans to occupy Norway, but that they were not as old as the German military plans and at the time of the invasion, the Nazi officials did not know about the existence of such plans; revealing documents were captured much later.[30] Moreover, the judges referred to several German internal documents that showed that no imminent threat was perceived regarding the British invasion of Norway. For instance, according to a 13 March 1940 note made by defendant Alfred Jodl 'the Fuehrer does not give order yet for "W" [Weser Exercise, invasion of Norway], he is still looking for an excuse.'[31] One day later, the same defendant noted: 'Fuehrer has not yet decided what reason to give for "Weser Exercise".'[32] The notes made by Alfred Jodl in his diary also shed light on Hitler's approach regarding any non-military, last resort measures. Accordingly, on 21 March 1940, Jodl noted: 'Fuehrer rejects any earlier negotiations, as otherwise calls for help go out to England and America. If resistance is put up, it must be ruthlessly broken'.[33]

---

[27] Ibid., p. 36 (Directive regarding the Weser Exercise, 1 March 1940).

[28] Ibid., p. 36.

[29] Ibid., p. 37.

[30] Ibid., pp. 37–38.

[31] Ibid., p. 37.

[32] Ibid.

[33] Ibid.

In upholding its judgment, the Tribunal also noted that the invasion of Norway and Denmark was envisaged as a long term solution. A German naval memorandum issued on 3 June 1940, discussed the use to be made of the two Scandinavian countries and proposed that the territories acquired should continue to be occupied and organized so that they could in the future be considered as German possessions.[34] This was another proof that the German military action went well beyond the purposes of a defensive measure, since its objective was to last much longer than any perceived threat of an Allied occupation.

7.4 The Trial and Judgment of the Japanese War Criminals (1946–1948)

The idea of an international tribunal to try the Japanese officials was first referred to in the Potsdam Declaration of July 1945.[35] Subsequently, on 19 January 1946, General Douglas McArthur, the supreme commander for the Allied powers in Japan issued an executive order by which he approved the Charter of the Tokyo Tribunal.

The Tokyo Charter defined three types of crimes: crimes against peace, crimes against humanity and war crimes [Article 5(a–c)]. The indictment of the Tokyo Tribunal classified crimes against peace as 'Group One' crimes, murder as 'Group Two' (it could amount to all three types of crimes) and conventional war crimes and crimes against humanity as 'Group Three' crimes.

The Tribunal in Tokyo prosecuted 28 individuals with crimes from all three groups (Class A defendants). Seven of the 28 defendants (including Tojo Hideki, prime minister during the attack on Pearl Harbour, and Hirota Koki, prime minister in 1936–1937), were sentenced to death by hanging. The others were given prison sentences ranging from life to 7 years' imprisonment.[36]

7.5 Self-Defence as Interpreted by the Tokyo Tribunal

The issue of self-defence came up in relation to the so-called Pacific War, more specifically the Japanese invasion of the Dutch East Indies. Count 1 for crimes against peace referred to the common plan or conspiracy of Japan to secure its military, naval, political and economic domination of East Asia and of the Pacific

[34] Ibid., p. 38.

[35] The Potsdam Declaration (Proclamation Defining Terms for Japanese Surrender) was a statement jointly issued by the US, UK and China on 26 July 1945 in which an ultimatum was given to Japan

[36] Röling 1993, pp. 3–4.

and Indian Oceans. Count 32 charged the accused with waging a war of aggression and a war in violation of international law against the Kingdom of the Netherlands.

According to the prosecution, the Netherlands East Indies, together with the Portuguese portion of the Island of Timor, were within Japan's area of interest and were designated as part of the 'Greater East Asia Co-Prosperity Sphere.'[37] This area—encompassing Burma, Malaya, the East Indies, Indo-China and the Philippines—was rich in supplies of rice as well as iron, gold, oil and many other raw materials that Japan sorely needed. The region, however, belonged to several Western nations: Britain, the Netherlands, France and the US.[38] The preparations of Japan to invade the Dutch East Indies were thus part of a greater campaign to assert its military dominance in the Far East.[39]

After Japan denounced its treaty with the Netherlands regarding the East Indies in 1940, it proposed a new one, which the Dutch government—at that time in exile —rejected.[40] According to the same indictment, the occupation by Japan of French Indo-China (commenced in September 1940 and completed in July 1941) as well as the attacks upon territories of the US and the British Commonwealth in December 1941 (notably the attack on Pearl Harbour on 7 December 1941), were all part of the plan which included an invasion of the Netherlands East Indies. On 8 December 1941, immediately after the bombing of Pearl Harbour took place, the Netherlands declared war on Japan in self-defence. In the weeks from January—March 1942, Japan successfully occupied the Dutch East Indies as part of its greater invasion plan.[41]

The contention of the defence that the invasion of the 'Co-Prosperity Sphere' was taken as a measure of self-defence against the US, UK, France and the Netherlands was rejected by the Tribunal. The judges did not seem convinced by the assertion that in the face of economic aggression from US, Britain, France and the Netherlands, Japan had no other way of preserving the welfare and prosperity of her nationals but to go to war.[42] The Tribunal held that the restrictive measures taken were entirely justifiable attempts to thwart Japan from its long-prepared aggressive military plans.[43] As a result, the Japanese invasion campaign was characterized as a suite of aggressive wars against the Allied powers.[44]

The judgment of 1 November 1948 reviewed the plans and policies adopted by Japan between July 1940 and December 1941 and concluded that the Pacific War

---

37 Appendix A, Sect. 10. In Trial of Japanese War Criminals 1946, p. 75.

38 Burma, Malaya and part of Borneo belonged to Britain; the remaining islands of the East Indies belonged to the Netherlands, whereas Indo-China was a French possession and the Philippines was under US protectorate. Dupuy 1963, Vol. 9, p. 3.

39 Appendix A, Sect. 10. In Trial of Japanese War Criminals 1946, pp. 75–76.

40 Ibid.

41 Ibid., pp. 75–76.

42 Röling and Rüter 1977, pp. 380–381.

43 Ibid., p. 381.

44 Ibid.

was a long premeditated campaign, aiming at expanding the 'Greater East-Asia Co-Prosperity Sphere.'[45] At first, in July 1940, Japan announced to the Netherlands that it was sending an economic mission to the East Indies.[46] Later that year, Japan sent out several espionage missions in contemplation of occupying the islands of Java, Sumatra and Bali.[47] In January 1941, the Japanese Diet discussed plans of military actions against the East Indies. The Dutch government was aware of that and became suspicious regarding further negotiations.[48] In October 1941 the Japanese leaders decided that it was time to start military action against several targets in the Pacific arena.[49] On 7 December 1941 the attack on Pearl Harbour took place. As a consequence, US and UK declared war on Japan. At the same time, the Netherlands, the Dutch East Indies, Australia, New Zealand, South Africa, Free France, Canada and China also declared war on Japan.[50] As expected by that time, Japan started its invasion of the Dutch East Indies in early January 1942.

On the basis of these findings, the arguments of self-defence on behalf of Japan were not upheld by the judgment. The underlying reasons for Japan's acts were identified as 'prompted by the desire to deprive China of any aid in the struggle she was waging against Japan's aggression and to secure for Japan the possessions of her neighbours in the South.'[51] The judges characterized the wars waged against the US, UK, France and the Netherlands as wars of aggression.[52]

The Tribunal also rejected the argument that in as much as the Netherlands took the initiative in declaring war on Japan, the ensuing war could not be described as a war of aggression by Japan.[53] The judgment emphasized that Japan had long planned the invasion of the Netherlands East Indies in order to secure its economic benefits. Accordingly, the judges noted that by the middle of 1941, it was apparent that Japan was in full preparations for invading and seizing the Netherlands East Indies.[54]

In contrast, the Tribunal regarded the declaration of war by the Netherlands as made in legitimate self-defence: 'The fact that the Netherlands, being fully appraised of the imminence of the attack, in self-defence declared war against Japan on 8 December and thus officially recognized the existence of a state of war

[45] Ibid., pp. 328–329.

[46] Ibid., p. 328.

[47] Ibid., p. 339.

[48] Ibid., pp. 346–347.

[49] Ibid., pp. 364–366.

[50] Ibid., pp. 379–380.

[51] Ibid., p. 381.

[52] Ibid., pp. 381–384.

[53] Ibid., p. 382.

[54] Ibid.

which had been begun by Japan, cannot change that war from a war of aggression on the part of Japan into something other than that.'[55]

Although the judgment of the Tokyo Tribunal did not elaborate on the concept of self-defence the way the Nuremberg judges did, it expressly acknowledged the legality of self-defence against an imminent threat of invasion.

7.6 Self-Defence in the Nuremberg and Tokyo Judgments

As shown above, the judgment of the Nuremberg Tribunal discussed the issue of self-defence in connection with the Nazi invasion of Norway. The judges referred to the *Caroline* incident in order to uphold the view that self-defence was justified if exercised in face of an imminent threat.[56] Although the judges did not expressly discuss the legality of preventive measures against a potential threat, by their reference to the Webster formula they confirmed that self-defence could only be invoked against an imminent danger.

The judges found the German invasion illegal, although, with hindsight, it became clear that the UK had planned to land in Norway at some point. The rejection of the self-defence claim was due to the fact that the German invasion plans were older than the British and there was no actual knowledge of the British plans at the time Norway was invaded. The judges thus based their assessment on what German officials knew at the time of the invasion.

From this point of view, the German invasion of Norway is in stark contrast with the British operation of sinking a part of the French fleet in 1940.[57] Accordingly, in case of 'Operation Catapult', the British government believed, in good faith, that, once returned to their ports, the French vessels could have been boarded and seized by German forces at any time and there would have been no obstacle in the Germans' way.[58] That threat was perceived by Churchill's War Cabinet at that time as giving rise to a present and inevitable necessity to act. Concerning the German invasion of Norway, no such perception, acquired in good faith, existed on behalf of the Nazi government at the time of the Weser Exercise.

The interpretations given to the concept of self-defence in the Nuremberg and Tokyo judgments are not dissimilar. Both judgments acknowledged the legality of self-defence against an imminent threat of invasion. In this respect, the interpretation of self-defence confirms the pre-Charter, narrow concept of the right. The judgments also strengthen the restrictions brought to preventive action (against a potential threat).

---

[55] Ibid.

[56] Ibid., p. 36.

[57] See *supra* 4.6.

[58] Gill 2007, p. 134.

The Charter of the UN was not taken into consideration when discussing the right of self-defence. This has prompted some authors to contend that, in relation to self-defence, the decisions of the Nuremberg and Tokyo Tribunals reflected the Pre-Charter law.[59] This approach is difficult to maintain upon a careful perusal of the two judgments. At Nuremberg, the judges expressly asserted that 'it must be remembered that preventive action in foreign territory *is justified* only in case of "an instant and overwhelming necessity for self-defence leaving no choice of means, and no moment of deliberation"'.[60] There was no discussion of the potential differences between the law applicable at the time of the German invasion and that applicable in 1946. The same can be said about the judgment of the Tokyo Tribunal. Save for the unlikely assumption that the judges at Nuremberg and Tokyo were not aware of a drastic change in the interpretation of self-defence, it is submitted that a better view is that the judgments reflect customary law *at the time* and *in the immediate aftermath* of the adoption of the Charter.

In the light of the inconclusive findings concerning the commonly understood content of Article 51 at the San Francisco Conference, the decision of the Nuremberg and Tokyo Tribunals aid in comprehending how self-defence was actually viewed at the time. Obviously, that does not exclude the possibility that subsequent, post-Charter state practice changed the understanding of self-defence. That possibility will be examined in the following chapters. It is, however, reasonable to maintain that the interpretation given to self-defence at the Nuremberg and Tokyo tribunals reflected the way in which that right was understood in the immediate aftermath of the adoption of the UN Charter.

References

Brownlie I (1963) International law and the use of force by states. Clarendon Press, Oxford

Corten O (2008) Le droit contre la guerre: l'interdiction du recours à la force en droit international contemporain. Pedone, Paris

Dupuy TN (1963) Asiatic land battles: Japanese ambitions in the Pacific. In: Dupuy TN (ed) The illustrated history of World War II, vol 9. Edmund Ward, London

Gill TD (2007) The temporal dimension of self-defence. In: Schmitt M, Pejic J (eds) International law and armed conflict: exploring the faultlines. Essays in honour of Yoram Dinstein. Martinus Nijhoff, Leiden, pp 113–155

Jackson RH (1949) Report on the International Conference on Military Trials: London, 1945, US Government Printing Office, Washington, D.C. http://avalon.law.yale.edu/imt/jack_titlep.asp. Accessed 13 March 2009

Marrus MR (1997) The Nuremberg War Crimes Trial 1945–46: A Documentary History. Bedford Books, Boston

Nazi Conspiracy and Aggression: Opinion and Judgment (1947) Office of the US Chief of Counsel for the Prosecution of Axis Criminality. Government Printing Office, Washington, D.C

[59] Brownlie 1963, pp. 258, 309–316; Corten 2008, pp. 631–632; Ruys 2010, p. 261.

[60] Nazi Conspiracy and Aggression 1947, p. 36 (emphasis added).

BVA Röling (1993) Cassese A (ed) The Tokyo trial and beyond: reflections of a peacemonger. Polity Press, Cambridge
Röling BVA, Rüter CF (1977) The Tokyo judgment: the International Military Tribunal for the Far East, 29 April 1946–12 November 1948. APA-University Press, Amsterdam
Ruys T (2010) 'Armed attack' and Article 51 of the UN Charter. Evolutions in customary law and practice. Cambridge University Press, Cambridge
Trial of Japanese War Criminals (1946) US Government Printing Office, Washington, D.C
Trial of the Major War Criminals before the International Military Tribunal: Proceedings, vol. 3. http://avalon.law.yale.edu/imt/12-04-45.asp. Accessed 13 March 2010
Trial of the Major War Criminals before the International Military Tribunal: Proceedings, vol. 14. http://avalon.law.yale.edu/imt/05-22-46.asp. Accessed 13 March 2010

Chapter 8
Self-Defence in State-to-State Conflicts

8.1 Introduction

This chapter will examine some of those post-Charter conflicts that had states as belligerent parties and in which claims of self-defence were contemplated or used. The aim of the chapter is to examine the temporal dimension of self-defence as interpreted by the state practice involving state-to-state conflicts. For this reason, only those instances of state practice will be examined that purported significant questions as to the temporality of self-defence (whether remedial or anticipatory). Cases where certain uses of force pertained to questions relevant for the concept of armed attack or proportionality alone, will not be examined.

Instances of state practice involving anticipatory action (contemplated or undertaken) will be first analysed. Further, some instances in which remedial action in self-defence was taken will be examined for comparative purposes. Lastly, some examples of exercise of self-defence involving both remedial and anticipatory action will be analysed. The aim of the comparison between cases entailing anticipatory action and those involving remedial action is to examine whether the limits of these two dimensions are identical or dissimilar in post-Charter state practice. As concluded in Part I, the limits of the pre-Charter, narrow concept of self-defence were the same, regardless of the temporal dimension of the right. It will be interesting to see if this is still the case in post-Charter state practice.

The specific cases will be tested against the variables identified in the introductory remarks of Part II. Accordingly, each instance of state practice will be analysed on the basis of necessity (the conditionality of an armed attack and immediacy) as well as proportionality.

The chapter will conclude on the overall significance of these variables regarding the outcome of the cases. Not only will legal or justifiable cases be examined, but also those instances that attracted criticism or outright condemnation. As noted in Chapter 1, the content and strength of a customary rule can be discerned not only from acquiescing action, but also from instances in which the

K. Tibori Szabó, *Anticipatory Action in Self-Defence*, DOI: 10.1007/978-90-6704-796-8_8,

rule was breached.[1] The outcome will be discerned from the reaction of states before the UN Security Council or General Assembly, the echoes in the legal literature and, where possible, official reports regarding the legality of specific instances of the use of force.

Each case will follow a similar structure. First, a summary of the facts will be provided. Secondly, the general reaction to the claims will be described. Thirdly, the variables and the outcome will be analysed.

8.2 The Anticipatory Dimension of Self-Defence

In this section, those instances of state practice will be given attention which purported a purely anticipatory dimension by way of action, claim or contemplation of exercise of self-defence. The following instances will be examined: the 1956 Sinai Campaign, the 1967 Six-Day War and the 1973 Yom Kippur War. On the basis of the factual circumstances, juridical variables and general reaction, the (il)legality of these cases will be discerned.

8.2.1 The Sinai Campaign (1956)

There are several instances in which self-defence was invoked in the Middle East in the past 60 years. Since the declaration of independence of Israel in May 1948, there has been continuous conflict between various Arab states and Israel, as well as between the Palestinian people and the Israeli government. This conflict several times escalated in wars and in those instances, one or both parties invoked the right to self-defence. In May 1948, after the Israeli declaration of independence, forces of Transjordan, Egypt, Syria and Iraq entered Palestine.[2] At that time, the representative of the Arab Higher Committee maintained that the Palestinian people possessed the unquestionable right to sovereignty over Palestine. Accordingly, by their declaration of independence, the Jewish minority created a dangerous threat and, for that reason, the Palestinian people asked the help of the neighbouring Arab countries.[3] The Security Council declared the situation a threat to the peace under Article 39 and ordered, pursuant to Article 40 'the Governments and authorities concerned' to desist from further military action and issue cease-fire orders to their military.[4]

---

1 See *supra* 1.3.6.2.

2 Laqueur and Rubin 2001, p. 81; Mansfield 2003, p. 236.

3 Repertoire 1946–1951, Chap. 8, pp. 493–494.

4 SC Res. 54 (1948).

A few years later, in 1954, after conducting a research on the country's security threats, Israeli Prime Minister David Ben-Gurion concluded that the Arab states could be ready for another war some time in 1956. Ben-Gurion saw the new Egyptian President, Gamal Abdul Nasser, as the primary threat facing Israel.[5] Both states were eager to arm themselves with the assistance of the US and European countries. After France, the UK and the US agreed to control the sale of weapons in the region, the Egyptian president turned to the Soviet Union to acquire the supplies he wanted.[6] That move made the Israeli government even more concerned; the possibility of Egypt overcoming the limitations of its inferior military equipment was viewed as a serious threat by the Israelis. Moreover, the involvement of the Soviet Union in Middle Eastern affairs was also an unwelcome development in the eyes of Ben-Gurion.[7] To make matters worse, in July 1956, Nasser, frustrated that the US and UK withdrew their funding for the Aswan high dam, decided to nationalize the Suez Canal, having earlier closed the Straits of Tiran to Israeli shipping.[8] The potential threat posed by Egypt against Israel was indeed serious, but there was no conclusive evidence that it was imminent as well. In fact, Ben-Gurion and some of his cabinet members long contemplated a preventive war against Egypt, but did not want to risk the criticism of their supporters.[9] As the then Israeli Defence Minister, Moshe Dayan, asserted, 'preventive war means an aggressive war initiated by Israel directly' and 'Israel cannot afford to stand against the entire world and be denounced as the aggressor.'[10]

Egyptian plans to nationalize the Suez Canal seemed to offer an adequate opportunity to launch the Israeli campaign. Moreover, the UK and France were also determined to seize the Canal by force.[11] As a consequence, on 29 October 1956, Israel launched its military offensive against Egypt and moved into the Sinai Peninsula. Two days later, after a foreseeable rejection of an Anglo-French ultimatum by Nasser, the UK and France launched airstrikes against Egypt. On 5 November, an Anglo-French force landed near Port Said, captured the city and advanced along the line of the Suez Canal.[12]

The 1956 invasion of Egypt received a very negative reaction from most members of the Security Council.[13] Before the UN General Assembly, Israel justified its actions as self-defence against the blocking of the Suez Canal and the support for raids of armed groups (*fedayeen*) by Egypt. Israel claimed that the

---

[5] Mueller et al. 2006, p. 191.

[6] Ibid., pp. 191–192; Sorenson 2008, p. 26.

[7] Mueller et al. 2006, p. 192.

[8] Ibid., p. 193, Sorenson 2008, p. 26.

[9] Mueller et al. 2006, p. 195.

[10] Ibid. (quoting Moshe Dayan).

[11] Mansfield 2003, pp. 256–257; Mueller et al. 2006, p. 196; Sorenson 2008, p. 26.

[12] Mansfield 2003, p. 257; Mueller et al. 2006, p. 196.

[13] SCOR, 11th Session, 749th and 750th meeting, UN Doc. S/PV.749 and S/PV.750.Rev.1 (30 October 1956).

'long and uninterrupted series of encroachments [...] constitute in its totality the essence and reality of an armed attack.'[14] This justification was rejected by most Member States. Although the nationalization of the Suez Canal did amount to a serious aggravation of the overall situation, between the announcement of such plans by Nasser at the end of July 1956 and the Israeli attack on 29 October 1956, Egypt showed willingness to negotiate and actively participated in talks organized by the US to solve the problem.[15] Moreover, Israel never offered conclusive proofs of the involvement of the Egyptian government in sponsoring guerrilla groups and never succeeded in demonstrating a magnitude of damage equivalent to an armed attack. According to a contemporary commentator, Quincy Wright, the existence of 'an instant and overwhelming danger of such attack' (armed attack) could not be maintained by Israel, because an armed attack had to threaten 'the territory, official agencies, or perhaps the lives of the citizens of the state,' whereas violation of the right of transit through a canal or stoppage of merchant vessels through a strait was less than that.[16]

The justifications brought by the UK and France received even less support. In their view, the invasion of Egypt was necessary to stop hostilities between Egypt and Israel, to prevent the nationalization of the Suez Canal and to prevent the stoppage of traffic, as well as to assure the future freedom of traffic.[17] As Wright opined at that time, such justifications could not possibly constitute 'the instant and overwhelming necessity for defence which justifies the use of armed force in international relations.'[18]

The Sinai campaign is an instance in which a claim of self-defence was condemned as unlawful. The blocking of naval passage—however serious—does not amount, by itself, to an imminent threat of an armed attack. Moreover, between July and October 1956, opportunities were present for negotiations; thus there was always a choice of means to solve the conflict and there was never a present and inevitable necessity to resort to self-defence. Moreover, the Israeli ground offensive and the British-French airstrikes could hardly be viewed as moderate responses to the situation under the requirement of proportionality.

8.2.2 The Six-Day War (1967)

The 1967 war was initiated by Israel with a pre-emptive strike against Egypt as a result of a dangerous escalation of events. Apart from the general backdrop of Arab-Israeli hostility, the build-up to the Six-Day War featured some additional,

---

[14] GAOR, 1st Emergency Spec. Session, UN Doc. A/PV.562 (1956), paras 105–145.

[15] Mueller et al. 2006, p. 196.

[16] Wright 1957, p. 272.

[17] Ibid.

[18] Ibid., p. 273.

highly risky elements. Dangerous developments were occurring on two fronts: on the Syrian–Israeli border and in Egypt.

The rise of the Ba'ath party in Syria greatly contributed to the increase of tensions between the two countries. Clashes on the Israeli-Syrian border became regular between 1964 and 1967. Tensions between the two countries were not only militarily expressed. Apart from organizing guerrilla attacks, the Syrian government also wanted to reduce the amount of water getting to Israel through the Jordan River.[19] A skirmish on the Syrian–Israeli border on 7 April 1967 increased the tension between the two sides.[20]

At the same time, Egypt was also increasingly hostile. The Soviet Union sent an informative note to Egypt warning it about Israeli troops massing on the Syrian–Israeli border. Nasser dispatched an envoy to Damascus to verify the Israeli troop deployments. The envoy reported back that he had seen nothing to confirm the Soviet note, but by that time Nasser had already mobilized Egyptian troops into the Sinai.[21]

One of the reasons Nasser was so determined about mobilizing troops was the pressure coming from the Syrian and Jordanian sides. He felt that he had to act because of that pressure, but not necessarily because of his firm belief in an imminent Israeli threat.[22]

The situation became even tenser when, on 14 May, Israel detected Egyptian troops crossing the Suez Canal and moving into the Sinai Peninsula. Three days later Nasser demanded the withdrawal of UNEF[23] and, on 23 May, he ordered the closing of the Straits of Tiran.[24] In addition, the Egyptian administration had been threatening with preventive action in case the Israelis developed a nuclear weapon at the Dimona nuclear reactor, in the Negev desert, close to the Egyptian border. Consequently, the moving of the Egyptian troops into the Sinai, increased Israeli fears of an aerial or land attack against Dimona.[25]

The Israelis were reluctant to start hostilities, especially because the US was aiming for a diplomatic solution. The Johnson administration proposed to organize an international armada to break the blockade of the Strait, but the operation never took place, because key countries refused to participate.[26] Israeli Prime Minister Eshkol ordered a limited mobilisation, in the hope of deterring the Egyptians and being careful not to obstruct potential diplomatic solutions. Eshkol held back the

[19] Mueller et al. 2006, p. 198.

[20] Ibid., pp. 198–199.

[21] Sorenson 2008, p. 27; Mueller et al. 2006, p. 199.

[22] Mueller et al. 2006, p. 200.

[23] United Nations Emergency Force, established in November 1956 as a result of UN General Assembly resolutions to supervise the cease-fire line in the aftermath of the Israeli Sinai campaign.

[24] Sorenson 2008, p. 26; Mueller et al. 2006, p. 200.

[25] Mueller et al. 2006, p. 200.

[26] Ibid.

military for three weeks, in hope of a diplomatic solution by the US, which never came.[27]

On 24 May 1967, two weeks before the outbreak of the war, Israel complained to the Security Council about 'massive troop concentrations' built up in the Sinai Peninsula. In Israel's view, the eviction of UNEF and the closing of the Straits 'were part of an overall plan, the design of which was unfolding' and 'the action of Egypt constituted a challenge of utmost gravity not only to Israel, but also to the whole international community.'[28] Over the next few days, Egyptian authorities issued numerous declarations concerning the existence of a 'state of war' with Israel and expressed their intention to launch a general assault against Israel.[29] A few days later, on 29 May, the representative of Egypt, referring to the Israeli–Syrian border incident of 7 April 1967 and to the 'accurate information' about Israeli troops-concentration on the same border, explicitly stated that 'the Government [of Egypt] had decided, in co-operation with its Arab allies, to defend the Arab nation by all measures.'[30] Further, the Egyptian representative asserted that the presence of UNEF would have conflicted with such a decision and 'also for the sake of the safety of the Force,' the Egyptian government decided to expel it, 'peacefully' restoring the situation back to the 1956 status quo.[31]

The Security Council proved to be incapable to calm the situation and war seemed inevitable. Consequently, Israel decided to resort to anticipatory action. On 5 June 1967, Israeli aircraft attacked Egyptian warplanes and destroyed most of the Egyptian air force. At the same time, Israeli forces crossed the Sinai and marched into the Gaza Strip. The next day, on 6 June, Jordanian troops opened fire on Israeli positions in Jerusalem, while Israeli troops captured towns on the Jordanian border.[32] On 7 June, Resolution 234 was unanimously passed by the Security Council calling for a ceasefire. Arab states, with the exception of Jordan, rejected it. Consequently, Israeli troops captured Sharm el-Sheikh, broke the blockade of Eilat and took Jericho in the West Bank.[33] Overwhelmed by the Israeli victories, Arab states accepted the ceasefire.

Several questions regarding the legal aspects of the Six-Day War have raised significant controversies. First, both sides have invoked the right of self-defence to justify their actions. Before the Security Council, the Egyptian delegate characterized Israel's actions as a 'treacherous aggression' and asserted that his country 'had no other choice than to defend itself by all means in accordance with Article

---

[27] Ibid., p. 202.

[28] Repertoire, Supp. 1966–1968, Chap. 8, p. 135.

[29] Statement of Mr. Eban (Israel), SCOR, 22th Session, 1348th meeting, UN Doc. S/PV.1348 (OR) (6 June 1967) para 150; Wright 1968, p. 9.

[30] Repertoire, Supp. 1966–1968, Chap. 8, p. 136.

[31] Ibid.

[32] Mueller et al. 2006, p. 204.

[33] Sorenson 2008, p. 27.

51 of the Charter of the United Nations.'[34] Israeli Minister of Foreign Affairs, Abba Eban argued, on the other hand, that the situation had already passed beyond the utmost point of danger when Israeli forces launched their attack. His country had thus 'responded defensively in full strength' in accordance with the 'inherent right of self-defence formulated in Article 51 of the United Nations Charter.'[35]

The sequence of events that led to the Israeli pre-emptive strike did indeed create a situation where an armed attack seemed unavoidable. Although the US was pressing for a diplomatic solution, its intention never materialised. The escalation of events in the last days of May and in the early days of June 1967 created a serious threat for Israel. The expulsion of UNEF, the closure of the Straits of Tiran, the extensive mobilizations on the Israeli border and the repeated threats coming from Nasser and other Egyptian representatives convinced the Israeli government that the threat of an armed attack was not only serious, but also imminent.[36] Although, taken separately, the Arab steps could not amount to an armed attack or a threat thereof, their aggregation was interpreted as showing the imminence of an invasion. It is irrelevant whether the situation was indeed as desperate as it seemed. Assuming that the Israeli authorities assessed the available information in good faith, their resort to a pre-emptive strike was justified. Hindsight knowledge should not play a role in assessing the legality of pre-emption, when the threat of an armed attack is seen as sufficiently credible and imminent to justify defence.[37] As Dinstein maintains, the legality of defensive action must be weighed 'on the ground of the information available' and on the basis of a reasonable interpretation at the moment of action.[38] Although it has been maintained since then that Nasser did not actually want to resort to force,[39] at that particular moment, the Israeli government saw itself facing an apparently hopeless situation. The perception of the threat by Israel can be compared with the perception the British War Cabinet had in 1940 when it decided to resort to *Operation Catapult*. Although, with hindsight knowledge, it could be established that the other side was in fact not preparing to attack, the threat was perceived as present and inevitable on the basis of the available information at the time, interpreted in good faith.[40]

Another thorny issue in relation to the Six-Day War was the annexation of Arab territories by Israel. Israeli forces managed to take East Jerusalem from Jordanian control and annex the Golan Heights, the Gaza Strip, the West Bank and the Sinai

---

[34] Statement of Mr. Kony (United Arab Republic), SCOR, 22th Session, 1347th meeting, UN Doc. S/PV.1347(OR) (5 June 1967) para 53.

[35] Statement of Mr. Eban (Israel), SCOR, 22th Session, 1348th meeting, UN Doc. S/PV.1348 (OR) (6 June 1967) paras 153, 155.

[36] Wright 1968, p. 27; Shapira 1971, pp. 75–76.

[37] Dinstein 2005, p. 192; Gill 2007, p. 139.

[38] Dinstein 2005, p. 192.

[39] Mueller et al. 2006, p. 200.

[40] See *supra* 4.6.

Peninsula.[41] Numerous authors have expressed their opinion that the continuous Israeli occupation of Arab territories suggested that the June 1967 actions went beyond the limits of self-defence.[42] The wording of Security Council Resolution 242 of November 1967 seems to confirm that opinion. The resolution did not condemn the Israeli action and attempted to secure a trade-off between the parties by restating the pre-war status quo. It affirmed, nevertheless, that 'the establishment of a just and lasting peace in the Middle East' had to include the 'withdrawal of Israel armed forces from territories occupied in the recent conflict.'[43] Arab states have interpreted this statement as a demand of immediate and unconditional withdrawal.[44] Israel has regarded that requirement conditional upon the satisfaction of another one, also affirmed by the Security Council in the same resolution: 'termination of all claims or states of belligerency and respect for and acknowledgement of the sovereignty, territorial integrity and political independence of every State in the area.'[45] The substantive issues arising from the different interpretations are numerous and they go beyond the purpose of the present research. It may suffice to note that the protracted occupation of territories annexed during armed action (be that defensive) cannot be justified within the limits of the right of self-defence.[46]

Some authors have maintained that the Six-Day War should not be considered an instance of anticipatory action in self-defence, because Israel had not characterized it as such before the Security Council.[47] While the specific claims advanced by a country in justification of its use of force are undoubtedly important, the acts of the particular state cannot be subdued by its statements. Allowing such an interpretation would mean to examine state practice only on the basis of what states say and not also on what they do. The Six-Day War is an instance of state practice in which anticipatory action in self-defence was *undertaken*. The legality of this particular exercise of self-defence was generally accepted by both states and legal publicists. Many commentators treat it as the *locus classicus* of anticipatory action in self-defence.[48]

The Israeli action meets the requirements of necessity. On the basis of the information available at the time and in the face of the escalating events, the Israeli Cabinet concluded, in good faith, that an armed attack was imminent and that it was absolutely necessary to act. From the point of view of proportionality, the

---

[41] Sorenson 2008, p. 28; Mueller et al. 2006, p. 204.

[42] Wright 1968, p. 27; Greig 1991, pp. 394–395; Mueller et al. 2006, p. 204. See *per a contrario*: Shapira 1971, pp. 77–79.

[43] SC Res. 242 (1967) para 1(i).

[44] Greig 1991, p. 395.

[45] SC Res. 242 (1967) para 1(ii). Greig 1991, p. 395.

[46] Constantinou 2000, pp. 72–74; *Per a contrario*: Schwebel 1970, pp. 344–347.

[47] Christakis 2005, pp. 215–216; Corten 2008, pp. 660–661; Gazzini 2005, p. 150; Ruys 2010, pp. 274–275.

[48] Gill 2007, pp. 138–139; Shapira 1971, pp. 75–76; Wright 1968, p. 27.

immediate actions of Israel were lawful. The continuous annexation of territories exceeded, however, the limits of self-defence.

8.2.3 The 'Yom Kippur War' (1973)

After the 1967 war, a series of smaller clashes occurred between Egyptian troops and the Palestine Liberation Organization, on one side, and Israeli forces, on the other. The 'War of Attrition', as it became known, was waged by Egypt in order to make Israel hand back the Sinai Peninsula.[49]

After the death of Nasser in September 1970, President Anwar Sadat attempted to soften the Israelis with a more peaceful rhetoric, calling for a diplomatic solution. Since that approach did not secure the desired result, President Sadat became more and more inclined to pursue a military solution.[50]

For most of 1973, Israeli intelligence saw the occurrence of war improbable.[51] Israel had been receiving numerous threats from all surrounding Arab states, which were all dismissed as regular large-scale military exercises or deterrence tactics.[52] Worrisome information only came a few days before the attack.[53] Nonetheless, Israel decided not to launch a pre-emptive strike. First, it was still not completely clear to Israeli intelligence that an attack would take place and, secondly, the Israeli government did not want to provoke a negative US reaction.[54] What the Israeli cabinet did do, however, was the mobilization of approximately 100,000 men in preparations for a potential attack.[55]

The so-called Yom Kippur War started with a double-attack of Egyptian forces from the Sinai and Syrian forces from Golan. The Israelis suffered great losses in the beginning, but regained their momentum towards the end of the war.[56]

The Israeli decision not to act pre-emptively is an example of state practice in which resort to self-defence was contemplated, but not pursued. Israeli intelligence did not have enough information to secure a credible justification of an anticipatory strike. Although the threat of an armed attack was perceived by Israel, there was no conclusive evidence of its imminence. For that reason, the Israeli government chose to sit and wait for the Arab offensive to begin. The fear of a negative US reaction should not be dismissed either. Without having

[49] Mueller et al. 2006, p. 206; Sorenson 2008, pp. 28–29.

[50] Mueller et al. 2006, p. 206.

[51] Ibid., p. 207; Sorenson 2008, p. 30. See *per a contrario*, Levite 1987, p. 153; Israel knew attack was coming: Envoy to the US asserts (1973), p. 1.

[52] Mueller et al. 2006, p. 207; Sorenson 2008, p. 30.

[53] Mueller et al. 2006, p. 207; Sorenson 2008, p. 30.

[54] Mueller et al. 2006, p. 207.

[55] Ibid.

[56] Mansfield 2003, pp. 294–295.

comprehensive information about the imminence of an Arab attack, Israel could have never convinced the US that its anticipatory action met the requirements of necessity.

8.3 The Remedial Dimension of Self-Defence

After discussing a few instances of state practice where the anticipatory dimension of self-defence was relevant, cases in which the remedial dimension was more dominant will be analysed. It is important to reiterate that only those cases will be discussed that purported significant questions as to the temporality of the use of force. These instances are the 1980–1988 Iran–Iraq War and the 1982 Falklands War. The analysis of these cases is necessary to see how the limits of self-defence were understood in remedial action and whether any significant difference from the limits of anticipatory action can be discerned.

8.3.1 The Iran–Iraq War (1980–1988)

Iran and Iraq had long disputed the border between them along the Shatt al-Arab river. In Algiers in 1975 the two countries finally reached an agreement that established the border to be running along the median course of the river.[57] This accord became to be known as the Algiers Agreement.[58]

In the immediate aftermath of the Islamic Revolution, the new Iraqi regime, led by Saddam Hussein, adopted an appeasing approach towards the government of Ayatollah Khomeini. In a speech in July 1979, Saddam Hussein expressed Iraq's desire to establish relations of friendship and co-operation with Iran, based on the principle of non-interference in internal affairs.[59] The Iranian regime, however, seemed to be far less amiable. Khomeini planned to disseminate his religious doctrine throughout the Muslim world.[60] He regarded Saddam an atheist and demanded the overthrow of his regime.[61]

By the end of 1979, both countries were fully engaged in blaming each other for subversive campaigns. Tehran was accused for aiding Kurdish separatists and Shiite movements in Iraq, whereas Iraq was blamed for supporting Arab elements

[57] Sorenson 2008, p. 34.
[58] Karsh 2002, pp. 12, 22.
[59] Ibid., p. 13.
[60] Karsh 2002, pp. 12–13.
[61] Sorenson 2008, p. 34.

in Iran.[62] Moreover, Iran was accused of organizing or supporting several terrorist and sabotage acts against the Iraqi population and some high-ranking officials.[63] Similar accusations were made by Iran as well: the 'continual dispatch of mercenaries and Ba'ath agents and armed groups' into several Iranian provinces as well as the provision of assistance to 'anti-revolutionary elements' and 'persons sought in Iran for having committed crimes against the population during the Shah's regime.'[64]

Against this background, the controversy that accelerated the sequence of events was related to the Shatt al-Arab border. On 7 September 1980, Iraq accused Iran of shelling Iraqi border towns.[65] The shelling was said to have taken place three days earlier, on 4 September 1980.[66] These border towns were located on the territory which, according to the Algiers Agreement, belonged to Iraq. Consequently, Iraq moved to 'liberate' them. In fact, it was deploying its army along the Iran–Iraq border.[67]

After both parties denounced the Algiers agreement, on 22 September 1980, Iraq launched a full-scale invasion against Iran. As justification, Iraq invoked its right of 'preventive self-defence to defend its people and territories' against the alleged Iranian shelling.[68] Since the military offensive covered a much greater area than that of the shelled towns, Iraq claimed that 'it was necessary to push the Iranian forces away from Iraqi towns situated within the range of Iranian heavy and long-range artillery capable of shelling.'[69] Consequently, Iraq maintained that 'the presence of the Iraqi military forces inside Iranian territories is solely for defensive purposes.'[70]

Instead of a quick victory for Iraq, the war dragged on, with both sides launching indecisive attacks and producing a large number of casualties.[71] Iraq was led by its belief that the Islamic Revolution had weakened Iran's military capabilities.[72] Although this was partly true, the Iranian forces regained their momentum and soon moved on to the offensive.[73] The war protracted for eight

---

[62] Karsh 2002, p. 13; Kaikobad 1992, pp. 52–53.

[63] Statement of Mr. Hammadi (Iraq), SCOR, 35th Session, 2250th meeting, UN Doc. S/PV.2250 (15 October 1980) paras 18–19, 21–22; Karsh, p. 13.

[64] Statement of Mr. Rajai (Iran), SCOR, 35th Session, 2251st meeting, UN Doc. S/PV.2251 (17 October 1980) para 18.

[65] Karsh, p. 14.

[66] UN Doc. S/14236 (1980).

[67] Karsh 2002, p. 14.

[68] UN Doc. S/14236 (1980).

[69] Ibid.

[70] Ibid.

[71] Sorenson 2008, p. 34.

[72] Ibid.; Karsh 2002, pp. 14, 19.

[73] Karsh 2002, pp. 33–42, 48–51.

years and it escalated to include missile attacks against cities in both countries, the use of chemical weapons by Iraq and attacks on oil tankers in the Gulf.[74]

During the war, the Security Council stopped short of condemning either side for aggression, although it repeatedly called for ceasefire and vehemently condemned the use of chemical weapons.[75] Nonetheless, in December 1991, the then UN Secretary-General, Javier Perez de Cuellar, characterized the Iraqi invasion as an aggression and thus, a clear violation of the prohibition to use force. In his view, the attack of 22 September 1980 against Iran could not be justified on the basis of the UN Charter.[76] Even if Iran was responsible for 'some encroachment on Iraqi territory,' such acts could not justify 'Iraq's aggression against Iran.'[77]

Assuming that Iran did indeed organize or support subversive campaigns and terrorist attacks against Iraq and assuming that it did shell a few towns on the border, the threat posed by its conduct was never of such gravity as to justify a full-scale invasion. Moreover, there was no evidence of Iran preparing for an armed action against Iraq and its subversive tactics never got close to overturning the Iraqi government. In other words, there was neither one major event, nor a sequence of events that could amount to an armed attack or an imminent threat thereof, certainly not one of a scale to justify the Iraqi invasion. Although Iraq invoked its right to 'preventive'[78] self-defence, the understanding given to self-defence at that time—on the basis of the UN Charter and customary law—did not justify Iraq's action. Iran, on the other hand, had all reasons to invoke the right of self-defence, at least in the beginning of the war. Ensuring the withdrawal of Iraqi forces from its territory and putting an end to the threat posed by those forces was within the limits of self-defence as understood at that time. The reaction of Iran has since been recognized as justifiable under Article 51 of the UN Charter.[79]

The Iran–Iraqi war has a double significance for the concept of self-defence. First, it pertains to an unjustified claim of self-defence on behalf of Iraq. The threat posed by Iranian subversive activities and alleged cross-border shelling never reached the threshold of imminence creating an immediate need for action. Consequently, the Iraqi claim of 'preventive'[80] self-defence did not meet the requirement of necessity. Secondly, this instance of state practice involves a justified claim of self-defence on behalf of Iran. The invasion of Iranian territory by Iraqi troops clearly amounted to an ongoing armed attack and created an immediate need to take action and oust the invader. The protracted nature of the conflict on both sides did, however, exceed the proportionality requirement of self-defence.

---

[74] Sorenson 2008, pp. 34–35.

[75] SC Res. 479 (1980); 514 and 522 (1982); 540 (1983), 554 (1984); 582 and 588 (1986); 598 (1987); 612 and 620 (1988).

[76] UN Doc. S/23273 (1991), para 6.

[77] Ibid., para 7. On the significance of this report, see Gray 2004, p. 97.

[78] UN Doc. S/14236 (1980).

[79] Dekker 1992, pp. 258–259.

[80] UN Doc. S/14236 (1980).

8.3.2 The Falklands War (1982)

Another instance of self-defence against invasion was the Falklands War of 1982 between Argentina and the UK. The sovereignty over the Falkland Islands (Las Malvinas) has been subject to a longstanding dispute between the two states. The dispute concerns both the question of discovery and that of ownership of the Islands.[81] Since 1833, the Falklands have been under British rule, but Argentina has maintained claims of sovereignty. Several rounds of negotiations took place in the second half of the twentieth century between the two countries, but no settlement was reached.[82]

The situation significantly deteriorated by the beginning of 1982, when Argentinean scrap-metal merchants landed on one of the islands, without permission from the British base and upon arrival hoisted the Argentine flag.[83] British ice patrol ship, the HMS *Endurance*, removed some of the workmen, but a small number remained.[84] In the ensuing diplomatic correspondence with his Argentinean counterpart, UK Foreign Secretary Lord Carrington pledged Britain's commitment to resolving the conflict by peaceful means, on condition that the remaining Argentinean workmen would leave South Georgia immediately.[85] Argentina rejected such a possibility and ordered instead the reinforcement of its own naval forces. In fact, the Argentinean Junta had been planning an invasion of the Falklands as early as January 1982. Fearing further British reinforcements, on 26 March, the Junta decided to invade in the beginning of April.[86] On the same day, the British intelligence source in Buenos Aires sent out warnings that an Argentine invasion of the Islands was imminent. Two days later, Argentina formally restated its claim to the Falkland Islands and Dependencies and refused further negotiations with Britain. A designated naval task force set sail on 28 March from Puerto Belgrano southwards. Three days later, the Argentinean task force changed course and headed directly to the Falklands.[87] At the same time, the British government ordered several warships to sail south from Gibraltar.[88]

In a letter dated 1 April 1982, Britain requested a UN Security Council meeting. In this letter, Britain decried the refusal of the Argentinean government to resolve the conflict by diplomatic means and warned of an imminent invasion of the Falkland Islands. The Argentinean representative contended that his country had been the victim of 150 years of repeated acts of aggression on behalf of the UK

[81] Freedman 2005, vol 1, pp. 3–8.

[82] Freedman and Gamba-Stonehouse 1991, pp. 7–13.

[83] Ibid., pp. 47–48.

[84] Freedman 2005, vol 1, pp. 184–185.

[85] Ibid., p. 182.

[86] Ibid., p. 187.

[87] Freedman and Gamba-Stonehouse 1991, p. 109.

[88] Ibid., p. 76.

and that the situation at hand amounted to a serious and imminent threat that left Argentina no choice than to resort to legitimate defence.[89]

Notwithstanding the ensuing statement of the Security Council to refrain from the use or threat of force, in the early hours of 2 April 1982, Argentina launched *Operation Rosario* and invaded the Falklands.[90] An emergency cabinet meeting in London on the same day approved the sending of a task force to liberate the Falkland Islands.[91]

The next day, the UN Security Council passed Resolution 502 determining 'the existence of a breach of peace in the region' and demanding an immediate withdrawal of all Argentinean forces from the Islands.[92]

Apart from the warships already sailing southwards, preparations for deployment of a British task force started on the same day, 3 April. By 7 April, the first wave of the task force was sailing towards the operation zone.[93] In the following days, several other ships and troops were sent to the South Atlantic.[94] Because of the great distance, it took the task force three to five weeks to reach the operation zone. On 26 April 1982, British forces retook South Georgia; the Argentinean forces on the Falkland Islands surrendered on 14 June 1982.[95] The war resulted in almost 300 British and more than 600 Argentinean casualties as well as substantial material losses on both sides.[96]

Although both parties invoked Article 51 of the UN Charter in justifying their actions,[97] the wording of Resolution 502 clearly favoured the British position. The unprovoked Argentinean attack on South Georgia and the Falkland Islands could hardly be characterized as a legitimate use of the right to self-defence.

The question remains whether the temporal remoteness of the British response can be justified within the limits of legitimate self-defence. The invasion of the Falklands occurred on 2 April 1982, whereas the actual hostilities between Argentinean and British forces started only four weeks after, when the naval force reached the operation zone. According to Neff, the British operation was not strictly-speaking self-defence, because the takeover had already occurred. It was rather a 'recovery operation, a reversal of a *fait accompli*.'[98] This opinion gives little attention to the geographical disparity between Britain and the South Atlantic

89 Repertoire, Supp. 1981–1984, Chap. 8, pp. 224–226.

90 The amphibious landing of some 200 Argentinean Marines with armoured vehicles was backed by air force. The aircraft carrier *25 de Mayo*, escorted by several destroyers, provided support with approximately 1000 Marines on board. Freedman 2005, vol 2, pp. 7–9.

91 Freedman and Gamba-Stonehouse 1991, p. 124.

92 SC Res. 502 (1982).

93 In addition to aircraft carriers *Hermes* and *Invincible*, three submarines, 11 destroyers and frigates as well as several other ships set sail. Freedman and Gamba-Stonehouse 1991, pp. 128–129.

94 Freedman 2005, vol 2, pp. 62–64.

95 Ibid., pp. 248–249, 651–652.

96 Ibid., pp. 772–780.

97 Repertoire, Supp. 1981–1984, Chap. 8, pp. 224–226.

98 Neff 2005, p. 330.

islands. Some 6,700 nautical miles separated Britain from its Southern Atlantic territories. In the absence of the geographical disparity, it would have been interesting to see where the parallel claims of self-defence against an 'imminent invasion' or 'imminent threat' could have led.[99]

In casu, even before the Argentinean invasion took place, the British ordered the deployment of several warships to the South Atlantic from either the Gibraltar or from home ports. All these precautionary measures were taken before the actual invasion occurred, but it took time until the ships arrived at their destination.

Secondly, on the very day of the Falklands attack, the British cabinet met up in an emergency session and decided to send a task force to liberate the Islands. That decision was endorsed by the House of Commons the next day, while South Georgia was being invaded.[100] Britain took prompt action in the face of an ongoing attack and decided the resort to self-defence while the invasion was still ongoing and in its immediate aftermath. Accordingly, after three days of hasty preparations, on 5 April the first ships of the task force pulled out of ports around Britain and from Gibraltar.[101] The geographical disparity between the departure points (home ports or Gibraltar) and the target (South Atlantic) as well as the amount of time needed for assembling a considerable amphibious task force are factors that cannot be ignored when considering the justifiability and timeliness of the British defensive action.

Thirdly, the expressed purpose of the British action was to 'secure the withdrawal of Argentine forces from the Islands.'[102] In other words, the aim of the British operation was to repel the attack of the occupying forces. The fact that it took four weeks for the British vessels to actually get to the Islands, engage in hostilities and drive out the Argentinean forces does not render the principal objective of the operation remote.

The Falklands War is an instance of state practice where a justified claim of self-defence was made against an invasion that clearly created an immediate need for action. It is an instance of remedial self-defence, when action was taken after the armed attack had occurred. The fact that the actual clash of forces occurred four weeks after the armed attack achieved its purpose is immaterial as long as the necessity to overcome that result existed.

8.4 Self-Defence Claims with Anticipatory and Remedial Dimensions

It is instructive to look at a few instances of state practice where both the anticipatory and the remedial dimension of self-defence is present. As will be shown below, most of such cases involve the exercise of self-defence against small-scale,

---

[99] Repertoire, Supp. 1981–1984, Chap. 8, pp. 224–226.

[100] Freedman and Gamba-Stonehouse 1991, p. 122.

[101] Ibid., p. 128.

[102] Biffen 1982, pp. 519–520.

repeated attacks (hit-and-run tactics).[103] Nonetheless, the South Ossetian War demonstrates that this is not always the case. The exercise of self-defence can take both anticipatory and remedial forms depending on the chronology of the relevant events. The aim of this section is to show that it is not always practical to talk about strictly anticipatory action or strictly remedial action in self-defence, because the two dimensions can be intrinsically interconnected.

8.4.1 The UK Bombing of a Yemeni Fort (1964)

In 1964, the UK bombed the Harib fort in Yemen in response to cross-border raids against the South Arabian Federation. Before the Security Council, the UK claimed that several of those incidents, all started by the Yemeni forces, had been registered over the previous year and reported to the Council.[104] Moreover, a fresh series of incidents had begun in March 1964, all of which had been reported to the Security Council.[105] These incidents had convinced the government of the South Arabian Federation and the government of the UK that 'a deliberate and increasing attack by Yemen against the Federation was under way.'[106] The UK considered itself responsible for the defence and protection of its territories, including the Federation, and 'it was in the fulfilment of that responsibility that the counter-attack of 28 March had been launched.'[107] The UK went on to show that the attack was directed at one particular target, the Harib fort, 'a military and isolated target about one mile outside Harib town itself.'[108] Moreover, before the attack, 'leaflets in Arabic were dropped in the area advising all persons to leave immediately.'[109] The weapons used (rockets and cannon fire) did not go astray and 'all possible measures had been taken to minimize the loss of life and property.'[110] The exposé of the UK representative was received with scepticism by the members of the Council. Several representatives (such as those of Iraq, Syria and Egypt) contended that the British action could not be characterized as a defensive response, but rather as an act of reprisal.[111] The British delegate rejected the accusations by asserting that the action was taken in response to an urgent request from the

[103] See *infra* 14.5.

[104] Repertoire, Supp. 1964–1965, Chap. 8, p. 128; UN Doc. S/5343 (1963); UN Doc. S/5424 (1963).

[105] UN Doc. S/5618 (1964); UN Doc. S/5628 (1964); UN Doc. S/5632 (1964).

[106] Repertoire, Supp. 1964–1965, Chap. 8, p. 128.

[107] Ibid.

[108] Ibid.; SCOR, 19th Session, 1106th meeting, UN Doc. S/PV.1106 (2 April 1964) para 54.

[109] Ibid.

[110] Repertoire, Supp. 1964–1965, Chap. 8, p. 128.

[111] Ibid.; SCOR, 19th Session, 1106th–1109th meeting, UN Doc. S/PV.1106–S/PV.1109 (2–7 April 1964).

Federation 'to protect the interests and integrity of their country.'[112] He went on to explain that there was a clear distinction between reprisals and self-defence. The former was of a retributive or punitive nature, whereas the latter was authorized by the Charter against an armed attack.[113] The British delegate contended that:

> The use of armed force to repel or prevent an attack—that is, legitimate action of a defensive nature—may sometimes have to take the form of a counter-attack. [...] The territory of the Federation had been subjected to a series of acts, over a considerable period, of an aggressive nature, against which the people of the Federation have asked to be defended.[114]

The Security Council was not convinced of the necessity and proportionality of the British intervention and, consequently, it condemned the action as a reprisal.[115] This instance of state practice involved a claim of self-defence against a hit-and-run type of an attack. The reason why the claim of self-defence put forward by the UK was rejected by the Security Council was that the sporadic attacks of Yemeni forces were not viewed as serious enough to amount to an armed attack that gave rise to the immediate need to act (necessity). Although the UK representative went to great lengths in emphasizing the carefully targeted nature of the airstrike (proportionality), the claim was overall rejected by the Security Council members. The approach of the Security Council to claims of self-defence against hit-and-run attacks will be elaborated in Chapter 10.

8.4.2 The Gulf of Tonkin Incident (1964)

Arguments similar to those of the UK regarding the Harib fort were put forward by the US in connection with its actions against North Vietnamese torpedo boats and supply facilities. On 2 August 1964, the US destroyer *Maddox* was cruising off the coast of North Vietnam, in the Gulf of Tonkin. The ship was authorized to gain intelligence on North Vietnamese radar facilities and to maintain communications with South Vietnamese commandos conducting raids along the North Vietnamese coast.[116] As it was patrolling three to five miles inside the 12-mile limit claimed by North Vietnam, it was approached by three high-speed North Vietnamese torpedo-boats in attack formation. All three attacking vessels directed machine-gun fire at the *Maddox* and two of them fired torpedoes which the destroyer evaded by changing course. After the attack was broken off, the *Maddox* continued on a

---

112 Repertoire, Supp. 1964–1965, Chap. 11, p. 194.

113 Ibid.

114 SCOR, 19th Session, 1109th meeting, UN Doc. S/PV.1109 (7 April 1964) paras 26–27.

115 SC Res. 188 (1964).

116 Martel 1993, p. 36.

southerly course in international waters. The US saw that as a 'clearly deliberate armed attack against a naval unit of the US on patrol on the high seas.'[117] Two days later, in the early evening hours of 4 August, officers of destroyers *Maddox* and *C. Turner Joy* believed that they were under attack from North Vietnamese torpedo boats. In a strong, sonar-distorting storm, the questionable sonar readings suggested that many torpedoes might have been launched against the ships, but since no sightings of torpedoes or vessels were confirmed and since neither destroyer sustained any damage, clear evidence of an actual attack could not be established.[118]

Nonetheless, the then US President Lyndon B. Johnson believed that the evidence was enough to order air attacks against four torpedo-boat bases and a major oil storage facility deep into the territory of North Vietnam.[119] Announcing the US response on television, the president referred to 'repeated acts of violence against the armed forces of the US and justified the raids as a necessary defensive response.[120] The same arguments were advanced before the Security Council. The US complained of 'deliberate and repeated armed attacks' against naval vessels 'on routine operations.'[121] Although the evidence of the second attack was far from being conclusive, the US delegate asserted before the Council that on 4 August, the destroyers *Maddox* and *C. Turner Joy* were again subjected to an attack by several motor torpedo-boats of the North Vietnamese Navy. Moreover, it was claimed that 'numerous torpedoes were fired' and that 'the attack lasted for over two hours.'[122] Accordingly, the US invoked its right to self-defence and justified the ensuing air attacks on this basis.[123] It characterized the raids as 'limited and relevant measures to secure its naval units against further aggression.'[124] The UK reacted favourably to the American argument. The British delegate stated that the US had a right in accordance with the principle of self-defence in international law to take action directed to prevent the recurrence of attacks on its ships. Accordingly, 'preventive action in accordance with that aim is an essential right which is embraced by any definition of that principle of self-defence.'[125] Conversely, the representative of Czechoslovakia contended that the US response exceeded the limits of self-defence, because the alleged Vietnamese attack had been immediately followed by an equally alleged act of self-defence.

---

117 Repertoire, Supp. 1964–1965, Chap. 8, p. 135; SCOR, 19th Session, 1140th meeting, UN Doc. S/PV.1140 (5 August 1964) paras 35–42.

118 Martel 1993, p. 36.

119 Ibid., p. 37.

120 Ibid.

121 SCOR, 19th Session, 1140th meeting, UN Doc. S/PV.1140 (5 August 1964) para 34.

122 Repertoire, Supp. 1964–1965, Chap. 8, p. 135; SCOR, Session, 1140th meeting, UN Doc. S/PV.1140 (5 August 1964) para 42.

123 SCOR, 19th Session, 1140th meeting, UN Doc. S/PV.1140 (5 August 1964) para 46.

124 Ibid., para 44.

125 Repertoire, Supp. 1964–1965, Chap. 11, p. 195.

Consequently, there was no need for the air attacks against naval bases in North Vietnam and the US response was in fact an act of reprisal.[126] No resolution was adopted by the Security Council on the issue, because of the veto powers of the US. Nonetheless, the reaction in the Security Council showed that the US claim failed on both the necessity and proportionality conditions. Assuming that the second attack on the US warships did indeed take place, the magnitude of the attacks, taken collectively, was far from amounting to an armed attack giving rise to an immediate need to carry out airstrikes deep into the territory of North Vietnam.

8.4.3 US Bombing of Libya (1986)

This instance of state practice involves another claim of self-defence against hit-and-run attacks. The air strikes took place against the background of a number of terrorist attacks against US nationals and property around the world during the course of 1985 and early 1986.[127] Libya was also suspected of harbouring and supporting several Palestinian and other armed groups that were accused of carrying out terrorist attacks in Western countries.[128] In 1984, a British policewoman was caught in cross fire outside the Libyan embassy in London and was shot dead by Libyan assailants.[129] In 1985, a Libyan diplomat at the United Nations was declared *persona non grata* in connection with a plot to kill Libyan dissidents in the US.[130] In December 1985, airline offices at airports in Rome and Vienna were bombed and Libya was widely suspected of involvement.[131] During the several years prior to the American air strike, the Libyan President, Colonel Qadhafi, made frequent public statements about 'exporting revolution' and forcing 'America to fight on a hundred fronts.'[132] Tensions were further aggravated with the bombing of a West-Berlin discotheque on 5 April 1986. The La Belle discotheque was frequented by American servicemen and the explosion killed two people (one US soldier and a Turkish woman) and injured more than 200 (including 50 US soldiers).[133]

---

126 Ibid. See also Schick 1968, p. 981.

127 Franck 2002, pp. 89–90; Greenwood 1987, p. 934.

128 Baker 1994, p. 104; Greenwood 1987, pp. 934–935; Intoccia 1987, pp. 180–181; McCredie 1987, p. 218.

129 Greenwood 1987, p. 934; Intoccia 1987, p. 181.

130 Intoccia 1987, p. 181.

131 Greenwood 1987, p. 934; Intoccia 1987, p. 182; McCredie 1987, p. 215.

132 Greenwood 1987, p. 934; Intoccia 1987, pp. 181–182

133 Greenwood 1987, p. 934. According to another account, two American soldiers died in the bombing and 154 persons were wounded, of which 50–60 were US servicemen (Intoccia 1987, p. 185). See also: The President's Address to the Nation, 14 April 1986, pp. 1–2 (for mentioning 230 wounded).

The US invoked its right of self-defence and characterized the air strikes as 'pre-emptive action against terrorist installations' that would 'not only diminish Colonel Qadhafi's capacity to export terror,' but would also 'provide him with incentives and reasons to alter his criminal behaviour.'[134] The aerial bombings targeted air fields, military barracks and training camps near Tripoli, Benina and Benghazi.[135] The bombing resulted in 37 dead and 93 wounded.[136] During the bombing of Qadhafi's military headquarters (which also served as his personal residence), his step-daughter was killed and two of his sons were wounded.[137]

Before the Security Council, US Ambassador Walters reiterated the claim of acting under 'the inherent right of self-defence' on the basis of which the US executed 'a series of carefully planned airstrikes against terrorist-related targets in Libya.'[138] Walters went on to explain that US forces had struck targets that were part of Libya's military infrastructure (command and control system, intelligence communication, logistics and training facilities), sites used 'to carry out Libya's harsh policy of international terrorism.'[139] The ambassador deplored the bombing of the West-Berlin discotheque and went on to say that:

> [I]in the light of that reprehensible act of violence—only the latest in an ongoing pattern of attacks by Libya—and of clear evidence that Libya was planning a multitude of future attacks, the US was compelled to exercise its right of self-defence. The US hopes that this action will discourage Libyan terrorist acts in the future.[140]

Ambassador Walters also pointed out that all prior efforts to stop Libyan terrorism—'quiet diplomacy, public condemnation, economic sanctions and demonstrations of military force'—had failed and the targeted bombing of military sites was the only effective solution left.[141]

The significance of Ambassador Walters's statement for claims of self-defence against hit-and-run attacks will be elaborated in Chapter 10.[142] It is enough to note at this point that despite the efforts of Walters to demonstrate that the airstrikes were both necessary and proportionate, the majority of the Security Council members rejected the explanation.[143] The US, the UK and France vetoed a draft

---

134 The President's Address to the Nation, 14 April 1986, pp. 1–2.

135 Intoccia 1987, p. 179; Greenwood 1987, p. 936.

136 Intoccia 1987, p. 179; McCredie 1987, p. 215. According to Greenwood, the number of civilian casualties was unknown, but press reports at the time spoke of a death-toll of approximately 100 persons and injuries to a greater number. Greenwood 1987, p. 936.

137 Intoccia 1987, p. 179.

138 SCOR, 41th Session, 2674th meeting, UN Doc. S/PV.2674 (15 April 1986) p. 13.

139 Ibid., pp. 13–14.

140 Ibid., p. 17.

141 Ibid., p. 16.

142 See *infra* 10.3.

143 SCOR, 41th Session, 2674th–2682nd meeting, UN Doc. S/PV.2674–S/PV.2682 (15–21 April 1986).

resolution that would have condemned the American airstrikes.[144] The UN General Assembly adopted, nonetheless, a resolution condemning them.[145]

The reaction to the US airstrikes was mixed, although many countries had later acquiesced to economic sanctions imposed upon Libya for its terrorist activities. Some authors have, nonetheless, defended the US line of argumentation.[146]

The claim of self-defence put forward by the US was rejected at the time by most Security Council members and the majority of states in the General Assembly.[147] It is important to highlight here that the claims of self-defence against hit-and-run tactics were based on a more complicated view on the requirements of necessity and proportionality. State-to-state conflicts were generally understood in terms of invasion or occupation (such as the Iran–Iraq War and the Falklands War). An invasion or an occupation was clearly viewed as an armed attack creating an immediate need for action by virtually all members of the United Nations. Hit-and-run attacks carried out by the regular armed forces of a state against the citizens or territory of another were seen as hardly reaching the threshold of an armed attack as required by Article 51, although there was nothing in pre-Charter customary law that would preclude such a conclusion.[148] The approach of the Security Council and the attitude of the legal literature to claims of self-defence against hit-and-run attacks will be elaborated in Chapter 10.[149]

8.4.4 US Missile Attack Against Iraqi Intelligence Headquarters (1993)

Tensions were running high between the US and Iraq after the Persian Gulf War. On 14 April 1993, as former US President George Bush was beginning a three-day visit in Kuwait City to attend a special ceremony in appreciation of his leadership in the previous war, Kuwaiti authorities uncovered an assassination plot against him. Fourteen men were arrested for smuggling plastic explosives into Kuwait intended to be used to assassinate the former president.[150]

The ensuing FBI and CIA investigative reports concluded that 'it was highly likely that the Iraqi Government originated the plot and more than likely that Bush

144 Ibid., 2682nd meeting, UN Doc. S/PV.2682 (21 April 1986) p. 43.

145 GA Res. 41/38 (1986).

146 Greenwood 1987, pp. 933–960; McCredie 1987, pp. 215–242. Dinstein characterized them as 'defensive armed reprisals'. Dinstein 2005, p. 229. For an elaboration of Greenwood's opinion, see *infra* 10.3.

147 Franck 2002, p. 90.

148 See *supra* 6.4.1.

149 See *infra* 10.3–10.5.

150 Baker 1994, pp. 101–102.

was the target.'[151] Additionally, the CIA independently reported that 'there was a strong case that Saddam Hussein directed the plot against Bush.'[152] As a consequence, President Bill Clinton ordered an airstrike against the headquarters of the Iraqi Intelligence Service (IIS). On 26 June 1993, US naval forces launched 23 cruise missiles against the IIS buildings in Baghdad. Three missiles missed their targets and hit a neighbouring residential area, killing eight Iraqi civilians.[153]

The US duly reported its action to the Security Council and justified it as self-defence under Article 51 of the UN Charter. Ambassador to the UN, Madeleine Albright claimed that the airstrike was carried out only after having concluded that there was no reasonable prospect that new diplomatic initiatives or economic pressure could influence the Iraqi government to cease planning such attacks against US citizens.[154] Further, she asserted that the target had been carefully chosen to minimize the risk of civilian casualties.[155]

Most of the Security Council members either endorsed or accepted the attack.[156] France, Hungary, Japan, New Zealand, Russia and the UK expressed their full support for the action.[157] Russia went as far as to assert that the US action was justified by the right of individual and collective self-defence in accordance with Article 51 of the Charter.[158] Brazil, Spain and the Group of Non-Aligned countries also accepted the attack, although their reaction was more moderate.[159] China was the only member of the Security Council that questioned the legality of the US airstrike.[160]

The US airstrikes against Iraq were another instance of self-defence against hit-and-run attacks carried out by regular forces of a state against the citizens of another. Assuming that the information available regarding the assassination attempt was interpreted in good faith by the US government and presupposing that the absence of any reasonable prospect to prevent the planning of such attacks in the future was clearly established, the US action could be regarded as meeting the requirement of necessity. The airstrikes were carried out with surgical accuracy, so the requirement of proportionality also seemed to be met. The specific issues raised by claims of self-defence against hit-and-run tactics will be elaborated in Chapter 10.

---

151 The FBI Laboratory 1997, section D.

152 Ibid.

153 Baker 1994, pp. 102–103; The FBI Laboratory 1997, section D.

154 UN Doc. S/26003 (1993); Franck 2002, p. 94.

155 UN Doc. S/26003 (1993); Franck 2002, p. 94.

156 Baker 1994, p. 103; Franck 2002, p. 94.

157 SCOR, 48th Session, 3245th meeting, UN Doc. S/PV.3245 (27 June 1993) pp. 13 (France), 16 (Japan), 21–22 (UK), 22 (Russia), 23 (New Zealand).

158 Ibid., p. 22.

159 Ibid., pp. 16–17 (Non-Aligned Countries), 17–18 (Brazil), 23–25 (Spain).

160 Ibid., p. 21.

8.4.5 The South Ossetia War (2008)

Another instance of state-to-state conflicts in which both the anticipatory and remedial dimensions of self-defence became relevant was the so-called South Ossetia War between Russia and Georgia. The historical and political background of the conflict between Russia and Georgia involves two sets of complex, overlapping relations between Georgia and Russia on one hand, and internal relations between Georgia and the breakaway territories of South Ossetia and Abkhazia on the other.[161] This duality was also reflected in the August 2008 armed conflict: there was both an internal conflict (between Georgia and South Ossetia and between Georgia and Abkhazia), and an international conflict between Georgia and Russia.[162] The present section will mainly focus on the conflict between Georgia and Russia, because it is the one that triggered self-defence claims. As regards the internal conflict between Georgia and its breakaway regions, suffice it to say that it involves historically complex claims of self-determination.[163] Nonetheless, it is important to note that one of the main bones of contention in the Georgian–Russian relationship has been the latter's peacekeeping role in Abkhazia and South Ossetia with Georgia repeatedly demanding an internationalisation of the peacekeeping mission to counterbalance Russian control.[164]

In the months leading up to August 2008, sporadic hostile actions and increasingly belligerent rhetoric marked Georgian–Russian relations. Tension in the Georgian-South Ossetian conflict zone started to rise in mid-June 2008 with explosions and mine incidents close to various Georgian- as well as South Ossetian-administrated villages.[165] After the July incident involving a Russian airplane admittedly flying over South Ossetia, Georgia recalled its ambassador to Russia.[166] Although both the Georgians and Ossetians launched numerous artillery attacks on each other's villages and checkpoints throughout July, many experts did not expect that either of the parties to the conflict could be rationally intending to open hostilities.[167]

During the evening and night of 1–2 August 2008, a series of intense and extensive exchange of sniper fire and mortar shelling occurred between the parties causing fatalities and casualties.[168] The exchange of fire continued in the nights of 2–3 and 3–4 August. According to the OSCE Mission to Georgia they were the most serious outbreak of hostilities since the 2004 conflict.[169] From the afternoon

---

161 Report of Fact-Finding Mission in Georgia 2009, p. 2.

162 Ibid., pp. 229–230.

163 Ibid., pp. 2–7; Higgins and O'Reilly 2009, pp. 567– 583.

164 Report of Fact-Finding Mission in Georgia 2009, p. 15.

165 Ibid., p. 204.

166 Ibid., p. 30.

167 Ibid., p. 31.

168 Ibid., p. 207.

169 Ibid., pp. 207–208. The 2004 conflict involved intense fighting between Georgian forces and South Ossetian militia between 8 and 19 August 2004 (see ibid., pp. 12–15).

of 6 August onwards fire was exchanged along the entire line of contact between the Georgian and South Ossetian sides.[170] The exchange of fire continued on 7 August with international observers noting movements of Georgian troops and equipment towards the conflict zone.[171] Diplomatic efforts undertaken that day between the Russian and Georgian sides did not bring any positive results. On the same day, in the afternoon, a ceasefire was observed by both parties that lasted until the evening hours.[172] Shortly before midnight, Georgian forces opened fire and in the early morning hours of 8 August launched a ground offensive against the city of Tskhinvali (the capital of South Ossetia).[173]

As a response, Russia engaged ground and air forces as well as the Black Sea Fleet, also attacking targets on Georgian territory outside South Ossetia.[174] As a result of the Russian armed action, by midnight on 10 August, most Georgian troops had left the territory of South Ossetia.[175] The withdrawing Georgian troops were followed by Russian forces, which crossed the administrative boundaries of South Ossetia and occupied a number of locations in Georgian territory.[176] The armed conflict continued in other parts of Georgia and on the Abkhazian front until 12 August 2008.[177]

According to Georgia, the Russian intervention started earlier than 8 August and was, *inter alia*, a breach of Article 2(4) of the UN Charter and international customary law.[178] Furthermore, according to the Georgian government, its response was confined entirely to its own sovereign territory, was reluctantly undertaken, and was a proportionate, necessary and wholly justified exercise of its customary and Charter right to use force in self-defence.[179]

According to Russia, the aggression perpetrated by the Georgian government against South Ossetia prompted the exercise of self-defence. The purpose of the defensive action was to protect the civilian population of the region and the

---

170 Ibid., p. 208.

171 Ibid.

172 Ibid., pp. 208–209.

173 Ibid., p. 209.

174 Ibid., p. 210.

175 Ibid., p. 211.

176 SCOR, 63rd Session, 5953rd meeting, UN Doc. S/PV.5953 (10 August 2008) p. 3; Report of the Fact-Finding Mission in Georgia 2009, p. 211.

177 SCOR, 63rd Session, 5953rd mtg., UN Doc. S/PV.5953 (10 August 2008) p. 4; Report of the Fact-Finding Mission in Georgia 2009, pp. 212–213.

178 Submission by Georgia entitled: 'Use of Force Issues Arising out of the Russian Federation Invasion of Georgia, 2008', in Report of Fact-Finding Mission in Georgia 2009, p. 186.

179 SCOR, 63rd Session, 5951st and 5952nd meeting, UN Doc. S/PV.5951 and S/PV.5952 (8 August 2008) p. 5 and p. 3, respectively; Submission by Georgia entitled: 'Use of Force Issues Arising Out of The Russian Federation Invasion of Georgia, 2008', in Report of Fact-Finding Mission in Georgia 2009, p. 186.

Russian peacekeeping contingent from the unprovoked Georgian aggression and preclude such armed attacks against them in the future.[180]

Virtually all members of the Security Council expressed grave concern over the escalation of the conflict and called for a diplomatic solution as well as a swift restoration of peace.[181] The representative of the US specifically called upon Russia to cease air and missile attacks against Georgia.[182] At the 10 August meeting of the Security Council, the US representative contended that the Russian action went beyond any reasonable measure to protect its peacekeepers and the civilian population.[183] The criticism as to the extent of the Russian armed action gradually increased over the following days. Other Security Council members, such as Costa Rica, France, Panama and the UK, adopted a more critical position regarding the Russian intervention.[184] The representative of Panama asserted that the Russian intervention was 'entirely disproportionate and, therefore, illegitimate,' because it abused the basic restrictions of the right of self-defence.[185]

The legality of the Georgia–Russia armed conflict as self-defence was assessed by an independent fact-finding mission appointed by the Council of the European Union.[186] The report found that self-defence claims could only be partly maintained. Accordingly, the on-the-spot reaction of Georgian forces to the shelling on 7 August 2008 as well as their defensive actions against Russian troops moving into Georgian territory could be justified as self-defence.[187] Nonetheless, the Georgian offensive of 8 August 2008 against South Ossetia did not meet the requirements of self-defence, because it exceeded the requirements of proportionality. The report stated:

> [I]t is not *per se* decisive that the offensive ordered by President Saakashvili exceeded the South Ossetian armed attacks on Georgian villages, police and peacekeepers by far in quality and the quantity. Proportionality must be judged on the basis of the answers to the following questions: Was the objective of the Georgian air and ground offensive indeed

---

[180] Submission by the Russian Federation entitled: 'Additional General Remarks on the Conflict in August 2008 on Georgia's Aggression against South Ossetia in August 2008', in Report of Fact-Finding Mission in Georgia 2009, pp. 188–189.

[181] SCOR, 63rd Session, 5951st meeting, UN Doc. S/PV.5951 (8 August 2008).

[182] Ibid., 5952nd meeting, UN Doc. S/PV.5952 (8 August 2008) p. 7.

[183] Ibid., 5953rd meeting, UN Doc. S/PV.5953 (10 August 2008) p. 6.

[184] Ibid., pp. 10 (France), 11 (UK), 14 (Costa Rica), 15 (Panama).

[185] Ibid., p. 15.

[186] On 2 December 2008, Ambassador Heidi Tagliavini was appointed Head of the Independent International Fact-Finding Mission on the Conflict in Georgia by the Council of the European Union. According to the Mission's mandate as agreed by the Council, the aim of the fact-finding mission was to investigate the origins and the course of the conflict in Georgia, including with regard to international law, humanitarian law and human rights, and the accusations made in that context (including allegations of war crimes). On 30 September 2009, the results of the investigation were presented in the form of a report to the parties to the conflict, the Council of the European Union, the Organisation for Security and Co-operation in Europe and the United Nations.

[187] Report of Fact-Finding Mission in Georgia 2009, pp. 249–250, 262.

> nothing else but the repulsion of the armed attacks on the Georgian villages, peacekeepers and police? Was there a reasonable relationship between the form, substance and strength of the attack on Tskhinvali and this objective?[188].

The report answered these questions in the negative and found that the Georgian offensive against the South Ossetian capital had a political objective rather than a defensive purpose.[189]

The report rejected the Georgian view that the Russian side carried out an armed attack prior to the Georgian offensive. It also rejected the view that the Russian military preparations of 7 August 2008 could be interpreted as an imminent armed attack. The report stopped short of discussing the legality *per se* of self-defence against an imminent threat of an armed attack. Instead it contended that there were only signs of an 'abstract danger' and not of a 'concrete danger of an imminent attack.'[190] Consequently, the mere Georgian expectation that Russia might plan an invasion did not justify Georgian self-defence.[191]

While the report admitted that there was a Georgian armed attack on Russian peacekeeping forces and military bases, it also asserted that the Russian response exceeded the requirements of necessity and proportionality.[192] While Russian peacekeepers had the right to an immediate response in self-defence, the expulsion of the Georgian forces from South Ossetia, and the defence of South Ossetia as a whole was not a legitimate objective for Russia.[193] Consequently, in the face of extended Russian military action into the territory of Georgia, the Georgian armed forces were acting in legitimate self-defence.[194]

In conclusion, it can be maintained that an armed attack existed on both sides, but at different times. The continuous shelling of Georgian positions on 7 August 2008 could only justify on-the-spot reaction. Instead, Georgian troops moved into offensive and attacked the capital of South Ossetia. That action qualified as an armed attack. Nonetheless, for the Russian side, that armed attack could only justify purely defensive action on the part of Russian peacekeepers and other military elements. Instead, the Russian response went beyond the remaining requirements of self-defence (immediacy and proportionality) and constituted a

---

[188] Ibid., p. 251.

[189] Ibid.

[190] The report found that despite all the tensions between the conflicting parties in the night of 7–8 August, and although there were Russian troops near the Georgian border north of the Roki tunnel, which had been deployed there for the 'Kavkaz 2008' exercise, it could not be verified that they were about to launch an attack on Georgia. Neither could an alleged 'large-scale incursion of Russian troops into Georgian territory' starting already in the morning of 7 August 2008 be verified by the Mission, although there were strong indications of some Russian military presence in South Ossetia beyond peacekeepers prior to 8 August 14.30 p.m. Report of Fact-Finding Mission in Georgia 2009, pp. 255–256.

[191] Ibid., p. 256.

[192] Ibid., pp. 269, 274–275.

[193] Ibid., p. 274.

[194] Ibid., p. 262.

further armed attack that triggered defensive action from the Georgian forces. The approach of the Security Council shows that, although members were reluctant to condemn the use of force *per se*, criticism as to the necessity and proportionality of the armed conflict was repeatedly voiced.

8.5 Concluding Remarks

This chapter analysed several instances of state practice which had two common elements. First, as with all instances analysed in Part II, they involved a claim of self-defence—used or contemplated. Secondly, specific for this chapter, they pertained to conflicts between states.

On the basis of these cases, it can be established that, in the case of state-to-state conflicts, the temporal dimension of the post-Charter concept of self-defence pertained to three moments: before, during and after an armed attack. The Six-Day War is an instance of the lawful exercise of anticipatory action in self-defence before an armed attack had occurred. The Israeli attitude before the outbreak of the Yom Kippur War is an instance of state practice where anticipatory action was not resorted to, although contemplated, because there was no perception of an imminent threat. The 1956 Sinai Campaign is an unlawful exercise of self-defence, because the limits of the anticipatory dimension were not respected.

The Iran–Iraq War is a case in which self-defence was exercised against an ongoing armed attack. The Falklands War involved the exercise of self-defence after an armed attack had occurred with the purpose of ousting the invader. The South Ossetia War involved both claims of anticipatory and remedial action in self-defence, although only some of the claims were justified.

The cases involving hit-and-run tactics (UK bombing of a Yemeni fort, the Gulf of Tonkin incident, the US bombing of Libya and the US airstrikes against Iraq) purport a more complicated temporal dimension of self-defence that will be discussed in Chapter 10.[195]

Table 8.1 illustrates how claims of self-defence are problematic regardless of their temporal dimension. The aim of the representation is to show the different nature of threats perceived by states contemplating or taking action in self-defence, the problematic issues of the action and the general reaction to them. The table also shows, however, that, most of the time, the fulfilment of the requirements of necessity and proportionality mirrors the reaction to the specific instance of use of force. On this basis, conclusions as to the perceived limits of self-defence can be drawn.

Concerning the conditionality of an armed attack, it is reasonable to conclude that in post-Charter state-to-state conflicts, a restrictive interpretation of that notion was perceivable. First of all, non-forceful 'attacks' were not accepted as bases for

---

[195] See *infra* 10.3–10.5.

Table 8.1 The temporality, limits and outcome of self-defence claims in state-to-state conflicts

Self-defence	Cases	Nature of threat faced		Breached limits		Reaction
Anticipatory dimension	1956	Israel Potential threat	Egypt Invasion	Israel All	Egypt –	Condemnation
	1967	Israel Imminent attack	Arab states Potential threat	Israel Proportionality concerning long-term occupation	Arab states –	Acceptance
	1973	Egypt Non-forceful	Israel Imminent attack	Egypt All	Israel None	Self-defence was only contemplated
Remedial dimension	1980	Iraq Potential threat	Iran Invasion	Iraq All	Iran (proportionality)	Acceptance Iran action / Condemnation Iraqi action
	1982	Argentina Potential threat	UK Invasion	Argentina All	UK None	Condemnation of Argentina / Controversial temporality of UK action
Combined dimension	1964	UK Repetition of attacks	Yemen –	UK (conditionality of armed attack) (immediacy)	Yemen –	Condemnation
	1964	US Repetition of attacks	N. Vietnam –	US All	N. Vietnam –	Condemnation
	1986	US Repetition of attacks	Libya –	US (conditionality of armed attack) (immediacy)	Libya –	Criticism
	1993	US Repetition of attacks	Iraq –	US (conditionality of armed attack) (immediacy)	Iraq –	Moderate acceptance
	2008	Russia Attack	Georgia – Potential attack – Invasion	Russia Proportionality	Georgia Proportionality	Criticism

Terms in brackets show the controversial nature of the issue, without signalling an outright breach of the specific limit self-defence.[196] Secondly, whereas 'attack' in the pre-Charter sense of the word could refer to many different forms of the use of force, in post-Charter state practice, 'armed attack' pertained to the most serious forms of force.[197] For that reason, self-defence against hit-and-run attacks was viewed with reluctance by most permanent and non-permanent members of the Security Council because of the question of proportionality between the attacks and the defensive response.[198]

The immediacy requirement was viewed as clearly met in cases where an invasion was unfolding. Certainly, an invasion amounted to an armed attack and created an immediate need for action. Therefore, in such cases, the requirement of necessity was viewed as automatically fulfilled without the need for much explanation on the part of the target state.[199] Nonetheless, in the case of the Falklands War, it was maintained that self-defence was obsolete, because the invasion was already completed by the time the British task force reached the operation zone.[200] In cases involving an anticipatory dimension, the immediacy requirement was not only disputed because of the lack of an armed attack, but rather because of the failure to demonstrate an imminent threat of such an attack. The reaction to the Six-Day War, on one hand, and to the Sinai Campaign, on the other, illustrated this tendency. As regards those instances where self-defence purported a combined dimension, the presence of an immediate need to act was highly debated, although not always rejected.

The requirement of proportionality in the illustrated cases was generally measured against the need to preclude the armed attack from happening or oust the invader. That view was expressly confirmed in the September 2009 Report of the Fact-Finding Mission on the Georgia conflict.[201] The content of the requirement of proportionality rendered some conflicts that passed the necessity test unlawful, because of the excessive use of force (Iran–Iraq War, South Ossetia War). The proportionality limit was considerably blurred when it came to self-defence against hit-and-run tactics. Accordingly, it was maintained by states that purported such claims that the defensive action was needed to preclude the occurrence of future attacks and, for that reason, it had to be proportionate to the need to neutralize the source of such attacks. Such reasoning led to defensive actions that were clearly bigger in scale than the hit-and-run attacks and that were prone to criticism on behalf of other states.[202]

---

[196] The rejection of the arguments of Arab states justifying the 1948 invasion illustrate this restrictive tendency (see *supra* 8.2.1). The reaction to the actions of the UK and France in the 1956 Sinai Campaign also confirm the trend.

[197] See *supra* 6.4.1.

[198] See *supra* 8.4.1, 8.4.2 and 8.4.3.

[199] See *supra* 8.3.1.

[200] Neff 2005, p. 330.

[201] See *supra* 8.4.5. Report of Fact-Finding Mission in Georgia 2009, p. 251.

[202] See *supra* 8.4.1, 8.4.2 and 8.4.3.

As said above, the examined cases of state-to-state conflicts involving claims of self-defence have shown that the temporal dimension of self-defence in such instances pertained to three moments: before, during and after the armed attack. Most of the cases analyzed, involved both an anticipatory and a remedial dimension of the right, although they have been discussed under one or the other category. Self-defence claims against hit-and-run tactics purported both dimensions because of the accumulative nature of the legal argument advanced (past attacks render the immediate need to resist to future attacks).

In comparison with the pre-Charter content of the limits of self-defence, the conditionality of an armed attack suffered visible changes. Unlike in pre-Charter state practice, in state-to-state conflicts, an armed attack was generally seen as a serious form of the use of force (invasion or bombardment). Nonetheless, the instances involving hit-and-run tactics were of considerably lower threshold than full-scale armed actions. The debate concerning their characterization as armed attack will receive further attention in Chapter 10.

The element of immediacy pertaining to necessity was acknowledged in all cases and acceptance or condemnation of specific instances of state practice was advanced on that basis. Despite the many generic referrals to Article 51 and customary law, no consistent limitation of immediacy can be discerned from these cases. Reaction was usually formulated along the lines of the need for immediate action, without a consistent delineation of temporal limits.

The requirement of proportionality continued to be viewed as limiting force to what was needed to ward off an attack. Nonetheless, some instances of self-defence, lawful in their necessity, failed the proportionality test, because of the excessive force used. This was the case regardless of the temporal dimension, although the instances involving hit-and-run tactics posed specific problems in this respect.

It is the conclusion of this chapter that no clear tendency of rejecting anticipatory action in self-defence can be discerned from the state practice analysed. Certainly, the one lawful exercise of self-defence through anticipatory action cannot support the converse conclusion that there is a discernable, broad and consistent acceptance of the anticipatory dimension. Rather, the analysed cases show that the key to a lawful exercise of self-defence was not in the occurrence of an armed attack, but in the existence of an immediate need to act in self-defence. If this necessity was absent, armed action could not be qualified as self-defence, regardless of its temporal dimension.

References

Baker SG (1994) Comparing the 1993 US airstrike on Iraq to the 1986 bombing of Libya: the new interpretation of Article 51. Ga J Int Comp Law 24:99–116

Biffen J (1982) Letter to Mr. George Foulkes, M.P., dated 20 May 1982. British Yearb Int Law 53:519–520

Christakis T (2005) Existe-t-il un droit de légitime défense en cas de simple "menace"?: une réponse au "groupe des personnalités de haut niveau" de l'ONU. In: Société française pour le droit international, Les métamorphoses de la sécurité collective: droit, pratique et enjeux stratégiques, Pedone, Paris, pp 197–222

Constantinou A (2000) The right of self-defence under customary international law and Article 51 of the United Nations Charter. Sakkoulas, Athens

Corten O (2008) Le droit contre la guerre: l'interdiction du recours à la force en droit international contemporain. Pedone, Paris

Dekker IF (1992) Criminal responsibility and the Gulf War of 1980–1989: the crime of aggression. In: Dekker IF, Post HHG (eds) The Gulf War of 1980–1989. Martinus Nijhoff, Dordrecht, pp 249–268

Dinstein Y (2005) War, aggression and self-defense. Cambridge University Press, Cambridge

Franck T (2002) Recourse to force: state action against threats and armed attacks. Cambridge University Press, Cambridge

Freedman L (2005a) The official history of the Falklands campaign, vol 1. Routledge, London

Freedman L (2005b) The official history of the Falklands campaign, vol 2. Routledge, London

Freedman L, Gamba-Stonehouse V (1991) Signals of war: the Falklands conflict of 1982. Princeton University Press, Princeton, N.J

Gazzini T (2005) The changing rules on the use of force in international law. Manchester University Press, Manchester

Gill TD (2007) The temporal dimension of self-defence. In: Schmitt M, Pejic J (eds) International law and armed conflict: exploring the faultlines. Essays in honour of Yoram Dinstein. Martinus Nijhoff, Leiden, pp 113–155

Gray C (2004) International law and the use of force. Oxford University Press, Oxford

Greenwood C (1987) International law and the United States' air operation against Libya. West Va Law Rev 89:933–960

Greig DW (1991) Self-defence and the Security Council: what does Article 51 require. Int Comp Law Q 40:366–402

Higgins N, O'Reilly K (2009) The use of force, wars of national liberation and the right to self-determination in the South Ossetian conflict. Int Crim Law Rev 9:567–583

Intoccia GF (1987) American bombing of Libya: an international legal analysis. Case West Reserve J Int Law 19:177–213

Laqueur W, Rubin B (eds) (2001) The Arab-Israeli reader: a documentary history of the Middle East conflict, 6th rev. edn. Penguin Books, London

Levite A (1987) Intelligence and strategic surprise. Columbia University Press, New York

Israel knew attack was coming: envoy to the US asserts (11 October 1973). New York Times, p. 1

Kaikobad KH (1992) "Jus ad Bellum": legal implications of the Iran–Iraq war. In: Dekker IF, Post HHG (eds) The Gulf war of 1980–1989. Martinus Nijhoff, Dordrecht, pp 51–70

Karsh E (2002) The Iran–Iraq war 1980–1988. Osprey, Oxford

Mansfield P (2003) A history of the Middle East. Penguin Books, London

Martel E (1993) Gulf of Tonkin. OAH Mag Hist 7(2):36–39

McCredie JA (1987) The April 14, 1986 bombing of Libya: act of self-defense or reprisal. Case West Res J Int Law 19:215–242

Mueller KP et al (2006) Striking first: preemptive and preventive attack in US National Security policy. RAND Project Air Force

Neff SC (2005) War and the law of nations: general history. Cambridge University Press, Cambrdige

Repertoire: Repertoire of the Practice of the Security Council http://www.un.org/en/sc/repertoire/

Report of the Independent International Fact-Finding Mission on the Conflict in Georgia (September 2009) http://www.ceiig.ch/Report.html. Accessed 2 June 2010

Ruys T (2010) 'Armed attack' and Article 51 of the UN Charter. Evolutions in customary law and practice. Cambridge University Press, Cambridge

Schick FB (1968) Some reflections on the legal controversies concerning America's involvement in Vietnam. Int Comp Law Q 17:953–995

Schwebel SM (1970) What weight to conquest? Am J Int Law 64:344–347
SCOR: Security Council Official Records http://documents.un.org/simple.asp
Shapira A (1971) The Six Day War and the right of self-defence. Israel Law Rev 6:65–80
Sorenson DS (2008) An introduction to the modern Middle East. Westview Press, Boulder
The FBI Laboratory: US Department of Justice, Office of the Inspector General (1997) The FBI laboratory: an investigation into laboratory practices and alleged misconduct in explosives-related and other cases, Part 3, section D: The Bush assassination attempt www.fas.org/irp/agency/doj/oig/fbilab1/05bush2.htm. Accessed 4 November 2008
The President's Address to the Nation, 14 April 1986 (June 1986). Department of State Bulletin 86:1–2
Wright Q (1957) Intervention 1956. Am J Int Law 51:257–276
Wright Q (1968) Legal aspects of the Middle East situation. Law Contemp Probl 33:5–31

Chapter 9
Self-Defence and Weapons of Mass Destruction

9.1 Introduction

Arguably the most important development of twentieth century warfare was the creation of the atomic bomb and the development of nuclear weapons. After the 1945 bombing of Hiroshima and Nagasaki, both the United States and the USSR entered into a (nuclear) arms race that saw the development of the thermonuclear (hydrogen) bomb, long-range bombers and ballistic missiles. The global dimension of the arms race was increased by the emergence of other nuclear weapon states (Britain in 1952, France in 1960 and China in 1964).[1] Despite the adoption of the Nuclear Non-Proliferation Treaty in 1970, several other states are known to have developed nuclear weapons (such as Israel, India and Pakistan) and others have invested considerable effort in doing so (North Korea, Iraq).[2]

As a consequence of the ongoing arms race, the fear that one side would have sufficient weapons of sufficient accuracy to destroy the other side's nuclear arsenal became mutual between the US and the USSR during the Cold War. The objective of both sides was to prevent the other from acquiring a position of meaningful superiority.[3] Part and parcel of this objective were the theory of deterrence and the principle of mutually assured destruction (MAD). The central concern of the former was to dissuade the other side from undertaking an attack.[4] The gist of the latter was that each side would have the capacity to destroy the other after being attacked.[5] These two theories intrinsically connected the use of force to the issue of

[1] Baylis and Smith 2001, p. 85.

[2] Ibid

[3] Ibid., p. 86.

[4] Ibid., p. 322; Allison 1971, pp. 98–99. Structural realist approach: Waltz 1990, pp. 732–736. For a social constructivist discussion of nuclear deterrence in general, see. Tannenwald 1999, pp. 433–468; Farrell and Lambert 2001, pp. 309–326.

[5] Baylis and Smith 2001, p. 86; Waltz 1990, pp. 732–733; Farrell and Lambert 2001, pp. 321–322.

K. Tibori Szabó, *Anticipatory Action in Self-Defence*, DOI: 10.1007/978-90-6704-796-8_9,

nuclear weapons. Despite this, states have been very cautious in resorting to force in crises connected to such weapons. The threat posed by nuclear weapons was later coupled with the dangers created by chemical and biological weapons. This way, one of the main security themes of the post-Charter era was the tackling of conflicts which could involve the use of weapons of mass destruction (WMD).

This chapter examines those conflicts of the twentieth and twenty-first centuries that involved the threat posed by such weapons and in which claims of self--defence were contemplated or used. The aim of this chapter is to examine the temporal dimension of self-defence as interpreted by the state practice involving WMD. The specific cases will be tested against the variables identified in the introductory remarks of Part II. Accordingly, each instance of state practice will be analysed on the basis of necessity (the conditionality of an armed attack and immediacy) as well as proportionality. There were two instances during the twentieth century and one instance during the twenty-first century when self-defence against the threat posed by WMD was contemplated. During the Cuban missile crisis, the emplacement of Soviet nuclear missiles in Cuba was met without resort to self-defence, although such an option was considered at some point. In the other two instances, the perceived threat of WMD led to armed action. Israel justified the 1981 bombing of the Osirak reactor as self-defence, whereas in 2003 the US claimed, *inter alia*, self-defence against the threat posed by alleged Iraqi possession of nuclear weapons.

None of these cases involved an actual attack or the imminent threat thereof. Nevertheless, their analysis is necessary in order to assess the validity of a claim of self-defence against *possession* and *development* of nuclear weapons. This analysis is very pertinent for the temporal dimension of self-defence, because it involves resort to defensive action well before the imminent threat of an armed attack is perceived.

9.2 The Cuban Missile Crisis (1962)

Soviet arms shipment to Cuba was not a novelty by 1962, but the United States government believed that such a build-up was confined to defensive systems.[6] The shipments had been discontinued in early 1962, but were resumed in July that year, after Raul Castro and other representatives of the Cuban government met with the Soviet Premier in Moscow and discussed a detailed plan for the deployment of Russian missiles in Cuba.[7] In particular, around 15 July 1962, Soviet cargo ships began moving out of the Black Sea for Cuba. Aerial reconnaissance showed that

[6] Chayes 1974, p. 8.

[7] Chayes 1974, p. 8; Garthoff 1988, p. 67.

they were 'riding high in the water,' meaning that the vessels carried unusually light cargo, typically a sign that military equipment was being transported.[8] The first clear sign that Soviet missiles were being transported to Cuba came in August 1962, when US surveillance flights discovered the presence of Soviet surface-to-air missile (SAM) batteries in several locations in Cuba.[9] The director of the Central Intelligence Agency (CIA) at that time, John McCone, assumed that such sites were potentially guarding valuable military equipment.[10] Clear evidence of the veracity of that assumption came on 14 October, when a U-2 aircraft photographed Soviet medium-range ballistic missile (MRBM) sites under construction around the island.[11] Three days later, US intelligence found out that intermediate-range ballistic missile (IRBM) sites were under construction as well.[12] While the construction of the MRBM sites was expected to be finished in one week's time, the finalization of the IRBM sites was calculated for December 1962. The MRBMs had ranges up to 1,100 nautical miles, whereas the range of the IRBMs was up to 2,200 nautical miles.[13] Both missile types could reach targets beyond the eastern seaboard and deep in the United States.[14] By 21 October, the inventory prepared by US intelligence showed that the Soviet arms build-up included 42 MRBMs, 12 IRBMs, 42 IL-28 jet light bombers, 144 SAM launchers, 39 MIG-21 jet fighters and 22,000 Soviet troops for the construction, operation and defence of these weapons.[15]

Several reasons were advanced by contemporary commentators to explain the Soviet build-up in Cuba.[16] The most widely accepted explanation was that the USSR was attempting to change the balance of power by altering the unfavourable strategic environment in which it found itself at the time.[17] The USSR wanted to achieve missile power parity by doubling the Soviet missile capability against the US and by counterbalancing the presence of US missiles in Turkey.[18] Although American strategic superiority was not altered by the Soviet move, attacks from

[8] 'The Cuban Missile Crisis: A Chronology of Events', in Chang and Kornbluh 1992, p. 352.

[9] Chang and Kornbluh 1992, p. 353.

[10] Ibid.

[11] Ibid., p 358; Mueller et al. 2006, pp. 172–173.

[12] Chang and Kornbluh 1992, p. 361.

[13] Allison 1971, p 104.

[14] Mueller et al. 2006, p. 175; SCOR, 17th Sess., 1022nd meeting., UN Doc. S/PV.1022(OR) (23 October 1962) paras 13, 71.

[15] Chang and Kornbluh 1992; Chayes 1974.

[16] For an overview of these hypotheses, see Allison 1971, pp. 43–56.

[17] Ibid., pp. 50–56

[18] Ibid., p. 54; Mueller et al. 2006, p. 174.

Cuba would have outflanked the US Ballistic Missile Early Warning System (BMEWS).[19]

Despite the fact that the Soviet build-up created a highly undesirable situation for the United States, at no time was there an imminent threat of a nuclear attack from the Soviet side. Nonetheless, two of the options considered by the president and the executive committee involved the use of force.[20] Several members of the committee proposed airstrikes against Cuba, either in the form of limited ('surgical') strikes against the relevant sites or a large air campaign against a multitude of targets. Moreover, a general ground invasion of Cuba was also considered.[21] The options of remaining passive or relying on diplomatic exchanges were also put forward.[22] All these options were, however, excluded. Apart from constituting costly and highly dangerous measures that could easily lead to devastating retaliation, airstrikes were also seen as difficult to justify to other states and the UN on behalf of a law-abiding US.[23]

As Abram Chayes, the then Legal Adviser to the State Department noted, the central difficulty with justifying the direct use of force as self-defence was that it seemed to create a very dangerous form of legal justification. Chayes explained that although the phrase 'armed attack' had to be construed broadly enough to permit some anticipatory response, the particularities of the Cuban crisis would have required an exaggeratedly expansive view on the issue. Anticipatory response could not be expanded 'to include threatening deployments or demonstrations that do not have imminent attack as their purpose or probable outcome'.[24] Chayes believed that to accept such an interpretation would have meant to make forceful response subject to unilateral national discretion. It would have also signalled that the US did not take the legal issues very seriously and values other than law would have been chiefly relied on as justification for action.[25]

The final decision was to impose a naval quarantine against Cuba.[26] That measure was communicated to the Security Council as well. The US requested an urgent meeting of the Security Council to 'deal with the dangerous threat to the peace and security of the world caused by the secret establishment in Cuba by the Union of Soviet Socialist Republics of launching bases and the installation of long-range ballistic missiles capable of carrying thermonuclear warheads to most of North and South America'.[27] The US invoked Articles 6 and 8 of the

---

[19] Allison 1971, p. 54.

[20] Ibid., pp. 58–61. For a composition of the Executive Committee, see Chayes 1974, pp. 13–14.

[21] Allison 1971, pp. 59–60; Mueller et al. 2006, pp. 176–177.

[22] Allison 1971, pp. 58–59; Mueller et al. 2006, pp. 176–177.

[23] Chayes 1974, p. 65; Mueller et al. 2006, pp. 176–177.

[24] Chayes 1974, p. 65.

[25] Ibid., pp 65–66.

[26] Chang and Kornbluh 1992, pp. 364–365.

[27] UN Doc. S/5181 (1962).

Inter-American Treaty of Reciprocal Assistance (Rio Treaty)[28] and signalled its reliance on the institution of regional arrangements provided by Articles 52 and 53 of the UN Charter.[29] On that basis, the US announced that it was initiating a 'strict quarantine of Cuba to interdict the carriage of offensive weapons to that country'.[30]

Cuba riposted to the naval quarantine and characterised the American action as 'an act of war', a 'unilateral and direct aggression' that created an 'imminent danger of war'.[31] The Soviet Union also characterized the quarantine as an unlawful naval blockade aimed at interfering in the internal affairs of Cuba to pursue aggressive American aims.[32] The USSR further contended that all weapons in its possession were serving 'the purposes of defence against aggressors' and that the assistance given to Cuba was 'exclusively designed to improve Cuba's defensive capacity'.[33]

The Security Council did not adopt any resolution given the obvious and insurmountable deadlock between two of its permanent members. The Council of the Organization of American States (OAS) did, however, adopt a resolution on 23 October 1962 in which it recommended that the member states 'take all measures, individually or collectively, including the use of armed force, which they may deem necessary to ensure that the Government of Cuba cannot continue to receive from the Sino-Soviet powers military material and related supplies which may threaten the peace and security of the Continent and to prevent the missiles in Cuba from ever becoming an active threat to the peace and security of the Continent'.[34]

The decision to refrain from other measures proved to be successful. On 23 October an exchange of correspondence between Kennedy and Khrushchev ensued, which resulted in 16 Soviet ships being returned from Cuba the next day.[35]

[28] The Inter-American Treaty of Reciprocal Assistance (commonly known as the Rio Treaty) was signed in 1947 between several American countries, including the US. The declared purpose of the Treaty was 'to provide for effective reciprocal assistance to meet armed attacks against any American State, and in order to deal with threats of aggression against any of them' (preamble). According to Article 6 of the Rio Treaty, in the event of an aggression, extra- or intra-continental conflict or other situation not amounting to an armed attack that affected the inviolability, territorial integrity, sovereignty or political independence of any American State, the Organ of Consultation had to meet up and discuss necessary measures. Article 8 of the Rio Treaty offered a list of measures that could be taken by the Organ of Consultation: 'recall of chiefs of diplomatic missions; breaking of diplomatic relations; breaking of consular relations; partial or complete interruption of economic relations or of rail, sea, air, postal, telegraphic, telephonic, and radiotelephonic or radiotelegraphic communications; and use of armed force.'

[29] UN Doc. S/5181 1962; Chayes 1974, pp. 16, 20.

[30] UN Doc. S/5181 1962.

[31] UN Doc. S/5183 1962.

[32] UN Doc. S/5186 1962.

[33] Ibid.

[34] Chayes 1974, p. 88; Wright 1963, p. 558.

[35] Mueller et al. 2006, pp. 174, 179.

On 26 October, the Soviet premier offered to withdraw missiles if the US pledged not to invade Cuba and to remove its missiles from Turkey. The next day, US President Kennedy publicly agreed not to invade Cuba and privately pledged to initiate the removal of missiles from Turkey.[36] From that point onwards, the pressure slowly started to drop. Evidence of that is the very cool-headed reaction of the US administration to the news of Soviet air defences being triggered by an American U-2 crossing into Russian air space, a SAM shooting down another U-2 aircraft over Cuba and US F-8 Crusaders taking antiaircraft fire when flying over the island.[37]

The Cuban missile crisis unfolded because of the prospect of nuclear weapons being deployed in Cuba by the Soviet Union. There was no threat of an imminent nuclear attack, but for the United States the presence or deployment of nuclear weapons in Cuba was a serious concern. Although several policy options were discussed, the US president decided to rely on the effects of a naval quarantine rather than resort to armed action in self-defence.

Several commentators analysed the US quarantine under Article 51 of the Charter.[38] A number of authors found that the quarantine could have been justified under the law of self-defence if 'traditional general community expectations' were considered.[39] Others asserted that the naval quarantine could not be justified as a measure of self-defence under Article 51, because it constituted a veritable naval *blockade*, which amounted to a resort to armed force without a prior armed attack taking place.[40] Both groups of authors relied on the assumption that the naval quarantine was tantamount to a naval blockade and that it amounted in some way to the use of force.[41] The then Deputy Legal Adviser to the US Department of State, Leonard Meeker explained, however, that the naval quarantine was not synonymous to a naval blockade and that it relied on provisions relating to regional arrangements rather than those connected to the use of force.[42] Accordingly, Meeker specified that the US naval quarantine was a lawful measure adopted by a regional organization in conformity with the provisions of the Rio Treaty and thus Chapter VIII of the UN Charter.[43] Although the quarantine relied on the use of naval force, it was a proportionate measure with a very clearly outlined objective and designed solely to prevent further build-up of strategic missile bases in Cuba.[44]

---

[36] Chang and Kornbluh 1992, pp. 377–80; Mueller et al. 2006, p. 180.

[37] Mueller et al. 2006, p. 180; Allison 1971, pp. 106.

[38] Campbell 1963, pp. 160–176; McDougal 1963, pp. 597–604; Meeker 1963, pp. 515–524; Wright 1963, pp. 546–565.

[39] McDougal 1963, p. 603; Campbell 1963, p.176.

[40] Wright 1963, pp. 554–557, 559–563; Dinstein 2005, p.186; Alexandrov 1996, pp. 156–157.

[41] McDougal 1963, p. 603; Campbell 1963, p. 160; Wright 1963, pp. 554–556.

[42] Meeker 1963, pp. 515–516, 523–524.

[43] Ibid., pp. 523–524.

[44] Ibid., p. 524. Also see Franck 2002, pp. 99–100.

Despite the 'eyeball-to-eyeball' stance of the two sides in the Cuban missile crisis, the deployment of nuclear missiles was never perceived as an imminent threat of a nuclear attack that created a present and inevitable necessity to act pre-emptively in self-defence. As Chayes explained, anticipatory action in self-defence could not be expanded 'to include threatening deployments or demonstrations that do not have imminent attack as their purpose or probable outcome'.[45] In other words, the necessity requirement of self-defence was not met, because there was neither an imminent threat of an armed attack nor a present and inevitable necessity to ward the attack off. The availability of (tense) diplomatic communications never disappeared. Multiple discussions and deliberations at both the executive committee level and between envoys occurred, thus there was no lack of choice of means to resolve the conflict. Moreover, launching a full-scale invasion or limited airstrikes because of the deployment of nuclear missiles in Cuba, would have exceeded the limits of proportionality of the defensive action.

9.3 The Israeli Bombing of the Iraqi Reactor (1981)

By the beginning of the 1980s, the number of nuclear states had grown to include several other states that either had developed (openly or covertly) nuclear weapons or were on their way to do so. Israel was suspected to belong to the first category, whereas Iraq was believed to pertain to the latter.[46]

Starting with the 1970s, the Iraqi President, Saddam Hussein embarked on an ambitious plan to develop nuclear weapons. Osirak, the nuclear reactor near Baghdad, was used by the Iraqi government to produce the fissile material for the future weapons.[47] According to Israeli intelligence, by July or September 1981, the Osirak reactor was to be fully fuelled and operational.[48] After that time, an attack on the reactor would have caused extensive civilian damage, because of the release of large amounts of nuclear fallouts.[49] Such a consequence would have resulted in serious repercussions for Israel on an international level.[50]

The threat perceived by the Israelis was connected to the reasons why Iraq was developing nuclear weapons and to Saddam Hussein's attitude towards Israel. Accordingly, the Israelis feared that, once in possession of a nuclear weapon, the Iraqi president would undoubtedly decide to use it against Israel and that

[45] Chayes 1974, p. 65.

[46] Baylis and Smith 2001, p. 86.

[47] Mueller et al. 2006, p. 212.

[48] UN Doc. S/14510 1981.

[49] Ibid.

[50] Mueller et al. 2006, pp. 212, 214; Gill 2007, p. 140.

retaliatory damage to the population of his own country would not deter him.[51] As grave as the threat sounded, there was no sign whatsoever of it being more than a mere possibility. Israeli intelligence did not acquire any sort of information that would suggest that Saddam Hussein had a plan of attack.[52] The circumstances were similar to the Cuban crisis inasmuch as the danger of *possessing* nuclear weapons was the threat and not the imminent possibility of *using* them. Nonetheless, the situation differed from the Cuban precedent in that Iraq was far from possessing such weapons. Israeli intelligence estimated that a crude nuclear device was to be finalized by 1985, thus four years away from even considering the imminence of an attack.[53]

Nonetheless, the Israelis decided to carry out a surgical strike on the reactor.[54] On 6 June 1981, eight fighter-bombers (F-16A) and six fighters (F-15A) flew across Jordanian and Saudi airspace and into Iraq at low level (to avoid detection), struck the target and returned to base without loss. The reactor was destroyed and ten people were killed.[55]

International reaction was negative, although Israel tried to justify its action as self-defence.[56] Before the Security Council, several states expressed their criticism as to the Israeli action.[57] Some representatives asserted that the Israeli action went well beyond the limits of pre-emptive or anticipatory defensive action against an imminent attack, without rejecting the legality of such options *per se*.[58] The Israeli airstrike was also coined as 'preventive war' the legality of which was seen as abolished by the Charter.[59] The Ugandan representative expressly referred to the *Caroline* incident and emphasized that 'the mere fact of having a nuclear research centre' could not, in any way, satisfy the requirements of the Webster-formula.[60] The Security Council unanimously adopted a resolution that condemned the Israeli

---

[51] Mueller et al. 2006, p. 213.

[52] Franck 2002, p. 106; Gill 2007, p. 141.

[53] Mueller et al. 2006, p. 212.

[54] Gill 2007, p. 141.

[55] Mueller et al. 2006, p. 213.

[56] SCOR, 36th Sess., 2280th meeting., UN Doc. S/PV.2280 (12 June 1981) para 58.

[57] Ibid., 2280th–2288th meeting., UN Doc. S/PV.2280–S/PV.2288 (12–19 June 1981).

[58] SCOR, 36th Sess., 2282nd meeting., UN Doc. S/PV.2282 (15 June 1981) paras 14–19; 2283rd meeting., S/PV.2283 (15 June 1981) paras 23–27; 2284th meeting., S/PV.2284 (16 June 1981) para 11.

[59] SCOR, 36th Sess., 2283rd meeting., UN Doc. S/PV.2283 (15 June 1981) paras 46, 117, 146; 2288th meeting., S/PV.2288 (19 June 1981) para 115. In one instance, the concepts of 'anticipation' and 'preventive aggression' were equated and deemed unlawful: 2283rd meeting., S/PV.2283 (15 June 1981) para 146 (Sierra Leone).

[60] SCOR, 36th Sess., 2282nd meeting., UN Doc. S/PV.2282 (15 June 1981) paras 14–19.

action and found it to be in clear violation of the Charter and the norms of international conduct.[61]

The bombing of the Iraqi reactor further expanded the question whether the mere possession of nuclear weapons could legitimize the use of force. Iraq did not even possess a nuclear weapon at that time; it was—arguably—in the process of building one. The feasibility of a potential nuclear attack on Israel was never thoroughly explored, because Israel, just like the US in 1962, was concerned by the fact of *possession*, before any questions of actual use might have been raised. The airstrikes were carried out in order to prevent the reactor from ever delivering a nuclear bomb. They thus amounted to a veritable preventive action against a threat not materialized and far from imminent.

Several commentators pointed out that the bombing did not fulfil the conditions of anticipatory or pre-emptive self-defence.[62] The more important question is, however, whether the airstrike fulfilled any of the conditions—necessity and proportionality—of the right of self-defence *per se*. There was no imminent threat of a nuclear attack by Iraq, thus there was no *present* need to act. Without that element of emergency, grave as the security concerns of Israel might have been, there was no clear proof that in the foreseeable future other means to address the problem might not have become available. Thus there was no clear proof that the need to act was also *inevitable*. Without a present and inevitable need to act, the immediacy element of necessity was clearly missing.[63] In other words, even if the gravity of the danger was perceived as raising serious concerns, action in self-defence could not be justified solely on the eventuality of an attack. The immediacy element also had to be present. Although the Israeli airstrikes were carried out in a surgical manner, not exceeding the force needed to destroy the reactor, such an action could not be regarded as lawful in self-defence, because the danger it was warding off lay not in the imminent use of force, but in the development and future possession of nuclear weapons.

Although, with the benefit of hindsight, one might realize that had Israel not struck in 1981, the reversal of Iraq's invasion of Kuwait a decade later might have been impossible, the legality of the use of force has to be assessed on the basis of the information available at the time of the forceful response interpreted in good faith by the targeted state.[64]

Consequently, on the basis of the information available in 1981, the Israeli airstrike resembled rather an instance of preventive use of force, which sought to prevent the mere possibility of a future threat (however great that could be) and to strengthen a certain security balance in favour of the attacker.

---

[61] SC Res. 487 (1981) para 1.

[62] Alexandrov 1996, p. 162; Franck 2002, pp. 105–106; Gill 2007, pp. 141–142; Greenwood 2003, p. 14.

[63] Franck 2002, p. 106.

[64] Ibid., p. 107; Gill 2007, p. 141.

9.4 The Nuclear Weapons Advisory Opinion (1996)

The relationship between the rules regarding the use of force and nuclear weapons was explored by the International Court of Justice in its advisory opinion on the *Legality of the Threat or Use of Nuclear Weapons*.[65] Although this is not an instance of state practice, it is important to discuss it as part of this chapter, because it addresses many issues regarding the use of self-defence against nuclear weapons. It also sheds light on the way the Court viewed the threat posed by such weapons.

Before addressing the legality of the threat or use of nuclear weapons under *jus ad bellum* and *jus in bello*, the Court noted that the nature of such weapons rendered them 'potentially catastrophic'.[66] The Court went on to specify that the provisions of the Charter relating to the threat or use of force did not refer to specific weapons. Nevertheless, 'a weapon that is already unlawful *per se*, whether by treaty or custom, does not become lawful by reason of its being used for a legitimate purpose under the Charter'.[67]

Concerning *jus ad bellum*, the Court found no rule in international customary or treaty law that would expressly authorize or prohibit the threat or use of nuclear weapons as such. The use of nuclear weapons was found to be unlawful if it was contrary to Article 2(4) of the Charter and if it failed to meet all the requirements of Article 51.[68] Regarding the threat to use nuclear weapons, the Court found it enough to only specify that if the envisaged use of force was itself unlawful according to the provisions of the Charter, then the stated readiness to use it would also be considered a threat prohibited by Article 2(4).[69]

The advisory opinion also addressed the question of the legality of possession of nuclear weapons. First, the Court admitted that possession of nuclear weapons could justify an inference of preparedness to use them. Nonetheless, an effective policy of deterrence had to discourage military aggression and thus necessitated that the intention to use nuclear weapons be credible.[70] Secondly, the Court contended that such a possession could only be rendered an unlawful threat under Article 2(4) if 'the particular use of force envisaged would be directed against the territorial integrity or political independence of a State, or against the Purposes of the United Nations or whether, in the event that it were intended as a means of defence, it would necessarily violate the principles of necessity and proportionality'.[71]

---

[65] Nuclear Weapons 1996, p. 226.

[66] Ibid., para 35.

[67] Ibid., para 39.

[68] Ibid., para 105 (C).

[69] Ibid., para 47.

[70] Ibid., para 48.

[71] Ibid.

In connection with the right of self-defence, the opinion discussed the relevance of the principle of proportionality for the threat or use of nuclear weapons. The Court contended that the proportionality principle could not in itself exclude the use of nuclear weapons in self-defence in all circumstances.[72] That statement was found to be correct by Matheson, who argued that the judgment of proportionality could not be made in the abstract for all possible uses of nuclear weapons, without knowing the circumstances of the particular case.[73] At the same time, the Court noted that a use of force that was proportionate under the law of self-defence had to, in order to be lawful, also meet the requirements of international humanitarian law.[74] The claim of certain states that the extremely strong risk of devastation that nuclear weapons posed rendered the compliance with the principle of proportionality impossible *per se* was thus not upheld. The Court only asserted, rather vaguely, that 'the very nature of all nuclear weapons and the profound risks associated therewith are further considerations to be borne in mind by states believing they can exercise a nuclear response in self-defence in accordance with the requirements of proportionality'.[75]

Regarding *jus in bello*, it was held that the threat or use of nuclear weapons 'would generally be contrary to the rules of international law applicable in armed conflict, and in particular the principles and rules of international humanitarian law'.[76] Nonetheless, the Court emphasized that it could not lose sight of the fundamental right of every state to survival, and thus the right to resort to self-defence, in accordance with Article 51 of the Charter, 'when its survival is at stake'.[77] The Court thus held that it could not conclude definitely whether the threat or use of nuclear weapons would be lawful or unlawful in an extreme circumstance of self-defence.[78]

This conclusion was criticized by a number of publicists.[79] Even some of the judges chose to distance themselves from this particular finding.[80] Judge Higgins regretted the vague formulation of rendering nuclear weapons 'generally' to be 'contrary to the rules of international law applicable in armed conflict'.[81] More importantly, Judge Higgins criticized the formula used by the Court in reserving

---

72 Ibid., para 42.

73 Matheson 1997, p. 424.

74 Nuclear Weapons 1996, para 42.

75 Ibid., para 43.

76 Ibid., paras 53–95 (discussion of the international law applicable in armed conflict), and 105 (E).

77 Ibid., para 96.

78 Ibid., para 105 (E).

79 Falk 1997, pp. 64–75; Grief 1997, pp. 681–688; Weston 1997, pp. 383–392. For a more positive opinion, see Matheson 1997, pp. 417–435.

80 Nuclear Weapons 1996, pp. 589–590 (dissenting opinion of Judge Higgins), 321–323 (dissenting opinion of Vice-President Schwebel), 376–377 (dissenting opinion of Judge Shahabuddeen), and 435 (dissenting opinion of Judge Weeramantry).

81 Ibid., p. 589 (dissenting opinion of Judge Higgins).

the possibility to use nuclear weapons in an extreme circumstance of self-defence. Accordingly, she asserted that through this formula the Court necessarily left open the possibility that a use of nuclear weapons contrary to humanitarian law might nonetheless be lawful.[82] She noted that this conclusion went beyond anything that was claimed by the nuclear weapon states appearing before the Court, who fully accepted that any lawful threat or use of nuclear weapons would have to comply with both the *jus ad bellum* and the *jus in bello*.[83] Similarly, Judge Weeramantry pointed out that the same formula opened 'a window of permissibility, however narrow' in which 'a nation may seek refuge, constituting itself the sole judge in its own cause'.[84]

Falk lamented the Court's failure to clarify its understanding of the restrictions to be placed upon a potential self-defence argument. He pointed out the contradiction between paragraph 97, where the use of nuclear weapons by a state was discussed in case *its* survival was at stake and the *dispositif* of the opinion, where self-defence was referred to in case the survival of 'a State' was at risk.[85] According to Falk, the wording of the *dispositif* allowed for collective self-defence, whereas paragraph 97 did not.[86] Matheson considered that the Opinion clearly permitted collective self-defence in which a nuclear weapon state used nuclear weapons to deter or defeat an armed attack that threatened the survival of an ally.[87]

Grief criticized the opinion for not elaborating on the 'extreme circumstances' of self-defence.[88] Matheson also acknowledged that the phrase 'the very survival of the state' was not specific enough, but he offered examples of state practice in which such a circumstance was present (the Korean War and the Persian Gulf War).[89]

There are several important inferences to be made from the Court's advisory opinion. First of all, the judges did not assign to nuclear weapons any 'special' illegality under *jus ad bellum*. The legality of the threat or use of such weapons was said to be governed by the Charter and customary law.[90]

Secondly, their use in self-defence had to meet the requirements of necessity and proportionality. The content of the necessity requirement was not expressly discussed by the Court, although its reference to the 'extreme circumstance' of self-defence when the 'very survival' of a state was at risk was interpreted as restricting the exercise of self-defence to instances where attacks impinged upon

82 Ibid., p. 590.

83 Ibid.

84 Ibid., p. 435 (dissenting opinion of Judge Weeramantry).

85 Falk 1997, p. 68.

86 Ibid.

87 Matheson 1997, p. 431.

88 Grief 1997, p. 687.

89 Matheson 1997, p. 430.

90 Nuclear Weapons 1996, para 105 (C).

the continued existence of the state.[91] The proportionality requirement was interpreted as intrinsically connected to the observance of the laws of armed conflict. The use of nuclear weapons in self-defence was thus proportionate only if it respected the rules of armed conflict.[92]

Thirdly, the possession *per se* of nuclear weapons was not unlawful. One could thus conclude that neither was the development of such weapons, if the developing state was not part of the Non-Proliferation Treaty. The Court went as far as to acknowledge the importance of the policy of deterrence that necessitated a credible intention to use nuclear weapons. In other words, the Court acknowledged that in certain circumstances the possession and threat of nuclear weapons was important to discourage military aggression.[93] The possession of nuclear weapons was unlawful only if the use of force 'envisaged' was directed against the territorial integrity or political independence of a state or was contrary to the purposes of the Charter or, if intended as a means of defence, it would have exceeded the requirements of necessity and proportionality.[94] The Court did not specify whether this 'envisaged' use of force had to be imminent on a short or medium term. Nor did it elaborate on the options available for states to handle such a situation. Nonetheless, it would be far-fetched to conclude that by rendering possession under such circumstances unlawful, the Court permitted the use of self-defence against the possessor state. Nor could the conclusion be drawn that self-defence was permitted against a state that was developing nuclear weapons for whatever purpose.

Lastly, the Court rendered the use of nuclear weapons to be 'generally' contrary to the laws of armed conflict.[95] If one corroborates this conclusion with the one made on the proportionality requirement of self-defence, it can be inferred that the use of nuclear weapons in self-defence would never be proportionate, because such weapons were generally contrary to the laws of armed conflict. Nonetheless, the *dispositif* of the opinion hinted at an exception to this qualification: in cases of an 'extreme circumstance' of self-defence when the 'very survival' of a state was at risk the Court declined to decide whether the use of nuclear weapons could be lawful or not.[96]

The Court shied away from making any reference to pre-emptive or anticipatory action under self-defence. Nor did it discuss the temporal dimension of self-defence ('extreme' or not) in warding off a threat of a nuclear attack. The importance of the advisory opinion lies however in its restrictive view on the proportionality of the use of nuclear weapons and in its conclusion that possession of nuclear weapons was not unlawful *per se*.

---

[91] Green 2009, p. 77.

[92] Nuclear Weapons 1996, para 42.

[93] Ibid., para 48.

[94] Ibid.

[95] Ibid., para 105 (E).

[96] Ibid.

9.5 The War Against Iraq (2003)

The 2003 Iraqi War (Second Gulf War) involved several complex legal arguments advanced by mainly the US and the UK. Primarily, the two governments relied on the effect of relevant Security Council resolutions calling upon Iraq to put an end to its nuclear, chemical and biological weapons programmes. Additionally, claims of self-defence against the threat of weapons of mass destruction and terrorism were also advanced by the United States. Lastly, the Iraqi invasion was also depicted as an armed intervention on humanitarian grounds.[97]

It is not the purpose of this book to elaborate on the claims pertaining to the effect of Security Council resolutions and humanitarian intervention. The main emphasis will be accorded to the claims of self-defence. Nonetheless, some preliminary points are necessary to be made. First, the claims of self-defence (against weapons of mass destruction and terrorism) were not as consistent and direct as the principal claim relying on SC resolutions.[98] Secondly, in order to put in the relevant context the claims of self-defence, a short review of the relevant public statements and strategy documents will have to be conducted. Thirdly, in order to assess the sustainability of the claim of self-defence against WMD, a succinct summary of the relevant Security Council resolutions and the last-minute UN and IAEA arms inspections will have to be made.

The following paragraphs will analyse the US claims of self-defence regarding the threat of Iraqi WMD. In Chapter 10 the US claims of self-defence regarding the threat of terrorism stemming from Iraq will be discussed.[99]

9.5.1 The 2003 Iraqi War: Setting the Context

In his State of the Union Address on 29 January 2002, President Bush characterized Iraq as one element of the 'axis of evil' that sought weapons of mass destruction and posed a grave and growing danger to the entire world.[100] Several months later, on 1 June 2002, the president declared in his US Military Academy speech that deterrence and containment meant nothing when 'unbalanced dictators with weapons of mass-destruction' could deliver such weapons on missiles or secretly provide them to 'terrorist allies'.[101] Bush was thus suggesting that in a world of 'unbalanced dictators' and 'terrorist allies' the cornerstone principles of the Cold War were not valid anymore.

---

[97] Greenwood 2005, pp. 399–404; Ignatieff 2003.

[98] Greenwood 2005, pp. 399–403.

[99] See *infra* 10.5.3.

[100] Bush (29 January 2002) State of the Union Address.

[101] Ibid., Bush (1 June 2002) Graduation Speech at West Point.

The new approach of the Bush administration to tackle these dangers became apparent with the publishing of the 2002 US National Security Strategy. After enunciating the obsolete nature of the Cold-War principles of deterrence and mutually assured destruction, Part V of the 2002 Security Strategy warned that 'new deadly challenges have emerged from rogue states and terrorists'.[102] Although none of the new dangers rivalled the threat posed in the past by the Soviet Union, the nature and motivations of the new adversaries and the greater likelihood that they could use weapons of mass destruction against American citizens, made the security environment more complex and dangerous.[103] Therefore, it was necessary 'to stop rogue states and their terrorist clients before they are able to threaten or use weapons of mass destruction against the United States and our allies and friends'.[104]

The new comprehensive strategy to tackle these threats also involved a reinterpretation of the existing law of self-defence. The Security Strategy openly admitted the legality of self-defence in the face of an imminent threat, but asserted that the rule was bound to be revisited given the new security concerns.[105]

> For centuries, international law recognized that nations need not suffer an attack before they can lawfully take action to defend themselves against forces that present an imminent danger of attack. Legal scholars and international jurists often conditioned the legitimacy of pre-emption on the existence of an imminent threat—most often a visible mobilization of armies, navies, and air forces preparing to attack.
>
> We must adapt the concept of imminent threat to the capabilities and objectives of today's adversaries. Rogue states and terrorists do not seek to attack us using conventional means. They know such attacks would fail. Instead, they rely on acts of terror and, potentially, the use of weapons of mass destruction—weapons that can be easily concealed, delivered covertly, and used without warning.[106]

The Strategy document went on to present the advantages of 'pre-emptive actions'. It is important to note at this point, however, that the document used the terms 'pre-emptive actions' and 'anticipatory action' to describe the need to *prevent* hostile acts even if uncertainty remained as to the time and place of the attack. The Strategy document thus made a deliberate confusion between pre-emptive or anticipatory action and the preventive use of force.[107]

> 'The United States has long maintained the option of pre-emptive actions to counter a sufficient threat to our national security. The greater the threat, the greater is the risk of inaction—and the more compelling the case for taking anticipatory action to defend ourselves, even if uncertainty remains as to the time and place of the enemy's attack. To forestall or prevent such hostile acts by our adversaries, the United States will, if necessary, act pre-emptively.

102 US National Security Strategy 2002, Part V.

103 Ibid.

104 Ibid.

105 Schmitt 2003, pp. 518-519.

106 US National Security Strategy 2002, Part V.

107 Gardner 2003, p. 587; Heisbourg 2003, p. 77.

> The United States will not use force in all cases to pre-empt emerging threats, nor should nations use pre-emption as a pretext for aggression. Yet in an age where the enemies of civilization openly and actively seek the world's most destructive technologies, the United States cannot remain idle while dangers gather.[108]

Lastly, the Security Strategy emphasized that:

> The purpose of our actions will always be to eliminate a specific threat to the United States or our allies and friends. The reasons for our actions will be clear, the force measured, and the cause just'.[109]

The new strategy was clearly one of preventive use of force, although the terms employed (pre-emptive, anticipatory) were the ones usually used to describe armed action against an imminent threat.[110] The new formula became to be known among legal scholars as the 'Bush doctrine' and played an important role in the 2003 invasion of Iraq.[111]

9.5.2 The 2003 Iraqi War: Disarmament and Security Council Resolutions

On 12 September 2002, a year after the 9/11 attacks, President Bush addressed the UN General Assembly.[112] In his speech, Bush warned that Iraq continued to withhold important information about its nuclear program and that it retained the physical infrastructure needed to build a nuclear weapon. If Iraq acquired fissile material, claimed Bush, it would be able to build a nuclear weapon within a year.[113] The US president noted that as early as 1991, Iraq had promised UN inspectors immediate and unrestricted access to verify its commitment to rid itself of weapons of mass destruction and long-range missiles. Nonetheless, Bush emphasized 'Iraq broke this promise, spending seven years deceiving, evading, and harassing UN inspectors before ceasing cooperation entirely'.[114] Bush also pointed out that it had been four years 'since the last UN inspector set foot in Iraq' and that was enough time for Saddam Hussein's regime to plan, develop and test weapons of mass destruction 'under the cloak of secrecy'.[115] After such a powerful exposé, the US president characterized the actions of the Iraqi regime as a threat to

[108] US National Security Strategy 2002, Part V.

[109] Ibid.

[110] Gardner 2003, p. 587; Sapiro 2005, p. 366.

[111] Gardner 2003, pp. 585–586; Henderson 2004, p. 6.

[112] Bush (12 September 2002) Remarks.

[113] Ibid.

[114] Ibid.

[115] Ibid.

the authority of the United Nations and a threat to peace. Therefore, if Iraq wished peace, it was obliged to: (1) disclose and remove or destroy all weapons of mass destruction; (2) end all support for terrorism and act to suppress it; and (3) cease persecution of its civilian population.[116]

The General Assembly speech of President Bush is noteworthy for two reasons. First, it summarized the main US arguments as to the possession of nuclear (and other mass destruction) weapons by Iraq. Secondly, the three main demands made by Bush are identical to the three main claims of legality advanced expressly or implicitly by the US in justification of the invasion of Iraq. The failure to disarm and the threat of nuclear (and other mass destruction) weapons became the main US argument calling for a use of armed force. Additionally, Saddam Hussein's links to terrorist organizations and the necessity of humanitarian intervention were also employed as justifications for the war.[117]

In the subsequent months after the president's General Assembly speech, the situation in Iraq became the focus of world attention.[118] European states were divided on the issue. France, Germany and Russia opposed the invasion of Iraq without further Security Council authorization. Britain, Italy, Portugal, Spain and several Central and Eastern European states expressed their support.[119] Most other states were opposed to the invasion.[120]

The Security Council adopted several resolutions dealing with Iraq before the invasion began.[121] Some of these resolutions dealt with the emergency of humanitarian supplies to the Iraqi people; none referred to the possibility of armed intervention on humanitarian grounds.[122] Resolution 1441 of November 2002 dealt with Iraq's failure in its disarmament obligations related to its weapons of mass destruction and long-range missile programs. The resolution found Iraq to be in 'material breach' of its obligations under various resolutions, including Resolution 687 (1991), in particular through its failure to cooperate with UN and IAEA inspectors.[123] The Security Council resolution put forward several reiterated and novel demands with which Iraq was called upon to comply.[124] In its last paragraph it warned Iraq that it would face serious consequences if it continued to disregard its obligations.[125] Although the findings and demands were made under

---

[116] Ibid. The US president made two other demands: disclosure of information about missing Gulf War personnel (from the 1990–1991 war) and end to the illicit trade outside the oil-for-food program.

[117] Greenwood 2005, pp. 399–404.

[118] Falk 2003, p. 592.

[119] McGoldrick 2004, pp. 13–15; Yoo 2003, p. 563.

[120] Johnstone 2005, p. 397; McGoldrick 2004, p. 62

[121] SC Res. 1441, 1443, 1447 and 1454 (2002).

[122] SC Res. 1443, 1447, 1454 (2002).

[123] SC Res. 1441 (2002) para 1.

[124] Ibid., paras 2–5, 8.

[125] Ibid., para 13.

Chapter VII, the Security Council made no reference whatsoever to collective enforcement actions, whether armed or not.[126]

Iraq agreed to comply with Resolution 1441 and re-admitted UN and IAEA inspectors in the country.[127] On 7 December 2002, Iraq published a report relating to its relevant weapons programs.[128] The ensuing January, February and March 2003 IAEA and UNMOVIC reports found that a genuine acceptance of the disarmament was still lacking and that Iraq had still not taken all the steps required by Resolution 1441.[129] None of these reports, however, ascertained the existence of functional nuclear, chemical or biological weapons programs in Iraq.[130]

At the Security Council meeting of 7 March 2003, despite his numerous criticisms as to the Iraqi compliance with Resolution 1441, Hans Blix, Executive Chairman of UNMOVIC, was forced to acknowledge that 'no evidence of proscribed activities has so far been found' in Iraq.[131] At the same meeting, a number of states saluted the improvements in Iraq's cooperation with the UN and IAEA inspectors and emphasized the need for the inspections to continue. Needless to say, these states—Germany, France, Russia, China, Syria and Pakistan—advocated a peaceful disarmament as opposed to the use of armed force.[132] The opinions expressed made the US and the UK understand that there was not going to be a Security Council endorsement of the use of force against Iraq.[133] In these circumstances, the US, the UK and Australia, supported by a number of other states (the 'coalition of the willing'), decided to take military action without a further resolution of the Security Council expressly endorsing it.[134]

Circumventing the absence of a Security Council resolution expressly approving the action, the US and the UK put forward a complex legal argument on the basis of which the 'material breach' of Resolution 687 (1991) ascertained by Resolution 1441 (2002) in fact revived the mandate of Resolution 678 (1990) that

---

[126] An earlier draft of what became paragraph 4 of Resolution 1441 had stated that 'such breach authorizes member states to use all necessary means to restore international peace and security in the area.' The text was opposed by France and Russia, thus was erased from the final version of the resolution. McGoldrick 2004., p. 62

[127] Defiant Saddam accepts UN team (14 November 2002) Guardian; UN weapons inspectors arrive in Iraq (18 November 2002) Guardian.

[128] Saddam risks war over arms dossier (8 December 2002) Guardian; Greenwood 2005, p 394.

[129] ElBaradei (27 January 2003); Blix (27 January 2003); ElBaradei (14 February 2003); Blix (14 February 2003); UN Doc. S/2003/232 (2003); ElBaradei (7 March 2003); Blix (7 March 2003). See also Greenwood 2005, pp. 394-395.

[130] ElBaradei (27 January 2003); Blix (27 January 2003); ElBaradei (14 February 2003); Blix (14 February 2003); ElBaradei (7 March 2003); Blix (7 March 2003).

[131] SCOR, 58th Sess., 4714th meeting., UN Doc. S/PV.4714 (7 March 2003) p. 3.

[132] Ibid., pp. 9 (Germany), 11 (Syria), 17 (Russia), 18–19 (France), 21 (China), 32–33 (Pakistan).

[133] Falk 2003, p. 595; Greenwood 2005, p. 395.

[134] Greenwood 2005, p. 395.

authorized the use of force against Iraq.[135] By not complying with Resolution 1441, they argued that Iraq had squandered the last opportunity for a peaceful solution, thus reviving the mandate of Resolution 678 (1990) was the only option left.[136]

Operation Iraqi Freedom commenced on 19 March 2003. The inter-state conflict lasted only a few weeks. On 1 May 2003, President Bush announced the end of 'major combat operations'. In June 2004, the US transferred sovereignty to Iraq, while the US combat mission ended in August 2010.[137]

9.5.3 The 2003 Iraqi War: Self-Defence Against WMD

In a memorandum published on 18 November 2002, the Legal Adviser of the US State Department, William H. Taft IV, claimed that the 2002 National Security Strategy relied upon 'the same legal framework applied to the British in *Caroline* and to Israel in 1981'.[138] He further elaborated that 'after the exhaustion of peaceful remedies and a careful, deliberate consideration of the consequences, in the face of overwhelming evidence of an imminent threat, a nation may take pre-emptive action to defend its nationals from unimaginable harm'.[139]

The first statement was intriguing for several reasons. First, it claimed that the 2002 National Security Strategy was written on the basis of the customary right of self-defence and following the conditions of the Webster-formula. In truth, what the 2002 Security Strategy advocated was a much broader right of unilateral use of preventive force that had hardly anything to do with the strict criteria set forth by Webster. Secondly, the Legal Adviser purported that the *Caroline* incident of 1837 and the Israeli bombing of the Osirak reactor in 1981 shared the same legal

[135] UN Doc. S/2003/351 (2003); UN Doc. S/2003/350 (2003); McGoldrick 2004, pp. 53–55, p. 286 (Appendix VII: The Advice of the United Kingdom Attorney-General, Lord Goldsmith, on 'The Legal Basis for the Use of Force against Iraq', 17 March 2003).

[136] UN Doc. S/2003/351 (2003); McGoldrick 2004, pp. 53–55, pp. 264–280 (Appendix V: Presentation of Colin Powell, US Secretary of State to the United Nations Security Council on 'Iraq–Failing to Disarm', 5 February 2003). Greenwood asserted that the governments that resorted to force against Iraq were right to conclude that they could rely on the authorization of military action in Res. 678, read together with Res. 687 and Res. 1441. Greenwood 2003, p. 36. For similar opinions, see Hill 2004, pp. 329–331; Pierson 2004, pp. 154–155; Taft and Buchwald 2003, pp. 557–563, Wedgwood 2003, pp. 576–585; Yoo 2003, pp. 571–574. For the rejection of the US argument see: Rapport Commissie-Davids, Conclusions (January 2010), paras 18–20.

[137] US combat mission in Iraq ends (31 August 2010) CNN.

[138] Taft 2002.

[139] Ibid.

framework. That statement was overlooking the controversy surrounding the Israeli action and the condemnation expressed by the Security Council.[140]

In his 20 March 2003 letter to the Security Council, US Ambassador Negroponte made no explicit reference to the right of self-defence in justifying the invasion of Iraq. Nonetheless, he emphasized that the actions of the coalition forces were necessary steps 'to defend the United States and the international community from the threat posed by Iraq and to restore international peace and security in the area'.[141] This timid allusion to the necessity of self-defence was more robustly acknowledged by Taft, who, on the same day, maintained before the US National Association of Attorneys General that 'the President may also, of course, always use force under international law in self-defence'.[142] These statements were interpreted by many commentators as the first application of the 2002 National Security Strategy put forward by the Bush administration.[143]

In order to assess the legality of the self-defence claim against the threat posed by Iraqi WMD, several issues have to be addressed. First, the nature of the danger that the US and its allies were allegedly facing needs elaboration. For that purpose, the question whether Iraq *possessed* such weapons and the threat stemming from that possible possession needs to be analysed. Secondly, the immediacy factor has to be given attention. In other words, the imminence of an Iraqi armed attack against the US or its allies has to be addressed. Thirdly, the proportionality of the 2003 invasion of Iraq has to be examined against the actual threat.

9.5.4 The 2003 Iraqi War: The Requirement of Necessity

9.5.4.1 Possession of WMD

According to the International Court of Justice, the possession of nuclear weapons was illegal only if it was intended for a threat or use of force unlawful under the rules of the Charter.[144] Since no armed attack had occurred, the US was bound to prove not only that Iraq was developing, possessed or was about to acquire WMD, but also that Saddam Hussein planned to use them against the US or other allied states.

At no time before the commencement of hostilities did the US or its allies demonstrate the possession of WMD by the Iraqi government. Moreover, the

---

140 Franck 2002, pp. 105–106; Greenwood 2003, p. 14; Gill 2007, pp. 141–142; Alexandrov 1996, p. 162; SCOR, 36th Sess., 2280th–2288th meeting, UN Doc. S/PV.2280–S/PV.2288 (12–19 June 1981).

141 UN Doc. S/2003/351 2003.

142 Taft 2003.

143 Gardner 2003, p. 588; Henderson 2004, p. 12; McGoldrick 2004, p. 68; Sapiro 2003, p. 602.

144 Nuclear Weapons 1996, para 48.

absence of such weapons was confirmed in an official report of the US Central Intelligence Agency after the war.[145] The UNMOVIC and IAEA reports preceding the invasion mentioned several difficulties in the disclosure of information and concerning compliance with SC resolutions in general. Nonetheless, none of the reports concluded that WMD existed at that time in Iraq. Moreover, none of the reports could infer that programs developing such weapons were functional in Iraq.[146]

Without demonstrating the possession of WMD, the US could have at least proved the ongoing development of such weapons and advance a precise timetable as to the dates when such weapons could have been ready for use. That is what Israel did in 1981 and was nevertheless criticized for not proving irrefutably the existence of an imminent threat of a nuclear attack.[147] Alternatively, the US could have shown that Iraq was about to acquire WMD from an external source. None of these scenarios were proven.

What the inspectors did find in Iraq were 12 empty chemical warheads (16 January 2003) and a number of al-Samoud II missiles that exceeded the maximum range of 150 km set down in the 1991 Gulf war ceasefire agreement (12 February 2003).[148] The warheads were empty, thus no evidence of chemical weapons was found.[149] The al-Samoud II missiles exceeded the 150 km maximum range with 33 km, a difference which was largely insignificant, because the 150-km range already allowed Iraq to hit targets in the border area of neighbouring countries.[150] The possession of the warheads and the missiles were indeed in contravention of Iraq's disarmament obligations, but neither could have been construed as evidence of existence of WMD. Likewise, inconclusiveness of information disclosed or gaps in the declarations of Iraq could not amount to enough evidence to conclude that WMD were hidden in the country.

The US had several times stressed that the possession of weapons of mass destruction by Iraq amounted to such a threat that not only the US but the entire world was endangered by it.[151] The Bush administration warned several times

---

[145] Comprehensive Report of the Special Advisor to the DCI on Iraq's WMD (September 2004). The report concluded that Saddam Hussein did not possess stockpiles of illicit weapons at the time of the US invasion in March 2003 and had not begun any program to produce them.

[146] ElBaradei (27 January 2003); Blix (27 January 2003); ElBaradei (14 February 2003); Blix (14 February 2003); ElBaradei (7 March 2003); Blix (7 March 2003).

[147] UN Doc. S/14510 (1981); Mueller et al., p. 212.

[148] Special Report Iraq, 'Iraq timeline: July 16, 1979 to January 31, 2004', Guardian; Iraq weapons inspectors find empty chemical warheads (17 January 2003) Guardian; UN team finds Iraq has illegal missiles (13 February 2003) Guardian.

[149] Iraq weapons inspectors find empty chemical warheads (17 January 2003) Guardian.

[150] Iraq's al-Samoud missile (3 March 2003) BBC World News. .

[151] A Decade of Deception and Defiance 2002 Bush (12 September 2002) Remarks; McGoldrick 2004, pp. 53–55, pp. 264–280 (Appendix V—Presentation of Colin Powell, US Secretary of State to the UN Security Council on 'Iraq: Failing to Disarm', 5 February 2003); Falk 2003, p. 592.

against the willingness and determination of Saddam Hussein to use such weapons once developed or acquired.[152] Determination to use WMD once acquired could indeed be viewed as a serious threat. The International Court of Justice also acknowledged that possession of nuclear weapons could indicate the preparedness to use them.[153] Nonetheless, as Franck said, propensity was immaterial in establishing conclusive evidence.[154] The fact that Saddam Hussein was inclined to use WMD did not offer irrefutable evidence of the fact that he *would* and *could* choose such an option.

9.5.4.2 The Immediacy Factor

For maintaining a claim of self-defence, the US should have also proven that the existing threat was also imminent. The US did not demonstrate the ongoing development, the possession or the nature of the threat of possessing and acquiring WMD by Iraq. The Bush administration offered even less evidence as to the feasibility—let alone imminence—of a future armed attack involving WMD.[155] As Beatty pointed out, the Iraqi war was 'fought in the subjunctive, based on a string of *ifs*':

> If Saddam possesses usable weapons of mass destruction and if, to take a scenario George W. Bush takes seriously, he builds a fleet of pilotless drones and if he somehow gets them out of Iraq and if he builds or hires ships and launches his drones from them and if he has found a way to make the drones spread weapons of mass destruction and if it is not a windy day and if our Army, Navy, Air Force, Coast Guard, CIA, and DIA are as asleep as they were on September 11, then Saddam will attack us.[156]

During the months preceding the invasion, Iraq signalled its willingness to comply with Resolution 1441 (2002).[157] It allowed weapons inspectors to return to the country, it provided declarations as to the weapons it possessed and asserted its openness to continue the inspection and disclosure procedure.[158] There were, obviously, criticisms as to its cooperation and straightforwardness.[159] Nonetheless, it never refused to continue the dialogue with UNMOVIC, the IAEA and the Security Council. Moreover, several members of the Security Council believed

---

[152] A Decade of Deception and Defiance (2002); Bush (12 September 2002) Remarks; McGoldrick, pp. 53–55, pp. 264–280 (Appendix V).

[153] Nuclear Weapons 1996, para 48.

[154] Franck 2002, p. 106.

[155] Henderson 2004, p. 14; Sapiro 2003, p. 603..

[156] Beatty 2003.

[157] Defiant Saddam accepts UN team (14 November 2002) Guardian.

[158] Ibid.; UN weapons inspectors arrive in Iraq (18 November 2002) Guardian; Saddam risks war over arms dossier (8 December 2002) Guardian; SCOR, 58th Sess., 4714th meeting., UN Doc. S/PV.4714 (7 March 2003) pp. 34–36.

[159] ElBaradei (27 January 2003); Blix (27 January 2003); ElBaradei (14 February 2003); Blix and February (2003)ElBaradei (7 March 2003); Blix (7 March 2003).

that the situation could be solved by peaceful disarmament.[160] There was always a choice of means to solve the conflict in a non-forceful manner. There was never a present and inevitable need to use force.[161]

The remoteness and vagueness of the future threat of an armed attack was indeed a vindication of the new Bush doctrine advocating preventive use of force against potential threats.[162] The threat perceived by the US was along the lines of the 2002 Security Strategy: compelling, even though 'uncertainty remains as to the time and place of the enemy's attack'.[163] As Sapiro noted, such a reinterpretation of limits eliminates the requirement that an impending threat be imminent.[164] Indeed, the administration did not put emphasis on the imminence of the threat. President Bush even asserted that 'in one year, or five years, the power of Iraq to inflict harm on all free nations will be multiplied many times over. [...] We choose to meet that threat now, where it arises, before it can appear suddenly in our skies and cities'.[165]

Notwithstanding the frequent reference to the magnitude of the Iraqi threat, by failing to demonstrate that Iraq was in possession or was developing WMD, the US failed to prove not only *when* and *where* the attack would occur, but also *if* it would ever happen.

There was no resemblance whatsoever of the new preventive approach with the anticipatory action permitted by the pre-Charter customary right of self-defence.[166] Nor was any resemblance between the anticipatory action accepted as legitimate in the Six-Day War and the US preventive approach.[167] Moreover, the US action exceeded even the limits of the 1981 Israeli bombing of the Osirak reactor, an instance of state practice condemned at a time for failing to demonstrate the immediacy factor.[168] The 2003 US action departed from the limits observed by the same country in the Cuban missile crisis. In 2003, the US administration chose to discard the view that anticipatory action in self-defence could not be expanded 'to include threatening deployments or demonstrations that do not have imminent attack as their purpose or probable outcome'.[169]

160 SCOR, 58th Sess., 4714th meeting., UN Doc. S/PV.4714 (7 March 2003) pp 9 (Germany), 11 (Syria), 17 (Russia), 18–19 (France), 21 (China), 32–33 (Pakistan).

161 Henderson 2004, p. 14.

162 Gardner 2003, p. 588; Henderson 2004, p. 12; Sapiro 2003, p. 602.

163 US National Security Strategy 2002, Part V; Sapiro 2005, p. 367.

164 Sapiro 2005, p. 367.

165 Bush (17 March 2003) Remarks.

166 Gardner 2003, p. 587; Sapiro 2005, p. 367.

167 See *supra* 8.2.2.

168 See *supra* 9.3.

169 Chayes 1974, p. 65.

The justification of the Iraqi war under the new doctrine of preventive use was not self-defence.[170] It could rather be described as a unilateral use of preventive force to tackle a situation that could—at an unknown point in time—become dangerous.[171] As Gardner observed, by expanding the right of pre-emption against an imminent attack into a right of preventive war against potentially dangerous adversaries, the Bush administration created a 'loaded weapon' that could be used against the United States and against the general interest in a stable world order.[172]

9.5.5 Proportionality

Assuming, for the sake of argument, that the US invasion of Iraq could have been characterized as an instance of self-defence, the question remains whether its exercise was proportionate.

In 1981, Israel was criticized for carrying out a surgical airstrike against the Osirak reactor. The airstrike targeted one reactor facility that was believed to produce the fissile material for the future weapons.[173] In 2003, the US and other coalition states launched a full-scale invasion against Iraq without having identified any facilities that were developing weapons of mass destruction. Putting aside all the other requirements for the legality of a claim of self-defence, the US war against Iraq lacked any proportionality whatsoever. It invaded a country, toppled and replaced the incumbent regime and assumed the responsibilities of an occupying power for several years without having the slightest proof that an imminent threat of an armed attack existed.

9.6 Concluding Remarks

This chapter analysed three instances of state practice which had two common elements. First, as with all instances analysed in Part II, they involved a claim of self-defence—used or contemplated. Secondly, specific for this chapter, they pertained to conflicts involving weapons of mass destruction (see Table. 9.1).

The instances of state practice presented above show a tendency to exceed the temporal dimension of self-defence when it comes to the use of force against weapons of mass destruction. In the Cuban missile crisis, the US government

---

[170] Lowe 2003, p. 865.

[171] For an author with similar views, see Gardner 2003, p. 588. For authors defending the new doctrine, see Hill 2004, pp. 329–331; Pierson 2004, pp. 174–176; Taft and Buchwald 2003, pp. 557–563; Wedgwood 2003, p. 584; Yoo 2003, pp. 571–574.

[172] Gardner 2003, p. 588.

[173] See *supra* 9.3. Mueller et al. 2006, p. 212.

Table 9.1 The nature of the threat, the limits and the outcome of claims of self-defence involving WMDs

	Nature of threat faced	Breached limits	Reaction
Cuban missile crisis (1962)	Emplacement of nuclear weapons in a neighbouring, hostile country	None (no forceful action taken apart from the naval quarantine)	Moderate acceptance (some criticism because of the naval quarantine)
Israeli bombing of the Iraqi reactor (1981)	Development of nuclear weapons	Immediacy	Condemnation
US war against Iraq (2003)	Presumed existence of nuclear weapons	Conditionality of attack Immediacy Proportionality	Condemnation

decided not to resort to self-defence, because it believed that there was no legal basis for anticipatory action in the absence of the threat of an imminent attack.[174] That instance of state practice followed the pre-Charter understanding of the temporal dimension of self-defence.

The Israeli bombing of the Osirak reactor went one step further. The airstrikes were justified as self-defence against the possibility of Iraq developing a nuclear weapon in the foreseeable future.[175] Grave as the threat of such a possibility would have been, self-defence does not allow the use of force against dangers that do not create a present and inevitable need to ward them off. In other words, without the immediacy factor, such an action could not meet the requirement of necessity in self-defence. It is important to note here that the Israeli airstrikes were criticized by states before the Security Council as exceeding the limits of anticipatory action. The parameters on the basis of which members of the Security Council put forward their criticism was in line with the pre-Charter understanding of anticipatory action.[176] One member even made reference to the *Caroline* incident in that respect.[177] The reaction of the SC members is very important on this point. By criticizing the Israeli action on the basis of the limits of anticipatory action in self-defence, the representatives acknowledged the validity of such action under strict parameters. This is in line with the ICJ's finding that unlawful instances of state practice can still confirm a rule if they are being treated as breaches of that rule.[178]

The 2003 US invasion of Iraq exceeded even the limits of the 1981 Israeli action. The 'Bush doctrine' served as the basis for the invasion and occupation of a

174 See *supra* 9.2.

175 See *supra* 9.3.

176 SCOR, 36th Sess., 2282nd meeting., UN Doc. S/PV.2282 (15 June 1981) paras 14-19; 2283rd meeting., S/PV.2283 (15 June 1981) paras 23–27; 2284th meeting., S/PV.2284 (16 June 1981) para 11.

177 SCOR, 36th Sess., 2282nd meeting., UN Doc. S/PV.2282 (15 June 1981) paras 14–19.

178 Nicaragua 1986, para 186.

country as well as the toppling of its regime without any evidence as to the existence of—let alone imminent threat to use— weapons of mass destruction. The two latter examples of state practice show a tendency to exceed the temporal dimension of self-defence by advocating preventive use of force against the development or possession of WMD. Conflicts involving WMD thus push the temporal dimension of self-defence towards prevention. That trend, however, is not conclusively supported by UN organs or legal doctrine. Comments characterizing such trend as signalling a lawful alteration of the temporal dimension of self-defence have been voiced in the legal literature, but the opinion is still a minority.[179] The approach of the Security Council has been negative; it condemned the Israeli reaction and it failed to endorse the US-led invasion of Iraq.[180] The International Court of Justice stopped short of characterizing possession of nuclear weapons unlawful *per se*, thus implicitly restricted the exercise of self-defence in such situations.[181] The majority of the legal doctrine is also considerably sceptical as to the lawfulness of the use of force against development and possession of nuclear weapons.[182]

The three instances of state practice presented in this chapter are also important for the perceived limits of anticipatory action in self-defence. Accordingly, as specified in the introductory remarks of Part II, the requirements of necessity and proportionality pertain to three limits: the conditionality of the attack, the immediacy factor and the moderate use of force. When it comes to conflicts involving weapons of mass destruction, the immediacy factor is affected the most. In the Cuban missile crisis, the US government chose to observe this element (in its pre-Charter form) and abstained from invoking self-defence because there was no present and inevitable need to resort to anticipatory action in self-defence. The immediacy factor was ignored both by Israel in 1981 and by the US in 2003. In fairness, the threat perceived by the Israeli government was considerably more realistic and possible than the one alleged by the US government in 2003. Nonetheless, on the basis of the available information at the time, there was no present and inevitable need to launch airstrikes against the Osirak reactor, because there was no imminent threat of an armed attack. Even if—from a strategic point of view—destroying the reactor was a crucial move, that action cannot be justified as self-defence. Without the immediacy element (present and inevitable need to act), the use of force cannot meet the necessity requirement. Even if the conditionality of the attack is present (it was shown that in four years' time, the reactor could have produced a nuclear weapon), that conditionality has to create an immediate need for action. This immediacy does not have to be measured in days

[179] Hill 2004, pp. 329–331; Pierson 2004, pp. 154–155; Taft and Buchwald 2003, pp. 557–563, Taft 2003; Wedgwood 2003, p. 584; Yoo 2003, pp. 571–574.

[180] See *supra* 9.3 and 9.5.2.

[181] See *supra* 9.4.

[182] Gardner 2003, pp. 587–588; Henderson 2004, p. 14; Lowe 2003, p. 865; Sapiro 2005, p. 367; Slaughter 2004, pp. 262–263.

or weeks, it only has to qualify the situation as creating a present and inevitable need for action. That qualification was not present in the 1981 and 2003 instances of state practice examined above. For this reason, it can be concluded that conflicts involving weapons of mass destruction push the temporal dimension of self-defence towards prevention by putting a strain on the immediacy factor of the requirement of necessity.

References

A decade of deception and defiance: Saddam Hussein's defiance of the United Nations (2002). The White House, Washington, D.C. http://www.gwu.edu/~nsarchiv/NSAEBB/NSAEBB80/wmd13.pdf. Accessed 15 February 2010.

Alexandrov S (1996) Self-defense against the use of force in international law. Kluwer, The Hague

Allison GT (1971) Essence of decision: explaining the Cuban missile crisis. Little Brown, Boston

Baylis J, Smith S (eds) (2001) The globalisation of world politics. Oxford University Press, New York

Beatty J (5 March 2003) In the name of God. Atlantic Online. www.theatlantic.com/magazine/archive/2003/03/in-the-name-of-god/3167. Accessed 20 February 2010.

Blix H, Executive Chairman UNMOVIC (27 January 2003) Briefing of the Security Council: an update on inspections. http://www.un.org/Depts/unmovic/Bx27.htm. Accessed 11 January 2010

Blix H, Executive Chairman UNMOVIC (14 February 2003) Briefing of the Security Council: an update on inspections. http://www.unmovic.org/. Accessed 11 January 2010

Blix H, Executive Chairman UNMOVIC (7 March 2003) Briefing of the Security Council: oral introduction of the 12th Quarterly Report of UNMOVIC http://www.unmovic.org/. Accessed 11 January 2010

Bush GW (29 January 2002) State of the Union Address http://georgewbush-whitehouse.archives.gov/news/releases/2002/01/20020129-11.html. Accessed 20 January

Bush GW (1 June 2002) Graduation speech at West Point http://georgewbush-whitehouse.archives.gov/news/releases/2002/06/20020601-3.html. Accessed 21 January 2010

Bush GW (12 September 2002) Remarks at the United Nations General Assembly, New York http://georgewbush-whitehouse.archives.gov/news/releases/2002/06/20020601-3.html. Accessed 26 January 2010

Bush GW (17 March 2003) Remarks by the President in Address to the Nation http://georgewbush-whitehouse.archives.gov/news/releases/2002/06/20020601-3.html. Accessed 26 January 2010

Campbell JS (1963) The Cuban crisis and the U.N. Charter: an analysis of the United States position. Stanf Law Rev 16:160–176

Chang L, Kornbluh P (eds) (1992) The Cuban missile crisis 1962. A national security archive documents reader. The New Press, New York

Chayes A (1974) The Cuban missile crisis. Oxford University Press, London

Comprehensive Report of the Special Advisor to the DCI on Iraq's WMD (September 2004). https://www.cia.gov/library/reports/general-reports-1/iraq_wmd_2004/index.html. Accessed 17 February 2010

Defiant Saddam accepts UN team (14 November 2002). Guardian www.guardian.co.uk/world/2002/nov/14/iraq.ewenmacaskill. Accessed 14 March 2010

Dinstein Y (2005) War, aggression and self-defense. Cambridge University Press, Cambridge

ElBaradei M, Director General IAEA (27 January 2003) Statement to the United Nations Security Council: the status of nuclear inspections in Iraq http://www.un.org/News/dh/iraq/elbaradei27jan03.htm. Accessed 11 January 2010

ElBaradei M, Director General IAEA (14 February 2003) Statement to the United Nations Security Council: the status of nuclear inspections in Iraq—an update http://www.un.org/News/dh/iraq/elbaradei-14feb03.pdf. Accessed 11 January 2010

ElBaradei M, Director General IAEA (7 March 2003) Statement to the United Nations Security Council: the status of nuclear inspections in Iraq—an update http://www.un.org/News/dh/iraq/elbaradei-7mar03.pdf. Accessed 11 January 2010

Falk RA (1997) Nuclear weapons, international law and the world court: a historic encounter. Am J Int Law 91:64–75

Falk RA (2003) What future for the UN Charter system of war prevention? Am J Int Law 97:590–598

Farrell T, Lambert H (2001) Courting controversy: international law, national norms and American nuclear use. Rev Int Stud 27:309–326

Franck T (2002) Recourse to force: state action against threats and armed attacks. Cambridge University Press, Cambridge

Gardner RN (2003) Neither Bush nor the "Jurisprudes". Am J Int Law 97:585–590

Garthoff RL (1988) Cuban missile crisis: the Soviet story. Foreign Policy 72:61–80

Gill TD (2007) The temporal dimension of self-defence. In: Schmitt M, Pejic J (eds) International law and armed conflict: exploring the faultlines. Essays in honour of Yoram Dinstein. Martinus Nijhoff, Leiden, pp 113–155

Green JA (2009) The International Court of Justice and self-defence in international law. Hart, Oxford

Greenwood C (2003) International law and the pre-emptive use of force: Afghanistan, Al-Qaida and Iraq. San Diego Int Law J 4:7–38

Greenwood C (2005) Legality of the use of force: Iraq in 2003. In: Bothe M, O'Connell ME, Ronzitti N (eds) Redefining sovereignty: the use of force after the Cold War. Transnational Ardsley, New York, pp 387–415

Grief N (1997) Legality of the threat or use of nuclear weapons. Int Comp Law Q 46:681–688

Heisbourg F (2003) A work in progress: the Bush doctrine and its consequences. Wash Q 26(2):73–88

Henderson C (2004) The Bush doctrine: from theory to practice. J Confl Secur Law 9:3–24

Hill C (2004) The Bush Administration preemption doctrine and the future of world order: remark. Am So Int Law Proceedings 98:329–331.

Ignatieff M (23 March 2003) I am Iraq. New York Times http://www.nytimes.com/2003/03/23/magazine/the-way-we-live-now-3-23-03-i-am-iraq.html. Accessed 13 March 2010

Iraq weapons inspectors find empty chemical warheads (17 January 2003). Guardian www.guardian.co.uk/world/2003/jan/17/iraq.ewenmacaskill. Accessed 21 March 2010

Iraq's al-Samoud missile (3 March 2003). BBC World News http://news.bbc.co.uk/1/hi/world/middle_east/2756987.stm Accessed 21 March 2010

Johnstone I (2005) Jus ad bellum: the next Iraq. ILSA J Int Comp Law 11:395–402

Lowe V (2003) The Iraqi crisis: what now? Int Comp Law Q 52:859–871

Matheson MJ (1997) The opinions of the International Court of Justice on the threat or use of nuclear weapons. Am J Int Law 91:417–435

McDougal MS (1963) The Soviet-Cuban quarantine and self-defense. Am J Int Law 57:597–604

McGoldrick D (2004) From "9–11" to the Iraq War 2003: international law in an age of complexity. Hart, Oxford

Meeker LC (1963) Defensive quarantine and the law. Am J Int Law 57:515–524

Mueller KP et al (2006) Striking first: preemptive and preventive attack in US national security policy. RAND Project Air Force

Nicaragua 1986: Military and paramilitary activities in and against Nicaragua (Nicaragua v. USA), Judgment of 27 June 1986, ICJ Rep. (1986)

Nuclear Weapons 1996: Legality of the threat or use of nuclear weapons, Advisory Opinion of 8 July 1996, ICJ Rep. (1996)

Pierson C (2004) Preemptive self-defence in an age of weapons of mass destruction: Operation Iraqi Freedom. Denver J Int Law Policy 33:150–178

Rapport Commissie-Davids: Rapport Commissie van Onderzoek Besluitvorming Irak (Rapport Commissie-Davids), Conclusions (January 2010) http://www.rijksoverheid.nl/onderwerpen/irak/documenten-en-publicaties/rapporten/2010/01/12/rapport-commissie-davids-conclusions.html. Accessed 2 June 2010

Saddam risks war over arms dossier (8 December 2002). Guardian www.guardian.co.uk/world/2002/dec/08/iraq. Accessed 21 March 2010

Sapiro M (2003) Iraq: the shifting sands of preemptive self-defense. Am J Int Law 97:599–607

Sapiro M (2005) Preempting prevention: lessons learned. NYU J Int Law Politics 37:357–371

Schmitt MN (2003) Preemptive strategies in international law. Mich J Int Law 24:513–548

SCOR: Security Council Official Records http://documents.un.org/simple.asp

Slaughter AM (2004) The use of force in Iraq: illegal and illegitimate. Am Soc Int Law Proc 98:262–263.

Special Report Iraq, Iraq timeline: July 16, 1979 to January 31, 2004. Guardian www.guardian.co.uk/Iraq/page/0,12438,793802,00.html. Accessed 21 March 2010

Taft 2002: Taft WH (18 November 2002) The legal basis for preemption. Council on Foreign Relations http://www.cfr.org/publication/5250/legal_basis_for_preemption.html. Accessed 17 February 2010

Taft 2003: Taft WH (20 March 2003) Remarks to the National Association of Attorneys General, Washington http://usinfo.org/wf-archive/2003/030321/epf516.htm. Accessed 17 February 2010

Taft WH, Buchwald TF (2003) Preemption, Iraq, and international law. Am J Int Law 97:557–563

Tannenwald N (1999) The nuclear taboo: the United States and the normative basis of nuclear non-use. Int Org 53:433–468

UN team finds Iraq has illegal missiles (13 February 2003) Guardian www.guardian.co.uk/world/2003/feb/13/iraq.garyyounge. Accessed 21 March 2010

UN weapons inspectors arrive in Iraq (18 November 2002). Guardian www.guardian.co.uk/world/2002/nov/18/iraq. Accessed 21 March 2010

US combat mission in Iraq ends (31 August 2010). CNN http://articles.cnn.com/2010-08-31/politics/iraq.us_1_training-of-iraqi-security-iraqi-violence-united-states-and-iraq?_s=PM:POLITICS. Accessed 15 October 2010

US National Security Strategy 2002: The National Security Strategy of the United States of America Part V. The White House. Washington, D.C.

Waltz KN (1990) Nuclear myths and political realities. Am Politi Sci Rev 84:731–745

Wedgwood R (2003) The fall of Saddam Hussein: Security Council mandates and preemptive self-defense. Am J Int Law 97:576–585

Weston BH (1997) Nuclear weapons and the World Court: ambiguity's consensus. Transl Law Contemp Probl 7:371–400

Wright Q (1963) The Cuban quarantine. Am J Int Law 57:546–565

Yoo J (2003) International law and the war in Iraq. Am J Int Law 97:563–576

Chapter 10
Self-Defence Against Non-State Actors

10.1 Introduction

Arguments justifying the use of self-defence against non-state actors have been advanced by many states throughout the twentieth century. Political violence between states and non-state actors has been given different names over time, from guerrilla war to insurgency or militant terrorism.[1] The present chapter will focus on those claims of self-defence that were made by states against non-state actors. The chapter will analyse several instances of state practice, but will also follow through the evolution of so-called terrorism from small, state-supported irregular bands to globalised networks of militants, relatively independent from the state apparatus.[2]

The aims of this chapter are threefold. First, it will analyse how states, the Security Council, the General Assembly and legal publicists viewed armed acts committed by non-state actors and whether they saw them as amounting to armed attack in the sense of Article 51 of the Charter. Secondly, it will assess how specific claims of self-defence against non-state actors have been perceived over the years after the adoption of the Charter. Thirdly, it will shed light on the evolution of the 'accumulation of events' theory and its relation to the temporal dimension of self-defence. In other words, it will be assessed in what way does the

---

1 For a classification of political violence between states and non-state actors, see Chaliand and Blin 2007, pp. 16–23.

2 The term 'terrorism' had many shifting and contested meanings over time and it is acknowledged to have a stigmatizing, delegitimizing, even dehumanizing connotation. In the light of the 'kaleidoscopic use of the term,' it is acknowledged by the present author that terrorism is very difficult to define (for an analysis of the use of the term, see Saul 2006, pp. 3–4). For that reason, in the present book 'terrorism' will be used to describe: 'criminal acts, including against civilians, committed with the intent to cause death or serious bodily injury, or taking of hostages, with the purpose to provoke a state of terror in the general public or in a group of persons or particular persons, intimidate a population or compel a government or ban international organization to do or to abstain from doing any act.' SC Res. 1566 (2004) para 3. Characterizations of acts as 'terrorist' made by states or publicists will be put in quotation marks.

K. Tibori Szabó, *Anticipatory Action in Self-Defence*, DOI: 10.1007/978-90-6704-796-8_10,

'accumulation of events' theory affect the anticipatory and remedial dimensions of self-defence and whether this theory signals a restrictive or a permissive trend in interpreting the limits of these dimensions.

The chapter is divided in four main sections. The first (Section 10.2) will focus on the conflict between Israel and Arab militant groups in the 1950s–1970s. Section 10.2 depicts the initial approach of the Security Council towards armed acts carried out by non-state actors and introduces the 'accumulation of events' theory. The second section (10.3) shows how this theory was used by other states and developed in legal literature in the 1960s–1980s. The third section (10.4) focuses on armed acts of non-state actors in the 1990s. It also examines the changing attitude of the Security Council towards such acts. The fourth section (10.5) discusses several claims of self-defence made by states against non-state actors in the 2000s. Section 10.5 also analyses how the 'accumulation of events' theory can be used for assessing the justifiability of a claim of self-defence.

10.2 Israel and Arab Militants

Confrontations between the Israeli and Palestinian communities erupted as early as the 1920s as a result of the Balfour Declaration legitimizing the creation of a Jewish state. That conflict escalated to involve neighbouring Arab states as well. One of its main characteristics was the use of non-state actors to carry out hit-and-run type of acts, such as those undertaken by regular armed forces in some of the conflicts discussed in Chapter 8 (the hit-and-run attacks that led to claims of self-defence by the UK and the US in 1964, the 1986 US bombing of Libya and the 1993 US bombing of Iraq). The same type of attacks—also coined as guerrilla warfare or terrorist-type of acts—were frequently resorted to by irregular armed groups.[3]

On the occasion of the 1956 Sinai campaign, Israel justified its actions as self-defence not only against the blocking of the Suez Canal but also against the raids of the *fedayeen* supported by Egypt.[4] At that time, Israel characterized the use of the *fedayeen* units as 'the spearhead of Egyptian belligerency.'[5] The Israeli Foreign Minister Abba Eban went on to explain that their use 'is a new device for making war and for making it with safety. The doctrine is one of unilateral belligerency. The Egyptian–Israel frontier is to be a one-way street. It is to be wide open for these armed Egyptian units to penetrate deeply into Israel to accomplish their mission and to return.'[6] Israel complained about the incursions and attacks of

---

[3] Chaliand and Blin 2007, pp. 212–213.

[4] GAOR, 1st Emergency Special Session, UN Doc. A/PV.562 (1956) paras 138–145.

[5] Ibid., para 143.

[6] Ibid.

the *fedayeen* in order to sustain its claim that the 'long and uninterrupted series of encroachment amounted to an armed attack that justified self-defence.'[7]

Similar arguments were raised by Israel to justify the repeated incursions into Jordanian and Lebanese territory to disable alleged bases of Palestinian organizations and armed units.[8] Between December 1968 and March 1969, Israel carried out concerted land and airborne attacks against alleged 'terror bases' deep inside Jordanian territory, reaching Amman.[9] On 27 March 1969, before the Security Council, Israel contended that 'more than 200 sabotage raids and firing attacks across the cease-fire lines' had been recorded since the beginning of that year.[10] They included 'attacks by small arms, mortar, bazooka and Katyushka fire' on several Israeli villages as well as 'sabotage raids with grenades and explosives directed against civilians, incidents of mining and six clashes with terror units.'[11] Israel went on to blame Jordan for supporting these operations and claimed that Jordanian territory served as 'the main jumping-off ground for attacks' and as 'the central base of the terror operations.'[12] Moreover, 'the terror organizations' units are free to roam the country, to cross the Jordan River for raids into Israel and enjoy full protection on the part of the regular Jordanian army.'[13] On this basis, Israel justified its armed action as self-defence against the repeated acts of the new 'terror warfare'.[14] During the enfolding discussion, the Russian representative characterized the Israeli raids as 'premeditated, planned acts of aggression.'[15] Similar opinions were expressed by the delegates of Algeria, Finland, France, Pakistan and China.[16] The US delegate, while deploring the loss of life and condemning Israel's 'indiscriminate actions', emphasized the responsibility of the

---

[7] Ibid., para 146. Israel used similar arguments to justify armed action against regular forces as well. In 1964 Israel carried out airstrikes against Syrian territory in response to 'repeated acts of aggression by Syrian armed forces against citizens and territory of Israel' and 'threats by official spokesmen of the Syrian government against the territorial integrity and political independence of Israel.' In the ensuing Security Council debate, the Israeli representative justified the action as a last resort and as an obligation of the Israeli government to defend the territory of the state and the life of its citizens, while the Syrian representatives coined the airstrikes as a premeditated aggression. The Syrian representative maintained that the Israeli 'defensive measure' was an abuse of right and that concepts such as 'exploratory self-defence' or 'preventive self-defence' should not be accepted. The Security Council failed to adopt a resolution, but the draft proposals submitted all concentrated on criticising Israel for its actions. See: UN Doc. S/6046 (1964); Repertoire, Supp. 1964–1965, Chapter VIII, pp. 139–140, 196.

[8] Alexandrov 1996, pp. 174–176.

[9] SCOR, 24th Session, 1466th meeting., UN Doc. S/PV.1466 (27 March 1969) paras 30, 69.

[10] Ibid., para 59.

[11] Ibid.

[12] Ibid., para 62.

[13] Ibid.

[14] Ibid., para 87.

[15] Ibid., 1467th meeting., UN Doc. S/PV.1467 (27 March 1969) para 6.

[16] Ibid., 1468th meeting., UN Doc. S/PV.1468 (28 March 1969) paras 3, 18, 34, 41; 1470th meeting., S/PV.1470 (29 March 1969) para 50.

Arab states for the frequent breaches of the ceasefire and for the various attacks carried out on population centres.[17] At the end of the discussions, the Security Council adopted a resolution in which it condemned the 'premeditated air attacks by Israel.'[18]

A few months later, Israel carried out similar air attacks against alleged 'bases of terror organizations' in Lebanon and justified its action as self-defence against 'repeated attacks'.[19] The Security Council adopted yet another resolution in which it condemned the Israeli air attacks.[20] Similar resolutions were adopted by the Security Council in May and September 1970 as well as in February and June 1972 condemning Israeli military action against Lebanon or demanding the withdrawal of its forces.[21] In the ensuing discussion after the June 1972 Israeli ground and air attacks on Lebanese territory, the representative of Belgium contended that the right of self-defence could only be used against 'a single case of armed aggression' and that the 'incidents' which provoked the Israeli reaction could not be described as an act of aggression.[22]

Israel continued to invoke self-defence against what it saw as 'terror warfare' and continuous attacks from armed groups based in the neighbouring Arab states.[23] In December 1975, Israel raided a complex of Palestinian bases in Lebanon, from which multiple attacks against Israeli territory had originated.[24] This time, the Security Council was unable to pass a resolution because of the veto exercised by the United States. During the discussions, the US delegate reminded the Council that the organizations which carried out acts of violence against Israel had publicly acknowledged their responsibility.[25] Moreover, progress could not be made with the adoption of 'one-sided resolutions' that left Israel believing that it was the victim of discrimination and bias on the part of the United Nations.[26]

The Israeli line of reasoning that had crystallized by that time was based on a concept of 'repeated attacks',[27] 'continuous warfare',[28] 'series of encroachment'[29] that amounted to armed attacks. There were two important arguments in this assertion: first, that the totality of the continuous attacks have caused serious harm

---

[17] Ibid., 1467th meeting., UN Doc. S/PV.1467 (27 March 1969) paras 48–49.

[18] SC Res. 265 (1969) para 3.

[19] UN Doc. S/9387 (1969).

[20] SC Res. 270 (1969) para 1.

[21] SC Res. 279, 285 (1970), 313, 316 (1972).

[22] SCOR, 27th Session, 1650th meeting., UN Doc. S/PV.1560 (26 June 1972) para 93.

[23] SC Res. 337 (1973) and 347 (1974).

[24] SCOR, 30th Session, 1860th meeting., UN Doc. S/PV.1860 (5 December 1975); Dinstein 2005, pp. 247–248; Alexandrov 1996, pp. 176–177.

[25] SCOR, 30th Session, 1860th meeting., UN Doc. S/PV.1860 (5 December 1975) para 3.

[26] Ibid., para 5.

[27] UN Doc. S/9387 (1969).

[28] SCOR, 24th Session, 1466th meeting., UN Doc. S/PV.1466 (27 March 1969) para 89.

[29] GAOR, 1st Emergency Special Session 1956, UN Doc. A/PV.562 (1956) para 146.

to the life of the Israeli citizens and second, that the repetition of these attacks prompted Israel to believe that more were yet to come.[30] The first argument raised the threshold of gravity to that of an armed attack, whereas the second justified defensive action against future threats. This assertion came to be known as the *Nadelstichtaktik*, 'needle-prick' approach or 'accumulation of events' theory.[31]

The 'accumulation of events' theory raised questions as to the necessity and proportionality requirements of self-defence. Accordingly, the 'needle-prick' approach saw a present and inevitable need to act both against already occurred acts and in the face of new threats. The notion of 'armed attack' had to be interpreted collectively to include a series of repeated attacks, 'pinpricks' that together created the immediate need to act. Furthermore, proportionality had to be measured against the need to neutralize the source of all future attacks.

Although self-defence against non-state actors was not an entirely new phenomenon in the legal history of the right, the general reaction to the Israeli claims showed that the members of the Security Council and the General Assembly were reluctant to accept that armed attacks could also be carried out by irregular forces and that the target state had the right to defend itself against them.[32]

Israel was not the only state to resort to the 'needle-prick' approach. As will be shown below, starting from the 1960s, other countries have raised similar claims to justify resort to armed force.

10.3 State Practice in the 1960s–1980s

The question whether armed acts of irregular bands, individually or collectively, could amount to an armed attack under Article 51 was discussed early on by several legal scholars.[33] Higgins, for instance, affirmed that if a state had been subjected, over a period of time, to border raids by nationals of another state, which were openly supported by the government of that state, to threats of a future and possibly imminent, large-scale attack, that state was entitled to use force in self-defence, provided it was proportionate, in nature and degree, to the prior illegality or the imminent attack.[34] Brownlie also acknowledged that 'a co-ordinated and general campaign by powerful bands of irregulars, with obvious or easily proven complicity of the government of a state from which they operate, would constitute an armed attack, more especially if the objective was the forcible

[30] Baker 1987, p. 42; Jacobson 1998, pp. 13–14.

[31] Bowett 1972, p. 12; Blum 1976, pp. 233; Gross 1983, p. 478; Schachter 1985, p. 293; Baker 1987, p. 42; Jacobson 1998, pp. 13, 16.

[32] Both the *Caroline* incident and the expedition in the pursuit of Pancho Villa involved non-state actors. See *supra* 3.2.2 and 3.2.2.1. See also Kelly 2005, pp. 225–227.

[33] Garcia-Mora 1962, p. 114; Higgins 1963, p. 201; Brownlie 1963, p. 279.

[34] Higgins 1963, p. 201.

settlement of a dispute or the acquisition of territory.'[35] Despite the increasing attention received in legal doctrine and state practice, many controversies remained regarding the gravity, number and purpose of armed acts carried out by irregular bands. Likewise, the 'accumulation of events' theory raised questions of necessity and proportionality of armed actions in self-defence. These controversies became apparent in virtually all instances when states justified their use of force in self-defence on the basis of the 'needle-prick' approach. These instances were not necessarily connected with non-state actors; states sometimes referred to the 'needle-prick' theory also in relation to repeated acts committed by regular forces.

One such instance was the 1964 UK bombing of a Yemeni fort, the details of which have been discussed in Chapter 8.[36] The UK claimed self-defence against 'a deliberate and increasing attack by Yemen'[37] against the South Arabian Federation. Although the British action was directed against regular armed forces of Yemen, the explanation brought up was very similar to that used by Israel in relation to the irregular armed groups on the territory of its Arab neighbours. The Security Council once again rejected such arguments and condemned the action as a reprisal.[38]

Similar arguments were put forward by the United States in connection with the Gulf of Tonkin incident, elaborated in Chapter 8.[39] The US characterized the raids carried out against North Vietnamese targets as 'limited and relevant measures to secure its naval units against further aggression.'[40]

Although the two examples mentioned above did not involve non-state actors, they are illustrative as to how the 'accumulation of events' theory was becoming increasingly relevant in claims of self-defence against repeated attacks.

Portugal invoked the right of self-defence to justify its military actions against Guinea, Senegal and Zambia between 1969 and 1971. Before the Security Council, Portugal repeatedly claimed that repeated attacks were being carried out against adjacent Portuguese territories by armed organizations based in Guinea, Senegal and Zambia.[41] The Security Council rejected all the justifications brought up by Portugal and condemned its military actions.[42]

Apartheid South Africa also made use of similar arguments. Between the late 1970s and the early 1980s, South Africa carried out several military actions across its borders against neighbouring countries (i.e., Angola, Mozambique, Zambia,

---

35 Brownlie 1963, p. 279.

36 See *supra* 8.4.1.

37 Repertoire, Supp. 1964–1965, Chapter VIII, p. 128.

38 SC Res. 188 (1964).

39 See *supra* 8.4.2.

40 SCOR, 19th Session, 1140th meeting., UN Doc. S/PV.1140 (5 August 1964) para 44.

41 SCOR, 24th Session, 1486th meeting., UN Doc. S/PV.1486 (18 July 1969) paras 69–70; 1516th meeting., S/PV.1516 (4 December 1969) para 103; 1524th meeting., S/PV.1524 (18 December 1969) paras 73–74; UN Doc. S/10255 (1971); Repertoire, Supp. 1969–1971, Chapter VIII, pp. 140–145.

42 SC Res. 273, 275 (1969); 294 (1971).

Zimbabwe, Lesotho, and Botswana) allegedly to protect its territory against guerrilla attacks.[43] South Africa claimed that these attacks were organized by the African National Congress and supported by the neighbouring countries.[44] The presence and activity of 'terrorist elements'[45] on the territory of the neighbouring countries proved, in South Africa's view, that these states were harbouring armed units that carried out repeated attacks against civilians in South Africa. These actions, it was claimed, hindered the government's reform process and disrupted civilian life in general.[46] For that reason, South Africa found that it had no other choice than 'take effective measures in self-defence to protect our country and population against threats.'[47] These claims were repeatedly rejected by the Security Council and several resolutions were adopted condemning the South African actions.[48]

Despite the numerous claims of self-defence based on the 'needle-prick' approach, the Security Council showed continuous reluctance to accept it and to acknowledge the potential gravity of (repeated) armed acts committed by irregular forces. Apart from the obvious political divides that dictated many of the opinions of Council members, genuine concern as to the necessity and proportionality of such responses was also considered.[49]

The 'accumulation of events' theory needed a widening of the context in which acts of self-defence were to be justified and emphasis was to be put not only on past incidents, but also on future ones.[50] The Security Council was unwilling to make such a concession and claims of self-defence against armed acts of irregulars were repeatedly rejected by the UN executive organ.

The Security Council's scepticism was somewhat counterbalanced by resolutions of the General Assembly and by legal doctrine. In 1970, the General Assembly adopted the so-called Friendly Relations Declaration, according to which states had to refrain from organizing or encouraging the organization of irregular forces or armed bands, including mercenaries, for incursion into the

---

43 Alexandrov 1996, p. 180; Higginbotham 1987, pp. 561–572.

44 Higginbotham 1987, p. 565; Repertoire, Supp. 1975–1980, Chapter XI, pp. 402–402; ibid., 1981–1984, Chapter IX, p. 326; SCOR, 41st Session, 2684th meeting., UN Doc. S/PV.2684 (22 May 1986) p. 22.

45 SCOR, 41st Session, 2684th meeting., UN Doc., S/PV.2684 (22 May 1986) p. 22.

46 Ibid., pp. 22–23.

47 Ibid., p. 26.

48 SC Res. 387, 393, 402 (1976); 428 (1978); 447, 454 (1979); 466, 475 (1980); 527 (1982); 545 (1983); and 546 (1984).

49 SCOR, 24th Session, 1468th meeting, UN Doc. S/PV.1468 (28 March 1969) paras 18–19 (Finland expressing concern about the loss of civilian life), 34 (France expressing doubt as to the proportionality of the Israeli action); SCOR, 27th Session, 1650th meeting., UN Doc. S/PV.1560 (26 June 1972) para 93 (Belgium claiming that Art. 51 allows self-defence only against a single case of armed aggression); SCOR, 30th Session, 1860th meeting., UN Doc. S/PV.1860 (5 December 1975) para 3 (the US calling for an analysis of the Israeli airstrikes in the context of the repeated acts of violence committed by irregulars).

50 Bowett 1972, pp. 6–7.

territory of another state. States also had the duty to refrain from 'organizing, instigating, assisting or participating in acts of civil strife or terrorist acts in another state or acquiescing in organized activities within its territory directed towards the commission of such acts.'[51]

Four years later, the General Assembly went one step further and adopted the Definition of Aggression, according to which 'the sending by or on behalf of a state or armed bands, groups, irregulars or mercenaries' which would carry out acts of armed force against another state of such gravity as to amount to acts performed by regular forces could amount to an act of aggression. Moreover, a state's substantial involvement in such activities was also seen as a potential act of aggression.[52]

The resolutions of the General Assembly did not touch upon the 'accumulation of events' theory; their purpose was, *inter alia*, to ascertain the gravity of armed acts performed by other than regular armed forces of a state. While the Friendly Relations Declaration equated organizing or encouraging the organization or irregular forces with an unlawful use of force that breached the provisions of the Charter, the Definition of Aggression went one step further and rendered such activities acts of aggression.

Both resolutions were acknowledged by the International Court of Justice as codifications of customary international law.[53] Moreover, in the *Nicaragua* case, the Court found that an armed attack could also be understood as including 'the sending by or on behalf of a State of armed bands' for the purposes described by Article 3(g) of the Definition of Aggression.[54] It is important to note, however, that the Court rejected the view according to which the provision of weapons or logistical or other forms of support to irregular bands would also amount to an armed attack.[55]

The accumulations of events theory received more attention in legal doctrine. In 1972, Bowett offered a thorough analysis of the concept and asserted that to focus on a particular incident and its cause without regard for 'the broader context of past relations between the parties and events arising therefrom, is to ignore the difficulties in which states may be placed, especially in relation to guerrilla activities.'[56] In other words, by rejecting the 'accumulation of events' theory and isolating an incident from its context, the Security Council not only found itself being accused of 'one-sidedness', but was also forced to characterize as illegal reprisals actions which, 'on a broader view of self-defence, might be regarded as legitimate.'[57] At the same time, Bowett pointed out that by condemning the

[51] GA Res. 2625, Friendly Relations Declaration, Part 1. See *infra* 11.1.

[52] GA Res. 3314, Definition of Aggression, Article 3(g). See *infra* 11.1.

[53] Nicaragua 1986, para 195.

[54] Ibid.

[55] Ibid. See *infra* 11.4.1.

[56] Bowett 1972, p. 9.

[57] Ibid., pp. 9–10.

disproportionate acts as reprisals and remaining silent or evasive on small-scale, cause-and-effect, relatively proportionate responses, the Security Council was in fact legitimizing proportionate, *de facto* reprisals.[58]

The same theory was given attention by Yehuda Blum, legal scholar and Israeli Ambassador to the UN (1978–1984) in an article that analysed the possible state responses to acts of terrorism.[59] Blum offered a comprehensive list of secondary legal sources that acknowledged as forms of indirect aggression support to and toleration of armed bands likely to carry out hostile incursions in the territory of another state.[60] He then went on to analyse the conditions under which 'acts of terrorism' could be considered an armed attack. As Bowett, he asserted that such a conclusion would greatly depend on whether one was inclined to give a narrow or a broad interpretation to the words 'if an armed attack occurs' of Article 51.[61] In Blum's opinion, an isolated terrorist act was bound to be treated differently from 'an act of terrorism which constitutes but one link in a long chain of such acts, particularly when it is obvious that acts of such intensity could not have been carried out without the encouragement, or at least knowledge or toleration, of the sanctuary state.'[62] In other words, although sporadic acts, taken separately, may not constitute an armed attack, their accumulation may demonstrate a systematic campaign which could amount to a veritable armed attack.[63] Blum went on to explain that the reason why 'terrorist organizations' engaged in protracted acts of violence was that they were incapable of achieving 'in one concentrated and direct blow' what they could accomplish in smaller, repeated acts of force.[64] If proportionality were to be measured to each of the acts, individually, hardly any response would qualify as proportionate. For that reason, Blum asserted, the 'needle-prick' approach helped in looking at the violent acts in their totality and assessing the proportionality of the response from such a perspective.[65]

The 'accumulation of events' theory was implicitly referred to by Roberto Ago in his report to the International Law Commission (ILC) on the draft articles for state responsibility.[66] Accordingly, Ago believed that self-defence could be justified against an armed attack consisting 'of a number of successive acts'. In such a case, the requirements of proportionality and immediacy had to be looked at 'in the light of those acts as a whole.'[67] Ago was very cautious in his wording, but he did admit that 'if a state suffers a series of successive and different acts of armed

---

[58] Ibid., pp. 11–12.
[59] Blum 1976, pp. 223–237.
[60] Ibid., pp. 230–231.
[61] Ibid., p. 233.
[62] Ibid.
[63] Ibid.; Gross 1983, p. 478; Jacobson 1998, p. 13.
[64] Blum 1976, p. 233.
[65] Ibid., p. 235.
[66] Ago 1980. See also *infra* 11.2.4.
[67] Ago 1980, pp. 69–70, para 121.

attack, from another state, the requirement of proportionality would certainly not mean that the victim state is not free to undertake a single armed action on a much larger scale in order to put an end to this escalating succession of attacks.'[68] It is important to note that Ago referred to repeated acts of *armed attack* of *states* (thus regular armed forces) and not to sporadic raids of irregular armed groups. That approach was criticized in the ensuing ILC discussions by Schwebel, who asserted that 'armed attack' had to be interpreted in such a way as to allow states to defend themselves against 'attacks by terrorist organizations and individuals.'[69]

In the 1980s, state practice showed a steady increase in invoking the *Nadelstichtaktik* against accumulated acts of armed groups. In 1981, Israel carried out airstrikes against Palestinian bases in Beirut and in 1982 invaded Lebanon to neutralize armed bases of the Palestine Liberation Organization (PLO). At the Security Council meeting of 17 July 1981, Israel justified its Beirut raids as defensive action against PLO's 'relentless campaign of murder against Israel and its people.'[70] The Israeli representative emphasized that the raids were targeted against 'concentrations of PLO terrorists in Lebanon' and not civilians. The unwanted civilian casualties were the result of the PLO choosing bases 'in villages and refugee camps' under Lebanese control.[71] The arguments put forward were once again criticized by the intervening Security Council members.[72] The resolution adopted called for the immediate cessation of 'all armed attacks', but stopped short of specifically condemning Israel, as was done in earlier years.[73]

One year later, on 6 June 1982, Israeli armed forces invaded southern Lebanon to push the PLO out of the range of northern Israeli settlements and to establish a 25 mile 'buffer zone' along the Israeli-Lebanese border.[74] For months prior to the invasion, Israel had expressed concerns over the build-up of PLO bases in southern Lebanon.[75] The act which triggered the invasion was the assassination attempt on the Israeli ambassador to Great Britain 2 days earlier. The attempt was staged by Palestinians in London, but the PLO denied responsibility for it.[76] Israel justified its armed intervention as self-defence against continuous shelling of its northern settlements and the repeated PLO attacks against Israel.[77] It was also claimed to be a defensive measure against the imminent threat posed by the growing stockpile of

---

[68] Ibid., pp. 69–70, para 121.

[69] Summary Record of the 1621st ILC meeting., UN Doc. A/CN.4/SR.1621 (1980) para 5.

[70] SCOR, 36th Session, 2292nd meeting., UN Doc. S/PV.2292 (17 July 1981) paras 40, 55.

[71] Ibid., paras 56–57.

[72] Ibid., paras 65–116.

[73] SC Res. 490 (1981) para 1.

[74] Gross 1983, p. 459.

[75] SCOR, 36th Session, 2292nd meeting., UN Doc. S/PV.2292 (17 July 1981) para 46.

[76] Gross 1983, pp. 458–459.

[77] SCOR, 37th Session, 2375th meeting., UN Doc. S/PV.2375 (6 June 1982) paras 39, 58, 65.

weapons at the PLO bases of southern Lebanon.[78] Again, the Security Council was not convinced and several resolutions were adopted in the following weeks demanding the withdrawal of the Israeli forces from Lebanon.[79]

The 1982 Israeli invasion of Lebanon drew further attention to the 'accumulation of events' theory. Several authors defended the theory and attempted to justify it on the basis of legal and policy arguments.[80] Gross opined that even if the Israeli invasion was of a much larger scale than the sporadic PLO attacks, the purpose of the intervention was to prevent future attacks that formed part of the same pattern. Under the *Nadelstichtaktik* approach, such a response could be justified.[81] Schachter asserted that it was not unreasonable to allow a state, the victim of an attack, to respond with force beyond the immediate area of attack when that state had good reason to expect a continuation of attacks from the same source. Such action could not be characterized as merely anticipatory, because prior attacks had taken place; nor would it be a reprisal, because its principal aim would be protective and not punitive.[82]

The validity of the 'accumulation of events' theory was suggested by the International Court of Justice as well. In the *Nicaragua* case, the Court stated that it had not enough evidence to decide whether Nicaraguan transborder incursions into Honduras and Costa Rica 'may be treated for legal purposes as amounting, singly or collectively, to an armed attack by Nicaragua.'[83]

The 'needle-prick' theory received increased attention as a result of the 1986 US airstrike against targets in Libya, discussed in Chapter 8.[84] Before the Security Council, US Ambassador Walters put forward a clear vindication of the 'accumulation of events' theory:

> [I]n the light of that reprehensible act of violence [the bombing of the West Berlin club, KTSz]—only the latest in an ongoing pattern of attacks by Libya—and of clear evidence that Libya was planning a multitude of future attacks, the United States was compelled to exercise its right of self-defence. The United States hopes that this action will discourage Libyan terrorist acts in the future.[85]

Clearly, the US claim of self-defence relied on the 'accumulation of events' theory. As with the early Israeli line of reasoning, both constitutive elements of the theory were asserted. First, that the ongoing pattern of attacks has seriously endangered American life and property abroad and second, that the repetition of these attacks prompted the US to believe that more were yet to come. Nonetheless,

---

[78] Gross 1983, p. 459; UN Doc. S/15271 (1982); SCOR, 37th Session, 2375th meeting., UN Doc. S/PV.2375 (6 June 1982) paras 45–46, 65.

[79] SC Res. 509, 515, 517, 520, 521 (1982).

[80] Gross 1983, pp. 458–492; Schachter 1985, p. 293.

[81] Gross 1983, p. 487.

[82] Schachter 1985, p. 293.

[83] Nicaragua 1986, para 231.

[84] See *supra* 8.4.3.

[85] SCOR, 41st Session, 2674th meeting., UN Doc. S/PV.2674 (15 April 1986) p. 17.

the majority of the Security Council members rejected the explanation.[86] The United Kingdom defended the American action by asserting that the evidence of ongoing terrorist activities of the Libyan government was beyond dispute and that the US had a right of self-defence which included destroying or weakening the capacity of one's assailant.[87] Other Western European countries criticised the US airstrikes, but condemned Libya's involvement in terrorist activities.[88] The US, the United Kingdom and France vetoed a draft resolution that would have condemned the American airstrikes. Australia and Denmark also voted against the resolution. Nine other members of the Council—Bulgaria, China, Congo, Ghana, Madagascar, Thailand, Trinidad and Tobago, the USSR and the United Arab Emirates—voted in favour of the resolution. Venezuela abstained.[89] The UN General Assembly adopted, nonetheless, a resolution condemning the airstrikes by 79 to 28 votes, with 51 states abstaining or absent.[90]

The reaction to the US airstrikes was mixed, though many countries had later imposed economic sanctions on Libya for its terrorist activities. Some authors have, nonetheless, defended the US line of argumentation.[91] Greenwood called for a reinterpretation of Article 51 of the UN Charter to include the 'accumulation of events' theory. In his view, if irregular or terrorist attacks, each one of which, taken separately, would be a relatively minor use of force, emanate from the same state and form a reasonably coherent pattern, their accumulation could amount to an ongoing armed attack. In such a case, the right of the victim state to take defensive action should be considered in the light of the whole of these attacks. Consequently, there would be no need for the victim state to show that another attack was imminent before it could react by using force in self-defence. In Greenwood's opinion, it would be sufficient that there was reason to believe that future attacks were likely to occur.[92]

By the beginning of the 1990s, the 'needle-prick' approach or 'accumulation of events' theory comprised several elements. First, there had to be a number of prior attacks, which, in their totality, would amount to an armed attack.[93] These acts, taken individually, did not need to be of increased gravity; it was enough if their totality resulted in great harm.[94] Secondly, these attacks had to emanate from an identifiable source, usually an armed group sent, supported or tolerated by another

[86] Ibid., 2674th–2682nd meeting., UN Doc. S/PV.2674–2682 (15–21 April 1986).

[87] Ibid., 2679th meeting., UN Doc. S/PV.2679 (17 April 1986) p. 27.

[88] Ibid., 2674th–2682nd meeting., UN Doc. S/PV.2674–2682 (15–21 April 1986); Intoccia 1987, pp. 187–188.

[89] SCOR, 41st Session, 2682nd meeting., UN Doc. S/PV.2682 (21 April 1986) p. 43.

[90] GA Res. 41/38 (1986). Franck 2002, p. 91.

[91] Greenwood 1987, pp. 933–960; McCredie 1987, pp. 215–242. Dinstein characterized them as 'defensive armed reprisals'. Dinstein 2005, p. 229.

[92] Greenwood 1987, p. 954.

[93] Brownlie 1963, p. 279; Gross 1983, p. 478; Greenwood 1987, p. 954; Schachter 1985, p. 293.

[94] Blum 1976, p. 233; Gross 1983, p. 478; Greenwood 1987, p. 954; Schachter 1985, p. 293.

state.[95] It was implicitly understood that the link between the armed group and the sending, sponsoring or harbouring state had to be established and evidence had to be brought that that state was either incapable or unwilling to tackle the problem.[96] Thirdly, the repeated nature of attacks had to create the conviction that more would follow in order to achieve the objective of the armed group.[97] On this basis, the targeted state was allowed to invoke self-defence to repel future attacks that were anticipated because of the very reoccurrence of past attacks.[98] Lastly, the proportionality of the use of armed force by the targeted state was to be weighed against the totality of past and future attacks and not against isolated incidents.[99]

The crystallization of the elements of the 'needle-prick' theory happened in spite of a generally negative attitude of the Security Council. In the early 1950s and 1960s, the theory was vehemently rejected by the Council. Starting with the 1960s, some states, including the US and the UK, gradually softened their position, especially as a result of instances of state practice in which they invoked a similar reasoning.[100] As a result, on some occasions when Israeli claims of self-defence were discussed, the US stressed the importance of analysing those claims against the general context of reoccurring violence and not in an isolated manner.[101] Although the reluctance of the Security Council to accept the validity of the 'needle-prick' theory lingered on, by the 1980s, it became less willing to condemn the Israeli actions and limited itself to call for the cessation of hostilities.[102] The attitude of the Security Council was counterbalanced by writings of publicists and resolutions of the UN General Assembly. Jurists drew attention to the growing dangers posed by armed acts of irregular groups and called for a validation of the 'needle-prick' approach within the limits of the principles of necessity and proportionality.[103] General Assembly resolutions limited themselves to enouncing that armed acts of irregular bands could amount to illegal use of force or acts of aggression. Moreover, even the International Court of Justice allowed for armed attacks to include acts of irregular bands, albeit under restrictive conditions.[104] Nonetheless, many controversies remained fuelled by the scepticism of the

---

[95] Blum 1976, p. 233; Greenwood 1987, p. 954; Gross 1983, p. 478; Schachter 1985, p. 293.

[96] Blum 1976, p. 233.

[97] Greenwood 1987, p. 954; Schachter 1985, p. 293.

[98] Blum 1976, p. 233; Greenwood 1987, p. 954; Gross 1983, p. 478; Higgins 1963, p. 201; Schachter 1985, p. 293.

[99] Blum 1976, p. 235; Gross 1983, pp. 486–487; Schachter 1985, p. 293.

[100] See *supra* 8.4.1 and 8.4.2.

[101] SCOR, 24th Session, 1467th meeting., UN Doc. S/PV.1467 (27 March 1969) paras 48–49; SCOR, 30th Session, 1860th meeting, UN Doc. S/PV.1860 (5 December 1975) paras 3–5.

[102] SC Res. 490 (1981); 509, 515 and 517 (1982). In SC Res. 520 and 521 (1982) the Security Council condemned Israel for renewed incursions into Beirut.

[103] Blum 1976, pp. 223–237; Greenwood 1987, pp. 933–960; Gross 1983, pp. 458–492; Schachter 1985, pp. 291–294.

[104] GA Res. 2625, Friendly Relations Declaration, Part 1; GA Res. 3314, Definition of Aggression, Article 3(g); Nicaragua 1986, para 195. See *infra* 11.4.1.

Security Council and a general distrust of public opinion towards the 'needle-prick' theory and its susceptibility for abuse.

The 1990s saw a gradual shift in public opinion in the face of an augmentation in both the number and scope of terrorist organizations and terrorist acts. Gradually, many of the controversies that characterized the debate of previous decades were renounced in the face of the changing nature of the threat posed by non-state actors.

10.4 Terrorist Attacks in the 1990s

While state-sponsored terrorism has remained active, starting with the 1990s, quasi-independent regional or global militant networks also started acquiring importance. These networks or organizations are only partly dependent on state support; private persons act as founders or sponsors, while harbouring states often prove to be incapable or unwilling to control their activity. They have also engaged in more or less legitimate businesses and have drawn considerable revenues from these independent sources of income.[105] Apart from a steadily broadening reach, assisted by modern information technology, these networks have also shown a growing preference for large-scale, lethal, indiscriminate attacks in public places.[106]

As a result of these developments, the attention of governments, intergovernmental organizations and legal publicists alike began to focus on efficient ways to prevent, ward off and punish terrorist acts. Among other questions concerning transnational cooperation and law enforcement, the issue of using armed force against such terrorist organizations was given more consideration than before.

Throughout the 1990s, the number of acts of international terrorism decreased. As a result, until the attacks of 11 September 2001, most Western governments considered that terrorist threats were in decline. Although the number of terrorist attacks has been, indeed, in decline, the lethality of such attacks has actually been increasing.[107] Moreover, during the 1990s, it became evident that the targets of terrorist attacks were, increasingly, US and other Western nationals.[108]

In 1990, the Tupac Amaru Revolutionary Movement bombed the US embassy in Lima, Peru. In the same year, the Philippine New People's Army killed two US soldiers in the Philippines. Two years later, in 1992, US businessmen were kidnapped in Manila by Philippine armed groups.[109]

---

105 Gunaratna 2004c, pp. 20–21.

106 Ibid., pp. 19, 29–30. For looking into the debate on the 'new terrorism', see Rose 1999, pp. 131–137; Tucker 2001, pp. 1–14; Kegley 2003; Morgan 2004, pp. 29–43; Gunaratna 2004a; Duyvesteyn 2004, pp. 439–454; Howard 2008, pp. 6–22; Jenkins 2008, pp. 23–31; Murphy 2009, pp. 281–293.

107 Gunaratna 2004c, p. 19; Gurr and Cole 2002, pp. 22–23.

108 Blin 2007, pp. 408–413.

109 Significant Terrorist Incidents, 1961–2003 (2004).

On 26 February 1993, the World Trade Center in New York was badly damaged when a car bomb exploded in an underground garage. The bomb left six people dead and ca. 1,000 people injured. The men carrying out the attack were led by Ramzi Yousef, trained in one of bin Laden's Al-Qaeda camps in Afghanistan.[110] He wanted the bomb to topple one tower, with the collapsing debris knocking down the second, bringing the entire complex down and killing what he hoped would be 250,000 people.[111] Instead, the bomb created a 30-m crater several stories deep and several more high.[112]

Deadly attacks continued throughout the second half of the 1990s. In 1995, Hamas claimed responsibility for the detonation of a bomb that killed six and injured over 100 persons, including several US citizens in Jerusalem. A year later, the US embassy in Athens was damaged by a fire rocket. The same year, in 1996, in Jerusalem, a suicide bomber blew up a bus, killing 26 persons, including three US citizens, and injuring some 80 persons, including three other US citizens. The attack was claimed by Hamas.[113] In June 1996, a fuel truck carrying a bomb exploded outside the US military's Khobar Towers housing facility in Dhahran (Saudi Arabia), killing 19 US military personnel and wounding 515 persons, including 240 US personnel.[114] On 17 December 1996, members of the Tupac Amaru Revolutionary Movement took several hundred people hostage at a party given at the Japanese ambassador's residence in Lima, Peru. Among the hostages were several US officials, foreign ambassadors and other diplomats, Peruvian government officials and Japanese businessmen. The group demanded the release of all Tupac Amaru members in prison and safe passage for them and the hostage takers. The terrorists released most of the hostages in December but held 81 Peruvians and Japanese citizens for several months.[115] In November 1997, gunmen shot and killed 58 tourists and four Egyptians and wounded 26 others at the Hatshepsut Temple near Luxor, Egypt.[116]

Although the listing above is only illustrative, it becomes evident that the impact and magnitude of the terrorist attacks had considerably changed by the second half of the 1990s. They became more lethal and pronouncedly more anti-Western, especially targeting US nationals abroad. As Wedgwood explained, modern terrorism featured independent ideological, political or ethnic factions rather than state-sponsored groupings. Such a faction was less vulnerable to international sanctions than states. 'With an uncertain membership and inchoate

---

110 Wright 2006, p. 177.

111 Ibid., p. 178.

112 FBI Headline Archives 1993 WTC Bombing.

113 Significant Terrorist Incidents, 1961–2003 (2004).

114 Wright 2006, pp. 237–239.

115 Significant Terrorist Incidents, 1961–2003 (2004).

116 Wright 2006, pp. 256–258.

form,' Wedgwood observed, 'terrorist networks lie outside the web of civil responsibility that constrains private and public actors in international society.'[117]

10.4.1 The Kenya and Tanzania Bombings

The bombings of the US embassies in Kenya and Tanzania were also evidence of the new type of terrorist attacks. On the morning of 7 August 1998, terrorists driving in a truck detonated a large bomb in the rear parking area of the American embassy in Nairobi, Kenya. A total of 213 people were killed, of whom 200 were Kenyan civilians and 12 were American citizens. Approximately 4,000 persons were injured by the blast.[118]

On the same morning, a truck laden with explosives drove up to the US embassy in Dar-Es-Salaam, Tanzania. Apparently unable to penetrate the perimeter because it was blocked by an embassy water tanker, the suicide bomber detonated his charge at a distance of about 35 feet from the outer wall of the chancery. The bomb attack killed eleven people and injured 85. No US citizens were among the fatalities, but many were injured, two of them seriously.[119]

Two weeks later, on 20 August 1998, Tomahawk Land Attack Missiles (TLAMs) were launched at targets in Afghanistan and Sudan associated with the Kenya and Tanzania explosions. The US contended that the Afghan targets were training camps used by a number of groups associated with the so-called 'bin Laden network'. According to the American findings, the bases housed 'the infrastructure for their funding and international travel and for training them in tactics and in the assembly and use of a wide variety of weapons.'[120] The Sudanese target was a chemical plant in northeast Khartoum, claimed to be 'involved in the production of chemical weapons agents' and associated with the bin Laden network.[121]

The then US President Clinton justified the airstrikes as necessary to address an 'imminent threat' to American National Security.[122] He further asserted that there was convincing intelligence information that the bin Laden network was responsible for the bombings. Moreover, the President stated that further compelling evidence showed that the network was planning to mount further attacks.[123]

The United States promptly informed the Security Council about the airstrikes and invoked the right of self-defence against 'a series of armed attacks' against US

[117] Wedgwood 1999, p. 559.

[118] Nairobi: Discussion and Findings 1999.

[119] Ibid.

[120] Fact Sheet 21 August 1998; Wedgwood 1999, p. 563.

[121] Fact Sheet 21 August 1998.

[122] Clinton 20 August 1998 Address to the Nation.

[123] Ibid.

embassies and nationals.[124] It asserted that the strikes were carried out in response to the Kenya and Tanzania terrorist attacks, and to prevent and deter their continuation.[125] The US permanent representative assured the Security Council that the airstrikes were carried out only after conclusive evidence showed the connection of the Afghan and Sudanese targets to the bin Laden network. Moreover, the representative pointed out that the American action was taken only after 'repeated efforts to convince the Government of the Sudan and the Taliban regime in Afghanistan to shut these terrorist activities down and to cease their cooperation with the bin Laden organization' had failed.[126] In a national address 3 weeks after the airstrikes, the then Secretary of State Madeleine Albright characterized the Tanzania and Kenya attacks as signals of 'the emergence of terrorist coalitions that do not answer fully to any government, that operate across national borders, and have access to advanced technology.'[127] In the face of 'well-financed terrorist leaders such as Osama bin Laden,' whose expressly acknowledged purpose was 'to kill Americans worldwide,' Albright pledged that the US would 'wage the struggle against terror on every front on every continent with every tool, every day.'[128]

The Security Council did not meet in public session to evaluate the US military action. International reaction was generally favourable, although a few prominent states condemned the US action.[129] Most US allies, including the United Kingdom, Germany, Australia, New Zealand and Israel expressed their support for the American choice of action. France and Italy showed moderate acquiescence. Russia, China, Pakistan, Libya and Iraq condemned the airstrikes.[130]

Several authors discussed the self-defence justifications brought by the US.[131] Wedgwood asserted that the military strikes of August 1998 could be justified as self-defence even according to the most stringent interpretation of the right. The magnitude of the Kenya and Tanzania bombings surely amounted to an armed attack, while US intelligence brought conclusive evidence of future attacks being planned by the bin Laden network.[132] At the same time, 'the prudent use of military force to prevent terrorist attacks and to degrade terrorist infrastructures' was a proportionate response to the bombings.[133] On the contrary, Campbell considered that the two airstrikes did little to eradicate the threat of the bin Laden network and they actually increased anti-American sentiment worldwide.[134] Moreover,

---

[124] UN Doc. S/1998/780 (1998).

[125] Ibid.

[126] Ibid.

[127] Albright (9 September 1998) Address to the American Legion Convention.

[128] Ibid.

[129] Franck 2002, p. 95.

[130] Ibid., p. 95; Lobel 1999, p. 538.

[131] Campbell 2000, pp. 1067–1096; Lobel 1999, pp. 537–557; Wedgwood 1999, pp. 559–576.

[132] Wedgwood 1999, pp. 564–565.

[133] Ibid., pp. 563, 575.

[134] Campbell 2000, pp. 1090–1092.

he asserted that although the Tanzania and Kenya bombings could amount to armed attacks, the US response failed to respect the requirements of necessity and proportionality.[135] Likewise, Lobel characterized the US air strikes as an 'assertion of imperial might and arrogance in opposition to international law.'[136]

The justification brought by the US for its air strikes was another vindication of the 'accumulation of events' theory. Certainly, the Tanzania and Kenya bombings could be construed as amounting to armed attacks, even if taken individually. It was also clear that they were committed against US citizens and property and they were carried out by non-state actors. Equally, there was virtually no debate on the veracity of the claim that the network of Osama bin Laden was behind the attacks.[137] Nonetheless, the factual link connecting these bombings to targets in Sudan and Afghanistan was widely debated.[138] Likewise, the assertion that future attacks were being planned from, or with the assistance of those targets, was—at the time of the airstrikes—less than unquestionably proven.[139] Moreover, the proportionality of the air strikes was also debated.[140] Still, general public reaction was relatively muted in comparison with past criticism of resort to force on the basis of similar justifications. According to Lobel, the reason for the lack of public protest and debate was the general disinterest of other states in Sudan and the awareness that a potential Security Council condemnation would be vetoed by the US.[141]

According to this author, the gradual realization that the danger posed by terrorist organizations and their armed acts was increasing in gravity played an important role in the relatively quiet public reaction. Governments and citizens alike began to understand that the new forms of terrorism needed a rethinking of the available responses and that states had to have different means to defend themselves against such threats.

If the requirements of necessity and proportionality are corroborated with the 'accumulation of events' theory, three interpretative points can be made regarding the East Africa bombings. First, the existent danger referred not only to the already occurred armed attacks in Tanzania and Kenya, but also to the threat lying in the planned future attacks. In other words, the conditionality of an armed attack (as an element of necessity) had to be interpreted to include both past and future events. Secondly, this collective conditionality of past and future attacks created a present and inevitable need to act (immediacy element of necessity). Furthermore, the proportionality of the US action had to be measured against the need to neutralize the source of all future attacks, thus it could involve a response that was considerably larger in scale than the attacks already occurred.

---

[135] Ibid., pp. 1093–1096.

[136] Lobel 1999, p. 557.

[137] Wright 2006, pp. 270–272.

[138] Lobel 1999, pp. 548–555; Campbell 2000, pp. 1089–1091.

[139] Clinton 20 August 1998 Address to the Nation; Campbell 2000, pp. 1090–1091.

[140] Campbell 2000, pp. 1093–1096. *Per a contrario*, see Wedgwood 1999, pp. 563, 575.

[141] Lobel 1999, pp. 556–557.

The relationship between the requirements of necessity and proportionally, on one hand, and the 'accumulation of events' theory, on the other, was further tested in the twenty-first century conflicts involving non-state actors.

10.5 Terrorist Attacks of the New Millennium

Although states began to focus more on the available responses to international terrorism, it was not until 9/11 that they began to fully appreciate the threat posed by the new terrorist groups. One of the main changes in anti-terrorism strategy was the re-definition of terrorism from a law-and-order problem to a national security threat.[142] As a result, the use of force in self-defence against terrorist organizations and terrorist attacks became one of the most relevant issues to address.

10.5.1 The Attack on the USS Cole *(2000)*

Two years after the Kenya and Tanzania bombings, the US was once again faced with the decision of whether to use force against a terrorist attack or to resort to other means. On 12 October 2000, in Aden (Yemen), a small dinghy, carrying explosives, rammed the destroyer *USS Cole*, killing 17 sailors and injuring 39 others.[143] The ensuing US investigation quickly linked the attacks to Al-Qaeda elements in Yemen and Afghanistan, but no conclusive evidence was uncovered at the time.[144] The then US President Bill Clinton believed that 'it was not responsible for a president to launch an invasion of another country just based on a preliminary judgment.'[145] If he had been given a definite answer from the intelligence agencies, he would have sought a Security Council ultimatum and given the Taliban a few days before taking further action against both Al-Qaeda and the Taliban.[146] The Bush administration took a similar stance in face of a 'strong circumstantial case,' which, however, lacked 'conclusive information on external command and control of the attack.'[147] As a result, the Bush administration decided to abandon the strategy of 'tit-for-tat' responses to terrorism and embarked on reassessing its anti-terrorist strategy.[148]

---

[142] Gunaratna 2004b, p. 3.

[143] Wright 2006, pp. 319–320.

[144] The 9/11 Commission Report 2004.

[145] Ibid., p. 195.

[146] Ibid.

[147] Ibid., p. 202.

[148] Ninth Public Hearing, Witness, Dr. Condoleezza Rice (8 April 2004); The 9/11 Commission Report 2004, pp. 202–203.

The lack of armed response to the attack on the *USS Cole* is an instance in which the US contemplated the use of force, but decided not to resort to it. Neither the Clinton nor the Bush administration considered at the time that the available evidence was enough to sustain a claim of self-defence or to request collective enforcement measures from the Security Council.

Two years after the attack on the *USS Cole*, on 3 November 2002, a CIA-operated Predator drone fired an AGM-114 Hellfire missile at a car on a highway in a rural area of Marib province (Yemen), destroying it and killing six militant Islamists, one of them a prime suspect in planning and authorizing the attack on the *USS Cole* and believed to be an Al-Qaeda senior in Yemen.[149] The strike was condemned as an extrajudicial killing by the UN Special Rapporteur on Civil and Political Rights.[150] Since the strike was carried out with the consent of the Yemeni government, the Special Rapporteur concluded that an alarming precedent might have been set for extrajudicial execution by consent of government.[151] According to Printer, the Predator strike was justified as a measure dictated by military necessity in conformity with *jus ad bellum*. He asserted that the strategic use of special forces and advanced aircraft against terrorists was not a disproportionate use of force.[152] It is important to note at this point that military necessity pertains to *jus in bello* rather than *jus ad bellum*. The conditions under which acts like the Predator strike are justifiable by military necessity pertain to the law of armed conflict rather than the principles regulating the use of force in general. It is beyond the purpose of this research to dwell into the (non-)applicability of the law of armed conflict to such situations and the relevant *jus in bello* rules relating to such strikes.[153] Nonetheless, it is the opinion of this author that targeted killings of individuals, the apprehension of whom is possible, falls outside the purpose and scope of the international law of self-defence.

10.5.2 The Attacks of 9/11 (2001)

10.5.2.1 Factual Background

The attacks of 11 September 2001 were of unprecedented magnitude not only for the US, but also for the entire world. On 11 September 2001, at 8:45 a.m., a hijacked passenger jet crashed into the north tower of the World Trade Center (WTC) in New York. Several minutes later, at 9:03 a.m., a second hijacked airliner

149 Mueller et al. 2006, p. 241.

150 UN Doc. E/CN.4/2003/3 (2003) paras 37–39.

151 Ibid., para 39.

152 Printer 2003, p. 357.

153 See Melzer 2010, pp. 277–301.

crashed into the south tower of the WTC. Forty minutes later, at 9:43 a.m., a third hijacked passenger jet crashed into the Pentagon in Washington. At 10:10 a.m. a fourth airliner, also hijacked, crashed on the field in Somerset County, Pennsylvania.[154] As a result, both towers of the WTC collapsed that day and the Pentagon was also badly damaged. Air traffic was completely halted in the US and several office buildings and headquarters were evacuated in New York and Washington.[155] Some 5,000 people lost their lives as a result of the attacks, the overwhelming majority civilians, including nationals from over 81 different countries.[156] Two days later the US Federal Bureau of Investigations (FBI) announced the list of the 19 hijackers believed to belong to the Al-Qaeda network and connected to Osama bin Laden.[157] The FBI claim was denied by Osama bin Laden until October 2004, when he claimed responsibility for the attacks.[158]

World reaction was very strong and overwhelmingly supportive of the US.[159] On 12 September 2001, the North Atlantic Council of NATO issued a statement in which it pledged that, if it was determined that the attacks were directed from abroad against the US, 'it shall be regarded as an action covered by Article 5 of the Washington Treaty, which states that an armed attack against one or more of the Allies in Europe or North America shall be considered an attack against them all.'[160] The Organization of American States issued a similar statement on 22 September 2001.[161] Unprecedented offers of air space and territory were made by various countries and even states that usually opposed US actions—such as Russia, China, Iran and Libya—pledged their support.[162]

Likewise, on 12 September 2001, the Security Council adopted Resolution 1368 and 'unequivocally' condemned 'in the strongest terms the horrifying terrorist attacks' of 11 September. It also asserted that such attacks were regarded as threats to international peace and security.[163] In the preamble of the same resolution, the Security Council referred to the inherent right to individual and collective self-defence in accordance with the Charter, acknowledging in this way the right of the US to resort to armed force.[164] The applicability of the same right was confirmed 2 weeks later in Resolution 1373 that established a wide range of

---

154 September 11: Chronology of terror (12 September 2001) CNN.

155 Ibid.

156 UN Doc. S/2001/946 (2001).

157 FBI National Press Release (13 September 2001).

158 Bin Laden says he wasn't behind attacks (17 September 2001) CNN; Bin Laden claims responsibility for 9/11 (29 October 2004) CBC News; God knows it did not cross our minds to attack the towers (30 October 2004) Guardian.

159 Beard 2002, pp. 568–573.

160 NATO Press Release (12 September 2001).

161 Beard 2002, pp. 568–569.

162 Ibid., pp. 571–573.

163 SC Res. 1368 (2001) para 1.

164 Ibid., preamble.

measures to combat terrorism.[165] In both resolutions, the Security Council combined measures under Chapter VII with the right of self-defence. Although it stopped short of calling for the use of force under Chapter VII, it called upon the adoption of a wide plethora of measures to combat international terrorism and to offer support to the United States and other coalition states.[166]

On 20 September 2001, in addressing the question of the identity of the attackers, the then US President George W. Bush stated: 'The evidence we have gathered all points to a collection of loosely affiliated terrorist organizations known as Al-Qaeda. They are some of the murderers indicted for bombing American embassies in Tanzania and Kenya and responsible for bombing the *USS Cole*.'[167] The president went on saying that Al-Qaeda and its leader, 'a person named Osama bin Laden,' were linked to many different organizations in different countries and that there were thousands of members in more than 60 countries. The leadership of Al-Qaeda, the president asserted, had great influence in Afghanistan and supported the Taliban regime in controlling most of that country.[168] Against that background, President Bush made a five-point demand to the Taliban: (1) deliver to US authorities all of the leaders of Al-Qaeda who were hiding in Afghanistan; (2) release all foreign nationals, including American citizens who had been unjustly imprisoned; (3) protect foreign journalists, diplomats and aid workers; (4) close immediately and permanently all terrorist training camps in Afghanistan and hand over members and their support structures to appropriate authorities; and (5) give the US full access to terrorist training camps.[169]

Taliban spokesman Abdul Salaam Zaeef promptly rejected the US demands and suggested that bin Laden was made a scapegoat by Washington.[170] As a result, the US government decided to resort to force and, together with British military forces, launched a massive aerial and ground campaign against the Taliban in Afghanistan. Before launching *Operation Enduring Freedom*, Zaeef put forward the offer of the Taliban to detain bin Laden and try him under Islamic law.[171] The offer was rejected by the US and military operations started on 7 October 2001.

On the same day, the US sent a letter to the Security Council in which it announced the measures taken and invoked the right of individual and collective self-defence. The US contended that it had gathered 'clear and compelling information' that linked Al-Qaeda harboured by the Taliban to the 9/11 attacks.[172]

---

[165] SC Res. 1373 (2001) preamble.

[166] Gill 2003, pp. 30–31.

[167] Transcript of President Bush's address to a joint session of Congress on Thursday night, 20 September 2001 (21 September 2001) CNN.

[168] Ibid.

[169] Ibid.

[170] Clerics answer "no, no, no!" and invoke fates of past foes (22 September 2001) New York Times; Taliban won't turn over bin Laden (21 September 2001) CBS News.

[171] U.S. rejects Taliban offer to try bin Laden (7 October 2001) CNN.

[172] UN Doc. S/2001/946 (2001).

The US further asserted that the objective of the measures taken was to 'prevent and deter further attacks on the United States' and that they were directed against 'Al-Qaeda terrorist training camps and military installations of the Taliban regime in Afghanistan.'[173] The United Kingdom put forward similar arguments in justifying its engagement in the operation. Accordingly, in a letter sent to the Security Council on 7 October 2001, the UK stated that Osama bin Laden and Al-Qaeda 'have the capability to execute major terrorist attacks, claimed credit for past attacks on United States targets, and have been engaged in a concerted campaign against the United States and its allies.'[174]

As of July 2011, *Operation Enduring Freedom* has been going on for more than 9 years. The initial purpose to oust the Taliban regime and neutralize Al-Qaeda camps has been changed to address insurgency movements. The NATO-led International Security Assistance Force (ISAF) has also been actively engaged in the conflict since 2001.

Several issues were discussed in the legal literature in relation to the 9/11 attacks and the US response. The most important ones pertained to the role of the Security Council in responding to the 9/11 attacks, the definition of 'armed attack', the responsibility of Afghanistan and the legality of the US use of force on the basis of the right of self-defence.

10.5.2.2 The Role of the Security Council

The unprecedented nature of the Security Council's reaction and the measures adopted received considerable attention.[175] Along with a great number of states, NATO and OAS, the Security Council also condemned the terrorist attacks and acknowledged the right of individual and collective self-defence of states against such attacks.

Cassese characterized Resolution 1368 (2001) as ambiguous and contradictory. He pointed out that the Security Council was wavering between the desire to take matters into its own hand and the acknowledgement of the right of the US to use force unilaterally.[176]

According to Gill and Ratner the unanimous adoption by the Security Council of Resolution 1368 (2001) and the unprecedented supportive reaction of various governments showed that the applicability of self-defence against attacks of non-state actors was widely accepted.[177] Ratner went as far as to suggest that the overwhelming support expressed by even the most unlikely governments showed a highly significant change in the views regarding the underlying legal norms that governed the relevant state of affairs.[178]

---

[173] Ibid.

[174] UN Doc. S/2001/947 (2001).

[175] Beard 2002, pp. 559–590; Cassese 2001, p. 996; Franck 2002, p. 54; Gill 2003, pp. 30–31.

[176] Cassese 2001, p. 996.

[177] Gill 2003, pp. 30–31; Ratner 2002, pp. 909–910.

[178] Ratner 2002, p. 910.

It is reasonable to assert that the unequivocal acknowledgement of the right of self-defence against an attack carried out by a non-state actor marked a significant change in the Security Council's approach. Implicitly, non-state actors were acknowledged as targets against which self-defence can be exercised and the long-upheld statist approach to the issue was discarded.

10.5.2.3 The 9/11 Attacks and the Definition of 'Armed Attack'

The obvious difference in magnitude between previous terrorist attacks and 9/11 was highlighted to show that terrorist attacks could unequivocally amount to armed attacks.[179] Beard asserted on this issue that:

> [T]he fact that the September 11 terrorist attacks occurred on the territory of the United States, that Al-Qaeda's ongoing terrorist attacks against American targets represent a sustained and continuing injury to the United States, and that the attacks caused an enormous loss of life and severe damage to both private and government property, bring these terrorist attacks into a category that would implicate a state's right to self-defence, even under a less permissive standard than that reflected in contemporary international practice.[180]

On the contrary, Murphy claimed that, on the basis of the ICJ's definition of an armed attack in the *Nicaragua* case, the nineteen hijackers could not be characterized as 'armed groups' or 'mercenaries', because they were a small group of persons carrying nothing but knives on them, who committed a conventional criminal act rather than an armed attack.[181] At the same time, Murphy acknowledged that the scale of the attacks, their impact and the public reaction to them showed that they could be equated to an armed attack.[182]

Gill stated that the effects of 9/11 in terms of both human casualties and material damage demonstrated without a doubt that the attacks 'exceeded the threshold of the term armed attack contained in Article 51 of the UN Charter.' He also asserted that they could almost certainly qualify as crimes against humanity.[183]

Conversely, Cassese asserted that by accepting that terrorist attacks could amount to armed attacks and that states could defend themselves against terrorist groups and harbouring states, the 'international community' was very close to opening a 'Pandora's Box', setting an extremely dangerous precedent for the use of force in self-defence.[184]

---

[179] Beard 2002, pp. 574–575; Brown 2003, pp. 24–25; Feinstein 2002, p. 279; Franck 2001, p. 840; Franck 2002, p. 54; Greenwood 2003, p. 16.

[180] Beard 2002, p. 575.

[181] Murphy 2002, pp. 45–46.

[182] Murphy 2002, pp. 47–50.

[183] Gill 2003, p. 30. Similarly, Brown 2003, p. 27.

[184] Cassese 2001, p. 998.

The magnitude of the 9/11 attacks rendered the question whether acts of non-state actors could amount to armed attacks obsolete and signalled the increased lethality and danger posed by such organizations and their actions. The 11 September attacks also prompted the emergence of a cascade of legal and international relations literature on the changing nature of the terrorist threat and the available strategies to respond to it.[185]

10.5.2.4 The Responsibility of the Taliban Regime for the 9/11 Attacks

The evidence adduced by the US to link the attacks to bin Laden and Al-Qaeda was analysed by a number of authors.[186] Charney warned against the dangerous precedent that the reluctance of the Bush administration to disclose the evidence linking the attacks to Al-Qaeda was creating.[187] In his opinion, the state resorting to self-defence against terrorist acts carried the burden of presenting evidence to support its actions; otherwise, it would become much easier for others to take unjustifiable military actions based on unsupported assertions of self-defence.[188] Although Franck agreed with the importance of providing conclusive evidence supporting the resort to force of the injured state, he emphasized that such requirement was relevant after the exercise of self-defence and not before. In his opinion, the right of the injured state to defend itself could not depend on its ability to convince the 15 members of the Security Council that it had indeed correctly identified the attackers and the host state.[189]

Indeed, there is nothing in the pre-Charter history and post-Charter use of the requirement of necessity that would require states to undoubtedly prove the justifiability of the use of force *prior* to their action. That would go against the immediacy factor embedded in the requirement of necessity. If a target state found itself facing a present and inevitable need to take action to ward off an attack, its right to defend itself should not be made dependent upon convincing the Security Council or any other official organ as to the accuracy of the evidence in its possession. That being said, the state would be obliged to offer an explanation during or after its defensive action. Article 51 requires reporting the use of force in self-defence to the Security Council. As it was done many times in state practice,

---

[185] See, for instance, Tucker 2001, pp. 1–14; Jenkins 2008, pp. 23–31; Murphy 2009, pp. 281–293.

[186] Beard 2002, pp. 575–578; Charney 2001, p. 836; Franck 2001, p. 843.

[187] Charney 2001, p. 836.

[188] Ibid.

[189] Franck 2001, p. 843.

the defending state would have ample opportunity to present evidence and justification of its action before the members of the Security Council.[190]

The attributability of the attacks to the Taliban regime for harbouring Al-Qaeda and, more generally, the question of responsibility of states for sponsoring and harbouring terrorists, also received attention.[191] Brown believed that even when states could not be held responsible for sending or organizing irregular bands, use of force against the armed groups on the territory of those states could be lawful, if certain conditions applied. Namely, the host state could give its consent to another state's use of force against them.[192] Further, if the host state was unwilling to prevent the use of its territory by terrorist groups, the injured state could have the right to respond against the non-state actor notwithstanding the sovereign status of the host state.[193] Moreover, when the host state inside which the terrorists operate was unable to prevent its territory from being used to launch attacks, the injured state could be allowed to resort to force against the authors of the attacks.[194] Greenwood and Feinstein were of the opinion that the unwillingness of the Taliban regime to prevent terrorist actions against the US justified the US use of force in Afghanistan.[195]

It is not the purpose of this research to dwell into the questions concerning the responsibility of states that support or harbour irregular groups accountable for the carrying out or the planning of armed attacks. For the sake of developing the arguments concerning self-defence against non-state actors, this author agrees that unwillingness or inability to prevent the use of its territory by irregular groups can be an essential factor in rendering the harbouring or sponsoring state responsible for the activities of such groups.[196]

---

[190] Higgins 1963, pp. 205–207.

[191] Brown 2003, pp. 30–32; Feinstein 2002, pp. 278–279.

[192] Brown 2003, p. 30.

[193] Ibid., pp. 30–31.

[194] Ibid., p. 31.

[195] Feinstein 2002, p. 279; Greenwood 2003, p. 25.

[196] Similar opinions: Feinstein 2002, p. 279; Greenwood 2003, p. 25. See also Prosecutor v. Dusko Tadić, ICTY Case No. IT-94-1-A, Judgment, Appeals Chamber, 15 July 1999, paras 131, 137. In *Tadić* the Appeal Chamber found that overall control by the state over organized and hierarchically structured groups was sufficient to deduce state responsibility. Such 'overall control' resided not only in equipping, financing or training and providing operational support to the group, but also in coordinating or helping in the general planning of its military or paramilitary activity. For a comparison of the *Nicaragua* and *Tadić* tests, see Cassese 2007, pp. 649–668.

10.5.2.5 The Legality of the US War in Afghanistan

The legality of the Afghanistan war on the basis of the right of self-defence (and other grounds) was addressed by several publicists.[197] Some contended that the US action was a lawful exercise of self-defence endorsed by the Security Council under Chapter VII.[198] Both Franck and Gill asserted that there was no contradiction in using both legal bases to justify the same armed action.[199] Conversely, Charney was of the opinion that the US relied solely on the right of self-defence and that such a stance was counterproductive given the wide support it enjoyed within the UN system after the 9/11 attacks.[200]

On the issue of 'anticipatory self-defence', Brown argued that it did not offer a sound legal basis for the use of force against terrorist attacks unless the existence of an imminent threat that goes beyond mere preponderance was proved.[201] Feinstein maintained the contrary: *Operation Enduring Freedom* was not only a lawful exercise of self-defence after an armed attack had occurred, but also a legal anticipatory action designed to prevent further serious injury.[202]

The legality of the US invasion of Afghanistan can be assessed both under the requirements of necessity and proportionality, on one hand, and the elements of 'accumulation of events' theory, on the other. As said above, the magnitude of the 9/11 attacks demonstrated that acts of non-state actors can, in themselves, amount to armed attacks. At the same time, the 11 September attacks can be viewed as part of a series of attacks directed against US targets.

Consequently, three interpretative points can be made regarding the 2001 US action. First, the existent danger referred not only to the 9/11 attacks, but also to past attacks (such as the 1993 New York, the 1998 East Africa and the 2000 Yemeni bombings) as well as to the threat lying in the planned future attacks. In other words, the conditionality of an armed attack (as an element of necessity) had to be interpreted to include both past and future events. Greenwood offered a clear explanation on this matter:

> The events of September 11 cannot be considered in isolation. Taken together with other events, such as the attacks on the US embassies in East Africa in 1998 and the attack on the USS Cole for which Al-Qaida had claimed responsibility, there were the clearest possible indications of further outrages to come. Moreover, in these circumstances there seems little difficulty in regarding the threat of future attacks from Al-Qaida as meeting the criteria of imminence.[203]

---

[197] For instance: Beard 2002; Brown 2003; Charney 2001; Cassese 2001; Feinstein 2002; Franck 2001; Gill 2003; Greenwood 2003; Murphy 2002; Ratner 2002.

[198] Franck 2001, p. 840, 841; Gill 2003, pp. 31–32.

[199] Gill 2003, p. 31.

[200] Charney 2001, p. 837.

[201] Brown 2003, p. 43.

[202] Feinstein 2002, p. 282.

[203] Greenwood 2003, p. 23.

Secondly, this collective conditionality of past and future attacks created a present and inevitable need to act (immediacy element of necessity). The intention of the US government was to preclude future attacks by Al-Qaeda. The re-occurrence of these attacks was evidenced by the available information that undoubtedly showed that the carrying out of armed attacks against US or Western targets was part and parcel of Al-Qaeda's anti-US, anti-Western political agenda.[204]

Thirdly, the proportionality of the US action had to be measured against the need to neutralize the source of all future attacks. According to Gill, the requirement of proportionality of the US response had to be measured in the light of the scale and effects of the attacks, the nature of the threat of further attacks posed by Al-Qaeda and its supporters, either directed against the US or against other states, the objectives pursued by Al-Qaeda as well as the feasibility of arriving at a cessation of armed activity by any other means.[205] On the basis of these factors, Gill concluded that there was no alternative than the one pursued by the US and its allies in invading Afghanistan. The Taliban refused to cut all ties with Al-Qaeda and there was little hope that it would have complied with Security Council resolutions to hand over the leadership of Al-Qaeda and cooperate in bringing to justice those responsible for terrorist acts.[206] Greenwood also pointed out that it was difficult to see how the US intervention could have succeeded in its aims of removing the Al-Qaeda bases in Afghanistan without overturning the leadership of that country.[207]

Cassese took a more restrictive approach. In his view, the use of force had to be aimed at detaining the persons allegedly responsible for the crimes and destroying military objectives used by the terrorists. The use of force could not aim at replacing Afghan leadership or destroying Afghan military installations if those had no connection to Al-Qaeda, unless they 'show by words or deeds that they approve and endorse the actions of terrorist organizations.'[208] For this author, it is hard to see how the refusal to hand over the Al-Qaeda leadership and close terrorist training camps does not show 'by words or deeds' that the Taliban approved and endorsed the actions of bin Laden's recruits.

In the opinion of this author, the US invasion of Afghanistan was a lawful exercise of self-defence that was also recognized by the Security Council in Resolution 1368 (2001).[209] The US response was lawful on the basis of the right of self-defence *per se*, as a measure taken *after* a series of armed attacks had occurred with the objective of warding off *future* attacks premeditated by Al-Qaeda.

---

[204] The 9/11 Commission Report 2004, pp. 47–48, 59.

[205] Gill 2003, p. 33.

[206] Ibid., pp. 33–34.

[207] Greenwood 2003, p. 25.

[208] Cassese 2001, p. 999.

[209] Franck 2002, p. 54.

Some authors have maintained that the attacks of 9/11 had a groundbreaking effect on the content of the right of self-defence.[210] Although the 11 September attacks had some important effects on the interpretation of self-defence, it is the opinion of this author that they did not alter the content or the temporal limits of that right. The most important development in the immediate aftermath of 9/11 was the explicit acceptance on behalf of the Security Council that armed acts carried out by non-state actors could justify resort to self-defence.[211] This was not a revolutionary development for the customary right of self-defence, but rather the result of a 'growing consistent pragmatism that is essentially fact-specific without being idiosyncratic.'[212] The pre-Charter understanding of the right had never restricted its exercise to armed acts carried out by states. Furthermore, there was nothing in Article 51 of the Charter that outlawed such an interpretation. Moreover, the justifiability of defensive action against non-state actors had been several times voiced in post-Charter state practice prior to 9/11. Consequently, the importance of the reaction to the 11 September attacks lies in the closing of the gap between state-, Security Council-practice and legal doctrine regarding the justifiability of self-defence against non-state actors. By accepting that armed acts of irregular groups could amount to armed attacks, the Security Council implicitly confirmed one of the elements of the 'accumulation of events' theory as well.

10.5.3 The War Against Iraq (2003)

Immediately after 11 September 2001, the then US President George W. Bush tasked some of its officials to conduct a survey of intelligence information about the possible involvement of Saddam Hussein in the 9/11 attacks.[213] The survey was sent on 18 September 2001 to the then Secretary of Defence Condoleezza Rice. The conclusion of the report was that there was no compelling evidence that Iraq had either planned or perpetrated the attacks.[214] The president thus decided to focus on Afghanistan, but ordered the US Defence Department to be ready to deal with Iraq if Baghdad acted against US interests.[215] On 20 September 2001, at a meeting with the then British Prime Minister Tony Blair, President Bush asserted

---

210 Cassese 2001, pp. 993, 995–998; Mégret 2002, pp. 361–399; Myjer and White 2002, pp. 5–17. See also Reisman 2003, pp. 142–143. Reisman maintains that the development of 'anticipatory self-defence' was prompted by the introduction of more destructive and rapidly delivered weapons, suggesting this way that anticipatory action in self-defence was a result of post-Charter developments.

211 SC Res. 1368 (2001) preamble. Franck 2002, pp. 66–67.

212 Franck 2002, p. 67.

213 The 9/11 Commission Report 2004, p. 334.

214 Ibid.

215 Ibid., p. 335.

that Iraq was not the immediate problem, although some members of his administration thought otherwise.[216]

The US invasion of Afghanistan was acknowledged by the Security Council both under Chapter VII and on the basis of the inherent right of self-defence. The government harbouring Al-Qaeda was overturned, significant damage was inflicted to terrorist facilities in Afghanistan and many of the Al-Qaeda leaders were either apprehended or killed in combat. The Bush administration did not stop at this. Apart from continuing its 'war on terror' against several targets all over the world, it also directed its attention towards Iraq. The road to the 2003 invasion and the legal arguments put forward were discussed in Chapter 9.[217] As maintained above, one of the grounds for invading Iraq was its alleged links with 'terrorism'.[218] In his speech given to the UN General Assembly on 12 September 2002, President Bush asserted that:

> In violation of Security Council Resolution 1373, Iraq continues to shelter and support terrorist organizations that direct violence against Iran, Israel, and Western governments. Iraqi dissidents abroad are targeted for murder. In 1993, Iraq attempted to assassinate the Emir of Kuwait and a former American President. Iraq's Government openly praised the attacks of September the 11th. And Al-Qaeda terrorists escaped from Afghanistan and are known to be in Iraq.[219]

That statement was reiterated on 17 March 2003, when the US president once again asserted that Iraq had 'aided, trained and harboured terrorists, including operatives of Al-Qaeda.[220] In the same national address the president maintained that the danger that Iraqi sponsorship of terrorism posed was 'clear': 'using chemical, biological or, one day, nuclear weapons, obtained with the help of Iraq, the terrorists could fulfil their stated ambitions and kill thousands or hundreds of thousands of innocent people in our country, or any other.'[221]

Notwithstanding such bold statements regarding Iraq's links to terrorists, the US did not produce any clear evidence to demonstrate that Iraq had any involvement in the 9/11 attacks or that it had any connection to Al-Qaeda.[222]

The 2003 war against Iraq raises questions similar to those relevant for the war against the Taliban regime of Afghanistan, but the answers differ considerably. First, the Security Council did not endorse the Iraqi war. There was no confirmation of the right of self-defence and no endorsement under Chapter VII. Secondly, since the link between the 9/11 attacks and the regime of Saddam Hussein was never proven, there was no possibility of blaming Iraq for what

[216] Ibid., p. 336.

[217] See *supra* 9.5.1 and 9.5.2.

[218] Bush (12 September 2002) Remarks.

[219] Ibid.

[220] Bush (17 March 2003) Remarks. See *supra* 9.5.4.

[221] Bush (17 March 2003) Remarks.

[222] Flynn 2008, p. 203; Henderson 2004, p. 15; Lowe 2003, p. 860; McGoldrick 2004, p. 17; Sapiro 2005, p. 360.

happened on 11 September 2001.[223] Iraq could not be held responsible for planning, organizing or supporting the completion of the 9/11 attacks. Moreover, there was no proof that individuals responsible for involvement in those attacks ever took refuge in Iraq.[224] Thirdly, there was no proof of the presence of Al-Qaeda or other terrorist elements on Iraqi territory. There was no proof that Iraq was involved in sponsoring or harbouring terrorist groups that planned future attacks on the US.[225] All in all, the existence of a credible (let alone imminent) terrorist threat involving Iraq was not proven by the US. Finally, the question of proportionality needs no answer. Without a legitimate ground for invoking self-defence against a terrorist threat originating from Iraq, the 2003 US-led war could not be rendered proportionate in any way.

As opposed to the US war in Afghanistan, no form of the 'accumulation of events' theory can be maintained for the 2003 invasion of Iraq. There were no armed acts amounting (individually or in their totality) to an armed attack that would render the future occurrence of other attacks imminent. Consequently, neither the requirement of necessity nor that of proportionality was met by the 2003 US invasion of Iraq.

10.5.4 Israeli Invasion of Lebanon (2006)

From 2000 through 2006, the Security Council adopted a series of resolutions in which it called on Lebanon to reassert its control over the southern part of the country.[226] During the 1990s, Israeli Defence Forces (IDF) and Hezbollah clashed several times and sustained week-long battles. In May 2000, Israeli troops withdrew from southern Lebanon and the UN established the 'Blue Line' as a border between the two countries.[227] The fighting between Israel and Lebanon continued, however, in a very predictable manner. Hezbollah launched rockets at Israel, targeted random Israeli citizens in a number of shootings and kidnapped Israeli soldiers and civilians.[228] In response, Israel carried out airstrikes, such as the one in September 2003, when warplanes hit targets in southern Lebanon in response to Hezbollah's firing antiaircraft missiles at Israeli planes in the area.[229] In Resolution 1559 (2004) the Security Council expressed its grave concern at the 'continued presence of armed militias in Lebanon, which prevent the Lebanese

---

223 The 9/11 Commission Report 2004, p. 334.

224 Henderson 2004, p. 15; Lowe 2003, p. 860; McGoldrick 2004, p. 17; Sapiro 2005, p. 360.

225 The 9/11 Commission Report 2004, p. 334.

226 For instance: SC Res. 1310 (2000); 1337, 1365 (2001); 1391, 1428 (2002); 1461 (2003); 1525, 1553, 1559 (2004); 1583, 1614 (2005); and 1655, 1680 (2006).

227 Sorenson 2008, pp. 33–34; Shiryaev 2007–2008, p. 80.

228 Wrachford 2007, p. 46.

229 Israeli jets fire on Lebanon (3 September 2003) BBC News; Wrachford 2007, p. 46.

government from exercising its full sovereignty over all Lebanese territory.'[230] Resolution 1559 called for the 'disbanding and disarmament of all Lebanese and non-Lebanese militias.'[231]

On 12 July 2006, Hezbollah launched a series of rocket attacks across the Blue Line against northern Israeli towns and IDF units patrolling the border with Lebanon. At the same time, Hezbollah fighters crossed into Israel and attacked an Israeli patrol. As a result of Hezbollah's *Operation True Promise*, eight Israeli soldiers and two civilians were killed. Two Israeli soldiers were captured and taken back to Lebanon.[232]

The next day, Israel launched *Operation Change Direction.* It first imposed a naval blockade on Lebanon and bombed several military and logistic targets in Lebanon. The naval and air blockade as well as the airstrikes continued in the following weeks, with Israeli ground troops crossing the border on 22 July 2006 and moving into Lebanon.[233] In response, Hezbollah fired countless Katyusha rockets targeting Haifa and a number of settlements in northern Israel.[234] The conflict lasted for over a month; it claimed the lives of some 116 Israeli soldiers, 28 Lebanese soldiers, 43 Israeli civilians and 1109 Lebanese civilians (of whom a part were Hezbollah fighters). Scores of people were wounded or forced to leave their homes.[235]

On the day the Hezbollah operations started, the Permanent Representative of Israel to the UN sent two identical letters to the UN Secretary-General Kofi Annan and to the president of the Security Council.[236] The Israeli representative reported that 'Hezbollah terrorists unleashed a barrage of heavy artillery and rockets into Israel, causing a number of deaths. In the midst of this horrific and unprovoked act, the terrorists infiltrated Israel and kidnapped two Israeli soldiers, taking them into Lebanon'.[237] The representative further noted that responsibility for these acts lay with the Lebanese government for 'ineptitude and inaction' as well as with the Iranian and Syrian governments for supporting and embracing those who carried out the attack. After declaring that the attacks posed a grave threat not just to Israel's northern border, but also to the region and the entire world, the representative justified Israel's armed response on the basis of the right of self-defence.[238]

---

230 SC Res. 1559 (2004) Preamble.

231 Ibid., para 3.

232 Schmitt 2008, p. 127; Shiryaev 2007–2008, pp. 80–81; Wrachford 2007, p. 47.

233 Schmitt 2008, p. 127; Wrachford 2007, pp. 47–48.

234 Ruys 2007, p. 266; Wrachford 2007, p. 48.

235 Ruys 2007, p. 266.

236 UN Docs. A/30/937 (2006) and S/2006/515 (2006).

237 Ibid.

238 Ibid.

Lebanon characterized the Israeli move as an act of aggression and asserted that it did not endorse the cross-border attacks and did not take responsibility for them.[239] Israel emphasized that after 'having shown unparalleled restraint for 6 years while bearing the brunt of countless attacks,' it had no choice but to respond to an 'absolutely unprovoked assault, whose scale and depth was unprecedented in recent years.' It was further maintained that although Israel held the Lebanese government responsible for these attacks, it was concentrating its response carefully, 'mainly on Hezbollah strongholds, positions and infrastructure.'[240]

Several members of the Security Council—Argentina, Australia, Brazil, Canada, Denmark, Greece, Guatemala, Peru, Slovakia, Turkey, the UK and the US—acknowledged Israel's right to self-defence.[241] The right of Israel to defend itself was recognized by Secretary-General Kofi Annan as well. He reiterated several times that Israel had a right of self-defence under Article 51 of the UN Charter as long as it observed proportionality.[242] Israel's right of self-defence was also recognized by the representative of Finland speaking on behalf of the European Union, while urging Israel to exercise utmost restraint and not to resort to disproportionate action.[243] Criticism as to the proportionality of Israel's actions was, however, frequently expressed in the later days of the conflict.[244] On 11 August, the Security Council adopted a resolution calling for the immediate cessation of hostilities on both sides.[245] It did not make reference to the right of self-defence, but refrained from condemning Israeli actions as it so frequently did in the past.

Such a wide recognition of Israel's right of self-defence against paramilitary attacks was unprecedented. The reaction to the 2006 Israeli invasion of Lebanon was a very good opportunity to assess how the opinion of the Security Council—and of a large group of states—had changed after the 9/11 attacks. There was nothing new in the line of reasoning put forward by Israel. It advanced the selfsame 'needle-prick' theory that had been rejected so many times in the past.[246] The Israeli government made reference to the long series of terrorist attacks that it had suffered, put the emphasis on the most recent ones and asserted that they together amounted to an ongoing armed attack. On that basis, Israel maintained

239 UN Doc. S/2006/517 (2006); SCOR, 61st Session, 5489th meeting., UN Doc. S/PV.5489 (14 July 2006) p. 4.

240 SCOR, 61st Session, 5489th meeting., UN Doc. S/PV.5489 (14 July 2006) p. 6.

241 Ibid., pp. 12, 14, 15, 17; ibid., 5493rd meeting., UN Doc. S/PV.5493 (21 July 2006) pp. 17, 19 and S/PV.5493 (Resumption1) (21 July 2006) pp. 9, 19, 27, 28, 39, 41.

242 SCOR, 61st Session, 5492nd meeting., UN Doc. S/PV.5492 (20 July 2006) p. 3.

243 Ibid., 5493rd meeting., UN Doc. S/PV.5493 (Resumption1) (21 July 2006) p. 16.

244 Ibid., 5497th meeting., UN Doc. S/PV.5497 (27 July 2006); Statement by the President of the Security Council, UN Doc. S/PRST/2006/34 (2006); SCOR, 61st Session, 5498th meeting., UN Doc. S/PV.5498 (30 July 2006) pp. 2–3; 5499th meeting., UN Doc. S/PV.5499 (30 July 2006); Statement by the President of the Security Council, UN Doc. S/PRST/2006/35 (2006).

245 SC Res. 1701 (2006).

246 See *supra* 10.2.

that it was necessary to resort to armed action to ward off such attacks in the near future.[247] The legal argument was old. The approach of the Security Council—and most of its members—was new. For the first time, the 'accumulation of events' theory was implicitly recognized by the Security Council.

Legal doctrine was more divided on the lawfulness of the 2006 invasion of Lebanon. Heinze cautiously noted that the Israeli move was the latest example of state practice that suggested an eased requirement of attribution for using force against states that harboured non-state actors engaging in trans-boundary violence.[248] Schmitt asserted that the 2006 Israeli action against Lebanon was 'an excellent illustration of the growing acceptability of cross-border counter-terrorist operations when the State in which terrorists are located fails to comply with the duty to police its own territory.'[249] Ruys maintained that Israel's actions could be justified as self-defence as the kidnapping of two of its soldiers did amount to an armed attack. Further, although Lebanon was not willingly harbouring Hezbollah, the latter had assumed the role of *de facto* government in some parts of the Lebanese territory and Israel was right in targeting its camps and facilities. Nonetheless, Ruys concluded that Israel exceeded the limits of self-defence by targeting governmental and civilian infrastructure in contravention with the principle of proportionality.[250] Schmitt also found the Israeli action justified as self-defence and emphasized that the proportionality of *Operation Change Direction* had to be assessed 'in the context of not only the 12 July Hezbollah attacks, but also those which had preceded them and those which likely would have followed.'[251] Wrachford took a middle-way approach: he found Israeli actions on Hezbollah-controlled territory justifiable as self-defence, while the incursions into territory not controlled by Hezbollah he characterized as illegal.[252]

The 2006 Israeli invasion of Lebanon was another instance in which the 'needle-prick' theory served as the basis for the claim of self-defence. For that reason, as with the US action against Afghanistan, the requirements of necessity and proportionality have to be analysed in corroboration with the elements of the 'accumulation of events' theory. Israel had been facing a series of Hezbollah attacks over the years, the one on 12 July 2006 being the latest in that protraction (collective conditionality of attacks). Further, the immediacy of the situation was given not only by the continuous shelling of northern Israeli towns, but also by the certainty of occurrence of future attacks by the same authors against similar targets. Consequently, both factors of the necessity requirement can be maintained if the elements of the 'accumulation of events' theory are accepted.

---

[247] Ibid.

[248] Heinze 2009, p. 100.

[249] Schmitt 2008, p. 164.

[250] Ruys 2007, p. 293.

[251] Schmitt 2008, pp. 163–164. *Per a contrario*, see Kattan 2007.

[252] Wrachford 2007, pp. 88–89.

Questions remain as to the proportionality of the Israeli armed action. The Security Council voiced serious concerns over specific incidents in July and August 2006, in which Israel seemed to resort to disproportionate measures. The proportionality of the Israeli invasion must be assessed on the basis of the 'accumulation of events' theory. Accordingly, the proportionality has to be weighed against the force needed to neutralize Hezbollah camps and facilities to stop future attacks. For this author, it is hard to see how operations directed against Lebanese targets, both military and civilian, can be rendered proportionate without clear evidence that such measures were absolutely needed to neutralize the threat coming from Hezbollah.[253] In this respect, the Israeli action exceeded the proportionality requirement of self-defence.

10.5.5 Turkish Incursion into Northern Iraq (2007–2008)

Another instance of state practice in which armed force was used to preclude the reoccurring of attacks by non-state actors was the 2007–2008 Turkish incursion in Northern Iraq against the forces of the Kurdistan Workers' Party (PKK). The Turkey—PKK conflict dates back to the late 1970s and purports several legal arguments including secessionist claims based on the principle of self-determination.[254] Although no official claim of self-defence was made on the part of Turkey, the armed action purported the main characteristics of self-defence against non-state actors.

On 21 February 2008, Turkey launched a major ground offensive into Northern Iraq to address the threat posed by PKK forces.[255] The incursion took place against a general background of increased violence between the parties that culminated in several armed incidents in 2007.[256] The cross-border attacks of 7 and 21 October 2007 resulted in the death of Turkish soldiers and thus pushed tensions to the limit.[257] After the attack of 7 October, some 100,000 Turkish grounds troops massed along the border with Iraq.[258] Following the 21 October attack, the Turkish

[253] Ducheine and Pouw 2009, pp. 71–72; Ruys 2007, p. 291.

[254] For details on the history of the conflict and the claims of the Kurdistan Workers' Party, see Doğu 2007, pp. 323–356.

[255] Turkey launches major land offensive into Northern Iraq (22 February 2008) Reuters; Ground Offensive against Separatists (2008) Keesing's Record of World Events, p. 48427.

[256] While in the 1990s the conflict unfolded in the south-eastern part of Turkey (a predominantly Kurdish region), after the capture of the PKK leader, Abdullah Ocalan, the conflict shifted to Northern Iraq, a region where the bulk of the PKK forces took refuge. Consequently, from 2004 onwards, the number of cross-border incidents had been increasing between the PKK rebels and Turkish forces. See Ruys 2008, pp. 334–335, 336–339.

[257] Ruys 2008, p. 338.

[258] Authorization of Incursions into Iraq (2007) Keesing's Record of World Events, pp. 48219–20; Ruys 2008, p. 338.

government ordered the carrying out of aerial bombardments, artillery attacks and small-scale hot pursuit in Northern Iraq against PKK positions and forces.[259] The aerial bombardment was increased in December 2007 and was followed by a ground offensive launched on 21 February 2008.[260]

Although the Turkish government did not advance any formal justification along the lines of self-defence, the background and purpose of the armed action was very similar to those undertaken by other states claiming self-defence against non-state actors. As with the Israeli invasion of Lebanon, the general reaction of states focused on the conduct of hostilities rather than on legality grounds.[261] On the day the ground offensive started, the European Union issued a statement in which it acknowledged 'Turkey's need to protect its population from terrorism,' but urged the government 'to refrain from any disproportionate military action' and to 'respect human rights and the rule of law.'[262] The UN Secretary-General issued a similar statement:

> While conscious of Turkey's concerns, he reiterates his appeal for utmost restraint, and for respect of the international borders between Iraq and Turkey. He also repeats his previous calls for an immediate end to continued incursions by PKK elements carrying out terrorist attacks in Turkey from Northern Iraq.[263]

Countries like the US, UK and France all emphasized the need for utmost restraint, while none of them condemned the underlying reasons of the Turkish offensive.[264]

Several questions arise as to the justifiability of the Turkish action as self-defence. First of all, the Turkish government did not report its actions to the Security Council, thus missing an opportunity to clarify the factual background and the legal issues at stake. Secondly, the Turkish government never made an official claim of self-defence and never referred to the 'accumulation of events' theory to justify its actions. The characteristics of the Turkish armed action nevertheless show considerable similarities with self-defence claims against non-state actors.

As to the conditionality of an armed attack, it can be argued that the long series of attacks of the PKK amounted to an armed attack in the understanding of the 'needle-prick' approach. That view was implicitly accepted by both the European

[259] Ruys 2008, p. 338.

[260] Offensive against PKK Positions in Northern Iraq (2007) Keesing's Record of World Events, p. 48316; Ground Offensive against Separatists (2008) Keesing's Record of World Events, p. 48427; Ruys 2008, p. 338.

[261] Ruys 2008, pp. 339–345.

[262] EU calls on Turkey to avoid "disproportionate" army action in Iraq (22 February 2008) EU Business.

[263] UN Doc. SG/SM/11436.

[264] Ruys 2008, p. 340.

Union and the UN Secretary-General in their acknowledgment of 'Turkey's concerns'.[265] Similarly, the answer of the Dutch foreign minister to a parliamentary question also confirmed that the actions of the PKK can be interpreted as the legal basis for self-defence.[266]

Matters are less straightforward when it comes to the immediacy element of self-defence. The Iraqi government instituted a number of measures aimed at stopping the cross-border attacks against Turkey, but it refused to extradite any Kurdish rebel or take armed measures against the PKK forces.[267] This put the Turkish government into a significant impasse, because the Iraqi measures were clearly not efficient enough to stop the PKK attacks.[268] Nonetheless, it is hard to discern from the available information whether that impasse led to a present and inevitable need to launch an aerial and ground offensive across the border into Northern Iraq. Javier Solana, the European Union's foreign policy chief asserted that the Turkish incursion was 'not the best response' and that diplomatic solutions should have been given priority.[269]

The repeated warnings as to the excessiveness of the Turkish military action also question the proportionality of the use of force.[270]

Although the Turkish government never made an official claim of self-defence in relation to its 2007–2008 Iraqi incursions, this instance of state practice is very similar to those in which states resort to armed action against repeated attacks carried out by non-state actors. As with the 2006 Israeli invasion of Lebanon, the general reaction as to the legality of such action was acquiescing rather than disapproving. The post-9/11 approach to self-defence against non-state actors (and, implicitly, to the 'accumulation of events' theory) had been once again confirmed by state practice.

10.5.6 The Gaza Crisis (2008–2009)

The Israeli military operations launched in December 2008 against strongholds of Palestinian armed groups in Gaza is another example of post-9/11 defensive measures against non-state actors. On 14 December 2008, Hamas political leader Khaled Meshaal announced that the 6-month ceasefire with Israel would not be extended. That ceasefire had been brokered by the Egyptian government and came

---

[265] EU calls on Turkey to avoid "disproportionate" army action in Iraq (22 February 2008) EU Business; UN Doc. SG/SM/11436.

[266] Verhagen (3 March 2008) Beantwoording.

[267] Ruys 2008, pp. 342–343.

[268] Ibid.

[269] EU calls on Turkey to avoid "disproportionate" army action in Iraq (22 February 2008) EU Business.

[270] Ruys 2008, pp. 339–345.

into effect on 19 June 2008. Consequently, it was due to expire on 18 December 2008.[271]

The ceasefire agreement included a commitment by Israel to cease its military operations in Gaza as well as a pledge by the Gaza authorities to stop attacks by Palestinian armed groups against Israel with immediate effect. Israel also reportedly agreed to ease its blockade of Gaza and gradually lift its ban on the import of a large number of commodities.[272] Throughout the months of the ceasefire, it became clear that none of the parties were able to keep to their commitments. The firing of rockets into Israel continued, whereas most of the Gaza crossings were progressively closed by Israeli authorities.[273] Israeli forces also launched several raids into Gaza and reportedly killed members of various Palestinian armed groups as well as a few civilians.[274]

From November 2008 onwards, the number of armed incidents significantly increased. On 4 November, Israeli forces entered into Gaza to close a cross-border tunnel that in Israel's view was intended to be used by Palestinian fighters to kidnap Israeli soldiers. In the ensuing fighting, one member of the Al-Qassam Brigades[275] was killed and several Israeli soldiers wounded. In response, the Al-Qassam Brigades fired more than 30 Qassam rockets into Israel. Israel responded with an air strike that left a further five members of the Al-Qassam Brigades dead.[276]

Throughout the month of November 2008, 125 rockets and 68 mortar shells were fired into Israel by Palestinian armed groups.[277] Rocket and mortar fire by Palestinian armed groups continued unabated throughout December 2008.[278]

On 18 December 2008, Hamas declared the end of the ceasefire with Israel.[279] That declaration was followed by an upsurge of rocket attacks.[280] On 24 December 2008, 30 rockets and 30 mortars were fired into Israel. The Israeli forces responded with air strikes on positions inside Gaza and the crossings into Israel remained closed.[281]

---

[271] HRC Report 2009, para 224; Timeline: Israeli-Hamas violence since truce ended (5 January 2009) Reuters.

[272] HRC Report 2009, para 225.

[273] Ibid., paras 227–253.

[274] Ibid., paras 230, 242 (raids), 230, 244, 245 (Palestinian groups casualties), 238, 247 (civilian casualties).

[275] Ezzedeen Al-Qassam Brigades (EQB) was established in the midst of the Palestinian Intifada (1987–1994) against the Israeli occupation. Their mission statement is available at www.qassam.ps/aboutus.html. Accessed 15 June 2010.

[276] HRC Report 2009, para 254.

[277] Ibid., para 257.

[278] Ibid., para 259.

[279] Ibid., para 262; Timeline: Israeli-Hamas violence since truce ended (5 January 2009) Reuters.

[280] HRC Report 2009, paras 263–265.

[281] Ibid., para 265.

On 27 December 2008, Israel started its military operations in Gaza.[282] In a wave of air and missile attacks on targets across Gaza, some 225 people were killed on that day, most of them policemen within the Hamas militant movement.[283] The Israeli military operations lasted until 18 January 2009 and resulted in some 1,400 Palestinian deaths.[284] The military operations included both an air and a land offensive with several hundred targets damaged or destroyed.[285] As the Israeli forces began withdrawing around 15 January 2009, there appeared to be a practice of systematically demolishing a large number of structures, including houses, water installations, such as tanks on the roofs of houses, and of agricultural land.[286] Moreover, whereas the strikes in the first days of the operation had been relatively selective, the last few days saw an increase in the number of strikes with several hundred targets hit, causing not only very substantial damage to buildings but also, according to some sources, underground structural damage.[287]

Before the Security Council, Israel claimed that it was acting in self-defence. The Israeli representative asserted:

> In the past 2 weeks, prior to Israel's reaction, we witnessed a steep escalation in Hamas attacks against Israel. Israel has been subjected to more than 300 rockets and mortar shells, which were launched indiscriminately, striking cities and towns, schools and playgrounds, commercial centres and synagogues. In its military operation Israel has exercised its inherent right to self-defence, which is enshrined in Article 51 of the United Nations Charter. Any other State would have acted in the same manner when faced with similar terrorist threats.[288]

Several members of the Security Council expressly accepted the Israeli claim of self-defence. Accordingly, the representatives of South Africa, Italy, Vietnam and Costa Rica all confirmed Israel's right to defend itself.[289] Other members—such as China, France, Panama, Russia, UK and the US—stressed the importance of a diplomatic solution and called for the immediate cessation of hostilities.[290] None of these members questioned the right of Israel to defend itself. Although the US did not expressly refer to the right of self-defence, it acknowledged that it was 'intolerable for Israel to live under the terror of rocket attacks.'[291] The representatives of Libya and Egypt expressly condemned the Israeli action as aggression

[282] Ibid., para 267.

[283] Gaza crisis: key maps and timeline (18 January 2009) BBC News.

[284] The percentage of civilians among the casualties varies from source to source. For an outline of the various sources, see HRC Report 2009, paras 350–358.

[285] Ibid., para 333.

[286] Ibid., para 349.

[287] Ibid.

[288] SCOR, 63rd Session, 6060th meeting., UN Doc. S/PV.6060 (31 December 2008) p. 6.

[289] Ibid., pp. 9 (South Africa), 13 (Italy and Viet Nam), 16 (Costa Rica).

[290] Ibid., pp. 9 (France), 10 (Panama), 11 (Russia), 12 (UK), 14 (US) and 15 (China).

[291] Ibid., p. 14.

and rejected the claim of self-defence.[292] Indonesia adopted a similar position, although it stopped short of condemning the Israeli military operation as aggression.[293] Nonetheless, all representatives have expressed concern or outrage as to the excessive use of force on the Israeli part.[294] That opinion was also shared by the Secretary-General. While refraining to comment on Israel's claim of self-defence, Ban Ki-moon stated:

> I condemn unequivocally and in the strongest possible terms the ongoing rocket and mortar attacks by Hamas and other Palestinian militants. But I also condemn the excessive use of force by Israel.[295]

The attitude of the Security Council members showed that Israel's claim of self-defence against the repeated attacks originating from various Palestinian armed groups was generally accepted. As with the 2006 Israeli invasion of Lebanon and, implicitly, the 2008 Turkish incursion into Northern Iraq, self-defence against non-state actors was not a controversial claim anymore. Accordingly, the reaction to the Gaza crisis again showed that repeated attacks carried out by non-state actors could lead to a situation in which both elements of necessity (armed attack and immediacy) were present. The relentless rocket and mortar attacks against Israel did indeed create an intolerable situation that led to a present and inevitable need to take armed action. Nonetheless, the extent of the armed action was heavily criticized by all members of the Security Council as well as independent agencies.[296] One of the main conclusions of the September 2009 Human Rights Council is particularly striking in this respect. Accordingly, the report asserts that 'while the Israeli Government has sought to portray its operations as essentially a response to rocket attacks in the exercise of its right to self-defence, the Mission (mandated by the Human Rights Council, KTSz) considers the plan to have been directed, at least in part, at a different target: the people of Gaza as a whole.'[297]

10.6 Concluding Remarks

This chapter analysed several instances of state practice which had two common elements. First, they involved a claim of self-defence. Secondly, specific for this chapter, they pertained to armed acts carried out by non-state actors.

On the basis of the state practice and legal doctrine discussed, it can be established that, in conflicts involving non-state actors, the temporal dimension of the post-Charter concept of self-defence is most of the time circular: the same

---

292 Ibid., pp. 7 (Libya), 18 (Egypt).

293 Ibid., p. 11.

294 Ibid., pp. 9–18.

295 Ibid., p. 3.

296 Ibid., pp. 9–18; HRC Report 2009, paras 1674–1692.

297 HRC Report 2009, para 1680.

defensive action is both remedial (against a string of past attacks) and anticipatory (against future attacks). The circularity stems from the 'accumulation of events' theory: the incidence of future attacks is expected because of the occurrence of past attacks. Defensive action on the basis of the 'accumulation of events' theory should not be regarded as exclusively remedial. The immediate need to act and the proportionality to use force has to be assessed by taking into consideration the threat posed by future threats. In fact, the way the anticipatory and remedial dimensions of self-defence work together in the 'accumulation of events' theory shows why the anticipatory considerents are intrinsically part of self-defence as such.

Needless to say, a single armed act carried out by a non-state actor can also amount to an armed attack (9/11). Moreover, the 'accumulation of events' theory can also be relevant for armed acts carried out by regular armed forces (Yemen, 1964; Libya, 1986; Iraq, 1993). Nonetheless, the state practice examined in this chapter has shown that the 'accumulation of events' theory is most of the time connected to claims of self-defence against non-state actors. From this respect, the temporal dimension of self-defence against non-state actors is mirroring the pre-Charter understanding of the right in its full form: defence being allowed before, during and after an armed attack.

The 'accumulation of events' theory clearly influences the interpretation of the necessity and proportionality requirements of self-defence. First, the existent danger refers both to already occurred armed attacks and to the threat lying in planned future attacks. In other words, the conditionality of an armed attack (as a factor of the necessity requirement) has to be interpreted to include both past and future events. Secondly, this collective conditionality of past and future attacks has to create a present and inevitable need to act (immediacy factor of the necessity requirement). Furthermore, the proportionality of the defensive action has to be measured against the need to neutralize the source of all future attacks, thus it can involve a response considerably larger in scale than the already occurred attacks (Fig. 10.1).

The 'accumulation of events' theory has given rise to many controversies since the adoption of the UN Charter. For long, the Security Council and a significant part of the legal doctrine did not accept the possibility of attributing armed attacks to non-state actors and thus rejected the 'needle-prick' approach as well.[298] This was in spite of the fact that pre-Charter customary law offered several examples of self-defence being invoked against non-state actors. Such a case was none else but the *Caroline* incident itself.[299] Since the 9/11 attacks, that approach has been undergoing some changes as evidenced by the considerably different attitude of the members of the Security Council to the 2006 Israeli invasion of Lebanon.[300] The necessity of defensive action against non-state actors was also acknowledged in relation to the Turkish incursions into Northern Iraq as well as the Gaza crisis.[301]

---

298 See *supra* 10.2. and 10.3.

299 See *supra* 3.2.2.1 and 6.4.1. See also Kelly 2005, p. 225.

300 See *supra* 10.5.4.

301 See *supra* 10.5.5 and 10.5.6.

'Accumulation of events'	Combined interpretation	Self-defence
Past and future attacks	Collective conditionality	Conditionality of armed attack
Repetition seen as an ongoing campaign	Present and inevitable need to stop the repetition of attacks	Immediacy
Need to neutralize the source of past and future attacks	Qualitative approach: force needed to neutralize the source, not necessarily proportionate to the attacks	Proportionality

Fig. 10.1 Elements of the 'accumulation of events' theory combined with the limits of self-defence

From this respect, the notion of armed attack has partly 'returned' to its pre-Charter meaning, in the sense that non-state actors are again accepted as potential authors of an armed attack.

Nonetheless, controversies still remain as to the elements of the 'accumulation of events' theory and their compatibility with the necessity and proportionality requirements of self-defence. As the last three instances of state practice showed, meeting the requirement of proportionality is especially problematic in large-scale defensive actions against non-state actors (or hit-and-run tactics in general). The relationship between the 'accumulation of events' theory and the necessity and proportionality requirements will be further discussed in Chapter 14 of this book.

References

Ago R (1980) Addendum to the eighth report on state responsibility. UN doc. A/CN.4/318/Add.5-7 (1980)

Albright M (9 September 1998) Address to the American Legion Convention New Orleans, Louisiana. http://avalon.law.yale.edu/20th_century/t_0025.asp. Accessed 29 November 2009

Alexandrov S (1996) Self-defense against the use of force in international law. Kluwer Law International, The Hague

Authorization of incursions into Iraq (2007) Keesing's Record of World Events 53:48219–48220

Baker MB (1987) Terrorism and the inherent right to self-defence (a call to amend Article 51 of the United Nations Charter). Houst J Int Law 10:25–49

Beard JM (2002) America's new war on terror: the case for self-defense under international law. Harv J Law Public Policy 25:559–590

Bin Laden says he wasn't behind attacks (17 September 2001). CNN http://archives.cnn.com/2001/US/09/16/inv.binladen.denial. Accessed 3 December 2010

Bin Laden claims responsibility for 9/11 (29 October 2004). CBC News http://www.cbc.ca/world/story/2004/10/29/binladen_message041029.html. Accessed 30 January 2010

Blin A (2007) The United States confronting terrorism. In: Chaliand G, Blin A (eds) The history of terrorism: from antiquity to Al-Qaeda. University of California Press, Berkeley, pp 398–419

Blum Y (1976) State response to acts of terrorism. Ger Yearb Int Law 19:223–237

Bowett DW (1972) Reprisals involving recourse to armed force. Am J Int Law 66:1–36

Brown D (2003) Use of force against terrorism after September 11th: state responsibility, self-defence and other responses. Cardozo J Int Comp Law 11:1–53

Brownlie I (1963) International law and the use of force by states. Clarendon Press, Oxford

Bush GW (12 September 2002) Remarks at the United Nations General Assembly, New York. http://georgewbush-whitehouse.archives.gov/news/releases/2002/09/20020912-1.html. Accessed 26 January 2010

Bush GW (17 March 2003) Remarks by the President in Address to the Nation. http://georgewbush-whitehouse.archives.gov/news/releases/2003/03/20030317-7.html. Accessed 26 January 2010

Campbell LM (2000) Defending against terrorism: a legal analysis of the decision to strike Sudan and Afghanistan. Tulane Law Rev 74:1067–1096

Cassese A (2001) Terrorism is also disrupting some crucial legal categories of international law. Eur J Int Law 12:993–1001

Cassese A (2007) The Nicaragua and Tadic tests revisited in light of the ICJ judgment on genocide in Bosnia. Eur J Int Law 18:649–668

Chaliand G, Blin A (eds) (2007) The history of terrorism. from antiquity to Al-Qaeda. University of California Press, Berkeley

Charney J (2001) The use of force against terrorism and international law. Am J Int Law 95:835–839

Clerics answer "no, no, no!" and invoke fates of past foes (22 September 2001). New York Times. http://www.nytimes.com/2001/09/22/world/nation-challenged-taliban-clerics-answer-no-no-no-invoke-fates-past-foes.html. Accessed 10 January 2010

Clinton W (20 August 1998) Address to the Nation. http://www.state.gov/www/regions/africa/strike_clinton980820a.html. Accessed 29 November 2009

Dinstein Y (2005) War, aggression and self-defense. Cambridge University Press, Cambridge

Doğu E (2007) PKK: the Kurdistan Workers' Party. In: Heiberg M, O'Leary B, Tirman J (eds) Terror, insurgency and the state: ending protracted conflicts. University of Pennsylvania Press, Philadelphia, pp 323–356

Ducheine P, Pouw E (2009) Operation Change of Direction: a short survey of the legal basis and the applicable legal regimes. NL-ARMS Netherlands Annual Review of Military Studies, pp. 51–95

Duyvesteyn I (2004) How new is the new terrorism? Studies in Conflict and Terrorism 27(5):439–454

EU calls on Turkey to avoid "disproportionate" army action in Iraq (22 February 2008). EU Business. http://www.eubusiness.com/news-eu/1203683534.57/?searchterm=None. Accessed 3 June 2010

Fact Sheet: U.S. Strike on facilities in Afghanistan and Sudan (21 August 1998). US Department of State. http://www.state.gov/www/regions/africa/fs_binladin_facilities.html. Accessed 30 November 2009

FBI Headline archives 1993 WTC bombing. http://www2.fbi.gov/page2/feb08/tradebom_022608.html. Accessed 25 November 2009

FBI National Press Release (13 September 2001). http://www.fbi.gov/news/pressrel/press-releases/fbi-announces-list-of-19-hijackers Accessed 30 January 2010

Feinstein BA (2002) Operation Enduring Freedom: legal dimensions of an infinitely just operation. J Transnatl Law Policy 11:201–295

Flynn MJ (2008) First strike. preemptive war in modern history. Routledge, New York

Franck T (2001) Terrorism and the right of self-defence. Am J Int Law 95:839–843

Franck T (2002) Recourse to force: state action against threats and armed attacks. Cambridge University Press, Cambridge

GAOR: General Assembly Official Records. http://documents.un.org/simple.asp

Garcia-Mora MR (1962) International Responsibility for Hostile Acts of Private Persons against Foreign States. Nijhoff, The Hague

GA Res. 2625: General Assembly Resolution 2625 (1970) Friendly Relations Declaration

GA Res. 3314: General Assembly Resolution 3314 (1974) Definition of Aggression

Gaza crisis: key maps and timeline (18 January 2009). BBC News. http://news.bbc.co.uk/2/hi/middle_east/7812290.stm. Accessed 12 June 2010

Gill TD (2003) The eleventh of September and the right of self-defence. In: Heere WP (ed) Terrorism and the military. international legal implications. T.M.C. Asser Press, The Hague, pp 23–37
God knows it did not cross our minds to attack the towers (30 October 2004). Guardian. www.guardian.co.uk/world/2004/oct/30/alqaida.september11. Accessed 30 January 2010
Greenwood C (1987) International law and the United States' air operation against Libya. W Va Law Rev 89:933–960
Greenwood C (2003) International law and the pre-emptive use of force: Afghanistan, Al-Qaida and Iraq. S Diego Int Law J 4:7–38
Gross LM (1983) The legal implications of Israel's 1982 invasion into Lebanon. Calif West Int Law J 13:458–492
Ground offensive against separatists (2008) Keesing's Record of World Events 54: 48427
Gunaratna R (ed) (2004a) The changing face of terrorism. Marshall Cavendish, Singapore
Gunaratna R (2004b) Change or continuity. In: Gunaratna R (ed) The changing face of terrorism. Marshall Cavendish, Singapore, pp 1–17
Gunaratna R (2004c) New threshold terrorism. In: Gunaratna R (ed) The changing face of terrorism. Marshall Cavendish, Singapore, pp 18–37
Gurr N, Cole B (2002) The new face of terrorism. Threats from weapons of mass destruction. I.B. Tauris, London
Heinze EA (2009) Non-state actors in the international legal order: the Israel–Hezbollah conflict and the law of self-defence. Global Governance 15:87–105
Henderson C (2004) The Bush doctrine: from theory to practice. J Confl Secur Law 9:3–24
Higginbotham FM (1987) International law, the use of force in self-defence and the southern African conflict. Columbia J Transnatl Law 25:561–572
Higgins R (1963) The development of international law through the political organs of the United Nations. Oxford University Press, London
Howard RD (2008) The new terrorism and weapons of mass destruction. In: Howard RD, Bajema NE (eds) Weapons of mass destruction and terrorism. McGraw-Hill, New York, pp 6–22
HRC Report 2009: Report of the United Nations Fact Finding Mission on the Gaza Conflict, Human Rights in Palestine and Other Occupied Arab Territories (2009). UN Doc. A/HRC/12/48 (2009)
Intoccia GF (1987) American bombing of Libya: an international legal analysis. Case West. Reserve J Int Law 19:177–213
Israeli jets fire on Lebanon (3 September 2003). BBC News. http://news.bbc.co.uk/2/hi/middle_east/3079072.stm. Accessed 4 April 2010
Jacobson MR (1998) War in the information age: international law, self-defense, and the problem of 'non-armed' attacks. J Strateg Stud 21(3):1–33
Jenkins BM (2008) The new age of terrorism. In: Howard RD, Bajema NE (eds) Weapons of mass destruction and terrorism. McGraw-Hill, New York, pp 23–31
Kattan V (2007) The use and abuse of self-defence in international law: the Israel–Hezbollah conflict as a case study. Social Science Research Network, working paper http://papers.ssrn.com/sol3/papers.cfm?abstract_id=994282
Kegley CW Jr (ed) (2003) The new global terrorism: characteristics, causes, controls. Prentice Hall, Upper Saddle River
Kelly MJ (2005) Critical analysis of the International Court of Justice ruling on Israel's security barrier. Fordham Int Law J 29:181–228
Lobel J (1999) The use of force to respond to terrorist attacks: the bombing of Sudan and Afghanistan. Yale J Int Law 24:537–557
Lowe V (2003) The Iraqi crisis: What now? Int Comp Law Q 52:859–871
McCredie JA (1987) The April 14, 1986 bombing of Libya: act of self-defense or reprisal. Case West Reserve J Int Law 19:215–242
McGoldrick D (2004) From "9–11" to the Iraq War 2003: international law in an age of complexity. Hart, Oxford
Mégret F (2002) "War"? legal semantics and the move to violence. Eur J Int Law 13:361–399

Melzer N (2010) Targeted killings in operational perspective. In: Gill TD, Fleck D (eds) Handbook of the international law of military operations. Oxford University Press, Oxford, pp 277–301
Morgan MJ (2004) The origins of the new terrorism. 34 Parameters: US Army War College 1:29–43
Mueller KP et al (2006) Striking first: preemptive and preventive attack in US National Security Policy. RAND Project Air Force
Murphy JF (2009) Challenges of the new terrorism. In: Armstrong D (ed) Routledge handbook of international law. Routledge, London, pp 281–293
Murphy SD (2002) Terrorism and the concept of "armed attack" in Article 51 of the UN Charter. Harv Int Law J 43:41–51
Myjer PJ, White ND (2002) The twin towers attack: an unlimited right to self-defence? J Confl Secur Law 7:5–17
Nairobi: Discussion and Findings: Report of the Accountability Review Boards on the Embassy Bombings in Nairobi, Kenya and Dar es Salaam, Tanzania on August 7, 1998 (1999). US Department of State, Washington, D.C. http://www.state.gov/www/regions/africa/board_nairobi.html. Accessed 1 December 2009
Ninth Public Hearing, Witness, Dr. Condoleezza Rice (8 April 2004). National Commission on Terrorist Attacks upon the United States. http://www.9-11commission.gov/archive/hearing9/9-11Commission_Hearing_2004-04-08.htm. Accessed 30 January 2010
Nicaragua 1986: Military and Paramilitary activities in and against Nicaragua (Nicaragua v. USA), Judgment of 27 June 1986, ICJ Rep. (1986)
NATO Press Release (12 September 2001) http://www.nato.int/docu/pr/2001/p01-124e.htm. Accessed 10 January 2010
Offensive against PKK positions in Northern Iraq (2007) Keesing's Record of World Events 53:48316
Printer NG Jr (2003) The use of force against non-state actors under international law: an analysis of the US Predator strike in Yemen. UCLA J Int Law Foreign Aff 8:331–383
Prosecutor v. Dusko Tadić, ICTY Case No. IT-94-1-A, Judgment, Appeals Chamber, 15 July 1999
Ratner SR (2002) Jus ad bellum and jus in bello after September 11. Am J Int Law 96:905–921
Reisman WM (2003) Self-defence in an age of terrorism: remarks. Am Soc Int Law Proc 97:142–143
Repertoire: Repertoire of the Practice of the Security Council. http://www.un.org/en/sc/repertoire/
Rose G (1999) It could happen here: facing the new terrorism. Foreign Aff 78:131–137
Ruys T (2007) Crossing the thin blue line: an inquiry into Israel's recourse to self-defence against Hezbollah. Stanf J Int Law 43:265–294
Ruys T (2008) Quo vadit jus ad bellum? A legal analysis of Turkey's military operations against the PKK in Northern Iraq. Melb J Int Law 9:334–364
Sapiro M (2005) Preempting prevention: lessons learned. NYU J Int Law Politics 37:357–371
Saul B (2006) Defining terrorism in international law. Oxford University Press, Oxford
Schachter O (1985) The lawful resort to unilateral use of force. Yale J Int Law 10:291–294
Schmitt MN (2008) "Change Direction" 2006: Israeli operations in Lebanon and the international law of self-defence. Mich J Int Law 29:127–164
SCOR: Security Council Official Records. http://documents.un.org/simple.asp
September 11: Chronology of terror (12 September 2001) CNN. http://articles.cnn.com/2001-09-11/us/chronology.attack_1_collapse-attacks-building?_s=PM:US. Accessed 8 January 2010
Shiryaev Y (2007–2008) The right of armed self-defense in international law and self-defense arguments used in the second Lebanon war. Acta Societatis Martensis 3:80–97
Significant terrorist incidents, 1961–2003: A brief chronology (2004) US Department of State, Office of the Historian, Bureau of Public Affairs. http://www.fas.org/irp/threat/terror_chron.html. Accessed 17 November 2009
Sorenson DS (2008) An introduction to the modern Middle East. Westview Press, Boulder

Taliban won't turn over bin Laden (21 September 2001). CBS News. http://www.cbsnews.com/stories/2001/09/11/world/main310852.shtml. Accessed 8 January 2010

The 9/11 Commission Report: Final Report of the National Commission on Terrorist Attacks upon the United States (2004). National Commission on Terrorist Attacks upon the United States, Washington, D.C

Timeline: Israeli-Hamas violence since truce ended (5 January 2009). Reuters. http://uk.reuters.com/article/idUKTRE50423320090105. Accessed 12 June 2010

Transcript of President Bush's address to a joint session of Congress on Thursday night, 20 September 2001 (21 September 2001). CNN. http://archives.cnn.com/2001/US/09/20/gen.bush.transcript. Accessed 8 January 2010

Tucker D (2001) What is new about the new terrorism and how dangerous is it? Terror Political Violence 13(3):1–14

Turkey launches major land offensive into Northern Iraq (22 February 2008). Reuters. http://uk.reuters.com/article/idUKL22614485._CH_.242020080222. Accessed 3 June 2010

US rejects Taliban offer to try bin Laden (7 October 2001). CNN. http://archives.cnn.com/2001/US/10/07/ret.us.taliban. Accessed 8 January 2010

Verhagen M (3 March 2008) Beantwoording vragen van het lid Van Bommel over een Turkse invasie in Noord-Irak. http://www.minbuza.nl/nl/Actueel/Kamerstukken/2008/03/Beantwoording_vragen_van_het_lid_Van_Bommel_over_een_Turkse_invasie_in_Noord_Irak. Accessed 5 June 2010

Wedgwood R (1999) Responding to terrorism: the strikes against bin Laden. Yale J Int Law 24:559–576

Wrachford JS (2007) The 2006 Israeli invasion of Lebanon: aggression, self-defence, or a reprisal gone bad? Air Force Law Rev 60:29–90

Wright L (2006) The looming tower. Al-Qaeda and the road to 9/11. Alfred Knopf, New York

Chapter 11
The Interpretation of Self-Defence and the United Nations

After discussing the main instances of state practice raising significant questions as to the temporality of self-defence, the influence of the United Nations system on the development of the concept will be explored. The aim of this chapter is to assess whether the temporal dimension and the juridical variables identified at the beginning of Part II (conditionality of armed attack, immediacy and proportionality) have been, in any form, addressed by various UN organs, and if so, what were the adopted approaches.

Two aspects of this influence will be analysed. First, the applicable work of the General Assembly, the International Law Commission as well as that of the 2004 UN High-Level Panel on Threats, Challenges and Change will be examined. Second, relevant judgments and advisory opinions delivered by the International Court of Justice will be discussed with a view on their impact on the understanding given to self-defence.

11.1 The General Assembly of the United Nations

Although GA resolutions are not binding, there is an important interplay between them and international customary law. As the ICJ pointed out in the *Nicaragua* case, *opinio juris* could be deduced from the attitude of states towards certain GA resolutions.[1] In other words, GA resolutions may be declaratory of existing customary law.[2]

Two of the most important GA documents connected to the prohibition to use force are the Friendly Relations Declaration [Resolution 2625 (1970)] and the Definition of Aggression [Resolution 3314 (1974)].

---

[1] Nicaragua 1986, para 188.

[2] Dixon 2000, pp. 45–47.

K. Tibori Szabó, *Anticipatory Action in Self-Defence*, DOI: 10.1007/978-90-6704-796-8_11,

Resolution 2625 (XXV) adopted the Declaration on the Principles of International Law Concerning Friendly Relations and Cooperation Among States, which set out several principles of international law. The preamble emphasized the importance of the codification of certain principles, including the prohibition of the threat or use of force. The declaration also stated that a war of aggression would be considered a crime against peace, for which there was responsibility in international law. Two obligations regarding the form of use of force are important to mention. First, states had to refrain from organizing or encouraging the organization of irregular forces or armed bands, including mercenaries, for incursion into the territory of another state. Secondly, states had the duty to refrain from 'organizing, instigating, assisting or participating in acts of civil strife or terrorist acts in another state or acquiescing in organized activities within its territory directed towards the commission of such acts.'[3] The declaration also expressly forbade the resort to 'acts of reprisal involving the use of force.'[4] Although neither the right of self-defence nor the concept of an armed attack was mentioned by the declaration, the resort to irregular use of force was acknowledged as a breach of the prohibition to use force. Moreover, the duties described by the declaration were characterized as principles embodied in the UN Charter and basic principles of international law.[5] Likewise, the ICJ interpreted the consent to the text of Resolution 2625 (XXV) as an acceptance of the validity of the rule or set of rules declared by the resolution itself.[6]

Resolution 3314 (XXIX) approved the Definition of Aggression, which identified several forms of use of armed force that amounted to an act of aggression. The resolution defined aggression as 'the use of armed force by a State against the sovereignty, territorial integrity or political independence of another state, or in any other manner inconsistent with the Charter of the United Nations.'[7] Apart from invasion, bombardment, blockade or other attacks by the armed forces of a state against the territory of another,[8] also certain indirect forms of force were listed as potential acts of aggression. Accordingly, 'the use of armed forces of one state which are within the territory of another state with the agreement of the receiving state' or 'the action of a state in allowing its territory [...] to be used by that other state for perpetrating an act of aggression against a third state' could also amount to an act of aggression.[9] The Definition of Aggression went one step further in relation to the use of irregular forces by states than the Friendly Relations Declaration did. Whereas the latter defined the organization of irregular forces as a breach of the prohibition to use force, the former qualified it as an act of

---

[3] GA Res. 2625, Friendly Relations Declaration, Part 1.

[4] Ibid.

[5] Ibid., Part 3.

[6] Nicaragua 1986, para 188.

[7] GA Res. 3314, Definition of Aggression, Art. 1.

[8] Ibid., Article. 3(a)–(d).

[9] Ibid., Article. 3(e) and (f).

aggression. Accordingly, 'the sending by or on behalf of a state of armed bands, groups, irregulars or mercenaries' which would carry out acts of armed force against another state of such gravity as to amount to acts performed by regular forces could also amount to an act of aggression. Likewise, a state's substantial involvement in such activities was also seen as a potential act of aggression.[10] Although the resolution does not make any connection between an 'act of aggression' and an 'armed attack', that connection was made by the ICJ in the *Nicaragua* case. Accordingly, the Court held that an armed attack had to be understood as including not merely action by regular forces across an international border, but also 'the sending by or on behalf of a State of armed bands, groups, irregulars or mercenaries' for the purposes described by Article 3(g) of the Definition of Aggression.[11] The Court made specific reference to that article in defining an armed attack by irregular forces and contended that the description 'may be taken to reflect customary international law.'[12]

The importance of the two GA resolutions is twofold. First, as maintained by the International Court of Justice, they reflect *opinio juris* as regards various forms of the use of force and the corollary obligations of states to refrain from them. Secondly, they shed some light on what the majority of the members of the United Nations view as illegal uses of force or aggression. Coupled with the interpretation of armed attack given by the Court, the two GA resolutions also help in better contouring the circumstances in which specific uses of force can serve as the basis for a lawful claim of self-defence.

11.2 The Work of the International Law Commission

The issue of self-defence also came up in the work of the International Law Commission on state responsibility.[13] The importance of codifying the principles of state responsibility was recognized by the Commission as early as 1949, although work only started in 1955. Several reports were prepared by various special rapporteurs over the years on all the important topics relevant to state responsibility.[14]

---

[10] Ibid., Article. 3(g).

[11] Nicaragua 1986, para 195.

[12] Ibid.

[13] Succinct references to 'anticipatory self-defence' were made during the discussions on diplomatic protection and on the draft Code of Crimes against Peace and Security of Mankind, but no elaborate discussions followed on the subject. See UN Doc. A/CN.4/506 (2000) p. 19, para 56, as well as Summary Record of the 2135th ILC meeting., UN Doc. A/CN.4/SR.2135 (1989) p. 297, para 47.

[14] The Work of the International Law Commission, 5th edn. 1996, pp. 121–122; Analytical Guide to the Work of the International Law Commission, 1949–1997, 1998, pp. 226–255.

Self-defence was first given detailed attention by Roberto Ago in the addendum of his eighth report on the principles of state responsibility.[15] He discussed state of necessity and self-defence as two of the circumstances precluding wrongfulness of an act of a state. He proposed the adoption of an article on self-defence that read as follows:

> The wrongfulness of an act of a State not in conformity with an international obligation to another State is precluded if the State committed the act in order to defend itself or another State against armed attack as provided for in Article 51 of the Charter of the United Nations.[16]

Ago's report was formulated in very cautious terms when it came to the more controversial questions of self-defence. He deferred a discussion of several 'problems of interpretation' and emphasized that such a task was for 'bodies responsible for interpreting and applying the Charter.'[17] Ago's report was discussed in several meetings of the Commission and the official ILC report of the 32nd session contained an equally cautious commentary to self-defence.[18] In this report, the wording of the article changed slightly to read:

> The wrongfulness of an act of a State not in conformity with an international obligation of that State is precluded if the act constitutes a lawful measure of self-defence taken in conformity with the Charter of the United Nations.[19]

After Special Rapporteur James Crawford revisited the work of the Commission on self-defence in 1999,[20] the ILC adopted a final version of the provision (now Article 21) that read:

> 'The wrongfulness of an act of a State is precluded if the act constitutes a lawful measure of self-defence taken in conformity with the Charter of the United Nations.'[21]

Some of the most important issues discussed regarding self-defence will be elaborated in the following paragraphs to shed light on the way the members of the International Law Commission viewed the role and limits of the defensive use of force.

---

15 Ago 1980.

16 Ibid., p. 70.

17 Ibid., p. 68, paras 117–118.

18 ILC Report 1980, p. 52.

19 Ibid.

20 UN Doc. A/CN.4/498/Add.2 1999. Crawford's report focused primarily on the question of whether use of force in self-defence precluded the wrongfulness of acts in breach of other international obligations, stemming from international humanitarian law, human rights law, environmental law (pp. 33–37). The same question was addressed by several members during the 2589th meeting. of the ILC. See Summary Record of the 2589th ILC meeting., UN Doc. A/CN.4/SR.2589 1999.

21 Draft Articles on Responsibility of States for Internationally Wrongful Acts, with Commentaries 2001, p. 74. The comments on Art. 21 (Self-Defence) focus on the question whether use of force in self-defence precludes the wrongfulness of acts in breach of other international obligations (pp. 74–75).

11.2.1 Self-Defence and 'General International Law'

Ago emphasized the dual basis of the right of self-defence by pointing out that since the adoption of the Charter, there had been no known case where it was argued that self-defence was admissible solely by virtue of Article 51 and not—'primarily'—by virtue of an 'absolute rule previously recognized by general international law.'[22] Ago also asserted that the meaning given to self-defence by the drafters of Article 51 was the one perceived as valid at the time of the adoption of the Charter.[23] Consequently, it was hard to believe that there was any difference whatsoever in content between the notion of self-defence in general international law and that endorsed by Article 51.[24]

That contention was criticized by Schwebel in the ensuing ILC discussion. Accordingly, Schwebel contended that although the Charter did codify the law governing the use of force in international relations, Article 51 had to be read in conjunction with other provisions of the Charter [such as Article 2(4) and Chapters VI and VII as a whole] to elucidate on the meaning given to self-defence. Article 51, taken alone, could not give a complete understanding of the notion of self-defence.[25] Vallat also asserted that the reference in Article 51 to self-defence as an 'inherent right' indicated that those who had drafted the Article had not attempted to codify the concept of self-defence.[26] Schwebel and Vallat thus agreed that there was more to self-defence than the wording of Article 51. Tsuruoka, the Japanese member of the ILC, approached the matter differently. He also disagreed with Ago's conclusion, but for totally different reasons. He noted that Japanese writers had emphasized that, in formulating Article 51, the authors of the Charter had taken an immense step towards pacifism by taking care to restrict the exercise of the right of self-defence to one clear-cut case. He disagreed thus on the point that Article 51 reflected a principle rooted in legal thinking at that time.[27]

On the subject of an armed attack, Ago criticized those authors who contended that Article 51 consecrated self-defence against the most important situations only, and that general international law allowed self-defence against other uses of force as well.[28] He placed advocates of 'preventative' self-defence in the same category, although pointing out that not all of them agreed with the existence of other grounds for self-defence than armed attack.[29] Ago did not assess the concrete

[22] Ago 1980, p. 61, para 104.

[23] Ibid., pp. 62–63, paras 107–108.

[24] Ibid., p. 63, para 108.

[25] Summary Record of the 1621st ILC meeting., UN Doc. A/CN.4/SR.1621 1980 para 2 (comment by Schwebel).

[26] Ibid., para 20 (comment by Sir Francis Vallat).

[27] Summary Record of the 1627th ILC meeting., UN Doc. A/CN.4/SR.1627 1980 para 3 (comment by Tsuruoka).

[28] Ago 1980, p. 64, paras 110–111.

[29] Ibid., pp. 64–65, paras 111–112.

relationship between the different arguments he claimed were part of the same school of thought. He merely asserted that the report was not the place for a detailed discussion of the merits or flaws of such arguments and that 'all the theses advanced by the advocates of that school of thought have been subjected to critical analysis and rejected one by one.'[30]

During the ensuing discussions of the report, several members of the ILC pointed out that the reference to 'armed attack' in Article 51 did raise some concerns and created confusion as to the significance of other forms of illegal use of force, such as an act of aggression in the sense of GA Resolution 3314.[31] Diaz Gonzalez went as far as to highlight that there were other types of aggression that could be far more effective in threatening or destroying a state, such as economic, ideological and cultural aggression and thus the concept of aggression should not be confined solely to an armed act.[32] Consequently, in the opinion of Diaz Gonzalez, the ILC was not in a position to state categorically when the use of force was lawful and when an act of aggression should be deemed to have taken place, because there was no definition of an act of aggression that justified self-defence.[33] Similar views were expressed by the then ILC Chairman Pinto, who emphasized that, through codification, self-defence was to be extended beyond armed attacks to encompass the ways in which a state could defend itself against threats to its economy or to its legitimate interests outside its territory or outside the territory of any state. The codified concept of self-defence had to take account of whether or not such threats involved the use of armed force, in the sense of full-scale military operations, or of some other form of coercion which fell short of military operations, and whether or not there had been overt aggression. It also had to determine whether defensive measures taken by a state aimed at warding off an armed attack at some time in the future, rather than an attack that was imminent or was actually taking place.[34] Barboza took a middle-way approach by contending that Article 51 in fact reflected general international law, while it also incorporated certain additional elements relating to the United Nations system of collective security. At the same time, he emphasized that Article 51 was not a comprehensive statement of international law on the matter of self-defence, because it made no mention of necessity and proportionality.[35]

---

[30] Ibid., pp. 65–66, paras 113–114.

[31] Summary Record of the 1620th ILC meeting., UN Doc. A/CN.4/SR.1620 (1980) paras 16 (comment by Ushakov), 20–21 (comment by Reuter); Summary Record of the 1621st ILC meeting., UN Doc. A/CN.4/SR.1621 (1980) paras 4 (comment by Schwebel), 20–21 (comment by Vallat); Summary Record of the 1628th ILC meeting., UN Doc. A/CN.4/SR.1628 (1980) para 13 (comment by Verosta).

[32] Summary Record of the 1627th ILC meeting., UN Doc. A/CN.4/SR.1627 (1980) para 5 (comment by Diaz Gonzalez).

[33] Ibid., para 6 (comment by Diaz Gonzalez).

[34] Ibid., para 21 (comment by Chairman Pinto).

[35] Ibid., paras 10–11 (comment by Barboza).

The contentions of Ago were transposed into the ILC report of the 32nd session. Accordingly, the report stated that the prevailing opinion in legal doctrine was that self-defence was applicable only against an armed attack and not other forms of the use of force.[36] No explicit reference to the connection between 'armed attack' and 'aggression' was made; however, the report later interchangeably used the terms of armed attack and aggression as legal grounds for self-defence.[37]

11.2.2 Armed Action Against Private Groups as 'State of Necessity'

While differentiating between 'state of necessity and self-defence', Ago emphasized that armed action undertaken by a state to ward off a danger emanating from private individuals or groups could not be defined as self-defence, because self-defence presupposed the wrongful conduct of a state. In such a case, the action undertaken was to be considered a 'state of necessity'.[38] Ago clearly based his line of reasoning on the assumptions that self-defence could only be invoked against a state and that there was no involvement whatsoever of a state in the activities of the private groups.

That point was questioned by Schwebel in his comments on the report. He asserted that states were surely entitled to defend themselves against 'attacks by terrorist organizations and individuals' and that he could not agree with Ago's interpretation on that point.[39] Notwithstanding that remark, the ILC report of the 32nd session took over Ago's comments on the possible response of states to armed acts of private groups and stated that, according to the prevailing opinion at the time, state action undertaken in such cases and for such purposes had to be explained on grounds other than self-defence.[40]

11.2.3 'Preventive' Self-Defence

Ago contended that the ILC could not take sides in the controversy regarding the admissibility of 'preventive' self-defence, 'particularly if the object of the preventive action is to halt, before it materializes, a thoroughly planned armed attack that is about to be launched.'[41] Ago did not discuss what exactly he meant by

---

[36] ILC Report 1980, p. 58, para 19.

[37] Ibid., p. 60, para 22.

[38] Ago 1980, pp. 61–62, para 106.

[39] Summary Record of the 1621st ILC meeting., UN Doc. A/CN.4/SR.1621 1980 para 5 (comment by Schwebel).

[40] ILC Report 1980, p. 57, para 16.

[41] Ago 1980, p. 67, para 116.

'preventive' self-defence and whether there was any difference between halting an armed attack that was 'about to be launched' and preventing another more remote in time. As a matter of fact, Ago seems to have equated 'preventive' self-defence with stopping an armed attack that was 'about to be launched.' Elsewhere, however, Ago admits that 'a state acting in self-defence, like a state acting in a state of necessity, acts in response to an imminent danger—which must in both cases be serious, immediate and incapable of being countered by other means.'[42] Similarly, he asserted that a defensive use of force was opposed to an offensive one inasmuch as it had as objective 'preventing another's wrongful action from proceeding, succeeding and achieving its purpose.'[43] This was—Ago admitted—'the core of the matter'[44]; and indeed it was, not only because it was a clear differentiation between defensive and offensive use of force, but also because the three crucial moments of self-defence were identified: before, during and after an armed attack.

During the discussion of the report, one of the members of the ILC (Barboza) pointed out that 'one of the main issues to be decided by the Commission was whether the concept of self-defence should extend to the use of force against the threat of imminent armed attack.'[45] Barboza further asserted that, in his understanding, self-defence related primarily to the use of force and 'possibly the threat of the use of force.'[46] Nonetheless, the Commission refused to take an official stance on the question of anticipatory action in self-defence.

11.2.4 Necessity and Proportionality

On the topic of necessity, Ago noted that its relevance was greater in case 'preventive' self-defence was admitted as lawful. Necessity meant that the state attacked or threatened with an imminent attack could not, in the particular circumstances, have had any means of halting the attack other than recourse to armed force. For that reason, necessity as a requirement was more important in case of defensive action against an imminent threat of an armed attack.[47]

Regarding proportionality, Ago offered a clear substantiation of the 'accumulation of events' theory. Accordingly, he contended that self-defence could be justified against an armed attack consisting 'of a number of successive acts.'

---

[42] Ibid., p. 53, para 88. That statement was almost literally transposed in the ILC Report 1980, p. 52, para 3.

[43] Ago 1980, p. 54, para 90. That statement was reiterated in a slightly changed form in the ILC Report 1980, p. 53, para 5.

[44] Ago 1980, p. 54, para 90.

[45] Summary Record of the 1627th ILC meeting., UN Doc. A/CN.4/SR.1627 (1980) para 10 (comment by Barboza).

[46] Ibid., para 11.

[47] Ago 1980, p. 69, para 120.

In such a case, the requirements of proportionality and immediacy had to be looked at 'in the light of those acts as a whole.'[48] Accordingly:

> If a state suffers a series of successive and different acts of armed attack, *from another state*, the requirement of proportionality would certainly not mean that the victim state is not free to undertake a single armed action on a much larger scale in order to put an end to this escalating succession of attacks.[49]

As a matter of fact, the requirement of proportionality had to be measured against 'the result to be achieved by the defensive action, and not the forms, substance and strength of the action itself.'[50]

Ago's observations on proportionality were upheld by Riphagen, one of the members of the ILC. In the ensuing discussions, Riphagen emphasized that 'the suffering of the aggressor State often exceeded that which it had intended to inflict on the victim State' and that, consequently, the requirement of proportionality needed more attention.[51] In his reply, Ago specified that when it came to self-defence, the assessment of the proportionality varied considerably from one case to another.[52] At times, the action taken in defence against an armed attack had to be out of proportion to that attack, because 'self-defence must aim at preventing the attack, and not at objectives going beyond that limit.' Notwithstanding the flexibility of the rule of proportionality in self-defence, Ago emphasized that a state could not profit from an armed attack to react not only by warding off the attack, but also by annexing the territory of the attacker.[53]

Several conclusions can be drawn from Ago's report and the ensuing discussions of ILC members. First, regarding the existence of an armed attack, Ago maintained that such an attack could only stem from a state. If armed acts were carried out by non-state actors, the targeted state could only respond on the basis of a state of necessity and not self-defence. That contention was questioned in the ensuing discussion, showing thus that there was no unanimity as to the potential authors of an armed attack among the members of the ILC. Moreover, the opinions expressed also showed that some lawyers still viewed self-defence as lawful against threats of non-forceful nature.

Secondly, Ago's reference to a danger immediate and incapable of being countered by other means echoed the immediacy factor of the necessity requirement. Nonetheless, Ago refrained from discussing whether anticipatory action in self-defence could be lawful on the basis of that factor. He only hinted at the

---

[48] Ibid., pp. 69–70, para 121.

[49] Ibid., (emphasis added). It has to be reiterated that Ago believed that self-defence could only be exercised against states. Ibid., pp. 61–62, para 106.

[50] Ibid., pp. 69, para 121.

[51] Summary Record of the 1620th ILC meeting., UN Doc. A/CN.4/SR.1620 (1980) para 4 (comment by Riphagen).

[52] Summary Record of the 1629th ILC meeting., UN Doc. A/CN.4/SR.1629 (1980) para 9 (comment by Ago).

[53] Ibid.

significance of the principle of necessity in the event that 'preventive' self-defence was admitted as lawful.

Thirdly, the Ago report defined proportionality in the same terms as the 'accumulations of events' theory. There was no contention on Ago's part as to any novelty in this interpretation and he was definitely not referring to non-state actors in his discussion of proportionality. Ago's views on proportionality were upheld by the Commission and no member expressed any contrary views on that interpretation.

Most importantly, perhaps, Ago's report gave a clear definition to the temporal dimension of self-defence when he asserted that the objective of such a right was 'preventing another's wrongful action from proceeding, succeeding and achieving its purpose.'[54]

All in all, the work of the ILC on self-defence contributed to all three elements of that right. It adopted a restrictive view on the conditionality of an armed attack by delimiting it to state action. It confirmed the immediacy factor and gave a clear definition of the temporal dimension of self-defence. As regards proportionality, the ILC's contribution was to strengthen the interpretation given to that principle by the 'accumulation of events' theory.

11.3 The Findings of the 2004 UN High-Level Panel

In September 2003, the then UN Secretary-General Kofi Annan announced plans to set up 'a high-level panel of eminent persons' to provide a common, comprehensive view on the nature of the threats faced and the appropriateness of the use of force to address them.[55]

The Panel delivered its report in December 2004. On the issue of self-defence, the report first noted that although the language of Article 51 of the Charter was restrictive, according to long established international law, a state could take military action as long as the threatened attack was imminent, there were no other means to deflect it and the action was proportionate.[56] Consequently, the question of legality did not relate to the use of force against such imminent threats, but to more remote threats, still claimed to be real 'for example the acquisition, with allegedly hostile intent, of nuclear weapons-making capability'.[57] In other words:

> Can a State, without going to the Security Council, claim in these circumstances the right to act, in anticipatory self-defence, not just pre-emptively (against an imminent or proximate threat) but preventively (against a non-imminent or non-proximate one)?[58]

---

[54] Ago 1980, p. 54, para 90. That statement was reiterated in a slightly changed form in the ILC Report 1980, p. 53, para 5.

[55] UN Doc. A/59/565 (2004), p. 1.

[56] Ibid., para 188, p. 54.

[57] Ibid.

[58] Ibid., para 189, p. 54.

The report answered the question in the negative. Accordingly, it held that if there were good arguments for preventive military action, with good evidence to support them, they had to be put to the Security Council, which could choose to authorize such action. If it chose not to do so, the availability of non-forceful strategies had to be explored, 'including persuasion, negotiation, deterrence and containment'.[59] The panel also left open the option to reconsider the use of force, but without specifying whether it was referring to the unilateral alternative or the collective one under Chapter VII.[60] Nonetheless, in the next paragraph the Panel seemed to distance itself from preventive action by asserting that the risk to the global order and the norm of non-intervention was too great for the legality of unilateral preventive action, as distinct from collectively endorsed action, to be accepted.[61] Accordingly, the Panel held that the rewriting or reinterpretation of Article 51 was not endorsed.[62]

The findings of the Panel are significant for two reasons. First, the legality of anticipatory action in self-defence against imminent threats was unequivocally endorsed. In fact, the report claimed that the legality of anticipatory action was long established in international law. Secondly, it shied away from endorsing preventive action against potential threats, because of the significant risks involved.[63]

11.4 The Work of the International Court of Justice

The ICJ touched upon the right of self-defence several times and addressed some of the most controversial questions regarding that right. A succinct analysis of the *Nicaragua*, the *Oil Platforms* and the *Armed Activities in Congo* cases as well as of the *Nuclear Weapons* and *Israeli Wall* advisory opinions will be conducted in order to discern the views adopted by the Court on the necessity and proportionality requirements as defined in the introductory remarks of Part II.[64]

The following paragraphs will review the Court's findings for each of the three elements pertaining to necessity and proportionality of self-defence.

[59] Ibid., para 190, p. 55.

[60] Ibid.

[61] Ibid., para 191, p. 55.

[62] Ibid., para 192, p. 55.

[63] For criticism of the report see: Corten 2007, pp. 217–232.

[64] For the factual background of these cases, see Nicaragua 1986, paras 18–25; Oil Platforms 2003, paras 23–26; Armed Activities in Congo 2005, paras 72–91. For background of the advisory opinions, see Nuclear Weapons 1996, paras 1, 20–22; Israeli Wall 2004, para 1.

11.4.1 The Conditionality of an Armed Attack

By far the most addressed issue pertaining to self-defence by the Court was the notion of armed attack, perceived by the Court as a condition *sine qua non* for lawful self-defence.[65] In the *Nicaragua* case, the Court referred to Article 3 of the Definition of Aggression to contend that an armed attack had to be understood as including not merely action by regular forces across an international border, but also 'the sending by or on behalf of a State of armed bands, groups, irregulars or mercenaries, which carry out acts of armed force against another State of such gravity as to amount to' an actual armed attack conducted by regular forces 'or its substantial involvement therein.'[66]

On this point, however, the Court expressed one of its most controversial opinions: the concept of 'armed attack' was not to be interpreted as including assistance to rebels in the form of the provision of weapons or logistical or other support. Such assistance could amount to a threat or use of force or could be regarded as intervention in the internal affairs of a state, but it could not be viewed as an armed attack.[67]

In the *Israeli Wall* advisory opinion, the Court asserted that Article 51 of the Charter recognized the existence of an inherent right of self-defence 'in the case of an armed attack by one state against another state.'[68] In the *Armed Activities in Congo* case, the judges declined to discuss 'whether and under what conditions contemporary international law provides for a right of self-defence against large-scale attacks by irregular forces,' because they believed that this was not necessary given the inability of Uganda to prove the existence of legal and factual circumstances for the exercise of self-defence.[69]

Some of the members of the Court disagreed with the state-based view on armed attack. In his dissenting opinion in the *Nicaragua* case, Judge Jennings contended that the provision of arms could be a 'very important element in what might be thought to amount to armed attack, where it is coupled with other kinds of involvement.'[70] He emphasized that the view adopted by the Court created a 'large area where both a forcible response to force is forbidden, and yet the United Nations employment of force, which was intended to fill that gap, is absent.'[71]

In her dissenting opinion in the *Israeli Wall* case, Judge Higgins adopted a similar view. She asserted that, in her opinion, there was nothing in the text of

---

[65] Green 2009, p. 30. Green also discusses the gravity threshold set by the Court for armed attack. Ibid., pp. 31–42.

[66] Nicaragua 1986, para 195; GA Res. 3314, Definition of Aggression.

[67] Nicaragua 1986, para 195.

[68] Israeli Wall 2004, para 139.

[69] Armed Activities in Congo 2005, para 147.

[70] Nicaragua 1986, p. 543 (dissenting opinion of Judge Jennings). *Per a contrario*, Gray 2004, pp. 109–110.

[71] Nicaragua 1986, p. 543–544 (dissenting opinion of Judge Jennings).

Article 51 stipulating that self-defence was available only when an armed attack was made by a state.[72] Similar points were made by Judge Buergenthal, who additionally emphasized that Security Council Resolutions 1368 (2001) and 1373 (2001) recognized self-defence against terrorism, thus implicitly acknowledging that an armed attack could be committed by non-state actors.[73] Judge Kooijmans noted that, although Article 51 was in the past interpreted as referring to an armed attack coming from another state, SC Resolutions 1368 (2001) and 1373 (2001) radically changed this view to interpret armed attacks as possibly being committed by non-state actors as well.[74]

Likewise, in his separate opinion in the *Armed Activities in Congo* case, Judge Simma contended that since the terrorist attacks of 11 September 2001, claims that Article 51 also covered defensive measures against terrorist groups were more favourably viewed.[75] Judge Kooijmans pointed out that because of its reluctance to discuss this matter 'the Court has missed a chance to fine-tune the position it took 20 years ago in spite of the explicit invitation by one of the Parties to do so.'[76]

The state-based approach of the Court was criticized by several authors as well.[77] According to Wedgwood, Article 51 did not link the right of self-defence 'to the particular legal personality of the attacker.'[78] Although in the past it was unlikely that non-state actors could mimic the force available to nation-states, according to Wedgwood, the events of 11 September 2001 had retired that assumption. The Security Council itself endorsed the right of self-defence against terrorist attacks. Wedgwood also pointed out that 'it would indeed be peculiar if states were legally unable to protect their civilians against repeated acts of terrorism, when they can use force against conventional armies attacking conventional targets.'[79] Kelly expressed similar views. He also emphasized that Article 51 only referred to an armed attack occurring against a state without specifying the author of the attack.[80] Although at the time of the adoption of the Charter there had not been as many instances of 'transnational terrorist actions not directly or not clearly attributable to a state,' there had been numerous examples of 'extraterritorial law enforcement and response to armed bands conducting cross-border activity.'[81] According to Kelly, the *Caroline* incident of 1837 'involved the contact of hostile activities by armed and organized citizens of the United States

[72] Israeli Wall 2004, p. 215 (separate opinion of Judge Higgins).

[73] Ibid., p. 242 (declaration of Judge Buergenthal).

[74] Ibid., pp. 229–230 (separate opinion of Judge Kooijmans).

[75] Armed Activities in Congo 2005, p. 337 (separate opinion of Judge Simma).

[76] Ibid., p. 313 (separate opinion of Judge Kooijmans).

[77] Wedgwood 2005, p. 58; Breau 2005, pp. 1007–1008; Kelly 2005, pp. 224–225; Murphy 2005, p. 62.

[78] Wedgwood 2005, p. 58.

[79] Ibid.

[80] Kelly 2005, p. 225.

[81] Ibid.

across the border in the British province of Canada, in support of a rebellion in that province.'[82] Likewise, Kelly noted, the US expedition in Mexico in pursuit of Pancho Villa also involved armed action against cross-border activities of armed bands.[83] Kelly concluded that the necessity of a state to defend itself against non-state actors had long been acknowledged by state practice and was not a novelty in itself, thus Article 51 could have not been envisaged to prevent a state from such course of action.[84] Murphy also expressed harsh criticism of the restrictive interpretation of armed attack. He noted that the position of the Court conflicted with 'the language of the UN Charter, its *travaux préparatoires*, the practice of states and international organizations, and common sense.'[85]

The same attitude was expressed by authors commenting on the Court's decision not to address the role of non-state actors in the *Armed Activities in Congo* case.[86] According to Barbour and Salzman, that case seemed to show that 'attacks carried out by non-State actors that are not attributable to a state are not armed attacks within the scope of Article 51, and therefore do not entitle the victim state to respond with force in self-defence.'[87]

The Court also set a high burden of proof as to the existence of an armed attack. In the *Oil Platforms* case, the Court found that although the evidence of Iranian responsibility for the attacks on US-flagged ships was 'highly suggestive', it was not conclusive enough to clearly establish such responsibility.[88] The Court did not rule out the possibility that an attack on a single vessel could amount to an armed attack.[89] Nonetheless, the Court held that the alleged attacks, even taken cumulatively, did not seem to constitute an armed attack, as a most grave form of the use of force.[90]

This approach was criticized by several authors. Taft characterized the *Oil Platforms* decision as 'regrettable', because of statements 'that might be read to suggest new and unsupported limitations on the ability of States to defend themselves from armed attacks.'[91] In particular, Taft referred to the limitations set by the judgment concerning the threshold and target of an armed attack.[92] Taft believed that such limitations would substantially and dangerously enlarge the

---

[82] Ibid., pp. 225–226.

[83] Ibid., pp. 226–227.

[84] Ibid., p. 227.

[85] Murphy 2005, p. 62. Wedgwood and Murphy have also dismissed the Court's contention that Israel, as an occupying power, could not defend its territory and nationals against armed attacks emanating from the occupied territory. Wedgwood 2005, pp. 58–59; Murphy 2005, pp. 68–69.

[86] Barbour and Salzman 2008, p. 62; Gathii 2007, p. 148; Verhoeven 2006, pp. 360, 363.

[87] Barbour and Salzman 2008, pp. 61–62.

[88] Oil Platforms 2003, paras 52–61, 71.

[89] Ibid., para 72.

[90] Ibid., para 64.

[91] Taft 2004, p. 306.

[92] Ibid., p. 299.

ability of states to undertake armed attacks without fear that such attacks will be defended against.[93] Gill asserted that the Court set a high burden of proof on the state invoking the right of self-defence, without clearly defining the standard of proof and it offered a number of rather ambiguous indications concerning the threshold for an armed attack.[94]

Consequently, the approach of the Court to the notion of armed attack can be characterized in three points. First, the mentioned judgments and advisory opinions put forward a restrictive, state-based approach regarding the authors of an armed attack. Accordingly, the Court repeatedly held that only states could be held responsible for armed attacks.[95] Secondly, the Court set a high burden of proof for showing the existence of an armed attack. Highly suggestive evidence, even corroborated, was deemed inconclusive. At the same time, the Court did not offer an explanation of how such burden of proof could be met in the absence of obvious evidence pertaining to the attacks.[96] Thirdly, there has been considerable division among the members of the Court as to the position adopted regarding the notion of armed attack. The gap between the mentioned judgments and advisory opinions, on one hand, and state practice and the legal literature, on the other, has been partly bridged by those dissenting opinions that adopted a more realistic view of armed attack. Accordingly, several judges have pointed out that the state-based approach was a matter of the past and that a reinterpretation was needed to meet the realities of twenty-first century state practice.[97]

11.4.2 Immediacy

In general, the Court shied away from discussing the requirement of necessity in general as well as immediacy or imminence in particular.[98] In the *Nicaragua* case, the Court declined to discuss the issue of self-defence against an imminent threat, because the parties had not referred to it. Likewise, in the *Armed Activities in Congo* case, the Court declined to discuss the lawfulness of a response to the imminent threat of an armed attack, because the issue had not been raised although the evidence adduced by Uganda showed the 'preventative nature' of many of its armed acts.[99]

---

[93] Ibid., p. 306.

[94] Gill 2007, p. 123.

[95] Nicaragua 1986, para 195; Israeli Wall 2004, para 139.

[96] Oil Platforms 2003, paras 52–61, 64, 71.

[97] Israeli Wall 2004, pp. 215 (separate opinion of Judge Higgins), 229–230 (separate opinion of Judge Kooijmans), 242 (declaration of Judge Buergenthal); Armed Activities in Congo 2005, pp. 313 (separate opinion of Judge Kooijmans), 337 (separate opinion of Judge Simma).

[98] On the marginalization of necessity and proportionality in general, see Gray 2004, pp. 122–123; Green 2009, pp. 105–107.

[99] Armed Activities in Congo 2005, para 143.

The Court implicitly acknowledged that the necessity requirement had to pertain to the inevitability of the danger in the *Oil Platforms* case. Accordingly, the Court found that not all the available options were explored by the US before resorting to armed force, because there was no evidence that it had complained to Iran about the military activities of the oil platforms.[100]

Apart from these timid references, the Court refrained from elaborating on the elements or limits of the necessity requirement of self-defence.[101]

11.4.3 Proportionality

In the *Nuclear Weapons* case, the Court asserted that a proportionate use of force in self-defence had to meet the requirements of international humanitarian law.[102] This way, the Court established a relationship between the *jus ad bellum* principle of proportionality and the *jus in bello* pertaining to armed conflict.

Also in relation to proportionality, in the *Oil Platforms* case, the Court held that the US response of 18 April 1988 was of a much greater scale than the incident that allegedly triggered it. The Court noted that 'it cannot close its eyes to the scale of the whole operation, which involved, *inter alia*, the destruction of two Iranian frigates and a number of other naval vessels and aircraft.'[103] Accordingly:

> [A]s a response to the mining, by an unidentified agency, of a single United States warship, which was severely damaged but not sunk, and without loss of life, neither "Operation Praying Mantis" as a whole, nor even that part of it that destroyed the Salman and Nasr platforms, can be regarded, in the circumstances of this case, as a proportionate use of force in self-defence.[104]

The discussion of the US operations in the *Oil Platforms* case suggested that the Court put more emphasis on the quantitative element of proportionality rather than the qualitative. Accordingly, it focused primarily on the scale of the original attacks rather than on the need to ward off the danger stemming from the author(s) of those attacks.[105]

11.4.4 The Customary Basis of Self-Defence

Despite the cautious approach taken by the International Court of Justice in relation to the right of self-defence, it made a very important contribution to the

---

[100] Oil Platforms 2003, para 76.

[101] Green 2009, pp. 105–107.

[102] Nuclear Weapons 1996, para 42.

[103] Oil Platforms 2003, para 77.

[104] Ibid.

[105] Ibid.

understanding of the basis of the right. Accordingly, the most important finding of the Court on self-defence related to the relationship between customary law and treaty law. In the *Nicaragua* case, the Court acknowledged that the customary right of self-defence coexisted with Article 51 and the latter did not supersede the former:

> On one essential point, this treaty itself [the UN Charter] refers to pre-existing customary international law; this reference to customary law is contained in the actual text of Article 51, which mentions the "inherent right" (in the French text the "*droit naturel*") of individual and collective self-defence, which "nothing in the present Charter shall impair" and which applies in the event of an armed attack.[106]

The Court went on interpreting Article 51 as being meaningless without reference to the 'natural' or 'inherent' right of self-defence, which could only be of customary nature.[107] The language used by the Court suggested that Article 51 was a bridge to customary law for interpreting the content of the right of self-defence. Although the Court admitted that the customary right of self-defence might have been subsequently confirmed or influenced by the Charter, it also emphasized that Article 51 did not directly regulate all aspects of this right.[108] As an illustration, the Court pointed out that there was no specification as to the necessity and proportionality of the measures taken and, equally, there was no definition provided for an armed attack. For that reason, one had to turn to customary law to seek answers to the issues not addressed in Article 51. Consequently, the Court was of the view that Article 51 could not be interpreted as a provision that subsumed and supervened customary international law.[109]

11.5 Concluding Remarks

The aim of this chapter was to assess whether the temporal dimension and the juridical variables identified at the beginning of Part II (conditionality of armed attack, immediacy and proportionality) have been, in any form, addressed by various UN organs, and if so, what were the adopted approaches.

It is reasonable to conclude that the work of UN organs relevant for the right of self-defence did not address in any elaborate form the temporal dimension of self-defence. In other words, no explicit rejection of the possible legality of anticipatory action in self-defence was made by any of the examined UN organs. In truth, both the ILC and the ICJ expressly declined to discuss the matter.[110] The only reference to anticipatory action came from the High-Level Panel set up by former Secretary-General Kofi Annan. The report of the panel acknowledged the legality

106 Nicaragua 1986, para 176.

107 Ibid.

108 Ibid.

109 Ibid.

110 Ago 1980, p. 67, para 116; Armed Activities in Congo 2005, para 143.

of anticipatory action against imminent threats, but stopped short of endorsing preventive action against potential threats. The report, however, did not elaborate on the conditions for anticipatory action. It only generically stated that pre-emptive action was legal as long as the threatened attack was imminent, there were no other means to deflect it and the action was proportionate.[111]

Regarding the influence of the work of UN organs on the elements of self-defence, three points are important to be made. First, both the International Law Commission and the International Court of Justice adopted a restrictive, statist approach to the definition of an armed attack. This gap was somewhat bridged by Resolution 1368 (2001) of the Security Council in which self-defence against terrorist attacks was recognized. Moreover, individual members of both the ILC and the ICJ pointed out that the definition of armed attack had to be reinterpreted to include non-state actors as authors.

Secondly, the factor of immediacy in self-defence was hardly ever addressed by the ICJ and ILC. The Court marginalized the discussion of the necessity requirement of self-defence in general. In its report before the ILC, Ago confirmed that the danger faced by the state exercising the right of self-defence had to be immediate and incapable of being countered by other means.'[112] Apart from this short reference to immediacy and the findings of the High-Level Panel, no elaborate discussion on the issue was taken up by any of the examined UN organs.

Thirdly, the requirement of proportionality received some attention in Ago's report, although there was no extensive discussion of the principle in the ensuing ILC meetings.[113] Ago primarily focused on the qualitative approach when defining proportionality and his view was not challenged by the other ILC members.[114] The ICJ placed more focus on the quantitative approach, though it shied away from giving thorough attention to the concept.[115]

The most important addition of the UN organs to the interpretation of self-defence originates from the ICJ. As shown in Sect. 11.4.4, the Court acknowledged the coexistence of customary law and treaty law regarding the right of self-defence. That statement followed the realities of post-Charter state practice on

[111] UN Doc. A/59/565 (2004), para 188, p. 54.

[112] Ago 1980, p. 53, para 88. That statement was almost literally transposed in the ILC Report 1980, p. 52, para 3.

[113] Ago 1980, p. 69, para 121; Summary Record of the 1620th ILC meeting., UN Doc. A/CN.4/SR.1620 (1980) para 4 (comment by Riphagen); Oil Platforms 2003, para 77.

[114] See *supra* 11.2.4. Ago asserted that the requirement of proportionality had to be measured against the result to be achieved by the defensive action, and not the forms, substance and strength of the action itself. Ago 1980, p. 69, para 121. Riphagen agreed, but warned against the abuse of the proportionality requirement. Summary Record of the 1620th ILC meeting., UN Doc. A/CN.4/SR.1620 (1980) para 4 (comment by Riphagen); Summary Record of the 1629th ILC meeting., UN Doc. A/CN.4/SR.1629 (1980) para 9 (comment by Ago).

[115] See *supra* 11.4.3. Oil Platforms 2003, para 77.

self-defence, in which references to the requirements of necessity and proportionality have often been made. The rest of the contributions shed light on many issues pertaining to the right of self-defence. Most of them point to the questions raised by the notion of armed attack. Nonetheless, the effect of these contributions, taken individually or cumulatively, cannot be interpreted as reflecting the emergence of a new customary rule that has significantly altered the pre-Charter content and temporal dimension of self-defence.

References

Ago R (1980) Addendum to the eighth report on state responsibility. UN Doc. A/CN.4/318/Add.5-7 (1980)

Analytical guide to the work of the International Law Commission, 1949–1997 (1998). United Nations, New York

Armed activities on the territory of the Congo (Democratic Republic of the Congo v. Uganda), Judgement of 19 December 2005, ICJ Rep. (2005)

Barbour SA, Salzman ZA (2008) "The tangled web": the right of self-defence against non-state actors in the Armed Activities case. NYU J Int Law Politics (special issue) 40:53–106

Breau SC (2005) Legal consequences of the construction of a wall in the occupied Palestinian territory: advisory opinion, 9 July 2004. Int Comp Law Q 54:1003–1022

Corten O (2007) Le débat sur la légitime défense préventive à l'occasion des 60 ans de l'ONU: nouvelles revendications, oppositions persistantes. In: Kherad R (ed) Légitimes défenses: colloque international organisé par le Laboratoire Angevin de Recherches sur les Actes Juridiques en collab. avec le Centre d'Études sur la Coopération Juridique International, LGDJ, Paris, pp 217–232

Dixon M (2000) Textbook on international law. Blackstone Press, London

Draft Articles on Responsibility of States for Internationally Wrongful Acts, with Commentaries (2001) Yearbook of the International Law Commission, vol 2, Part II. pp 31–143

GA Res 2625: General Assembly Resolution 2625 (1970) Friendly Relations Declaration

GA Res. 3314: General Assembly Resolution 3314 (1974) Definition of Aggression

Gathii JT (2007) Armed activities on the territory of the Congo (Democratic Republic of the Congo v. Uganda). Am J Int Law 101:142–149

Gill TD (2007) The temporal dimension of self-defence. In: Schmitt M, Pejic J (eds) International law and armed conflict: exploring the faultlines. Essays in honour of Yoram Dinstein. Martinus Nijhoff, Leiden, pp 113–155

Gray C (2004) International law and the use of force. Oxford University Press, Oxford

Green JA (2009) The International Court of Justice and self-defence in international law. Hart, Oxford

ILC report 1980: Report of the International Law Commission to the General Assembly on the work of its 32nd Session, 5 May–25 July 1980, UN Doc. A/35/10 (1980)

Israeli Wall 2004: Legal consequences of the construction of a wall in the occupied Palestinian territory. Advisory Opinion of 9 July 2004, ICJ Rep. (2004)

Kelly MJ (2005) Critical analysis of the International Court of Justice ruling on Israel's security barrier. Fordham Int Law J 29:181–228

Murphy SD (2005) Self-defence and the Israeli Wall advisory opinion: an ipse dixit from the ICJ? Am J Int Law 99:62–76

Nicaragua 1986: Military and paramilitary activities in and against Nicaragua (Nicaragua v. USA), Judgment of 27 June 1986, ICJ Rep. (1986)

Nuclear Weapons 1996: Legality of the threat or use of nuclear weapons, Advisory Opinion of 8 July 1996, ICJ Rep. (1996)

Oil Platforms (Islamic Republic of Iran v. United States of America), Judgment of 6 November 2003, ICJ Rep. (2003)
Taft WH (2004) Self-defense and the Oil Platforms decision. Yale J Int Law 29:295–306
The work of the International Law Commission (1996) 5th edn. United Nations, New York
Verhoeven S (2006) A missed opportunity to clarify the modern Ius ad Bellum: case concerning armed activities on the territory of the Congo. Military Law Law War Rev 45:355–368
Wedgwood R (2005) The ICJ advisory opinion on the Israeli security fence and the limits of self-defense. Am J Int Law 99:52–61

Chapter 12
The Temporal Dimension of Post-Charter Self-Defence

The aim of Part II was to analyse the development of post-Charter customary law on self-defence. It was the conclusion of Part I that the pre-Charter, natural-law concept of self-defence always had an anticipatory aspect and it was limited by the requirements of necessity (attack and immediate need for action) and proportionality (moderation).[1] Against this background, Part II assessed whether post-Charter developments have brought about the emergence of a new customary rule on self-defence that has affected the pre-Charter understanding of that right.

Although at the time of the adoption of the Charter, Article 51 was seen as a good compromise between the drafters, the wording of that article has since given rise to inexhaustible debate. As the comparative study of Part II has shown, controversies have emerged in relation to the temporal dimension of self-defence and all of its three elements: the conditionality of an attack and immediacy (necessity) as well as proportionality.

The purpose of this chapter is to draw conclusions as to the temporal dimension of post-Charter self-defence on the basis of the comparative analysis of Part II. The concluding remarks of this chapter will assess the place of anticipatory action within that temporal dimension. The significance of the findings and the discussion of the necessity and proportionality requirements will be elaborated in Part III.

Depending on the nature of the conflict, the temporal dimension of self-defence has been shifting from anticipatory action to remedial response and *vice versa*.

12.1 Temporal Dimension of Self-Defence in State-to-State Conflicts

In the case of state-to-state conflicts (Chapter 8), it was shown that the temporal dimension of the post-Charter concept of self-defence pertained to all three moments: before, during and after an armed attack.

[1] See *supra* 6.4.

K. Tibori Szabó, *Anticipatory Action in Self-Defence*, DOI: 10.1007/978-90-6704-796-8_12,

The Six-Day War was an instance in which anticipatory action in self-defence was found to be legitimate by most commentators.[2] In June 1967, Israel launched an anticipatory action against an imminent threat of invasion from its Arab neighbours.[3] The Israeli cabinet took into consideration the escalation of events beforehand and was able to predict both the manner and purpose of the invasion.[4] The Israeli attitude before the outbreak of the Yom Kippur War was an instance of state practice where anticipatory action was not resorted to, although contemplated, because there was no perception of an imminent threat.[5] The reluctance to resort to anticipatory action in the absence of specific knowledge as to the imminence of the threat is an example of omission—as part of state practice—that acknowledges the immediacy requirement of self-defence. The 1956 Sinai Campaign was an example of state practice where resort to force was condemned, because the purported threat—although serious—did not necessitate immediate action.

Regarding the legality of anticipatory action in general, a significant number of authors agree that an imminent threat of an armed attack can justify the exercise of self-defence.[6] Most of these authors consider the *Caroline* criteria as the standard for 'anticipatory self-defence'.[7]

Although legal doctrine has devoted thorough attention to the question of anticipatory action in self-defence, the International Court of Justice has always avoided addressing the issue of anticipatory action against an imminent threat. The only judicial bodies that expressly acknowledged the lawfulness of anticipatory action in self-defence against an imminent threat were the Nuremberg and Tokyo tribunals.[8]

Moreover, as shown in Chapter 11, the International Law Commission has also avoided adopting a conclusive approach to anticipatory action in self-defence, although the manner in which the Ago report formulated the temporality of self-defence left the possibility of legal anticipatory action open.[9]

---

[2] Beres 1991, p. 267; Dinstein 2005, pp. 191–192 (Dinstein characterized the Six-Day War as an instance of 'interceptive self-defence'); Franck 2002, p. 105; Gill 2007, pp. 138–139. Shapira 1971, pp. 75–76. The 'escalation of events' theory should not be confused with the 'accumulation of events' theory. For the description of the former, see *supra* 8.2.2. The latter pertains to hit-and-run tactics and was thoroughly examined throughout Chap. 10. Some authors rejected the legality of the Six-Day War: Alexandrov 1996, pp. 153–154.

[3] See *supra* 8.2.2.

[4] See ibid.

[5] See *supra* 8.2.3.

[6] Bowett 1958, pp. 188–189; Fleck 1988, pp. 176–177; Gill 2007, pp. 145–147; Greenwood 2003, pp. 12–16; Higgins 1963, p. 199; Malanczuk 1987, pp. 247–248; McDougal and Feliciano 1961, pp. 231–236; Schachter 1991, p. 151; Schwebel 1972, p. 481; Waldock 1952, pp. 497–499.

[7] Bowett 1958, pp. 188–189; Greenwood 2003, pp. 12–16; McDougal and Feliciano 1961, pp. 231–236; Schachter 1991, p. 151; Waldock 1952, pp. 497–499.

[8] See *supra* 7.3, 7.5 and 7.6. Nazi Conspiracy and Aggression 1947, p. 36; Röling and Rüter 1977, p. 382.

[9] Ago 1980, p. 54, para 90.

The only UN-level discussion of the legality of anticipatory action came from the 2004 High-Level Panel set up by former Secretary-General Kofi Annan. The report put together by the panellists acknowledged the legality of self-defence before an attack as long as the threatened attack was imminent, there were no other means to deflect it and the action was proportionate.[10]

The Iran–Iraq war was an instance in which self-defence was exercised against an *ongoing* armed attack the purpose of which was not yet accomplished.[11] In this case, the armed attack materialised in the form of a full-scale invasion in the sense of classic, state-to-state warfare, where armed forces of the belligerent states clash over a protracted amount of time. The Iran–Iraq war also formed the quintessential example of self-defence in the literal confines of Article 51, although, it took the UN a few years to affirm the right of Iran to defend itself against the Iraqi invasion.[12]

The Iran–Iraq war also mirrors the opinion of those authors who maintain that self-defence should be understood on the basis of a strict reading of Article 51 which limits the use of force to instances where an armed attack has already occurred.[13]

The Falklands war involved the exercise of self-defence after an armed attack had already occurred. The naval forces of the UK engaged in battle with the Argentinean forces four weeks after the Junta regime accomplished the occupation of the Falklands islands and South Georgia in the South Atlantic.[14] Nonetheless, preparations for the use of force in self-defence were made as soon as the armed attack had started. The geographical disparity between the home ports of the British naval forces and the zone of operations delayed the exercise of self-defence.[15]

Although the Security Council acknowledged the legality of the British action, there has been some debate as to the timeliness of defensive action when the armed attack has already achieved its purpose.[16] Accordingly, the Falklands war was coined the reversal of a *fait accompli* rather than self-defence, because the takeover had already occurred.[17] Likewise, the contention was made that allowing self-defence in cases where the armed attack had already achieved its purpose

[10] UN Doc. A/59/565 (2004), para 188, p. 54.

[11] See *supra* 8.3.1.

[12] See ibid.

[13] Abi Saab 1987, p. 371; Badr 1980, p. 25; Brownlie 1963, pp. 275–278; Cassese 2005, pp. 361–362 (Cassese offers *de lege ferenda* proposal for a possible future regulation of 'anticipatory self-defence', ibid., pp. 362–363); Constantinou 2000, pp. 120–121; Corten 2008, p. 619; Gray 2004, pp. 98–99; Henkin 1991, pp. 44–46; Jessup 1948, p. 166; Kolesnik 1989, p. 154; Kunz 1947, p. 878; Ruys 2010, pp. 259–262.

[14] See *supra* 8.3.2.

[15] See *supra* 8.3.2.

[16] See *supra* 8.3.2.

[17] Neff 2005, p. 330. See *supra* 8.3.2.

would open the possibility of advancing defensive claims long after the injurious action had occurred.[18]

Some instances of state practice on self-defence have also involved hit-and-run tactics, where official elements of one state have carried out a series of small-scale, sporadic attacks on the territory or against the citizens of another state. Such instances were the hit-and-run tactics that led to the UK bombing of a Yemeni fort, the Gulf of Tonkin incident, the US bombing of Libya and the US airstrikes against Iraq. They purported a more complicated temporal dimension of self-defence that will be analysed within the temporal dimension of self-defence against non-state actors.[19] In the ensuing claims of self-defence, the defending states claimed that both remedial and anticipatory action was necessary to neutralize the source of the threat. Accordingly, in 1964, the UK maintained that a series of incidents had convinced the government of the South Arabian Federation and the government of the United Kingdom that 'a deliberate and increasing attack by Yemen against the Federation was under way.'[20] Similarly, the US complained of 'deliberate and repeated armed attacks' against its naval vessels from North Vietnamese torpedo boats.[21] In 1986, the US justified the bombing of Libya by claiming that there was 'an ongoing pattern of attacks by Libya' as well as 'clear evidence that Libya was planning a multitude of future attacks.'[22] Likewise, in 1993, the US ambassador to the UN claimed that the airstrike against the Iraqi Intelligence Headquarters in Baghdad was carried out only after having concluded that there was no reasonable prospect that diplomatic initiatives or economic pressure could influence the Iraqi government to cease the planning such attacks against US citizens.[23]

The US claims in the Gulf of Tonkin incident were condemned because of lack of clear information about the 'deliberate and repeated armed attacks' the government claimed it suffered. The mixed reaction to the other instances (condemnation for UK in 1964, criticism for US in 1986 and muted acceptance in 1993)[24] was due to the peculiarity of the argument for self-defence: defending oneself against past attack to preclude the occurrence of future ones.

Legal doctrine has been divided on the issue. A number of authors have expressly or implicitly endorsed what came to be known as the 'accumulation of events' theory.[25] Others have rejected it as a dangerous extension of the understanding given to the right of self-defence.[26]

---

[18] Badr 1980, p. 25; Schachter 1985, p. 292.

[19] See *infra* 12.3.

[20] Repertoire, Supp. 1964–1965, Chap. 8, p. 128.

[21] SCOR, 19th Session., 1140th meeting., UN Doc. S/PV.1140 (5 August 1964) para 34.

[22] SCOR, 41st Session., 2674th meeting., UN Doc. S/PV.2674 (15 April 1986) p. 17.

[23] UN Doc. S/26003 (1993); Franck 2002, p. 94.

[24] See *supra* 8.4.1, 8.4.3 and 8.4.4.

[25] Baker 1987, p. 42; Blum 1976, pp. 233; Bowett 1972, p. 12; Brownlie 1963, p. 279; Gross 1983, p. 478; Higgins 1963, p. 201; Jacobson 1998, pp. 13, 16; Schachter 1985, p. 293.

[26] Henkin 1995, pp. 126–127.

12.2 Temporal Dimension of Self-Defence in Conflicts Involving WMD

In the case of conflicts involving weapons of mass destruction (Chapter 9), it was shown that there was a perceivable tendency to exceed the temporal dimension of self-defence. In the Cuban missile crisis, the US government decided not to resort to self-defence, because it believed that there was no legal basis for anticipatory action in the absence of the threat of an imminent attack.[27] That instance of state practice followed the pre-Charter understanding of the temporal dimension of self-defence.

The 1981 Israeli bombing of the Iraqi nuclear reactor went one step further. The Israeli cabinet justified the airstrikes as self-defence against the possibility of Iraqi government developing a nuclear weapon in the foreseeable future.[28] The Israeli airstrikes were criticized by states before the Security Council as exceeding the limits of anticipatory action.[29]

The 2003 US invasion of Iraq exceeded even the limits of the 1981 Israeli action. The 2002 US National Security Strategy (also known as the 'Bush doctrine')[30] served as the basis for the invasion and occupation of Iraq as well as the toppling of its regime without any evidence as to the existence—let alone imminent threat to use—weapons of mass destruction. The 1981 Israeli and the 2003 US actions show a tendency to exceed the temporal dimension of self-defence by advocating preventive use of force against the development or possession of WMD.

The preventive trend is not conclusively supported by UN organs or legal doctrine.[31] The approach of the Security Council has been negative; it unanimously condemned the Israeli reaction and failed to endorse the US-led invasion of Iraq.[32] The International Court of Justice stopped short of characterizing the possession of nuclear weapons unlawful *per se*, thus implicitly restricting the exercise of self-defence in such situations.[33] Moreover, the 2004 UN High-Level Panel asserted that unilateral preventive action against non-imminent threats

---

[27] See *supra* 9.2.

[28] See *supra* 9.3.

[29] Ibid.

[30] Gardner 2003, pp. 585–586; Henderson 2004, p. 6.

[31] SCOR, 36th Session., 2282nd meeting., UN Doc. S/PV.2282 (15 June 1981) paras 14–19; 2283rd meeting., S/PV.2283 (15 June 1981) paras 23–27, 46, 117, 146; 2284th meeting., S/PV.2284 (16 June 1981) para 11; 2288th meeting., S/PV.2288 (19 June 1981) para 115. In one instance, the concepts of 'anticipation' and 'preventive aggression' were equated and deemed unlawful: 2283rd meeting., S/PV.2283 (15 June 1981) para 146 (Sierra Leone). See also Alexandrov 1996, p. 162; Franck 2002, pp. 105–107; Gardner 2003, p. 587; Gill 2007, pp. 141–142; Greenwood 2003, p. 14; Sapiro 2005, p. 367.

[32] See *supra* 9.3 and 9.5.2.

[33] See *supra* 9.4.

carried great risks for the world order and the principle of non-intervention and that such action should rather be taken after a collective endorsement under Chapter VII.[34]

The majority of the legal doctrine is also considerably sceptical as to the lawfulness of the use of force against development and possession of nuclear weapons.[35] Comments characterizing that trend as signalling a lawful alteration of the temporal dimension of self-defence have been voiced in the legal literature, but the opinion is still a minority.[36]

12.3 Temporal Dimension of Self-Defence in Conflicts Involving Non-State Actors

When it comes to conflicts involving non-state actors (Chapter 10), the temporal dimension of the post-Charter concept of self-defence is circular: the same defensive action is both remedial (against a string of past attacks) and anticipatory (against future attacks). The circularity stems from the 'accumulation of events' theory: the incidence of future attacks is expected because of the occurrence of past attacks.

This circularity of the temporal dimension was already perceived when analysing certain instances of state-to-state conflicts. The hit-and-run tactics employed by official elements of a state on the territory or against the citizens of another state, have led to similar arguments in self-defence than those used against non-state actors.[37]

The 'accumulation of events' theory has given rise to many controversies since the adoption of the UN Charter. For long, the Security Council and a part of the legal doctrine did not accept the possibility of attributing armed attacks to non-state actors and thus rejected the 'needle-prick' approach as well.[38] Nonetheless, there have also been lawyers who endorsed the theory and pointed out its usefulness for facing the threats posed by non-state actors.[39]

In the immediate aftermath of the 9/11 attacks, the Security Council expressly acknowledged the right to resort to self-defence against terrorist acts.[40] With that

---

[34] UN Doc. A/59/565 (2004), para 191, p. 55.

[35] Gardner 2003, pp. 587–588; Henderson 2004, p. 14; Lowe 2003, p. 865; Sapiro 2005, p. 367.

[36] Hill 2004, pp. 329-331; Pierson 2004, pp. 154–155; Taft and Buchwald 2003, pp. 557–563, Taft 2003; Wedgwood 2003, pp. 584; Yoo 2003, pp. 571–574.

[37] See *supra* 8.4.1–8.4.4.

[38] See *supra* 10.2 and 10.3. For a critical opinion on the 'accumulation of events' theory, see Lubell 2010, pp. 51-54.

[39] Baker 1987, p. 42; Blum 1976, pp. 233; Bowett 1972, p. 12; Brownlie 1963, p. 279; Gross 1983, p. 478; Higgins 1963, p. 201; Jacobson 1998, pp. 13, 16; Schachter 1985, p. 293.

[40] SC Res. 1368 (2001) preamble.

acknowledgement, the members of the Security Council also implicitly admitted that armed attacks could be carried out by non-state actors as well.[41] That acknowledgement was in line with the pre-Charter understanding of self-defence, in which non-state actors were viewed as potential authors of an armed attack. Moreover, the attitude of the SC members to the 2006 Israeli invasion of Lebanon, the 2007–2008 Turkish incursion into northern Iraq and the 2008–2009 Gaza crisis signalled an implicit acceptance of the 'accumulation of events' theory, although all these instances were criticized for their disproportionate use of force.[42]

The growing concerns as to the nature of the twenty-first century terrorism have also fuelled arguments for 'preventive' self-defence, much in the same way as the anxiety over possession of WMD by unfriendly states did. These opinions form a minority part of the relevant legal doctrine.[43]

Generally speaking, the circularity of the temporal dimension of self-defence against non-state actors is very similar to the pre-Charter understanding of that right. Accordingly, pre-Charter self-defence (in its narrow sense, of course), pertained to three moments: before, during and after an armed attack. That understanding is best mirrored in the post-Charter understanding of self-defence against non-state actors: defensive action against past attacks to preclude the occurrence of new ones.

12.4 Concluding Remarks

The aim of this chapter was to draw conclusions as to the temporal dimension of post-Charter self-defence on the basis of the comparative analysis of Part II. This brief appraisal was needed in order to assess the place of anticipatory action within that temporal dimension.

It is the conclusion of this chapter—and of Part II as well—that the anticipatory dimension of self-defence could be discerned in all major groups of state practice discussed in the comparative analysis. All themes—state-to-state conflicts, conflicts involving WMD and conflicts involving non-state actors—confirmed the pre-Charter dimensions of self-defence: anticipatory and remedial. Moreover, all themes included cases in which self-defence had an anticipatory dimension, whether independently or in combination with a remedial aspect.

The basis on which the various claims of anticipatory action have been criticized or accepted pertained to the same elements that limited the pre-Charter concept of self-defence. For this reason, this author does not agree with the contention of some publicists that post-Charter state practice has outlawed

[41] Franck 2002, pp. 54, 66–67.

[42] See *supra* 10.5.4–10.5.6.

[43] Hill 2004, pp. 329–331; Pierson 2004, pp. 154–155; Taft and Buchwald 2003, pp. 557–563, Taft 2003; Wedgwood 2003, pp. 584; Yoo 2003, pp. 571–574.

anticipatory action in self-defence as a result of its questionable legal basis or its rare use.[44] Looking at a few instances of state practice to reject (or justify) 'anticipatory self-defence' is insufficient. Although the instances in which states resorted to 'purely' anticipatory *action* (before an armed attack occurs) are rare, the anticipatory *dimension* of self-defence is present in many instances of state practice that are not necessarily treated as pre-emptive strikes. The small number of pure anticipatory *actions* certainly shows a precaution of states in exercising self-defence before an armed attack occurs, but that should not be interpreted as illustrating the unlawful basis of such actions. The anticipatory *dimension* of self-defence is apparent in most cases analysed and that dimension allows the use of force not only to prevent the re-occurrence of past attacks, but also to preclude a first armed attack from commencing.

Against this background, the practice of the Security Council cannot be interpreted as rejecting defensive anticipatory action *per se*. In fact, the legality of 'anticipatory self-defence' in general was many times endorsed by members of the Security Council, even when specific instances of state practice involving self-defence were harshly criticized.[45]

The International Court of Justice, the International Law Commission as well as the General Assembly have refrained from making qualifications on the temporal dimension or anticipatory aspect of self-defence.[46] The 2004 UN High-Level Panel has, however, acknowledged the legality of anticipatory action in self-defence.[47]

Moreover, legal doctrine is still divided on the legality of anticipatory action in self-defence, although a significant number of authors justify it on the basis of the *Caroline* criteria.[48]

If the findings regarding state practice are corroborated with the influence exercised by the Security Council, the International Court of Justice and other UN organs as well as with the current state of the academic debate, it can be concluded that no new customary rule has emerged since the adoption of the Charter that

[44] Brownlie 1963, p. 260; Christakis 2005, pp. 215–219; Gazzini 2005, p. 151; Gray 2004, p. 130; Henkin 1995, pp. 121–122.

[45] See, for instance, the discussions regarding the 1981 Israeli airstrike against the Osirak reactor, SCOR, 36th Session., 2282nd meeting., UN Doc. S/PV.2282 (15 June 1981) paras 14–19; 2283rd meeting., S/PV.2283 (15 June 1981) paras 23–27; 2284th meeting., S/PV.2284 (15 June 1981) para 11. On the inconclusiveness of Security Council practice on 'anticipatory self-defence', see Gray 2004, p. 96.

[46] See *supra* 11.1, 11.2 and 11.4. On the silence of the General Assembly on the issue, see Gray 2004, p. 95.

[47] UN Doc. A/59/565 (2004), para 188, p. 54.

[48] Those for 'anticipatory self-defence': Bowett 1958, pp. 188–189; Fleck 1988, pp. 176–177; Gill 2007, pp. 145–147; Greenwood 2003, pp. 12–16; Higgins 1963, p. 199; Malanczuk 1987, pp. 247–248; McDougal and Feliciano 1961, pp. 231–236; Schachter 1991, p. 151; Schwebel 1972, p. 481; Waldock 1952, pp. 497–499. Those against: Abi Saab 1987, p. 371; Badr 1980, p. 25; Brownlie 1963, pp. 275–278; Cassese 2005, pp. 361–362; Constantinou 2000, pp. 120–121; Corten 2008, p. 619; Gray 2004, pp. 98–99; Henkin 1991, pp. 44–46; Jessup 1948, p. 166; Kolesnik 1989, p. 154; Kunz 1947, p. 878; Ruys 2010, pp. 259–262.

eliminated the anticipatory dimension of self-defence. Undoubtedly, the various post-Charter developments on the subject have influenced the particularities of the limits of self-defence, but they cannot be interpreted as outlawing the pre-Charter anticipatory dimension of that right. On that basis, it remains to be seen what the coordinates of the current customary law on anticipatory action in self-defence are.

References

Abi Saab G (1987) Cours general du droit public. Recueil des Cours 207(1987-VII):9–463.
Ago R (1980) Addendum to the eighth report on state responsibility. UN Doc. A/CN.4/318/Add.5–7 (1980)
Alexandrov S (1996) Self-defense against the use of force in international law. Kluwer, The Hague
Badr GM (1980) The exculpatory effect of self-defence in state responsibility. Ga J Int Comp Law 10:1–28
Baker MB (1987) Terrorism and the inherent right to self-defence (a call to amend Article 51 of the United Nations Charter). Houst J Int Law 10:25–49
Beres LR (1991) After the Gulf war: Israel, preemption and anticipatory self-defence perspective. Houst J Int Law 13:259–280
Blum Y (1976) State response to acts of terrorism. Ger Yearb Int Law 19:223–237
Bowett DW (1958) Self-defense in international law. Manchester University Press, Manchester
Bowett DW (1972) Reprisals involving recourse to armed force. Am J Int Law 66:1–36
Brownlie I (1963) International law and the use of force by states. Clarendon Press, Oxford
Cassese A (2005) International law. Oxford University Press, Oxford
Constantinou A (2000) The right of self-defence under customary international law and Article 51 of the United Nations Charter. Sakkoulas, Athens
Corten O (2008) Le droit contre la guerre: l'interdiction du recours á la force en droit international contemporain. Pedone, Paris.
Dinstein Y (2005) War, aggression and self-defense. Cambridge University Press, Cambridge
Fleck D (1988) Rules of engagement for maritime forces and the limitation of the use of force under the UN Charter. Ger Yearb Int law 31:165–186
Franck T (2002) Recourse to force: state action against threats and armed attacks. Cambridge University Press, Cambridge
Gardner RN (2003) Neither Bush nor the "jurisprudes". Am J Int Law 97:585–590
Gill TD (2007) The temporal dimension of self-defence. In: Schmitt M, Pejic J (eds) International law and armed conflict: exploring the faultlines. Essays in honour of Yoram Dinstein, Martinus Nijhoff, Leiden, pp 113–155
Gray C (2004) International law and the use of force. Oxford University Press, Oxford
Greenwood C (2003) International law and the pre-emptive use of force: Afghanistan, Al-Qaida and Iraq. S-Diego Int Law J 4:7–38
Gross LM (1983) The legal implications of Israel's 1982 invasion into Lebanon. Calif West Int Law J 13:458–492
Henderson C (2004) The Bush doctrine: from theory to practice. J Confl Secur Law 9:3–24
Henkin L (1991) The use of force: law and US policy. In: Henkin et al (eds) Right v. might. International law and the use of force. Council on Foreign Relations Press, New York, pp 37–69
Henkin L (1995) International law: politics and values. Martinus Nijhoff, Dordrecht
Higgins R (1963) The development of international law through the political organs of the United Nations. Oxford University Press, London

Hill C (2004) The Bush Administration preemption doctrine and the future of world order: Remark. Am Soc Int Law Proc 98:329–331
Jacobson MR (1998) War in the information age: international law, self-defense, and the problem of 'non-armed' attacks. J Strateg Stud 21(3):1–33
Jessup PC (1948) A modern law of nations: an introduction. Macmillan, New York
Kolesnik DN (1989) The development of the right to self-defence. In: Butler WE (ed) The non-use of force in international law. Nijhoff, Dordrecht, pp 153–159
Kunz J (1947) Individual and collective self-defence in Article 51 of the Charter of the UN. Am J Int Law 41:872–879
Lowe V (2003) The Iraqi crisis: what now? Int Comp Law Q 52:859–871
Lubell N (2010) Extraterritorial use of force against non-state actors. Oxford University Press, Oxford
Malanczuk P (1987) Countermeasures and self-defence as circumstances precluding wrongfulness in the International Law Commision's Draft Articles on States Responsibility. In: Spinedi M, Simma B (eds) United Nations codification of state responsibility. Oceana, New York, pp 197–286
McDougal MS, Feliciano FP (1961) Law and minimum world public order: the legal regulation of international coercion. Yale University Press, New Haven
Nazi Conspiracy and Aggression: Opinion and Judgment (1947) Office of the United States Chief of Counsel for the Prosecution of Axis Criminality, Government Printing Office, Washington, D.C.
Neff SC (2005) War and the law of nations: general history. Cambridge University Press, Cambrdige
Pierson C (2004) Preemptive self-defence in an age of weapons of mass destruction: Operation Iraqi Freedom. Denver J Int Law Policy 33:150–178
Repertoire: Repertoire of the Practice of the Security Council http://www.un.org/en/sc/repertoire/
Röling BVA, Rüter CF (eds) (1977) The Tokyo judgment: the international military tribunal for the Far East, 29 April 1946–12 November 1948. APA-University Press, Amsterdam
Ruys T (2010) 'Armed attack' and Article 51 of the UN Charter. Evolutions in customary law and practice. Cambridge University Press, Cambridge
Sapiro M (2005) Preempting prevention: lessons learned. NYU J Int Law Politics 37:357–371
Schachter O (1985) The lawful resort to unilateral use of force. Yale J Int Law 10:291–294
Schachter O (1991) International law in theory and practice. Martinus Nijhoff, Dordrecht
Schwebel SM (1972) Aggression, intervention and self-defence in modern international law. Recueil des Cours 136(1972-II):411–497
SCOR: Security Council Official Records http://documents.un.org/simple.asp
Shapira A (1971) The Six Day War and the right of self-defence. Israel Law Rev 6:65–80
Taft 2003: Taft WH (20 March 2003) Remarks to the National Association of Attorneys General, Washington. http://usinfo.org/wf-archive/2003/030321/epf516.htm. Accessed 17 February 2010
Taft WH, Buchwald TF (2003) Preemption, Iraq, and international law. Am J Int Law 97:557–563
Waldock CHM (1952) The regulation of the use of force by individual states in international law. Recueil Des Cours 81(1952-II):451–517
Wedgwood R (2003) The fall of Saddam Hussein: Security Council mandates and preemptive self-defense. Am J Int Law 97:576–585
Yoo J (2003) International law and the war in Iraq. Am J Int Law 97:563–576

Part III
Anticipatory Action in Self-Defence and International Customary Law

The present research examined the conditions under which anticipatory action in self-defence was legal under public international law. As it was explained in Chapter 1, the questions pertaining to anticipatory action have always been intrinsically connected to the content and temporal dimension of the right of self-defence *per se*. For that reason, the research conducted focused on the right of self-defence as a whole and analysed anticipatory action together with that right.

The controversies surrounding the wording of Article 51 have made reliance on the customary basis of self-defence necessary.[1] Accordingly, in order to assess the legality of anticipatory action under public international law, this research has relied primarily on the relevant customary rules.

With that view in mind, two main research questions have been identified in the first chapter. The first question inquired whether anticipatory action in self-defence was part of contemporary customary international law. The second research question was reliant on the first and focused on the limits of anticipatory action in self-defence under customary international law.

Part III will answer these two questions on the basis of the findings of Part I and Part II. Accordingly, the conclusions of Parts I and II will be examined in order to answer the first research question. On that basis, the findings of both Part I and Part II will be discussed to address the second research question.

---

[1] See *supra* 1.2 and 11.4.4.

Chapter 13
The Legality of Anticipatory Action in Self-Defence

As explained in Chapter 1, the adoption of the UN Charter is seen by many as a key moment for the development of the right of self-defence.[1] It was then that the right of self-defence was expressly acknowledged as the only legal exception to the unilateral use of force.[2] At the same time, the adoption of the Charter gave rise to several controversies affecting the customary right of self-defence.[3] One of these contentions related to the temporal dimension of self-defence and the legality of anticipatory action against imminent threats.

Since the drafters of the Charter included the right of self-defence as an 'inherent' (i.e., customary) right, it was necessary to clarify what was covered by the concept at the time of the adoption of the Charter and what was the intention of the drafters with Article 51. In order to understand the drafters' intention as regards self-defence, a legal-historical analysis was conducted to explain the evolution of the right and the form in which it was accepted as legal at the end of the Second World War. Further, a comprehensive analysis of the drafting process of Article 51 was carried out and the various treaty interpretation approaches were applied to clarify the intention of the drafters at the conference. On this basis, further analysis was conducted to assess if and how the pre-Charter content and temporal dimension of self-defence altered under the influence of the UN Charter. For this purpose, several themes that characterized the post-World War II use of force were used to examine those claims of self-defence that had a significant impact on the temporality of self-defence and the legality of anticipatory action.

On this basis, the first main research question inquired whether anticipatory action in self-defence was part of customary international law. This chapter will draw conclusions from the findings of Parts I and II as to the legality of anticipatory action in self-defence.

---

1 See *supra* 1.3.2.

2 Brownlie 1963, p. 265; Simma 1995, p. 663; Neff 2005, pp. 316–317; Dixon 2000, p. 297.

3 See *supra* 1.2.

K. Tibori Szabó, *Anticipatory Action in Self-Defence*, DOI: 10.1007/978-90-6704-796-8_13,

13.1 Findings of Part I

The objective of Part I was to trace the evolution of pre-Charter customary law on self-defence from its ancient Greek natural-law roots to the time of the adoption of the UN Charter. This legal–historical research was necessary to understand how the content and temporal dimension of self-defence was viewed in 1945. On that basis, Part I drew conclusions on whether anticipatory action was seen as part of self-defence at the time the Charter was adopted.

The concept of self-defence was traced through three succeeding normative frameworks that regulated war: the Christian natural-law, the positivist and the emerging international law frameworks. In each of these frameworks, the concept of self-defence was identified and explained on the basis of the available works and relevant state practice.

It was one of the conclusions of the legal–historical research that the pre-Charter concept of self-defence was viewed as a right given by nature to both individuals and states. As a result of this dual discussion, two forms of defensive wars came to be recognized and employed in practice, although only one of them could be correctly characterized as 'self-defence'. The natural right of self-defence acknowledged for individuals purported to the *narrow* understanding of this right. This understanding was also applied to the state in a slightly more permissive manner, when it came to 'imperfect wars' and 'measures short of war'.[4] Conversely, when waging a 'perfect', officially declared, full-scale war for various defensive purposes, a much *broader* understanding of defence was employed. On the basis of the natural law-based, narrow understanding, defence was allowed against an imminent or an ongoing attack as well as against an attack that had already occurred, but only with the purpose of warding off a future attack.[5] The broader understanding of defence allowed the waging of preventive wars.[6]

The legal–historical research traced the evolution of both strands, but it mainly focused on the narrow understanding of self-defence. Accordingly, one of the findings of Part I was that the natural-law, pre-Charter concept of self-defence had always been seen as having an intrinsic anticipatory aspect. There was no strict differentiation made between 'self-defence' and 'anticipatory self-defence', because the right *as such* had an anticipatory meaning. Remedial action in self-defence was allowed only if a new attack had to be warded off.[7]

The research conducted in Part I also showed that, as a result of the gradual restriction of the broader conception of defensive wars in the third normative framework (late nineteenth and early twentieth centuries), the narrow, natural-law

---

[4] See *supra* 2.4.4. Grotius 1964, Book II, Chap. 1 (xvi), p. 184. See also *supra* 3.3 and 4.7.

[5] See *supra* 2.5. Gratian, question I, in Reichberg et al. 2006, pp. 109–110; Aquinas, question 41, article 1, in Reichberg et al. 2006, pp. 182–183; Pisan, Part III, Chap. 12, in Reichberg et al. 2006, p. 219.

[6] Gentili 1933, Book I, Chap. 14, p. 66.

[7] See *supra* 6.2–6.4.

form of self-defence was the one accepted as customary law in the period immediately preceding and at the time of the adoption of the UN Charter. This understanding of self-defence—pertaining to the time before, during and after an attack—was taken into consideration when the compromise of Article 51 was reached.[8]

The intrinsic anticipatory aspect of the pre-Charter concept of self-defence was also highlighted by Bowett, who contended that 'the right has, under traditional international law, always been "anticipatory", that is to say its exercise was valid against imminent as well as actual attacks or dangers.'[9] The same conclusion was reached by Waldock, who asserted that 'self-defence belongs to preventive justice' in the sense that self-defence was strictly confined 'to the object of stopping or preventing the infringement and reasonably proportionate to what is required for achieving this object.'[10]

In view of the conclusions of Part I, this research has referred to 'anticipatory action in self-defence' rather than 'anticipatory self-defence'. The choice of the phrase was made in order to highlight the intrinsic aspect of anticipatory action within the concept of self-defence as a whole. Furthermore, the phrase has been used to suggest that there is no separate 'anticipatory self-defence' along a standard right of self-defence.[11] Naturally, the notion of 'anticipatory self-defence' was also used when direct quotes or specific references to legal doctrine as well as state—or UN practice rendered it necessary.

13.2 Findings of Part II

The aim of Part II was to analyse the development of post-Charter customary law on self-defence. In view of the conclusion of Part I, that the pre-Charter, natural-law concept of self-defence always had an anticipatory aspect,[12] Part II had to assess whether post-Charter developments have brought about the emergence of a new customary rule on self-defence affecting the anticipatory aspect of that right.

It is essential to emphasize that the aim of Part II was *not* to ascertain the existence of a clear customary rule justifying anticipatory action in self-defence. That objective was reached by Part I by concluding that there existed such a customary rule before and at the time of the adoption of the UN Charter. Therefore, what Part II needed to assess was whether a *new* customary rule *prohibiting* anticipatory action had emerged since the adoption of the Charter. For that reason, Part II embarked on a comparative analysis of several instances of state practice,

---

[8] See *supra* 5.4 and 6.5.

[9] Bowett 1958, pp. 188–189.

[10] Waldock 1952, p. 464.

[11] Remarks also made *supra* 2.5, 3.2.2.1, and 6.5.

[12] See *supra* 6.5.

organized under various themes, and examined the temporal dimension of self-defence as a whole to ascertain potential alterations in the concept of self-defence. Both anticipatory and remedial actions in self-defence were given attention.

On the basis of the comparative analysis, Part II found that the anticipatory dimension of self-defence could be discerned in all major groups of state practice discussed. All themes—state-to-state conflicts, conflicts involving WMD and conflicts involving non-state actors—included cases in which self-defence had an anticipatory dimension. Although the instances in which states resorted to 'purely' anticipatory *action* (before an armed attack occurred) were few, the anticipatory *dimension* of self-defence was present in many instances of state practice that were not necessarily treated as pre-emptive strikes. The anticipatory dimension of self-defence was found to allow use of force not only to prevent the re-occurrence of past attacks, but also to preclude a first armed attack from commencing.

Furthermore, in conflicts involving WMD the anticipatory dimension was very strong; though two of the cases discussed pushed that dimension beyond its pre-Charter limits towards prevention. The temporal dimension of self-defence against non-state actors was found to be both anticipatory and remedial. In other words, it reflected the pre-Charter understanding of the right in its full form: defence being allowed before, during and after an armed attack.

The findings regarding state practice were coupled with the influence exercised by the practice of the Security Council, the International Court of Justice and other UN organs as well as with the current state of the academic debate. The resulting picture showed that there was no conclusive evidence of a new customary rule eliminating the pre-Charter anticipatory dimension of self-defence.

13.3 The Legality of Anticipatory Action in Self-Defence in International Law

On the basis of the corroborated findings of Parts I and II, this research concludes that anticipatory action is still part of the contemporary customary understanding of self-defence. Undoubtedly, the various post-Charter developments on the subject have shaped the conditions under which anticipatory action in self-defence is legal under international law. Their influence is addressed in Chapter 14. Nonetheless, the temporal dimension of the contemporary customary right to self-defence has retained an anticipatory aspect, which—under certain conditions—may be deemed lawful under international law.

In order to place the present argument in the context of the current debate on the legality of anticipatory action in self-defence, a short examination of the relevant literature is necessary. Only the main contentions in the debate will be depicted, in order to place the present opinion in their context.

Those who reject the legality of 'anticipatory self-defence' (restrictive approach) employ a combination of treaty interpretation and contextualization.

Accordingly, relying on a literal analysis of Article 51, certain authors maintain that self-defence before an armed attack was outlawed by the negotiators of Article 51.[13] Furthermore, these publicists contend that the adoption of the Charter was a big leap forward for the regulation of the use of force and that many traditional norms were left behind.[14] Likewise, the outlawry of anticipatory action in self-defence is also deduced from the assessment of post-Charter state practice.[15] Accordingly, it has been asserted that because the actual invocation of the right to 'anticipatory self-defence' is rare in practice, such a justification for the use of force can hardly be maintained under contemporary customary international law.[16] On that basis, it is contended that even if the drafters of the Charter did not intend to outlaw anticipatory action, subsequent state practice, under the influence of the Charter, has done so.[17]

Conversely, those advocating the legality of 'anticipatory self-defence' (permissive approach) maintain that the purpose of Article 51 was to preserve the customary understanding of the right, as prescribed by the *Caroline* criteria.[18] These authors also maintain that the *travaux préparatoires* do not show any intention in defining or restricting self-defence to instances where an armed attack has already occurred.[19] Some writers also point out that the French version of the phrase 'if an armed attack occurs' (*dans un cas où un Membre des Nations Unies est l'objet d'une aggression armée*) is considerably less restrictive.[20] This part of the legal doctrine often makes reference to specific instances of state practice that involved anticipatory action in self-defence and maintains, on their basis, that 'anticipatory self-defence' may still be lawful under strict conditions.[21] It is also

[13] Abi Saab 1987, p. 371; Brownlie 1963, p. 275; Cahier 1985, p. 73; Christakis 2005, pp. 208–212; Constantinou 2000, pp. 120–121; Corten 2008, pp. 619–624; Gray 2004, p. 98; Jessup 1948, p. 166; Kolesnik 1989, p. 154; Kunz 1947, pp. 877–878; Lachs 1980, pp. 162–164; Ruys 2010, pp. 259–262; Wright 1963, pp. 560–561. This view was also maintained by Franck, although he belongs to the legal doctrine that accepts the legality of anticipatory action in self-defence under certain circumstances. Franck 2002, p. 50.

[14] See *supra* 11.2.1. Summary Record of the 1627th ILC mtg., UN Doc. A/CN.4/SR.1627 (Lachs 1980) para 3 (comment by Tsuruoka).

[15] Christakis 2005, pp. 215–219; Corten 2008, pp. 630–631; Gazzini 2005, p. 151; Gray 2004, pp. 98–99, 130.

[16] Brownlie 1963, p. 260; Gray 2004, p. 130; Henkin 1995, pp.121–122.

[17] Brownlie 1963, p. 260; Gray 2004, pp. 98, 130; Zoller 2004, pp. 333–337.

[18] Bowett 1958, pp. 188–189; Fleck 1988, pp. 176–177; Higgins 1963, p. 199; Malanczuk 1987, pp. 247–248; McDougal and Feliciano 1961, pp. 231–236; Schachter 1991, pp. 150–152; Schwebel 1972, p. 481; Waldock 1952, pp. 497–499.

[19] Bowett 1958, p. 188; Dixon 2000, p. 301; McDougal and Feliciano 1961, pp. 234–235; Waldock 1952, p. 497.

[20] Higgins 1963, p. 199; Waldock 1952, p. 497.

[21] Fleck 1988, pp. 176–177; Franck 2002, pp. 107–108; Higgins 1963, pp. 199-203.

contended by this group that modern warfare technology and modern threats make resort to anticipatory action in self-defence necessary.[22]

Some observations are needed in order to better illustrate the place of the present argument in the relevant debate. First of all, those advocating for a restrictive approach claim that by the time the Charter was adopted, customary law allowed only a narrow right of self-defence.[23] This is undoubtedly true. The analysis of the pre-Charter legal history has shown two strands—a narrow and a wider understanding—of self-defence.[24] The broader understanding of self-defence allowed for preventive action against possible and probable dangers, in the sense put forward by Gentili and Vattel.[25] This understanding was indeed considerably restricted by the beginning of the twentieth century and was generally viewed as unlawful at the time of the adoption of the Charter.[26] Conversely, the narrow understanding of self-defence continued to be accepted as customary law at the time of the Charter. On its basis, self-defence could be exercised against imminent threats or ongoing attacks as well as after an attack had already occurred if a new attack had to be warded off.[27]

Furthermore, there is documentary evidence suggesting that some delegates of the United States at the San Francisco Conference wanted to restrict self-defence to the time after an armed attack.[28] Their proposal, however, was met with scepticism by other US delegates who believed that the right would be unduly restricted.[29] Moreover, these proposals were not put forward before the relevant committee, so no intergovernmental discussion ensued on the topic.[30] Therefore, no clear conclusion can be drawn solely from the records as to the temporal dimension attributed to self-defence by the various negotiators. Likewise, there is no conclusive evidence of a common or at least generally shared intention of restricting the right of self-defence to exclude anticipatory action.[31]

---

[22] Malanczuk 1987, pp. 247–248; McDougal and Feliciano 1961, p. 238; McDougal 1963, p. 601; Schwebel 1972, p. 481.

[23] Brownlie 1963, pp. 257–261; Christakis 2005, pp. 201–207; Gray 2004, p. 98.

[24] See *supra* 6.1–6.3.

[25] See *supra* 2.4.4 and 3.1.3. Gentili 1933, Book I, Chap. 14, p. 61; Vattel 1964, Book III, Chap. 3, Section 42, p. 248.

[26] See *supra* 4.7 and 5.4.

[27] See *supra* 6.2 and 6.4.1.

[28] For the expressed intention of some of the US delegates at the San Francisco Conference to limit self-defence to the time after an armed attack occurred, see *supra* 5.3. See also: Franck 2002, p. 50; Ruys 2010, p. 260.

[29] See *supra* 5.3. Minutes of the Forty-eighth meeting (Executive Session) of the United States Delegation, Held at San Francisco, 20 May 1945, in Foreign Relations of the US Foreign Relations of the United States: Diplomatic Papers 1945, vol. 1, p. 818; Minutes of the Thirty-eighth meeting of the United States Delegation, Held at San Francisco, 14 May Foreign Relations of the United States: Diplomatic Papers 1945, in ibid., pp. 707–709.

[30] See *supra* 5.3.

[31] Ibid.

Likewise, the Nuremberg and Tokyo judgments do not seem to confirm the view that Article 51 brought drastic changes to the interpretation of self-defence as a big leap forward in prohibiting the use of force.[32] Certainly, the prohibition in Article 2(4) was a crucial step in outlawing unilateral use of force, but that move did not seem to substantially affect the content of the right of self-defence in the immediate aftermath of the adoption of the Charter. It can thus hardly be maintained—by any side in the temporal debate—that the adoption of Article 51 solved the issue of the temporality of self-defence.

Finally, the status of anticipatory action in post-Charter developments cannot be ascertained only by looking at specific instances of state practice invoking 'anticipatory self-defence'. Episodic references to the *Caroline* incident (for pre-Charter practice) and the Six-Day War (for post-Charter practice) cannot offer a comprehensive view on how the temporal dimension of self-defence has evolved in the last two centuries. General policy moves, implicit definitions in diplomatic correspondence, negotiators' interests, decisions not to resort to force, armed action not carrying an expressed defensive claim as well as condemned and criticized instances of state practice have to be taken into consideration to discern the way the protagonists viewed and are viewing the temporal limits of self-defence. The status of pre- and post-Charter anticipatory action can only be understood if the temporal dimension of the right of self-defence as a whole is analysed. The legal–historical research of Part I has shown that self-defence had both an anticipatory and remedial aspect. The comparative analysis of Part II has shown that sometimes the two dimensions combine as well so that neither of them is void of controversy. The picture that emerges as a result of the corroborated analysis of all these aspects shows the anticipatory dimension of self-defence resurfacing in all the main themes of post-Charter state practice: state-to-state conflicts, conflicts involving WMD as well as conflicts involving non-state actors. At worst, anticipatory action in self-defence is a legal basis for the use of force that can easily be abused as a result of a general lack of regulation of its content in UN practice. At best, anticipatory action in self-defence is a legal basis for the use of force that is acquiring increased relevance in twenty-first century conflicts and, for that reason, needs to be better defined.

References

Abi Saab G (1987) Cours general du droit public. Recueil des Cours 207(VII):9–463
Bowett DW (1958) Self-defense in international law. Manchester University Press, Manchester
Brownlie I (1963) International law and the use of force by states. Clarendon Press, Oxford
Cahier P (1985) Changements et continuité du droit international: cours général de droit international public. Recueil des Cours 195(VI):9–374

---

[32] See *supra* 11.2.1. Summary Record of the 1627th ILC mtg., UN Doc. A/CN.4/SR.1627 (Lachs 1980) para 3 (comment by Tsuruoka).

Christakis T (2005) Existe-t-il un droit de légitime défense en cas de simple "menace"?: une réponse "groupe des personnalités de haut niveau" au de l'ONU. In: Société française pour le droit international, Les métamorphoses de la sécurité collective: droit, pratique et enjeux stratégiques. Pedone, Paris, pp 197–222
Constantinou A (2000) The right of self-defence under customary international law and Article 51 of the United Nations Charter. Sakkoulas, Athens
Corten O (2008) Le droit contre la guerre: l'interdiction du recours à la force en droit international contemporain. Pedone, Paris
Dixon M (2000) Textbook on international law. Blackstone Press, London
Fleck D (1988) Rules of engagement for maritime forces and the limitation of the use of force under the UN Charter. Ger Yearb Int Law 31:165–186
Foreign Relations of the United States: Diplomatic Papers 1945, vol 1: General (1967). US Government Printing Office, Washington, D.C.
Franck T (2002) Recourse to force: state action against threats and armed attacks. Cambridge University Press, Cambridge
Gazzini T (2005) The changing rules on the use of force in international law. Manchester University Press, Manchester
Gentili A (1933) De jure belli libri tres (trans: Rolfe JC). Clarendon Press, Oxford
Gray C (2004) International law and the use of force. Oxford University Press, Oxford
Grotius H (1964) De jure belli ac pacis libri tres (trans: Kelsey FW). Oceana, New York
Henkin L (1995) International law: politics and values. Martinus Nijhoff, Dordrecht
Higgins R (1963) The development of international law through the political organs of the United Nations. Oxford University Press, London
Jessup PC (1948) A modern law of nations: an introduction. Macmillan, New York
Kolesnik DN (1989) The development of the right to self-defence. In: Butler WE (ed) The non-use of force in international law. Nijhoff, Dordrecht, pp 153–159
Kunz J (1947) Individual and collective self-defence in Article 51 of the Charter of the UN. Am J Int Law 41:872–879
Lachs M (1980) The development and general trends of international law in our time. Recueil des Cours 169(IV):9–377
Malanczuk P (1987) Countermeasures and self-defence as circumstances precluding wrongfulness in the International Law Commision's Draft Articles on States Responsibility. In: Spinedi M, Simma B (eds) United Nations Codification of State responsibility. Oceana, New York, pp 197–286
McDougal MS (1963) The Soviet-Cuban quarantine and self-defense. Am J Int Law 57:597–604
McDougal MS, Feliciano FP (1961) Law and minimum world public order: the legal regulation of international coercion. Yale University Press, New Haven
Neff SC (2005) War and the law of nations: general history. Cambridge University Press, Cambrdige
Reichberg GM, Syse H, Begby E (eds) (2006) The ethics of war: classic and contemporary readings. Blackwell, Malden
Ruys T (2010) 'Armed attack' and Article 51 of the UN Charter. Evolutions in customary law and practice. Cambridge University Press, Cambridge
Schachter O (1991) International law in theory and practice. Martinus Nijhoff, Dordrecht
Schwebel SM (1972) Aggression, intervention and self-defence in modern international law. Recueil des Cours 136(II):411–497
Simma B (ed) (1995) The Charter of the United Nations, a commentary. Oxford University Press, Oxford
de Vattel E (1964) The law of nations or the principles of natural law: applied to the conduct and to the affairs of nations and of sovereigns. Oceana, New York
Waldock CHM (1952) The regulation of the use of force by individual states in international law. Recueil Des Cours 81(II):451–517
Wright Q (1963) The Cuban quarantine. Am J Int Law 57:546–565
Zoller E (2004) The law applicable to the preemption doctrine. Am Soc Int Law Proc 98:333–337

Chapter 14
The Limits of Anticipatory Action in Self-Defence

The approach taken by the different opinion groups discussed in Chapters 1, 13 as to the temporal dimension of self-defence elucidated another important question: if anticipatory action in self-defence was legal, could it be exercised against not only an imminent, but also a potential threat? As a consequence, the second main research question explored the limits of anticipatory action in self-defence under customary international law.

In order to identify the temporal limits of self-defence, the legal–historical research conducted in Part I also focused on the elements of self-defence in the three pre-Charter normative frameworks analysed. Accordingly, a recognizable pattern of limits was identified in pre-Charter customary law, which seemed to be valid at the time of the adoption of the Charter. That pattern was tested in Part II, in order to show whether it suffered any significant alterations and whether new factors have emerged affecting the limits of anticipatory action. On this basis, the present chapter will draw conclusions from the findings of Parts I and II as to the limits of anticipatory action in self-defence under customary international law.

14.1 Findings of Part I

Since anticipatory action was an intrinsic part of the natural-law of self-defence, one of the findings of the legal–historical research was that the elements limiting the exercise of the narrow understanding of self-defence were applicable to anticipatory action.[1]

In all the three normative frameworks identified in Part I the same recognizable pattern of elements of self-defence could be contoured. First, self-defence always entailed the conditionality (occurrence or expectation) of an attack. Secondly, this attack (its occurrence or its expectation) had to give rise to an immediate (present and inevitable) need to take action. Thirdly, the exercise of self-defence had to be

[1] See *supra* 6.5.

K. Tibori Szabó, *Anticipatory Action in Self-Defence*, DOI: 10.1007/978-90-6704-796-8_14,

moderate. The first two elements have been found to be intrinsically linked to each other and were therefore treated under the general heading of 'necessity'. The third condition pertained to the modality of the exercise of self-defence and was treated under the heading of 'moderation' or 'proportionality'.

14.2 Findings of Part II

The three elements identified in Part I were employed as 'juridical variables' in the comparative analysis of Part II and were used to assess the various claims of self-defence voiced in state practice. The variables were also employed as the basis for examining the influence of UN organs on the content of self-defence. It was the conclusion of each chapter of the comparative analysis that the three elements—under the headings of necessity and proportionality—continued to contour the content of self-defence and, implicitly, the limits of anticipatory action.

14.3 Parameters of Analysis

On the basis of the combined findings of Parts I and II, Part III will set out the content, applicability and controversies regarding each element of self-defence and will thus demarcate the parameters under which anticipatory action may be lawful. It is essential to note at this point, that in order to demarcate the parameters of anticipatory action, attention will be given to the immediacy element, because it is the one directly pertaining to the temporal dimension of self-defence. Although the other two elements (conditionality of an armed attack and proportionality) are closely connected to immediacy and cannot be examined in an isolated manner, they will receive less attention, because they do not directly pertain to the temporal dimension of self-defence.

In order to analyse the content of each element, distinction has been made between standard-type armed attacks (invasion, large-scale or surgical airstrikes or any armed attack of a considerable scale) and so-called hit-and-run tactics (small-scale and re-occurring gunfire, shelling, explosions, bomb-attacks as well as small, repeated cross-border incidents). As explained in the concluding remarks of Part II, hit-and-run tactics (whether performed by non-state actors or regular forces) have a circular temporal dimension that need specific attention.[2] Furthermore, self-defence against such tactics is significantly more controversial than against standard armed attacks, because it involves the application of the 'accumulation of events' theory.[3] Therefore, the elements of self-defence will first be discussed for armed attack in the standard sense and subsequently, for hit-and-run tactics.

---

[2] See *supra* 12.1 and 12.3.

[3] See *supra* 10.6 and 12.3.

It is important to reiterate at this point, that it is not the purpose of this book to discuss unit self-defence. Nonetheless, this author believes that the armed forces of a country are permitted, under strict conditions, to defend themselves on a unit-to-unit level. For instance, the crew of the *USS Cole* could have issued a warning against the approaching dinghy boat and opened fire on it in case it refused to stop. Likewise, the on the-spot-reaction of the Georgian forces to the shelling on 7 August 2008 was a legitimate act of unit self-defence. Such an act could have been carried out on the exclusive basis of unit self-defence, without any need to trigger *jus ad bellum* questions pertaining to 'national self-defence'.[4] The conditions under which unit self-defence is allowed pertain to the law of military operations and are outside the scope of this research.[5]

14.4 Standard-Type Armed Attacks

As explained above, those claims of self-defence will first receive attention, which have been invoked against standard-type armed attacks. Accordingly, in this section the notion of 'armed attack' will be used to describe the standard-type understanding of the term.

As said above, this category mainly involves acts that have been traditionally understood as armed attacks: invasion, airstrikes, armed attack of large-scale and effect. The instances of state practice involving WMD will also be treated within this category, because the relevant threat in these cases (however remote) was that of an armed attack of significant magnitude. Likewise, instances of state practice where resort to self-defence was contemplated, but not used belong to this category if the threat faced was a large-scale armed attack (however remote). Accordingly, the following conflicts pertain to this part of the analysis: the Sinai Campaign (1956), the Cuban missile crisis (1962), the Six-Day War (1967), the Yom Kippur War (1973), the Iran–Iraq War (1980–1988), the Israeli bombing of the Osirak reactor (1981), the Falklands War (1982), the US war against Iraq (2003) and the South Ossetian War (2008). Additionally, some instances of pre-Charter state practice will also be mentioned for comparison purposes.

14.4.1 Necessity: Conditionality of an Armed Attack and Immediacy

On the basis of the findings of Parts I and II, two intertwined elements of the necessity requirement could be discerned: the conditionality of an armed attack and immediacy.[6]

---

[4] For examples of on the-spot-reaction, see Dinstein 2005, pp. 220–221.

[5] See, for instance, Boddens Hosang 2010, pp. 415–427.

[6] See *supra* 6.4.1 and introductory remarks of Part II.

The *conditionality of an attack* denotes both the occurrence and expectation of an armed attack. As regards the notion of 'armed attack', pre-Charter customary law offered no precise definition. In case of individuals, it was accepted that both the life and property of private persons could be defended.[7] In case of sovereigns, reference was usually made to an 'attack',[8] 'danger'[9] or 'invasion'[10] without laying down the specific conditions. Nonetheless, it was generally understood that, for the narrow understanding of self-defence, such an attack had to involve the use or threat of armed force.[11] Neither was there a common understanding of what such attack had to endanger; the territory, the independence, the government of the state as well as its nationals could all be the objects of such an attack.[12] Article 51 of the Charter employed the term 'armed attack' to describe this condition. Nonetheless, no definition of the term was provided by the drafters.[13] Post-Charter practice has not completely remedied the definitional problems of armed attack. Although it is widely accepted that it involves the most serious forms of threat or use of force, there is no commonly agreed definition of what constitutes armed attack and what does not.[14] Moreover, conflicts involving non-state actors have further complicated the definition of armed attack (as will be shown in Sect. 14.5).

It is beyond the purpose of this research to elaborate on all the questions pertaining to the definition of armed attack. On the basis of the examined instances of state practice, it can nevertheless be maintained that an armed attack usually denotes the most serious forms of the use of force endangering political independence, territorial integrity as well as the security and life of citizens.[15]

Although self-defence was sometimes invoked against injuries not involving the use of force, such claims found no support in state practice. In 1948, Transjordan, Egypt, Syria and Iraq maintained a claim of self-defence against the Jewish declaration of independence.[16] Likewise, in 1956, Israel justified its Sinai Campaign as self-defence against the blocking of the Suez Canal and raids of the

---

[7] Vitoria 1991b, p. 299; Grotius 1964, Book II, Chap. 1 (ii), p. 172.

[8] For instance: Gratian, question II, canon 1, in Reichberg et al. 2006, p. 113; Grotius 1964, Book II, Chap. 1 (iii), p. 172 (attack by violence) and Chap. 2 (xvi), p. 184 (act of violence); June 23 Note, in Miller 1928, pp. 213–214.

[9] Gentili 1933, Book I, Chap. 14, p. 62.

[10] June 23 Note, in Miller 1928, p. 214.

[11] For instance: Suárez 1944, Disputation XIII, Section 1 (6), p. 804; Grotius 1964, Book II, Chap. 1 (v), p. 173; Webster 1841, p. 1138.

[12] The *Caroline* incident and the *Virginius* affair involved private citizens and property (see *supra* 3.2.2.1 and 3.2.2.2). The Japanese invasion of Manchuria and the Italian invasion of Ethiopia endangered the territorial integrity and political independence of the occupied states (see *supra* 4.5.1 and 4.5.2). See also Bowett 1958, p. 5.

[13] See *supra* 5.3.

[14] Constantinou 2000, pp. 63–64, 74–75, 76; Green 2009, pp. 41–42; Lubell 2010, pp. 48–55; Malanczuk 1987, pp. 243–244.

[15] Higgins 1963, pp. 204–205; Gray 2008, pp. 147–148; Schachter 1991, p. 164.

[16] See *supra* 8.2.1; Repertoire, Supp. 1946–1951, Chap. 12, pp. 493–494.

fedayeen supported by Egypt.[17] Neither of the arguments found support as grounds for invoking self-defence. In 1948, the Security Council characterized the actions of the Arab states as a threat to peace under Article 39 of the Charter and demanded the parties concerned to desist from further military action and issue ceasefire orders.[18] Although no condemnatory resolution was adopted on the occasion of the 1956 Sinai Campaign, the general reaction in the Security Council to the endeavours of Israel, Britain and France was highly negative.[19]

Despite the fact that it is widely maintained that 'armed attack' denotes the most serious forms of the use of force, there is little agreement on what exactly such forms entail. Pre-Charter customary law did not limit self-defence to the gravest uses of force. Since the narrow understanding of self-defence was relevant for 'imperfect wars' and measures short of war, it was also admitted that small-scale uses of force could trigger self-defence as well.[20] The *Caroline* incident, for instance, involved self-defence against a small-scale danger posed by rebels and sympathizers of the Canadian insurrection.[21]

In post-Charter state practice, emphasis has been put on the scale of force in trying to point at the threshold of an armed attack.[22] Invasion and large-scale bombardments are generally agreed to constitute armed attacks, whereas smaller scale uses of force are assessed on a case-by-case basis.[23]

In the opinion of the present author, the modality of the use of force (its geographical and temporal scope as well as the employed weapons) coupled with the effect of the force (the impact on the state or society) has to trigger serious consequences in order to denote an armed attack. In case of an armed attack already ongoing, the modality and effect of the force used can be more easily assessed. For instance, the 1950 invasion of South Korea by North Korea not only affected the territorial integrity and the political independence of that state, but also disrupted society and caused great loss of life.[24] When it comes to a threat of an armed attack, it is more problematic, although not impossible, to discern the modality and effect of the expected use of force. In June 1967, Israel expected that the combined attack of Arab states against its territory would not only cause great

---

[17] See *supra* 8.2.1. GAOR, 1st Emergency Special Session, UN Doc. A/PV.562 (1956) paras 105–145.

[18] See *supra* 8.2.1. SC Res. 54 (1948).

[19] See *supra* 8.2.1.

[20] Bowett 1958, p. 5.

[21] See *supra* 3.2.2.1.

[22] Gray 2008, pp. 147–148; McDougal and Feliciano 1961, pp. 238–240. See also *supra* 11.4.1. For an appraisal of the ICJ's position on the required gravity of an armed attack, see Green 2009, pp. 31–42.

[23] On the discussion of the scale and gravity of an armed attack, see, for instance, Gray 2008, pp. 128–133, 147–148; Lubell 2010, pp. 50–51; Schachter 1991, p. 164.

[24] For an elaboration of the history of the Korean war, see Alexandrov 1996, pp. 257–261; Spanier 1959; Stanley 1952; Stueck 1997. For the significance of the 38th parallel as the demarcation line of the two Koreas, see Grey 1951.

casualties, but would also aim at occupying significant parts of the country. Moreover, it was the expressed intention of several Arab officials to bring an end to Israel as an independent state.[25] The modality of the use of force can be discerned, *inter alia*, from the likely target and the scale of the expected airstrikes, the geographic scope of the expected ground offensive or the proximity of population centers to the military targets likely to be hit. The envisaged effect of the use of force has to point at, for instance, a significant loss of civilian life, substantial damage to property and/or a considerable and long-lasting disruption of the functioning of society.

Suffice it to say at this point, that if the combination of the modality of force (to be used) and of the (envisaged) effect leads to grave consequences, the first element of necessity should be seen as met.

The second element of necessity can be described as *immediacy* and flows from the dangers posed by the conditionality of the armed attack. Simply put, because of the modality of the force (to be) used and the (envisaged) effect, an immediate need for action is created.

Webster's famous formula suggests the same conclusion. He referred to a 'necessity of self-defence, instant, overwhelming, leaving no choice of means, and no moment for deliberation.'[26] Although his formula very colourfully describes the immediate need for action that (the threat of) an armed attack might create, another, simpler phrase used by him describes immediacy in the best terms. Accordingly, Webster contended that the actions of the British government had to stem from a necessity, 'present and inevitable'.[27]

These two adjectives, present and inevitable, describe very well what the immediacy factor is about. First, the need for action must be 'present' in the sense that a state of emergency is created in which measures must be taken. In the standard Webster-formula, the phrase of 'no moment for deliberation' is the equivalent. As evidenced by the examination of state practice in various chapters of Part II, this author has given preference to the term 'present', because it more reasonably describes the state of emergency created. While 'no moment for deliberation' poses the danger of being literally interpreted, the term 'present' describes an actual, real emergency, which nevertheless gives room for last-minute military preparations or talks with allies.[28]

Secondly, the emergency situation has to be 'inevitable'. In the Webster-formula, the phrase 'leaving no choice of means' is the corresponding description. As evidenced by the presentation of state practice in Part II, this author has given preference to the term 'inevitable', because it is a more realistic description of the unavoidability of the danger faced.

---

[25] See *supra* 8.2.2. Statement of Mr. Eban (Israel), SCOR, 22nd Session, 1348th meeting, UN Doc. S/PV.1348(OR) (6 June 1967) para 150; Wright 1968, p. 9.

[26] Webster 1841, p. 1138.

[27] Ibid.

[28] Gill 2007, p. 153; Jessup 1948, p. 164; Lubell 2010, p. 44.

The two features—present and inevitable—form the immediacy factor. Both of them are needed to have an immediate need for action. If the need to act is not present, then there will probably be no way of knowing whether the danger is inevitable. For example, in 1981, Israel carried out airstrikes against an Iraqi nuclear reactor believing that if that reactor produced a nuclear bomb, Saddam Hussein would not shy away from using it. Even if one accepts that that was a legitimate fear based on adequate information, the reactor was four years away from producing a crude nuclear device. The need to act was not present and, for that reason, there was no way of knowing that within those four years other choice of means would have not presented themselves. Hindsight is immaterial in assessing whether the immediacy element was present at the time of the action.[29] Conversely, if the need to act is present, but the danger can be avoided by alternative means (such as negotiations), claims of self-defence cannot be justified.

After this succinct general presentation of the immediacy factor, its application to the remedial and anticipatory dimensions of self-defence will be examined. Accordingly, distinction will be made between claims of self-defence against imminent, ongoing and already occurred armed attacks.

14.4.1.1 Precluding an Armed Attack from Occurring

As Ago asserted, the objective of self-defence was to preclude 'another's wrongful action from proceeding, succeeding and achieving its purpose.[30]'

Precluding an armed attack from proceeding or occurring entails the existence of an imminent threat of armed attack. In other words, the threat has to be inevitable and present. Thus when it comes to self-defence against an imminent threat, the immediacy factor takes the form of imminence, but its two underlying features (presence and inevitability) remain unchanged. Accordingly, in order to render a threat imminent, it must be shown that it could not be neutralised in any other way than force. More specifically, the defending state must demonstrate that the attack could not have been precluded by non-forceful means, such as negotiations, mediation or fulfilment of certain legitimate and reasonable requests. For instance, if the Johnson administration had succeeded in securing the reopening of the Straits of Tiran and further diplomatic talks had ensued, the inevitability of the Arab attack would have probably not seemed as obvious as it did before the Six-Day War.[31]

Furthermore, the defending state has to show that the elapse of time would have not ameliorated the situation and that there was an urgent need to act. The difficulty in proving the emergency of the situation was one of the reasons why Israel chose not to act pre-emptively in the face of the Yom Kippur War.[32]

---

[29] See *supra* 9.3. Gill 2007, p. 141.

[30] Ago 1980, p. 54.

[31] See *supra* 8.2.2.

[32] See *supra* 8.2.3. Mueller et al. 2006, p. 207.

The urgent and inevitable need to preclude the commencement of an attack can also be deduced from an escalation of events that renders any non-forcible solution inadequate, as it happened in the Six-Day War.[33] A general background of hostility is not sufficient to render a threat imminent. Hostile, but non-forceful measures aimed at disrupting the normal functioning of society—as serious as they may be—cannot, in themselves, show an escalation that renders an attack imminent. For instance, the blocking of naval passage (as it happened before the Sinai Campaign), non-compliance with bilateral or multilateral agreements affecting the free movement of persons and goods between the two states, the overt or covert development of weapons of mass destruction, unfriendly statements made by public officials, etc. cannot be construed, in themselves, to show the imminence of an attack. They can, however, add to the escalation of events if they are coupled with specific military measures that show a clear preparedness to resort to force. Not all military measures show such preparedness. Military exercises, by themselves, should not amount to an imminent threat. Likewise, the testing of missile-firing capability, *per se*, cannot be evidence of an imminent attack. There has to be a corroboration of forceful (and non-forceful) hostile measures that gradually increase the tension. If a state regularly tests its missile-firing capacity, while it continuously expresses its enmity towards another state, the escalation of events is not necessarily present. But if that same state suddenly increases the number of missile tests, issues an ultimatum for the fulfilment of certain requests and refuses to negotiate the demands, the conditions for rendering an attack imminent might be present. Nonetheless, there has to be information (from autochthonous or third-party intelligence) as to the range, possible target, guidance system and imperceptibility of the expected missile attack. If the missile can be intercepted after its launch, then anticipatory action is not necessary. If, because of the type of the missile, the absence of a missile defence system or the proximity between the launching site and the target, the interception of an already launched missile would be impossible, the option of anticipatory action can be judiciously considered. Even so, the targeted state must assure itself that the attack is not only imminent, but also inevitable. In this scenario, it has to consider whether the demands are legitimate and whether it is reasonable to fulfil them. Not fulfilling legitimate demands will not render the missile attack lawful, but will affect the legality of anticipatory action in self-defence, because not all non-forceful options had been previously explored. Further, the targeted state has to make sure that no third state or international organization is capable to diffuse the tension, bring the parties to the negotiation table or apply political pressure on the threatening state. Certainly, the factual circumstances have to be interpreted on a case-by-case basis. Abstract conditions or generic examples—as the one mentioned above—cannot be used as universal models for anticipatory action against imminent threats.

The targeted state does not have to demonstrate the incidence of these conditions to third parties prior to the exercise of self-defence, but it has to be

[33] Ibid.

convinced, on the basis of the available information, that an attack is imminent (see Sect. 14.6).

14.4.1.2 Precluding an Armed Attack from Achieving its Purpose

Full-scale invasions lead to situations in which defence is exercised against an ongoing armed attack that has not yet reached its purpose. Such an instance was the Iran–Iraq War.[34] The armed attack materialised in the form of a full-scale invasion in the sense of classic, state-to-state warfare, which allowed armed forces of the belligerent states to clash over a protracted amount of time. Such an attack forms the quintessential example of Article 51 measures of self-defence.[35]

As with claims of self-defence against imminent threats, the immediacy factor has to be shown through the existence of a present and inevitable need to act. In cases of ongoing invasions, the immediacy factor is met in a very apparent way.[36] If the armed forces of an attacking state are engaged in large-scale operations against those of the defending state, the fact that an armed attack is underway and that immediate action is needed is more than obvious. Therefore, the requirement of objectively demonstrating a present and inevitable need to act is more easily met than in cases of imminent threats.[37]

Some authors have distinguished between cases where there is an ongoing armed attack and where an armed attack has already commenced, but has not reached its purpose. The proponents of this division assert that attacks in progress, but which have not yet crossed an international border or have not yet reached the target, render the exercise of self-defence legal under Article 51, as opposed to anticipatory action against an imminent attack.[38] This author is not convinced of the utility of this division. If an armed attack has already begun, in whatever incipient form it may be, the defending state is faced with an ongoing attack, regardless of the fact that the target has not yet been hit. Dinstein discusses different scenarios of the US intercepting the Japanese fleet before the attack on Pearl Harbour.[39] In his opinion, the US would have been allowed to shoot down the Japanese aircraft after launching from the carriers and would have also been permitted to attacked the Japanese fleet on its way to the operation zone, if it possessed conclusive evidence as to its mission.[40] The US could have not, in

---

34 See *supra* 8.3.1.

35 Ibid. SC Res. 83 (1950); UN Doc. S/23273 (1991) para 6.

36 Schmitt 2003, p. 530.

37 Schachter 1991, p. 152.

38 Dinstein 2005, pp. 190–192; Gazzini 2005, pp. 151–3. See also: Abi Saab 1987, p. 371; Christakis 2005, pp. 211–212; Constantinou 2000, pp. 125–126; Corten 2008, pp. 626–627; Kolb 2004, pp. 123–125; Lachs 1980, p. 164; Ruys 2010, p. 266.

39 Dinstein 2005, pp. 190–191.

40 Ibid.

Dinstein's view, attack the Japanese fleet before it sailed and while it was still training or preparing for the mission, because the attack had not yet commenced.[41] The example used by Dinstein raises the question of when an armed attack actually begins. Is the act of setting sail the beginning or is the launching of the aircraft the decisive moment? In the opinion of this author, the US would have been allowed to attack the Japanese fleet before it sailed, if US intelligence was in possession of conclusive evidence as to the Japanese mission and if a successful neutralization of the fleet while at sea was not feasible. Certainly, the operation could have been called off while the fleet was still training. Nonetheless, as Dinstein acknowledged, the mission could have been aborted also after the fleet set sail or the aircraft was launched.[42]

Undoubtedly, when there is a considerable geographical and temporal disparity between source and target, discussing various instances of interception of an already commenced attack is unproblematic. Indeed, if time and space allows interception of an attack that has already started, but has not yet struck the target, such an option should be favoured against anticipatory action. Nonetheless, such an alternative might not always be present. Those authors who distinguish between interceptive and other forms of self-defence adduce the example of the launched missile or aircraft that has not yet hit the target.[43] While it is indeed more prudent, from a legal point of view, to intercept an already launched missile as opposed to pre-emptively destroying the launching site that option might not always be available. Temporal and geographic proximity, the type of the missile and the capabilities of the existing missile defence system can render that alternative impracticable. In such cases, the appropriateness of anticipatory action, under all required conditions, can be explored.

In conclusion, since 'interceptive self-defence' relates to those instances where an armed attack has already commenced, this author does not see the utility of distinguishing between that situation and one in which there is an ongoing invasion. As soon as an armed attack is commenced, the remedial dimension of self-defence is activated and a state has the right to defend itself, although the attack has not yet achieved its purpose.

14.4.1.3 Precluding an Armed Attack from Maintaining its Purpose

In some cases, an armed attack reaches its purpose before the defending state has a chance to riposte. The Falklands War was such an instance.[44] It has been maintained that in such cases, claims of self-defence could not be upheld, because the attack that would have given rise to a defensive action was already finished.[45]

41 Ibid., p. 191.

42 Ibid., pp. 190–191.

43 Gazzini 2005, pp. 151–153; Ruys 2010, pp. 253; Singh 1956, pp. 24–26.

44 See *supra* 8.3.2.

45 Badr 1980, p. 25.

Such a view stems from a literal transposition of the self-defence permitted under criminal law to the domain of public international law. Indeed, the natural-law concept of private self-defence (pertaining to individuals) allowed a strike after the first attack only if a second assault was expected.[46] Simply put, if a person is punched by someone and the attacker leaves the scene immediately, the victim is not entitled to run after him or her to punch them back. Instead, the victim would have to rely on law enforcement and file a complaint against the aggressor. Conversely, if after receiving the first blow it becomes evident that the attacker wants to continue the assault, the victim would be allowed to fight back to ward off the danger upon him. These scenarios cannot be literally transposed to inter-state relations. There is no police force in the legal domestic sense on which a state could rely when it becomes the victim of an armed attack. As Gill explained, the international legal order is characterized by a degree of decentralization and horizontalism which radically differs from a stable domestic legal order.[47]

Consequently, it would be unreasonable to maintain that a state was not allowed to defend itself in cases where the armed attack has already achieved its purpose. Undoubtedly, such a liberty could not extend endlessly after the armed attack. As Schachter warned, without a limitation 'self-defence would sanction armed attacks for countless prior acts of aggression and conquest.'[48] To avoid such abuses, Schachter suggested that a response had to be made close in time to the attack.[49] While it is unquestionably true that the immediacy factor has its temporal confines, the better view would be to rely on the emergency and inevitability of the danger rather than on physical temporal limits.

In other words, although the armed attack has already achieved its purpose, it has to be apparent that preparations to repel the armed attack had been started as soon as information about the attack became available. That would show that the target state found itself in a present and inevitable need to act, but preparations for the defensive action took more time than the attack itself.

Accordingly, the naval forces of the UK engaged in battle with the Argentinean forces four weeks after the Junta regime accomplished the occupation of the Falklands Islands in the South Atlantic.[50] Nonetheless, even before the Argentinean invasion took place, the British ordered the deployment of several warships to the South Atlantic from either Gibraltar or from home ports. Furthermore, on the very day of the attack, the British cabinet met up in an emergency session and decided to send a task force to liberate the Islands.[51] Accordingly, after three days of hasty preparations, further ships of the task force pulled out of ports around

---

[46] See *supra* 6.2.

[47] Gill 2007, p. 152.

[48] Schachter 1985, p. 292.

[49] Schachter 1985, p. 292.

[50] See *supra* 8.3.2.

[51] Freedman and Gamba-Stonehouse 1991, p. 122.

Britain and from Gibraltar.[52] The geographical disparity between the departure points (home ports or Gibraltar) and the target (South Atlantic) as well as the minimal time needed for assembling a considerable amphibious task force are factors that cannot be ignored when considering the justifiability and timeliness of the British defensive action.

The Persian Gulf War serves as an alternative example. *Operation Desert Storm* started after Iraqi troops had completed the invasion and occupation of Kuwait.[53] Apart from the fact that it only took a few days for the Iraqi forces to occupy Kuwait, the fact that the Security Council and coalition states were attempting to find a non-forceful solution to the conflict is also important.[54]

In both cases the immediacy factor was present. The armed attacks created an emergency situation which could only be avoided by the use of force. Neither the UK nor Kuwait (and its allies) were, however, in position to respond immediately. Nonetheless, last-minute attempts of negotiations and rapid military preparations had been started as soon as the conflict erupted. Accordingly, as long as the immediacy factor—in the form of a present and inevitable need to act—is present, states are allowed to exercise self-defence even though the armed attack has already achieved its purpose. A contrary position would lead to the very undesirable consequence of not being allowed to oust invading forces from a country.

Moreover, as Gill warned, such a restrictive view would favour the more powerful states, always in a position to respond immediately, whereas the less powerful ones would be barred from defending themselves.[55]

Certainly, demonstrating the present and inevitable need to act would have the same importance in these cases as in the instances involving imminent threats. Accordingly, a state would have to prove that it resorted to remedial action in self-defence, because it found that no other solution was available. On the basis of the combined objective and subjective criteria, the state would have to show that the information available interpreted in good faith led to no other conclusion than that armed action was necessary to overturn the purpose of the armed attack.

14.4.1.4 Immediacy and Time

As shown above, the immediacy factor pertains to a present and inevitable need to act in both anticipatory and remedial actions in self-defence. A present and inevitable need to act will always have to be identified on the basis of the factual circumstances of each case. They can relate to several aspects: the military strength of the attacking and defending states, the (envisaged) scale and effect of

---

[52] Ibid., p. 128.

[53] For a portrayal of the conflict see Khadduri and Ghareeb 1997.

[54] SCOR, 45th Session, 2932nd meeting, UN Doc. S/PV.2932 (2 August 1990) pp. 8, 11; SC Res. 660 (1990) paras 1 and 2; SC Res. 661 (1990) para 3.

[55] Gill 2007, pp. 153–154.

an attack or of a threat thereof, the availability of non-forceful solutions, the openness of allies to come to the assistance of the victim state, the approach of the Security Council to the issue, the underlying historical and political conditions and the like. The discussed instances of state practice offer sufficient examples—precedents—of factors that can render the immediacy element present or absent. On the basis of this multitude of factors, in most cases it will be possible to discern whether there was a present and inevitable need to act. There is no need to link immediacy to a given time span measurable in days or weeks. Obviously, in some cases the time span would play an important role. For instance, the Osirak reactor was four years away from producing a crude nuclear device when it was destroyed by Israel. In that case, the four-year time span did play a role in rendering the Israeli claim of self-defence untenable. Nonetheless, in general terms, immediacy should not denote an obligation on the part of a state to take action within a given, physically defined time limit. Measuring immediacy in days or weeks would shift the emphasis away from the most essential question: whether the need to act was in truth present and inevitable. That conclusion can be more efficiently drawn from quality-based factors (as those listed above), rather than quantity-oriented considerations (how many days did it take the British task force to reach the South Atlantic).

This preference for given time limits also stems from the literal transposition of the rationale and content of private self-defence (for individuals) to the realities of inter-state warfare. As explained above, that transposition is untenable because of the radically different nature of the international legal order.

14.4.2 Proportionality

The analysis of both pre-Charter and post-Charter customary law showed the continuity of the proportionality requirement for self-defence. Pre-Charter customary law acknowledged the principle of moderation, on the basis of which one could not exceed the force needed to ward off an attack.[56] That requirement was also reiterated by Webster, when he called upon the British government to show that its forces 'did nothing unreasonable and excessive'[57] in their operation against the *Caroline*. Although Article 51 does not mention proportionality, the analysis of subsequent state practice shows the continued applicability of the principle.[58]

It is beyond the purpose of this research to address all the questions pertaining to the proportionality principle. Nonetheless, some comments will be made provided that they are necessary for depicting the anticipatory and remedial dimensions of self-defence. For that purpose, it can be maintained that proportionality is

[56] See *supra* 6.4.2.

[57] Webster 1841, p. 1138.

[58] See *supra* 8.5, 9.6 and 10.6.

generally understood to limit the use of force in self-defence—both quantitatively and qualitatively—to what is required to ward off an attack.[59]

The quantitative element of proportionality refers to the relationship between the scale of the armed attack suffered and that of the defensive action. The qualitative element concerns the use of force needed to ward off the armed attack. The two elements work together. The quantitative element focuses on the scale of the armed attack (or the threat thereof) and thus indicates the danger created by it. By understanding the existing danger, the qualitative element helps to assess the use of force needed to ward it off.

At times, the quantitative element was given more emphasis by suggesting that proportionality had to be measured primarily against the expected or suffered attack.[60] The approach adopted by the ICJ in the *Oil Platforms* case seemed to suggest the same interpretation.[61] Many commentators have, however, asserted that proportionality needed to be weighed against the use of force required to preclude an attack from occurring, achieving or maintaining its purpose.[62]

Both the quantitative and qualitative elements are important when it comes to proportionality, although the qualitative one is the more relevant in deciding the extent of the force needed in the exercise of self-defence. The rationale of proportionality is best understood in case of an anticipatory action in self-defence. For example, if a state was facing an imminent threat of an amphibious invasion, the proportionate pre-emptive action would not necessarily mean carrying out an amphibious counter-attack against the threatening state. Such an action would be 'proportionate' in a purely quantitative sense of the word. Nonetheless, the imminent threat might be better avoided if the pre-empting state carried out surgical airstrikes against the crucial home ports or on the sailing fleet of the threatening state, rendering it incapable to land its troops. That action would be proportionate to the use of force needed to preclude the attack from taking place.

Likewise, in the instances where self-defence is exercised against an ongoing armed attack or one that has already occurred, proportionality should pertain to the use of force needed to stop the armed attack or overturn its achieved purpose.

The following section will examine the content of all three elements in cases where self-defence is invoked against hit-and-run tactics. Many conclusions relevant to standard-type armed attacks will be relied upon in the subsequent paragraphs.

[59] Ibid. See also *supra* 6.4.2.

[60] Higgins 1963, p. 201; Schachter 1991, p. 153.

[61] Oil Platforms 2003, para 77. See *supra* 11.4.3.

[62] Ago 1980, pp. 69, para 121; Dinstein 1992, p. 57; Gardam 1993, p. 404; Gardam 2004, pp. 156–159; Gray 2004, p. 121; McDougal and Feliciano 1961, pp. 242–243; Schmitt 2003, p. 532; Waldock 1952, p. 464. See also *supra* 8.14.

14.5 Hit-and-Run Tactics and the Limits of Self-Defence

When it comes to hit-and-run tactics, the temporal dimension of self-defence is circular: the same defensive action is both remedial (against a string of past attacks) and anticipatory (against future attacks). The circularity stems from the 'accumulation of events' theory: the incidence of future attacks is expected because of the occurrence of past attacks.

Hit-and-run tactics are most often employed by non-state actors, thus all the instances described in Chapter 10 are relevant for the present analysis. At times, regular forces also resort to such acts, as evidenced by some of the cases examined in Chapter 8: the UK bombing of a Yemeni fort (1964); the Gulf of Tonkin incident (1964); the US bombing of Libya (1986); and the US airstrikes against the headquarters of the Iraqi intelligence service (1993). In these four cases, the governments claiming self-defence resorted to the use of force as a result of a string of past attacks directed against the territory under their control as well as against their armed forces and citizens.[63] When referring to such acts, apart from the 'hit-and-run tactics' denomination, 'terrorist acts' will also be used, in the sense explained in Sect. 10.4.

Claims of self-defence against hit-and-run acts have been made in a particular fashion. The approach came to be known as the 'accumulation of events' theory or the 'needle-prick', or 'pinprick' approach.[64] The theory has several elements. First, there has to be a number of prior attacks, which, in their totality, amount to an armed attack.[65] These acts, taken individually, need not be of increased gravity; it is enough if their totality results in great harm.[66] Secondly, these attacks have to emanate from an identifiable source, usually an armed group sent, supported or tolerated by another state.[67] It is implicitly understood that the link between the armed group and the sending, sponsoring or harbouring state has to be established and evidence has to be brought that that state is either incapable or unwilling to tackle the problem.[68] Thirdly, the repeated nature of attacks has to create the conviction that more would follow in order to achieve the objective of the armed group.[69] On this basis, the targeted state is allowed to invoke self-defence to repel future attacks that are expected because of the reoccurrence of past attacks.[70] Lastly, the proportionality of the use of armed force by the targeted state is to be

---

[63] See *supra* 8.4.1–8.4.4.

[64] Bowett 1972, p. 12; Blum 1976, pp. 233; Gross 1983, p. 478; Schachter 1985, p. 293; Baker 1987, p. 42; Jacobson 1998, pp. 13, 16.

[65] Brownlie 1963, p. 279; Gross 1983, p. 478; Greenwood 1987, p. 954; Schachter 1985, p. 293.

[66] Blum 1976, p. 233; Gross 1983, p. 478; Greenwood 1987, p. 954; Schachter 1985, p. 293.

[67] Blum 1976, p. 233; Greenwood 1987, p. 954; Gross 1983, p. 478; Schachter1985, p. 293.

[68] Blum 1976, p. 233.

[69] Greenwood 1987, p. 954; Schachter 1985, p. 293.

[70] Blum 1976, p. 233; Greenwood 1987, p. 954; Gross 1983, p. 478; Higgins 1963, p. 201; Schachter 1985, p. 293.

weighed against the totality of past and future attacks and not against isolated incidents.[71]

As with the analysis of standard-type armed attacks, the immediacy element of self-defence will be given the most attention. For that reason, questions pertaining to the third element of the 'accumulation of events' theory will be examined most thoroughly. For the sake of a comprehensive representation, however, some attention will be given to the other elements as well.

14.5.1 Necessity: Collective Conditionality of Attacks and Immediacy

As many times reiterated above, the principle of necessity entails two intertwined elements: the conditionality of an armed attack and immediacy. Because of the complex nature of the 'accumulation of events' theory, the conditionality of the attack and immediacy are even more entangled in claims of self-defence against hit-and-run tactics than in those against standard-type armed attacks.

Regarding the *conditionality of an armed attack*, several difficulties can be discerned. One of them concerns the authorship of the attack. For long, the Security Council and a part of the legal doctrine condemned or criticized claims of self-defence against non-state actors and thus rejected the 'needle-prick' approach as well.[72] This was in spite of the fact that pre-Charter customary law offered several examples of self-defence being invoked against non-state actors. Such a case was none else but the *Caroline* incident itself.[73] In the immediate aftermath of the 9/11 attacks, the Security Council expressly acknowledged the right to resort to self-defence against terrorist acts.[74] With that acknowledgement, the members of the Security Council also implicitly admitted that armed attacks could be carried out by non-state actors as well.[75] The notion of armed attack thus partly 'returned' to its pre-Charter meaning, in the sense that non-state actors were again accepted as potential authors of an armed attack.

The question of the authorship of armed attack also involves the issue of sponsoring and harbouring states. It is beyond the purpose of this research to dwell into the questions concerning the responsibility of states for the acts of irregular groups that they support or harbour. For the purpose of the present analysis, it is asserted that the sending of armed groups by or on the behalf of a state to carry out attacks against another state is considered as amounting to an armed attack, in line

---

[71] Blum 1976, p. 235; Gross 1983, pp. 486–487; Schachter 1985, p. 293.

[72] See *supra* 10.2 and 10.3. For a critical opinion on the 'accumulation of events' theory, see Lubell 2010, pp. 51–54.

[73] See *supra* 3.2.2.1 and 6.4.1. See also Kelly 2005, p. 225.

[74] SC Res. 1368 (2001) preamble.

[75] Franck 2002, pp. 54, 66–67.

with the view expressed in the *Nicaragua* case.[76] Furthermore, exercising overall control on such groups is also considered as potentially amounting to an armed attack.[77] Lastly, unwillingness or inability to prevent the use of its territory by irregular groups are seen as essential factors in rendering the harbouring or sponsoring state responsible for the activities of such groups.[78]

All other questions pertaining to the necessity requirement of self-defence against hit-and-run tactics directly or indirectly involve the *immediacy* element. For that reason, the specificities of the relationship between necessity and the 'accumulation of events' theory will be treated without a strict differentiation between the conditionality of armed attack and immediacy.

While it is accepted by the Security Council and a significant part of the legal literature that a single terrorist act, because of its scale and effect, can amount to an armed attack, it is widely debated under what conditions can a string of less serious attacks reach the same threshold.[79]

When a series of past attacks, taken individually, do not amount to an armed attack, the claim of self-defence becomes more complicated. Relevant state practice shows that repeated attacks are carried out on the territory of another state or against its citizens on the basis of a specific political agenda.[80] In recent times, that political agenda is being clearly expressed through video recordings or internet sites.[81] Notwithstanding this, a significant amount of information regarding the activities of the armed groups is not readily available. Although their political agenda, target group and/or operation zone is often known, the approximate time and place of their next attack is extremely difficult to ascertain. For that reason, the burden of proof pertaining to the immediacy of the danger has to be interpreted differently. In case of an imminent threat of a standard-type armed

---

[76] Nicaragua 1986, para 195.

[77] The ICJ stopped short of qualifying support of irregulars as basis for enquiring responsibility for the armed attack. Nicaragua 1986, p. 103, para 195. This view was criticized by Judge Jennings in his dissenting opinion. Ibid., p. 543. For an elaboration of the Court's contentions and Judge Jenning's opinion, see *supra* 11.4.1. See also Prosecutor v. Dusko Tadić 1999, paras 131, 137. The Appeal Chamber found that overall control by the state over organized and hierarchically structured groups was sufficient to deduce state responsibility. Such 'overall control' resided not only in equipping, financing or training and providing operational support to the group, but also in coordinating or helping in the general planning of its military or paramilitary activity. See also: Ducheine 2008, pp. 184–188. For the difficulties of transposing norms of attribution from one international law field to another, see: Nollkaemper 2005, pp. 140–141.

[78] Similar opinions: Feinstein 2002, p. 279; Greenwood 2003, p. 25; Schachter 1991, p. 165.

[79] The fact that a single terrorist attack can amount to an armed attack was implicitly admitted by the Security Council in the preamble of Res. 1368 (2001) when it acknowledged the right of self-defence against terrorist attacks. Several authors agree with this view: Beard 2002, pp. 574–575; Brown 2003, pp. 24–25; Feinstein 2002, p. 279; Franck 2001, p. 840; Franck 2002, p. 54; Gill 2003, p. 30; Greenwood 2003, p. 16.

[80] Gunaratna 2004b, pp. 10–13. See also Schachter 1991, pp. 167–168.

[81] Gunaratna 2005, pp. 14–16.

attack, the defending state needs to demonstrate that, on the basis of the available information interpreted in good faith, the attack cannot be avoided by non-forceful means and the emergency of the threat requires swift action. That burden of proof entails an approximate knowledge of the specific parameters of the attack.

The same logic cannot be applied to terrorist acts, because of the clandestinity surrounding their activities.[82] For that reason, certain additional considerations have to play a role in deciding whether a claim of self-defence could be justified. According to the 'accumulation of events' theory, a string of past attacks has to occur in order to expect new attacks from the same source.[83] Accordingly, a series of auxiliary factors can be discerned.

First, as mentioned above, there has to be evidence of a clear political agenda. For instance, the political agenda of Al-Qaeda includes the ending of Western (US) influence in the Middle East as well as the ousting of US forces from Afghanistan and Iraq.[84] Secondly, the political agenda has to be 'active', in the sense that there has to be a string of past attacks carried out on its basis. In the case of Al-Qaeda, the 1993 WTC bombing, the East Africa bombings, the attack on the *USS Cole* and 9/11 were all part of a series of attacks on Western targets. If the political agenda has thus been 'put in practice', it is reasonable to conclude that, without a drastic change in circumstances, future attacks will occur as well.[85]

More specifically, if the hit-and-run tactics form a certain pattern (specific region and/or specific targets), it can again be reasonably concluded that the pattern will continue. If armed groups are particularly active in a certain part of a country, where they sporadically carry out attacks against civilians, soldiers or specific facilities, it can be expected that that pattern will continue. For instance, relevant state practice has shown that Palestinian armed groups several times shelled settlements in the northern part of Israel.[86] Furthermore, if an armed group repeatedly carries out attacks against the citizens of a certain country, regardless of their whereabouts, it can be reasonably concluded that such attacks will continue. This was the case with Libya in the 1980s, when Qaddafi had an expressed political agenda of fighting the US 'on a hundred fronts.[87]' Likewise, the 1993 assassination attempt against former President George Bush was believed to be only one instance of a string of future attempts by Iraqi authorities to murder US officials.[88] Similarly, the political agenda of Al-Qaeda undoubtedly includes past

[82] On the interplay between secrecy and intelligence, see Gunaratna 2005, pp. 22–24.

[83] Blum 1976, p. 233; Greenwood 1987, p. 954; Gross 1983, p. 478; Higgins 1963, p. 201; Schachter 1985, p. 293.

[84] Atwan 2006, pp. 225–226.

[85] Brownlie points at a 'co-ordinated and general campaign'. Brownlie 1963, p. 279. Schachter refers to a 'pattern of terrorist attacks' that entail a 'series of attacks accompanied by bellicose statements' and that are convincing indications that future attacks will occur. Schachter 1991, p. 167. Schmitt points at an 'ongoing campaign of terror.' Schmitt 2003, p. 547.

[86] See *supra* 10.2, 10.3 and 10.5.6.

[87] See *supra* 8.4.3. Greenwood 1987, p. 934; Intoccia 1987, pp. 181–182.

[88] See *supra* 8.4.4. UN Doc. S/26003 (1993); Franck 2002, p. 94.

and future attacks against US and other Western citizens.[89] In most of these cases, the expressed political agenda of the armed group will shed light on their motivation and general objectives.

An 'active' political agenda thus identified will highlight the dangers posed by all past attacks (taken collectively) and also by the reoccurrence of such attacks. This greater picture will then have to be used to assess whether the danger posed by the armed group (or, as with Libya in the 1980s, by a state) creates a present and inevitable need to resort to armed force in self-defence. Needless to say, such an assessment will have to be made in good faith on the basis of all available information.[90]

As explained above, both the modality of the force (to be) used and the (envisaged) effect have to be taken into consideration when assessing an armed attack.[91] In the case of hit-and-run tactics the *modality* of the use of force is seldom substantial. The 19 hijackers of 9/11 carried only knives upon them and still managed to crash four planes. Therefore, the (envisaged) *effect* of hit-and-run acts will usually be more important than the modality of the force they used. The effect of the 9/11 was comparable with a large-scale bombardment: thousands of dead and financial losses measured in billions.[92]

Consequently, in assessing the significance of terrorist attacks, the overall effect that such attacks are creating must be given specific attention. If a string of (small-scale) attacks carried out over a period of time results in considerable casualties or damages, disrupts public order, public security or the normal functioning of a society or renders certain regions uninhabitable, use of force in self-defence can be analysed as an option. Undoubtedly, the effect of such attacks is not the only factor that needs to be taken into consideration. The inevitability element of immediacy is particularly important in this case. After establishing that the series of hit-and-run acts have a significantly disrupting effect, the concerned government will have to assess whether there is any non-forceful solution to the problem. Most importantly, it will have to assess whether measures of law enforcement are available and whether negotiations or mediation with the host state(s) would lead to any acceptable result.

Consequently, the obligations of the state on the basis of both the 'accumulation of events' theory and the requirement of necessity pertain to three points. First, it has to make clear that the political agenda of the armed group (or state, in some cases) is directed against its territory or its citizens and it has been 'activated' by a string of past attacks. Secondly, it has to show that the cumulative effect of the

89 Atwan 2006, pp. 225–226.

90 On the challenges faced by intelligence work and investigation for identifying terrorist threats, see Borum 2005, pp. 65–67.

91 See *supra* 14.4.2.

92 2010 9/11 by numbers. New York Magazine.

attacks causes serious disruptions to public security or the normal functioning of society. Thirdly, it has to demonstrate that the members of the armed group cannot be apprehended (by its own or third-party forces), no other non-forceful measures are practicable and, consequently, there is a present and inevitable need to resort to armed action.

Perhaps even more prominently than in the case of standard-type armed attacks, the futility of applying a physical time limit to immediacy is obvious when it comes to hit-and-run tactics. In this case, the temporal dimension of self-defence is all-encompassing and circular. Self-defence against hit-and-run tactics is both remedial and anticipatory. Moreover, the relevant conflict may encompass a string of attacks protracted over a significant period of time. For instance, the 1993 WTC bombing, the 1998 East Africa bombings, the 2000 attack on *USS Cole* and the 9/11 attacks were all said to be part of the same string of acts pertaining to Al-Qaeda's political agenda.[93] Measuring immediacy in days or weeks is therefore counterproductive in such cases. Instead, attention has to be given to the factual circumstances of each conflict: how powerful the armed group is; what is the effect of its attacks on security and society; what are the objectives they are trying to reach; what are the possible non-forceful solutions; can international law enforcement cooperation offer an efficient alternative, etc. Focusing on such considerations would shed light on whether armed action in self-defence in truth stems from a present and inevitable need to act.

14.5.2 Proportionality

As reiterated above, proportionality is generally understood to limit the use of force in self-defence to what is required to ward off an attack.[94] According to the 'accumulation of events' theory, proportionality has to be measured against the need to neutralize the source of all past and future attacks.[95]

The proportionality issue has given rise to countless controversies in relation to claims of self-defence against non-state actors (and hit-and-run tactics in general).[96] For long, most members of the Security Council were reluctant to accept that the proportionality of the defensive steps had to be measured against the

---

93 Greenwood 2003, p. 23; Schmitt 2003, pp. 535–536.

94 See *supra* 6.4.2, 8.5, 9.6 and 10.6.

95 Blum 1976, p. 235; Gross 1983, pp. 486–487; Schachter 1985, p. 293.

96 SCOR, 24th Session, 1468th meeting, UN Doc. S/PV.1468 (28 March 1969) paras 18–19 (Finland expressing concern about the loss of civilian life), 34 (France expressing doubt as to the proportionality of the Israeli action); SCOR, 27th Session, 1650th meeting, UN Doc. S/PV.1560 (26 June 1972) para 93 (Belgium claiming that Art. 51 allows self-defence only against a single case of armed aggression); SCOR, 30th Session, 1860th meeting, UN Doc. S/PV.1860 (5 December 1975) para 3 (the US calling for an analysis of the Israeli airstrikes in the context of the repeated acts of violence committed by irregulars).

general context of reoccurring violence.[97] At times, the need to look beyond the individual attacks and see the reoccurring pattern was pointed out by some members of the Council.[98] Such a need was also pointed out by Ago in his report to the International Law Commission. Although he was discussing acts of states, Ago asserted that self-defence could be justified against an armed attack consisting 'of a number of successive acts.' In such a case, the requirements of proportionality and immediacy had to be looked at 'in the light of those acts as a whole.'[99] He pointed out that if a state suffered a series of successive and different acts of armed attack, the requirement of proportionality would not mean that the victim state was prohibited from undertaking a single armed action on a much larger scale in order to put an end to the escalation of attacks.[100] A part of the legal doctrine also advocates such a perspective.[101]

This author agrees with the argument put forward by Ago, with the *proviso* that it should be considered applicable to non-state actors as well. If it has been established that the 'active' political agenda leads to a present and inevitable need to resort to force, the exercise of self-defence will have to aim at neutralizing the danger. Inflicting an equivalent damage on the attacker would only lead to a tit-for-tat method that would only prolong the conflict. For that reason, the magnitude of the defensive action can exceed that of the repeated attacks, as long as it is aimed at neutralizing the source of the attacks. In other words, the defensive action will have to aim at destroying military bases, training camps, stockpiles of weapons and other essential, infrastructure-related facilities used for preparing and launching attacks. The defensive action may therefore be of a larger scale than the individual attacks launched by the armed groups. Nonetheless, the defensive force cannot go beyond what is necessary to neutralize the source of attacks. There are many questions regarding the lawfulness of targeting certain facilities that are equally used by civilians and the military. Moreover, the consequences of civilians' direct participation in hostilities, especially in irregular warfare, further complicates the problem. However, these questions pertain to the law of armed conflict and will not be addressed in this research.[102] Nonetheless, it is necessary to emphasize that defensive action going beyond what is required to stop the reoccurring of attacks should be deemed disproportionate. For instance, although the necessity requirement was met by Israel in 2006, some of its ensuing actions were

---

[97] See *supra* 10.2 and 10.3.

[98] SCOR, 24th Session, 1467th meeting, UN Doc.S/PV.1467 (27 March 1969) paras 48–49; SCOR, 30th Session, 1860th meeting, UN Doc. S/PV.1860 (5 December 1975) paras 3–5.

[99] Ago 1980, pp. 69–70, para 121.

[100] Ibid.

[101] Blum 1976, p. 235; Gross 1983, pp. 486–487; Schachter 1985, p. 293; Schmitt 2003, pp. 532–533.

[102] See, for instance, Schmitt 2010, pp. 245–275.

rightfully criticized as disproportionate, because they destroyed targets that had no identifiable connection to the paramilitary activities of Hezbollah.[103]

On the basis of the analysis put forward above, it is the opinion of this author that the 'accumulation of events' theory does not render the traditional, pre-Charter limitations of self-defence obsolete. The elements of the theory can be successfully corroborated with the necessity and proportionality requirements. Further attention to the combination of these elements is needed, but it is important to note that the centuries-old limitations of necessity (conditionality of an attack and immediacy) and proportionality (moderation) are flexible enough to meet new challenges and robust enough to nevertheless maintain their rationale.

14.6 Demonstrating the Fulfilment of the Conditions of Necessity and Proportionality

The question arises whether the state defending itself against an imminent threat must prove *prior* to the defensive action the justifiability of its claim. It has been maintained that the state resorting to self-defence should offer justifying arguments before the defensive action. Accordingly, 'while conclusory official statements might be acceptable when the victim state has no time or opportunity to present the requisite evidence, the facts justifying its actions should otherwise be revealed prior to taking the necessary defensive steps. When such disclosure is not feasible, it should be made at the earliest time thereafter.[104]

This author does not support such a view. As Franck asserted, the right of the targeted state to defend itself could not depend on its ability to convince the fifteen members of the Security Council that it had indeed correctly identified the attackers and the host state.[105]

Indeed, there is nothing in the legal history of the requirement of necessity that would require states to unquestionably prove the justifiability of their claims prior to the defensive action. That would go against the immediacy factor embedded in the requirement of necessity. If a target state found itself facing a present and inevitable need to ward off an imminent attack, its right to defend itself should not be made dependent upon convincing the members of the Security Council or any other official body as to the accuracy of the evidence in its possession. That being said, the target state would be obliged to offer an explanation during or after its defensive action. Article 51 requires reporting the use of force in self-defence to

---

[103] SCOR, 61st Session, 5497th meeting, UN Doc. S/PV.5497 (27 July 2006); Statement by the President of the Security Council, UN Doc. S/PRST/2006/34 (2006); SCOR, 61st Session, 5498th meeting, UN Doc. S/PV.5498 (30 July 2006) pp. 2–3; 5499th meeting, 30 July 2006, S/PV.5499; Statement by the President of the Security Council, UN Doc. S/PRST/2006/35 (2006). See also Ducheine and Pouw 2009, pp. 71–72; Wrachford 2007, pp. 88–89.

[104] Charney 2001, p. 836.

[105] Franck 2001, p. 843.

the Security Council. The defending state would thus have ample opportunity to present evidence and justification of its action before the members of the Security Council. States have used such an opportunity in the majority of cases where claims of self-defence were invoked to sustain specific armed actions.[106]

What such a report would have to show is that, on the basis of the available information (objective criterion) interpreted in good faith (subjective criterion), the relevant officials of the state reached the conclusion that a threat of an armed attack was imminent. Both objective and subjective criteria have to be met.

The subjective criterion is of utmost importance. Its absence will always render a claim of self-defence untenable. For instance, before the Nuremberg Tribunal, the defence of the accused argued that the invasion of Norway was a measure of prevention, as Britain and France were contemplating to occupy the country and use it as a basis for further military operations.[107] Although the availability of evidence of a potential British occupation of Scandinavia was (arguably) demonstrated, the facts of the case showed that the Nazi attack had been planned long before any question of British occupation of Norway had been raised.[108] Accordingly, the available information as to the British plans was used to justify a long-planned move of Nazi Germany aimed at improving its strategic and operational position in the war-theatre.[109] Conversely, the British operation against the concentration of French ships at Mers-el-Kebir was carried out on the basis of the strong conviction that had the Nazis seized the vessels, the waters around Britain would have become an open avenue for a German invasion force.[110] Although there was no irrefutable evidence of a clear German intention to take control of the French fleet, once returned to their French ports, the vessels could have been boarded and seized by German forces at any time and the British could have done nothing about it.[111] On the basis of the available information interpreted in good faith, Churchill's War Cabinet concluded that there was a present and inevitable need to act in the face of such a threat.

The objective criterion relates to the information in possession of the targeted state. While official statements of the parties, conclusions of negotiation and mediation meetings as well as diplomatic correspondence (including that of third parties) can shed light on the emergency and inevitability of the threat, most of the times accurate intelligence will have to be acquired to fill the gaps of knowledge. The imminence of a threat cannot be deduced from official communications alone. There has to be specific intelligence on the preparedness of the threatening state, the military measures undertaken or envisaged and the potential targets in order to

[106] For instance, *supra* 8.4.1–8.4.3 as well as 10.2 and 10.3. See also Higgins 1963, pp. 205–207.

[107] See *supra* 7.3.

[108] Ibid.

[109] See *supra* 7.3. Nazi Conspiracy and Aggression 1947, p. 35.

[110] Brown 1997.

[111] Gill 2007, p. 134.

examine the feasibility and appropriateness of a pre-emptive action. The targeted state need not know all the elements of the threat, but the information at hand has to lead to the conviction that an attack is imminent.

14.7 Conclusions as to the Limits of Anticipatory Action in Self-Defence

In order to answer the second research question, Part III analysed the content, applicability and controversies of the three elements limiting self-defence: the conditionality of an armed attack and immediacy (under the requirement of necessity) and proportionality. These three elements were analysed from the point of view of standard-type armed attacks and hit-and-run tactics.

The answer to the second research question—under what conditions anticipatory action in self-defence is lawful in international law—can be summarized in three points.

First, the conditions under which anticipatory action is lawful pertain to the right of self-defence as a whole. They limit the exercise of self-defence regardless of its temporal dimension. In other words, anticipatory action is limited by the same requirements as remedial action in self-defence.

Secondly, these conditions pertain to the necessity and proportionality of self-defence. Necessity entails the conditionality of an armed attack and the factor of immediacy (urgency and inevitability); whereas proportionality relates to the required amount of force to ward off the attack. As regards anticipatory action, the combination of these elements can be put in a simple formula: the perceived threat of an armed attack must create a present and inevitable need to use proportionate force to stop the attack from taking place.

Thirdly, the defending state must demonstrate that it perceived the applicability of all three elements on the basis of the available information (objective criterion) interpreted in good faith (subjective criterion).

If all these conditions are met, anticipatory action in self-defence—just as remedial action—may be deemed lawful.

14.8 Self-Defence: What It Is and What It Is Not

The essence of the centuries-old content of self-defence allows states to undertake proportionate armed action as long as the armed attack or threat thereof creates a present and inevitable need to use force. The temporal dimension of self-defence pertains thus to the time before, during and after an armed attack. In other words, self-defence has both an anticipatory and a remedial dimension.

The anticipatory dimension of self-defence has been criticized as opening the door to abuse.[112] State practice offers a plenitude of examples for abuse of the right of self-defence, regardless of its temporal dimension. The solution is not to unduly restrict the temporal dimension of self-defence as a whole, but to better delineate the conditions that need to be met in its exercise. The present work attempted to address this task. It demarcated three elements of self-defence: the conditionality of an armed attack and immediacy (as elements of necessity) and proportionality.

These elements also assist in distinguishing self-defence from other uses of force. Understanding what does *not* constitute self-defence is as important as comprehending what makes up that right.

Self-defence is not a form of collective security. The seventeenth–nineteenth-century right to wage 'perfect' wars does not belong to individual states anymore. The greater part of that right was transferred to the Security Council at the time of the adoption of the Charter.[113] The Security Council may take collective enforcement measures to address a threat to international peace and security, a breach of peace or aggression. It may take action to achieve various objectives: restore constitutional order, put an end to an armed conflict, stop atrocities against the civilian population, prevent the outbreak of war and so on. These prerogatives are part and parcel of the collective security system of the UN and presuppose the existence of a Security Council resolution calling for or acquiescing to multilateral action. Self-defence cannot be exercised in pursuance of such objectives. Self-defence requires the existence of an armed attack or a threat thereof that creates a present and inevitable need to use force. No security threat, crisis or violation of international law justifies the exercise of self-defence if the above-mentioned conditions are not met. The conditionality of an armed attack and immediacy—as elements of necessity—are thus instrumental in distinguishing self-defence from any use of force belonging to the realms of collective security.

Self-defence must be distinguished from reprisals. According to the classic temporal differentiation between self-defence and reprisals, the former pertained to the time before and during the attack, whereas the latter became applicable after the attack had already occurred.[114] That differentiation ascertained the intrinsically anticipatory character of self-defence. Today, when self-defence also has a remedial aspect, a more purpose-based differentiation between the two forms of use of force is pertinent. A reprisal always had a punitive character. Its objective is to punish the author of the attack by inflicting damage proportionate to the one suffered. That is not the objective of self-defence. Even in its remedial dimension, self-defence is meant to put an end to an armed attack or precluding that attack from achieving its purpose. In that respect, self-defence stems from a necessity,

---

[112] Cassese 2005, pp. 361–362; Gray 2008, pp. 164–165; Mégret 2002, p. 376.

[113] See *supra* 5.3 and 5.4.

[114] For instance: Suárez 1944, Disputation XIII, Section 1 (6), p. 804; Grotius 1964, Book II, Chap. 1 (ii), p. 172; Vattel 1964, Book II, Chap. 5, Sections 67–68, p. 135, and Book III, Chap. 1, Section 5, p. 236.

present and inevitable, to address the dangerous situation by resorting to force. There is no such necessity when it comes to reprisals. Nonetheless, there are many contemporary instances of state practice where defensive actions turn into reprisals. When the use of force exceeds what is necessary to put an end to an armed attack, the armed action transforms and becomes a reprisal. Although the existence of an armed attack is established, both the immediacy and the proportionality elements are overlooked. Disproportionate use of force often renders an originally legal claim of self-defence unjustifiable. Remedial action in self-defence is thus considerably susceptible to abuse. The only way self-defence can be distinguished from a reprisal is to observe the relevance and applicability of the elements of immediacy and proportionality.

Self-defence is not preventive use of force. Customary law does not require the existence of an armed attack to justify self-defence. The existence of a threat is also accepted as a legal ground for defensive action. Such a threat—in much the same way as an existing armed attack—has to create a present and inevitable need to use force. Only an imminent threat can create such a necessity. A remote danger of being attacked at some point in the future does not meet the requirements of immediacy. In the case of hit-and-run tactics, where the place and time of the future attack is seldom known, the existence of a series of past attacks coupled with the dangers posed by future attacks can amount to a present and inevitable need to act. In such cases, the danger is not remote, it is very much real and confirmed by the series of attacks that had already occurred. The immediacy element is not met when force is used to tackle a potentially dangerous situation, even if the circumstances show a probable escalation of security concerns. In many cases, the security concerns are grave and raise considerable fears of conflict. Nonetheless, as long as this does not translate into a present and inevitable need to act in response to an imminent threat of attack, the right of self-defence is not available. Even if the current collective security systems creates loopholes in which states are left undefended against potentially grave dangers, the immediacy element must be used to distinguish self-defence from preventive use of force. Simply put, there is no 'preventive self-defence'. The term is a paradoxical construction, as it denies one of the main elements of self-defence: immediacy. One can refer to preventive use of force, preventive war or preventive measures, but not to preventive self-defence.

The three elements (conditionality of an armed attack, immediacy and proportionality) are instrumental in distinguishing self-defence from other uses of force. They have remained unchanged despite the passing of time and the changing nature of conflicts. They could be discerned in all three normative frameworks of pre-Charter customary law. They were identified in post-Charter state practice. Regardless of the protagonists of the conflict or the weapon technology used, the essential elements of self-defence retained their significance and function. Even if they are categorized and classified in different manners, their core understanding remains the same: moderate action in self-defence is allowed as long as the armed attack or the threat thereof creates a present and inevitable need to use force.

The core understanding of self-defence is the sole basis for differentiating this centuries-old right from other forms of use of force. Strict observance of the three essential elements of self-defence is the only way an abuse of the right can be identified and, in the future, avoided. For that purpose, more attention should be given by judicial and other law-related bodies as well as by legal doctrine to the analysis of the manner in which these three elements work in practice.

References

9/11 by numbers. New York Magazine. http://nymag.com/nymetro/news/sept11/features/n_7692/. Accessed 19 June 2010

Abi Saab G (1987) Cours general du droit public. Recueil des Cours 207(VII):9–463

Alexandrov S (1996) Self-defence against the use of force in international law. Kluwer, The Hague

Ago R (1980) Addendum to the eighth report on state responsibility. UN Doc. A/CN.4/318/Add.5–7 (1980)

Atwan AB (2006) The secret history of Al-Qaida. Saqi Books, London

Badr GM (1980) The exculpatory effect of self-defence in state responsibility. Ga J Int Comp Law 10:1–28

Baker MB (1987) Terrorism and the inherent right to self-defence (a call to amend Article 51 of the United Nations Charter). Houst J Int Law 10:25–49

Beard JM (2002) America's new war on terror: the case for self-defence under international law. Harv J Law Pub Policy 25:559–590

Blum Y (1976) State response to acts of terrorism. Ger Yearb of Int Law 19:223–237

Boddens Hosang JFR (2010) Force protection, unit self-defence, and extended self-defence. In: Gill TD, Fleck D (eds) Handbook of the international law of military operations. Oxford University Press, Oxford, pp 415–427

Borum R (2005) Counter-terrorism training post-9/11. In: Gunaratna R (ed) Combating terrorism. Marshall Cavendish, Singapore, pp 62–73

Bowett DW (1958) Self-defence in international law. Manchester University Press, Manchester

Bowett DW (1972) Reprisals involving recourse to armed force. Am J Int Law 66:1–36

Brown D (2003) Use of force against terrorism after September 11th: state responsibility, self-defence and other responses. Cardozo J Int Comp Law 11:1–53

Brown RJ (1997) Operation Catapult: naval destruction at Mers-el-Kebir. World War II http://www.historynet.com/operation-catapult-naval-destruction-at-mers-el-kebir.htm. Accessed 5 June 2009

Brownlie I (1963) International law and the use of force by states. Clarendon Press, Oxford

Cassese A (2005) International law. Oxford University Press, Oxford

Charney J (2001) The use of force against terrorism and international law. Am J Int Law 95:835–839

Christakis T (2005) Existe-t-il un droit de légitime défense en cas de simple "menace"?: une réponse au "groupe des personnalités de haut niveau" de l'ONU. In: Société francçaise pour le droit international, Les métamorphoses de la sécurité collective: droit, pratique et enjeux stratégiques. Pedone, Paris, pp 197–222

Constantinou A (2000) The right of self-defence under customary international law and Article 51 of the UN Charter. Sakkoulas, Athens

Corten O (2008) Le droit contre la guerre: l'interdiction du recours à la force en droit international contemporain. Pedone, Paris

Dinstein Y (2005) War, aggression and self-defence. Cambridge University Press, Cambridge

Ducheine P (2008) Krijgsmacht, geweldgebruik & terreurbestrijding: Een onderzoek naar juridische aspecten van de rol van strijdkrachten bij de bestrijding van terrorisme. Wolf Legal Publishers, Nijmegen
Ducheine P, Pouw E (2009) Operation Change of Direction: a short survey of the legal basis and the applicable legal regimes. NL-ARMS Netherlands Annual Review of Military Studies, pp 51–95
Feinstein BA (2002) Operation Enduring Freedom: legal dimensions of an infinitely just operation. J Transnatl Law Policy 11:201–295
Franck T (2001) Terrorism and the right of self-defence. Am J Int Law 95:839–843
Franck T (2002) Recourse to force: state action against threats and armed attacks. Cambridge University Press, Cambridge
Freedman L, Gamba-Stonehouse V (1991) Signals of war: the Falklands conflict of 1982. Princeton University Press, Princeton
GAOR: General Assembly Official Records http://documents.un.org/simple.asp
Gardam JG (1993) Proportionality and force in international law. Am J Int Law 87:391–413
Gardam JG (2004) Necessity, proportionality and the use of force by states. Cambridge University Press, Cambridge
Gazzini T (2005) The changing rules on the use of force in international law. Manchester University Press, Manchester
Gentili A (1933) De jure belli libri tres (trans: Rolfe JC). Clarendon Press, Oxford
Gill TD (2003) The eleventh of September and the right of self-defence. In: Heere WP (ed) Terrorism and the military international legal implications. T. M. C. Asser Press, The Hague, pp 23–37
Gill TD (2007) The temporal dimension of self-defence. In: Schmitt M, Pejic J (eds) International law and armed conflict: exploring the faultlines. Essays in honour of Yoram Dinstein. Martinus Nijhoff, Leiden, pp 113–155
Gray C (2004) International law and the use of force. Oxford University Press, Oxford
Gray C (2008) International law and the use of force. Oxford University Press, Oxford
Green JA (2009) The International Court of Justice and self-defence in international law. Hart, Oxford
Greenwood C (1987) International law and the US' air operation against Libya. West Va Law Rev 89:933–960
Greenwood C (2003) International law and the pre-emptive use of force: Afghanistan, Al-Qaida and Iraq. S.-Diego Int Law J 4:7–38
Grey AL (1951) The 38th parallel. Foreign Aff 29:482–487
Gross LM (1983) The legal implications of Israel's 1982 invasion into Lebanon. Calif West Int Law J 13:458–492
Grotius H (1964) De jure belli ac pacis libri tres (trans: Kelsey FW). Oceana, New York
Gunaratna R (2004) Change or continuity. In: Gunaratna R (ed) The changing face of terrorism. Marshall Cavendish, Singapore, pp 1–17
Gunaratna R (2005) Military and non-military strategies for combating terrorism. In: Gunaratna R (ed) Combating terrorism. Marshall Cavendish, Singapore, pp 1–36
Higgins R (1963) The development of international law through the political organs of the UN. Oxford University Press, London
Intoccia GF (1987) American bombing of Libya: an international legal analysis. Case West Reserve J Int Law 19:177–213
Jacobson MR (1998) War in the information age: international law, self-defence, and the problem of 'non-armed' attacks. J Strateg Stud 21(3):1–33
Jessup PC (1948) A modern law of nations: an introduction. Macmillan, New York
Kelly MJ (2005) Critical analysis of the International Court of Justice ruling on Israel's security barrier. Fordham Int Law J 29:181–228
Khadduri M, Ghareeb E (1997) War in the Gulf, 1990–91: the Iraqi-Kuwait conflict and its implications. Oxford University Press, New York

Kolb R (2004) Self-defence and preventive war at the beginning of the millennium. Zeitschrift für öffentliches Recht 59(2):111–134
Lachs M (1980) The development and general trends of international law in our time. Recueil des Cours 169(IV):9–377
Lubell N (2010) Extraterritorial use of force against non-state actors. Oxford University Press, Oxford
Malanczuk P (1987) Countermeasures and self-defence as circumstances precluding wrongfulness in the International Law Commision's Draft Articles on States Responsibility. In: Spinedi M, Simma B (eds) UN codification of state responsibility. Oceana, New York, pp 197–286
McDougal MS, Feliciano FP (1961) Law and minimum world public order: the legal regulation of international coercion. Yale University Press, New Haven
Mégret F (2002) "War"? legal semantics and the move to violence. Eur J Int Law 13:361–399
Miller DH (1928) The Peace Pact of Paris: a study of the Briand–Kellogg Treaty. G.P. Putnam's Sons, New York
Mueller KP et al (2006) Striking first: preemptive and preventive attack in US national security policy. RAND project air force
Nazi Conspiracy and Aggression: Opinion and Judgment (1947) Office of the United States Chief of Counsel for the Prosecution of Axis Criminality. Government Printing Office, Washington
Nicaragua 1986: Military and paramilitary activities in and against Nicaragua (Nicaragua v. USA), Judgment of 27 June 1986, ICJ Rep. (1986)
Nollkaemper A (2005) Attribution of forcible acts: connections between the law on the use of force and the law of state responsibility. In: Blokker NM, Schrijver NJ (eds) The Security Council and the use of force: theory and reality, a need for change?. Nijhoff, Leiden, pp 133–171
Oil Platforms (Islamic Republic of Iran v United States of America), Judgment of 6 November 2003, ICJ Rep. (2003)
Prosecutor v. Dusko Tadić, ICTY Case No. IT-94-1-A, Judgment, Appeals Chamber, 15 July 1999
Reichberg GM, Syse H, Begby E (eds) (2006) The ethics of war: classic and contemporary readings. Blackwell, Malden
Repertoire: Repertoire of the Practice of the Security Council http://www.un.org/en/sc/repertoire
Ruys T (2010) 'Armed attack' and Article 51 of the UN Charter. Evolutions in customary law and practice. Cambridge University Press, Cambridge
Schachter O (1985) The lawful resort to unilateral use of force. Yale J Int Law 10:291–294
Schachter O (1991) International law in theory and practice. Martinus Nijhoff, Dordrecht
Schmitt MN (2003) Preemptive strategies in international law. Michigan J Int Law 24: 513–548
Schmitt MN (2010) Targeting in operational law. In: Gill TD, Fleck D (eds) Handbook of the international law of military operations. Oxford University Press, Oxford, pp 245–275
Singh MN (1956) The right of self-defence in relation to the use of nuclear weapons. Indian Yearb Int Aff 5:3–26
Spanier JW (1959) The Truman–MacArthur controversy and the Korean war. Belknap Press of Harvard University Press, Cambridge
Stanley GFG (1952) The Korean dilemma. Int J 7(4):278–282
Stueck W (1997) The Korean War: an international history. Princeton University Press, Princeton
Suárez F (1944) The three theological virtues: on charity. Reprinted In: Brown Scott J (ed) Selections from three works of Francisco Suárez SJ (trans: Williams GL et al). Clarendon Press, Oxford, pp 799–865
E Vattel de (1964) The law of nations or the principles of natural-law: applied to the conduct and to the affairs of nations and of sovereigns. Oceana, New York
F Vitoria de (1991) De jure belli. Reprinted in Pagden A, Lawrance J (eds) Vitoria: political writings. Cambridge University Press, Cambridge
Waldock CHM (1952) The regulation of the use of force by individual states in international law. Recueil Des Cours 81(II):451–517

Webster 1841: Letter from Daniel Webster, US Secretary of State, to Henry Fox, British Minister in Washington, 24 April 1841. In: British and Foreign State Papers, 1840–1841, vol 29 (1857). James Ridgway and Sons, London, pp 1129–1139

Wrachford JS (2007) The 2006 Israeli invasion of Lebanon: aggression, self-defence, or a reprisal gone bad? Airf Law Rev 60:29–90

Bibliography

Abi Saab G (1987) Cours general du droit public. Recueil des Cours 207(1987-VII): 9–463.
Akehurst M (1976) Custom as a Source of International Law. British Yearbook of International Law 47:1–53.
Alexandrov S (1996) Self-Defense against the Use of Force in International Law. Kluwer Law International, The Hague.
Allison GT (1971) Essence of Decision: Explaining the Cuban Missile Crisis. Little Brown, Boston.
Anzilotti D (1928) Corso di diritto internationale. Atheneum, Roma.
Aristotle (1959) The 'Art' of Rhetoric, trans. by Freese JH. William Heinemann, London.
Aristotle (1967) Politics, trans. by Rackham H. William Heinemann, London.
Aristotle (1968) XIX The Nicomachean Ethics, trans. by Rackham H. William Heinemann, London.
Atwan AB (2006) The Secret History of al-Qaida. Saqi Books, London.
Augustine (1994) City of God, reprinted in Fortin EL et al. (eds) Political Writings/Augustine, Hackett, Indianapolis, Ind.
Augustine (1955) The Problem of Free Choice (De libero arbitrio), trans. by Pontifex M. Newman Press, Westminster Maryland.
Aust A (2007) Modern Treaty Law and Practice. Cambridge University Press, Cambridge.
Badr GM (1980) The Exculpatory Effect of Self-Defence in State Responsibility. Georgia Journal of International and Comparative Law 10:1–28.
Baker MB (1987) Terrorism and the Inherent Right to Self-Defence (A Call to Amend Article 51 of the United Nations Charter). Houston Journal of International Law 10:25–49.
Baker SG (1994) Comparing the 1993 US Airstrike on Iraq to the 1986 Bombing of Libya: The New Interpretation of Article 51. Georgia Journal of International and Comparative Law 24:99–116.

K. Tibori Szabó, *Anticipatory Action in Self-Defence,* DOI: 10.1007/978-90-6704-796-8,

Barbour SA, Salzman ZA (2008) "The Tangled Web": The Right of Self-Defence against Non-State Actors in the Armed Activities Case. NYU Journal of International Law and Politics (Special Issue) 40:53–106.

Barker E (1959) The Political Thought of Plato and Aristotle. Dover Publications, New York.

Baylis, J, Smith S (eds) (2001) The Globalisation of World Politics. Oxford University Press, New York.

Beard JM (2002) America's New War on Terror: The Case for Self-Defense under International Law. Harvard Journal of Law and Public Policy 25:559–590.

Beaulac S (2000) The Westphalian Legal Orthodoxy: Myth or Reality? Journal of the History of International Law 2:148–177.

Bellamy AJ (2006) Just Wars: From Cicero to Iraq. Polity Press, Cambridge.

Benes E (1932) The League of Nations: Successes and Failures. Foreign Affairs 11:66–80.

Benes E, Politis N (1924) Report on the Protocol, submitted to the Fifth Assembly. League of Nations Official Journal (Special Supp. No. 23) 483.

Beres LR (1991) After the Gulf War: Israel, Preemption and Anticipatory Self-Defence Perspective. Houston Journal of International Law 13:259–280.

Biffen J (1982) Letter to Mr. George Foulkes, M.P., dated 20 May 1982. British Yearbook of International Law 53:519–520.

Blin A (2007) The United States Confronting Terrorism. In: Chaliand G, Blin A (eds), The History of Terrorism: From Antiquity to Al-Qaeda, University of California Press, Berkeley, pp. 398–419.

Blum Y (1976) State Response to Acts of Terrorism. German Yearbook of International Law 19:223–237.

Boddens Hosang, JFR (2010) Force Protection, Unit Self-Defence, and Extended Self-Defence. In: Gill TD, Fleck D (eds), Handbook of the International Law of Military Operations, Oxford University Press, Oxford, pp. 415–427.

Bono E de (1937) Anno XIIII. The Conquest of an Empire. Cresset Press, London.

Borum R (2005) Counter-Terrorism Training Post-9/11. In: Gunaratna R (ed), Combating Terrorism, Marshall Cavendish, Singapore, pp. 62–73.

Bowett DW (1958) Self-Defense in International Law. Manchester University Press, Manchester.

Bowett DW (1972) Reprisals Involving Recourse to Armed Force. American Journal of International Law 66:1–36.

Breau SC (2005) Legal Consequences of the Construction of a Wall in the Occupied Palestinian Territory: Advisory Opinion, 9 July 2004. International Comparative Law Quarterly 54:1003–1022.

Brown D (2003) Use of Force against Terrorism after September 11th: State Responsibility, Self-Defence and Other Responses. Cardozo Journal of International and Comparative Law 11:1–53.

Brown RJ (1997) Operation Catapult: Naval Destruction at Mers-el-Kebir. World War II www.historynet.com/operation-catapult-naval-destruction-at-mers-el-kebir.htm. Accessed 5 June 2009.

Brownlie I (1963) International Law and the Use of Force by States. Clarendon Press, Oxford.

Brownlie I (1986) Comparative Approaches to the Theory of International Law: Remarks. American Society of International Law Proceedings 80:154-157.

Butler NM (1939–1940) Across the Busy Years: Recollections and Reflections. Scribner, New York.

Byers M (1999) Custom, Power and the Power of Rules: International Relations and Customary International Law. Cambridge University Press, Cambridge.

Cahier P (1985) Changements et continuité du droit international: cours général de droit international public. Recueil des Cours 195(1985-VI):9–374.

Campbell JS (1963) The Cuban Crisis and the U.N. Charter: An Analysis of the United States Position. Stanford Law Review 16:160–176.

Campbell LM (2000) Defending against Terrorism: A Legal Analysis of the Decision to Strike Sudan and Afghanistan. Tulane Law Review 74:1067–1096.

Canyes MS (1945) The Inter-American System and the Conference of Chapultepec. American Journal of International Law 39:504–517.

Cassese A (2001) Terrorism is also Disrupting Some Crucial Legal Categories of International Law. European Journal of International Law 12:993–1001.

Cassese A (2005) International Law. Oxford University Press, Oxford.

Cassese A (2007) The Nicaragua and Tadic Tests Revisited in Light of the ICJ Judgment on Genocide in Bosnia. European Journal of International Law 18:649–668.

Chaliand G, Blin A (eds) (2007) The History of Terrorism. From Antiquity to Al-Qaeda. University of California Press, Berkeley.

Chang L, Kornbluh P (eds) (1992) The Cuban Missile Crisis 1962, A National Security Archive Documents Reader. The New Press, New York.

Charney J (2001) The Use of Force against Terrorism and International Law. American Journal of International Law 95:835–839.

Chayes A (1974) The Cuban Missile Crisis. Oxford University Press, London.

Chayes A (1991) The Use of Force in the Persian Gulf. In: Damrosch LF, Scheffer DJ (eds), Law and Force in the New International Order, Westview Press, Boulder, pp. 3–12.

Cheng B (1965) United Nations Resolutions on Outer Space: 'Instant' International Customary Law? Indian Journal of International Law 5:23–48.

Christakis T (2005) Existe-t-il un droit de légitime défense en cas de simple "menace"?: une réponse au "groupe des personnalités de haut niveau" de l'ONU. In: Société française pour le droit international, Les métamorphoses de la sécurité collective: droit, pratique et enjeux stratégiques, Pedone, Paris, pp. 197-222.

Christopher P (2004) The Ethics of War and Peace. An Introduction to Legal and Moral Issues. Pearson/Prentice Hall, Upper Saddle River, N.J.

Cicero, MT (1968) De Officiis, trans. by Miller W. Heinemann, London.

Ciobanu D (1970) The Contribution of the Advisory Committee of Jurists to the Drafting of the UN Charter. Rivista di Diritto Internazionale 53:300–333.

Clausewitz C von (1976) On War. Princeton University Press, Princeton.

Constantinou A (2000) The Right of Self-Defence under Customary International Law and Article 51 of the United Nations Charter. Sakkoulas, Athens.

Corten O (2007) Le débat sur la légitime défense préventive à l'occasion des 60 ans de l'ONU: nouvelles revendications, oppositions persistantes. In: Kherad R (ed), Légitimes défenses: colloque international organisé par le Laboratoire Angevin de Recherches sur les Actes Juridiques en collab. avec le Centre d'Études sur la Coopération Juridique International, LGDJ, Paris, pp. 217–232.

Corten O (2008) Le droit contre la guerre: l'interdiction du recours à la force en droit international contemporain. Pedone, Paris.

D'Amato AA (1971) The Concept of Custom in International Law. Cornell University Press, Ithaca.

Détais J (2007) Les critères du droit de légitime défense dans la jurisprudence de la Cour International de Justice. In: Kherad R (ed), Légitimes défenses: colloque international organisé par le Laboratoire Angevin de Recherches sur les Actes Juridiques en collab. avec le Centre d'Études sur la Coopération Juridique International, LGDJ, Paris, pp. 149–171.

Dekker IF (1992) Criminal Responsibility and the Gulf War of 1980–1989: The Crime of Aggression. In: Dekker IF, Post HHG (eds), The Gulf War of 1980–1989, Martinus Nijhoff, Dordrecht, pp. 249–268.

Dinstein Y (1992) Implementing Limitations on the Use of Force – The Doctrine of Proportionality and Necessity: Remarks. American Society of International Law Proceedings 86:54–58.

Dinstein Y (2005) War, Aggression and Self-Defense. Cambridge University Press, Cambridge.

Dixon M (2000) Textbook on International Law. Blackstone Press, London.

Doğu E (2007) PKK: the Kurdistan Workers' Party. In: Heiberg M, O'Leary B, Tirman J (eds), Terror, Insurgency and the State: Ending Protracted Conflicts. University of Pennsylvania Press, Philadelphia, pp. 323–356.

Draft Articles on the Convention of the Law of Treaties with Commentaries (1966), Yearbook of the International Law Commission, Vol. II

Draper GIAD (1990) Grotius' Place in the Development of Legal Ideas about War. In: Bull H, Kingsbury B, Roberts A (eds), Hugo Grotius and International Relations. Clarendon Press, Oxford, pp. 177–207.

Ducheine P (2008) Krijgsmacht, geweldgebruik & terreurbestrijding: Een onderzoek naar juridische aspecten van de rol van strijdkrachten bij de bestrijding van terrorisme. Wolf Legal Publishers, Nijmegen.

Ducheine P, Pouw E (2009) Operation Change of Direction: A Short Survey of the Legal Basis and the Applicable Legal Regimes. NL-ARMS Netherlands Annual Review of Military Studies, pp. 51–95.

Dupuy TN (1963) Asiatic Land Battles: Japanese Ambitions in the Pacific, Vol. 9. In Dupuy TN, The Illustrated History of World War II, Edmund Ward, London.

Duyvesteyn I (2004) How New is the New Terrorism? Studies in Conflict and Terrorism 27(5):439–454.

Evans GJ (2008) The Responsibility to Protect: Ending Mass Atrocity Crimes Once and for All. Brookings Institution Press, Washington, D.C.

Everson S (1997) Aristotle on the Foundations of the State. In: Dunn J, Harris I (eds), Aristotle, Vol. 2, Edward Elgar, Cheltenham, pp. 292–304.

Falk RA (1997) Nuclear Weapons, International Law and the World Court: A Historic Encounter. American Journal of International Law 91:64–75.

Falk RA (2003) What Future for the UN Charter System of War Prevention? American Journal of International Law 97:590–598.

Farcau BW (1996) The Chaco War: Bolivia and Paraguay, 1932–1935. Praeger, Westport, Conn.

Farrell T, Lambert H (2001) Courting Controversy: International Law, National Norms and American Nuclear Use. Review of International Studies 27:309–326.

Feinstein BA (2002) Operation Enduring Freedom: Legal Dimensions of an Infinitely Just Operation. Journal of Transnational Law and Policy 11:201–295.

Ferrell RH (1952) Peace in Their Time: The Origins of the Kellogg-Briand Pact. Yale University Press, New Haven.

Fleck D (1988) Rules of Engagement for Maritime Forces and the Limitation of the Use of Force under the UN Charter. German Yearbook of International Law 31:165–186.

Flynn MJ (2008) First Strike. Preemptive War in Modern History. Routledge, New York.

Fontane J (2000) Isidore de Seville: genese et originalite de la culture hispanique au temps des Visigoths. Brepols, Turnhout.

Ford TK (1936) The Genesis of the First Hague Peace Conference. Political Science Quarterly 51:354–382.

Franck T (2001) Terrorism and the Right of Self-Defence. American Journal of International Law 95:839–843.

Franck T (2002) Recourse to Force: State Action against Threats and Armed Attacks. Cambridge University Press, Cambridge.

Freedman L (2005) The Official History of the Falklands Campaign, Vol. 1. Routledge, London.

Freedman L (2005) The Official History of the Falklands Campaign, Vol. 2. Routledge, London.

Freedman L, Gamba-Stonehouse V (1991) Signals of War: The Falklands Conflict of 1982. Princeton University Press, Princeton, N.J.

Garcia-Mora MR (1962) International Responsibility for Hostile Acts of Private Persons against Foreign States. Nijhoff, The Hague.

Gardam JG (1993) Proportionality and Force in International Law. American Journal of International Law 87:391–413.

Gardam JG (2004) Necessity, Proportionality and the Use of Force by States. Cambridge University Press, Cambridge.

Gardner RN (2003) Neither Bush Nor the "Jurisprudes". American Journal of International Law 97:585–590.

Garthoff RL (1988) Cuban Missile Crisis: The Soviet Story. Foreign Policy 72:61–80.

Gathii JT (2007) Armed Activities on the Territory of the Congo (Democratic Republic of the Congo v. Uganda). American Journal of International Law 101:142–149.

Gazzini T (2005) The Changing Rules on the Use of Force in International Law. Manchester University Press, Manchester.

Gentili A (1933) De jure belli libri tres, trans. by J.C. Rolfe. Clarendon Press, Oxford.

Gill TD (1989) The Second Gulf Crisis and the Relation between Collective Security and Collective Self-Defence. Grotiana 10:47–76.

Gill TD (1992) The Forcible Protection, Affirmation and Exercise of Rights by States under Contemporary International Law. Netherlands Yearbook of International Law 23:105–173.

Gill TD (2003) The Eleventh of September and the Right of Self-Defence. In: Heere WP (ed), Terrorism and the Military. International Legal Implications. T.M.C. Asser Press, The Hague, pp. 23–37.

Gill TD (2007) The Temporal Dimension of Self-Defence. In: Schmitt M, Pejic J (eds), International Law and Armed Conflict: Exploring the Faultlines. Essays in Honour of Yoram Dinstein. Martinus Nijhoff, Leiden, pp. 113–155.

Gill TD, Fleck D (eds) (2010) Handbook of the International Law of Military Operations. Oxford University Press, Oxford.

Gray C (2004) International Law and the Use of Force. Oxford University Press, Oxford.

Gray C (2008) International Law and the Use of Force. Oxford University Press, Oxford.

Green JA (2009) The International Court of Justice and Self-Defence in International Law. Hart, Oxford.

Greenwood C (1987) International Law and the United States' Air Operation against Libya. West Virginia Law Review 89:933–960.

Greenwood C (2002) International Law and the "War against Terrorism". International Affairs 78:301–317.

Greenwood C (2003) International Law and the Pre-Emptive Use of Force: Afghanistan, Al-Qaida and Iraq. San Diego International Law Journal 4:7–38.

Greenwood C (2005) Legality of the Use of Force: Iraq in 2003. In: Bothe M, O'Connell ME, Ronzitti N (eds), Redefining Sovereignty: The Use of Force after the Cold War. Transnational, Ardsley, N.Y., pp. 387–415.

Greig DW (1991) Self-Defence and the Security Council: What Does Article 51 Require. International and Comparative Law Quarterly 40:366–402.

Grewe WG (2000) The Epochs of International Law, trans. by M. Byers. De Gruyter, Berlin.

Grey AL (1951) The 38th Parallel. Foreign Affairs 29:482–487.

Grief N (1997) Legality of the Threat or Use of Nuclear Weapons. International and Comparative Law Quarterly 46:681–688.

Gross LM (1983) The Legal Implications of Israel's 1982 Invasion into Lebanon. California Western International Law Journal 13:458–492.

Grotius H (1964) De jure belli ac pacis libri tres, trans. by F.W. Kelsey. Oceana, New York.

Gunaratna R (ed) (2004a) The Changing Face of Terrorism. Marshall Cavendish, Singapore.

Gunaratna R (2004b) Change or Continuity. In: Gunaratna R (ed), The Changing Face of Terrorism. Marshall Cavendish, Singapore, pp. 1–17.

Gunaratna R (2004c) New Threshold Terrorism. In: Gunaratna R (ed), The Changing Face of Terrorism. Marshall Cavendish, Singapore, pp. 18–37.

Gunaratna R (2005) Military and Non-Military Strategies for Combating Terrorism. In: Gunaratna R (ed), Combating Terrorism. Marshall Cavendish, Singapore, pp. 1–36.

Gurr N, Cole B (2002) The New Face of Terrorism. Threats from Weapons of Mass Destruction. I.B. Tauris, London.

Haggenmacher P (1997) On Assessing the Grotian Heritage. In: Dunn J, Harris I (eds), Grotius, Vol. 2, Edward Elgar, Cheltenham, pp. 365–375.

Hall LB, Coerver DM (1990) Revolution on the Border: The United States and Mexico 1910–1920. University of New Mexico Press, Albuquerque.

Hall WE (1880) International Law. Clarendon Press, Oxford.

Halleck HW (1861) International Law or Rules Regulating the Intercourse of States in Peace and War. H.H. Bancroft, San Francisco.

Heinze EA (2009) Non-State Actors in the International Legal Order: the Israel-Hezbollah Conflict and the Law of Self-Defence. Global Governance 15:87–105.

Heisbourg F (2003) A Work in Progress: The Bush Doctrine and Its Consequences. The Washington Quarterly 26(2):73–88.

Henderson C (2004) The Bush Doctrine: From Theory to Practice. Journal of Conflict & Security Law 9:3–24.

Henkin L (1991) The Use of Force: Law and US Policy. In: Henkin et al. (eds), Right v. Might. International Law and the Use of Force, Council on Foreign Relations Press, New York, pp. 37–69.

Henkin L (1995) International Law: Politics and Values. Martinus Nijhoff, Dordrecht.

Higginbotham FM (1987) International Law, the Use of Force in Self-Defence and the Southern African Conflict. Columbia Journal of Transnational Law 25:561–572.

Higgins N, O'Reilly K (2009) The Use of Force, Wars of National Liberation and the Right to Self-Determination in the South Ossetian Conflict. International Criminal Law Review 9:567–583.

Higgins R (1963) The Development of International Law Through the Political Organs of the United Nations. Oxford University Press, London.

Higgins R, Flory M (eds) (1997) Terrorism and International Law. LSE/Routledge, London.

Hill C (2004) The Bush Administration Preemption Doctrine and the Future of World Order: Remark. American Society of International Law Proceedings 98:329–331.

Hobbes T (1991) Leviathan. Cambridge University Press, Cambridge.

Holk LE van (1983) Hugo Grotius, 1583–1645: A Biographical Sketch. In: Holk LE van, Roelofsen CG (eds), Grotius Reader: A Reader for Students of International Law and Legal History, T.M.C. Asser Instituut, The Hague, pp. 23–44.

Howard RD (2008) The New Terrorism and Weapons of Mass Destruction. In: Howard RD, Bajema NE (eds), Weapons of Mass Destruction and Terrorism, McGraw-Hill, New York, pp. 6–22.

Hueck IJ (2001) The Discipline of the History of International Law: New Trends and Methods on the History of International Law. Journal of the History of International Law 3:194–217.

Intoccia GF (1987) American Bombing of Libya: An International Legal Analysis. Case Western Reserve Journal of International Law 19:177–213.

Jacobson MR (1998) War in the Information Age: International Law, Self-Defense, and the Problem of 'Non-Armed' Attacks. Journal of Strategic Studies 21(3):1–33.

Jenkins BM (2008) The New Age of Terrorism. In: Howard RD, Bajema NE (eds), Weapons of Mass Destruction and Terrorism. McGraw-Hill, New York, pp. 23–31.

Jennings RY (1938) The Caroline and McLeod Cases. American Journal of International Law 32:82–99.

Jessup PC (1948) A Modern Law of Nations: an Introduction. Macmillan, New York.

Jinks D (2003) Self-Defence in an Age of Terrorism: Remarks. American Society of International Law Proceedings 97:144–146.

Johnstone I (2005) Jus Ad Bellum: The Next Iraq. ILSA Journal of International and Comparative Law 11:395–402.

Kaikobad KH (1992) "Jus ad Bellum": Legal Implications of the Iran-Iraq War. In: Dekker IF, Post HHG (eds), The Gulf War of 1980–1989, Martinus Nijhoff, Dordrecht, pp. 51–70.

Kalshoven F (2005) Belligerent Reprisals. Martinus Nijhoff, Leiden.

Karsh E (2002) The Iran-Iraq War 1980–1988. Osprey, Oxford.

Kattan V (2007) The Use and Abuse of Self-Defence in International Law: The Israel-Hezbollah Conflict as a Case Study. Social Science Research Network, Working Paper http://papers.ssrn.com/sol3/papers.cfm?abstract_id=994282

Keen MH (1965) The Laws of War in the Late Middle Ages. Routledge & Kegan Paul, London.

Kegley CW Jr (ed) (2003) The New Global Terrorism: Characteristics, Causes, Controls. Prentice Hall, Upper Saddle River, N.J.

Kelly MJ (2005) Critical Analysis of the International Court of Justice Ruling on Israel's Security Barrier. Fordham International Law Journal 29:181–228.

Kelsen H (1939) Théorie du droit international coutumier. Revue International de la Theorie du Droit (New Series) 1:25–57.

Kelsen H (1966) Principles of International Law. Holt, Rinehart and Winston, New York.

Khadduri M, Ghareeb E (1997) War in the Gulf, 1990–91: The Iraqi-Kuwait Conflict and Its Implications. Oxford University Press, New York.

Kolb R (2004) Self-Defense and Preventive War at the Beginning of the Millennium. Zeitschrift für öffentliches Recht 59(2):111–134.

Kolesnik DN (1989) The Development of the Right to Self-Defence. In: Butler WE (ed), The Non-Use of Force in International Law, Nijhoff, Dordrecht, pp. 153–159.

Kooijmans PH (2004) Is There a Change in the Ius ad Bellum and, if so, What Does It Mean for the Ius in Bello? In: Lijnzaad L et al. (eds), Making the Voice of Humanity Heard, Martinus Nijhoff, Leiden, pp. 225–237.

Kooijmans PH (2009) The Legality of the Use of Force in the Recent Case Law of the International Court of Justice. In: Yee S, Morin JY (eds), Multiculturalism and International Law – Essays in Honour of Edward McWhinney, Martinus Nijhoff, Leiden, pp. 455–466.

Koskenniemi M (1989) From Apology to Utopia: The Structure of International Legal Argument. Lakimiesliiton Kustannus, Helsinki.

Koskenniemi M (2001) Why History of International Law Today? Rechtsgeschichte 4:61–66.

Krasner SD (1995–1996) Compromising Westphalia. International Security 20(3): 115–151.

Kunz J (1947) Individual and Collective Self-Defence in Article 51 of the Charter of the UN. American Journal of International Law 41:872–879.

Lachs M (1980) The Development and General Trends of International Law in Our Time. Recueil des Cours 169(1980-IV):9–377.

Laffan RGD (ed) (1929) Select Documents of European History: 800–1492. Henry Holt, New York.

Laqueur W, Rubin B (eds) (2001) The Arab–Israeli Reader: A Documentary History of the Middle East Conflict, 6th rev. edn., Penguin Books, London.

Lasterle P (2003) Could Admiral Gensoul Have Averted the Tragedy of Mers el-Kébir? The Journal of Military History 67:835–844.

League Council meeting of 13 March 1924 (1924). League of Nations Official Journal 5: 523–529.

League Council meeting of 25 January 1932 (1932). League of Nations Official Journal 13: 326–333.

League Council meeting of 15 May 1933 (1933). League of Nations Official Journal 14:752–760.

Legnano G da (1917) Tractatus De Bello, De Represaliis et De Duello, ed. by Holland TE. Oxford University Press, Oxford.

Levite A (1987) Intelligence and Strategic Surprise. Columbia University Press, New York.

Lillich RB (ed) (1986) Humanitarian Intervention and the United Nations. University Press of Virginia, Charlottesville.

Lisska AJ (1996) Aquinas's Theory of Natural Law. An Analytic Reconstruction. Clarendon Press, Oxford.

Llewellyn P (1970) Rome in the Dark Ages. Faber & Faber, London.

Lobel J (1999) The Use of Force to Respond to Terrorist Attacks: The Bombing of Sudan and Afghanistan. Yale Journal of International Law 24:537–557.

Lowe V (2003) The Iraqi Crisis: What Now? International and Comparative Law Quarterly 52:859–871.

Lubell N (2010) Extraterritorial Use of Force against Non-State Actors. Oxford University Press, Oxford.

Machiavelli N (1970) Discourses on the First Decade of Livy. Reprinted in: Crick B, Walker LJ (eds), Niccolo Machiavelli: The Discourses, Penguin, London.

Machiavelli N (2004) The Prince & The Art of War. Collector's Library, London.

Malanczuk P (1987) Countermeasures and Self-Defence as Circumstances Precluding Wrongfulness in the International Law Commision's Draft Articles on State Responsibility. In: Spinedi M, Simma B (eds), United Nations Codification of State Responsibility, Oceana, New York, pp. 197–286.

Malanczuk P (1997) Akehurst's Modern Introduction to International Law. Routledge, London.

Mansfield P (2003) A History of the Middle East. Penguin Books, London.

Marrus MR (1997) The Nuremberg War Crimes Trial 1945–46: A Documentary History. Bedford Books, Boston.

Martel E (1993) Gulf of Tonkin. OAH Magazine of History 7(2):36–39.

Matheson MJ (1997) The Opinions of the International Court of Justice on the Threat or Use of Nuclear Weapons. American Journal of International Law 91:417–435.

Mattox JM (2006) Saint Augustine and the Theory of Just War. Continuum, London.

May L et al. (2006) The Morality of War: Classical and Contemporary Readings. Pearson Prentice Hall, Upper Saddle River, N.J.

McCredie JA (1987) The April 14, 1986 Bombing of Libya: Act of Self-Defense or Reprisal. Case Western Reserve Journal of International Law 19:215–242.

McDougal MS (1963) The Soviet-Cuban Quarantine and Self-Defense. American Journal of International Law 57:597–604.

McDougal MS, Feliciano FP (1961) Law and Minimum World Public Order: The Legal Regulation of International Coercion. Yale University Press, New Haven.

McGoldrick D (2004) From "9-11" to the Iraq War 2003: International Law in an Age of Complexity. Hart, Oxford.

Meeker LC (1963) Defensive Quarantine and the Law. American Journal of International Law 57:515–524.

Mégret F (2002)"War"? Legal Semantics and the Move to Violence. European Journal of International Law 13:361–399.

Melzer N (2010) Targeted Killings in Operational Perspective. In Gill TD, Fleck D (eds), Handbook of the International Law of Military Operations, Oxford University Press, Oxford, pp. 277–301.

Miller DH (1928) The Peace Pact of Paris: A Study of the Briand-Kellogg Treaty. G.P. Putnam's Sons, New York.

Mitchell K, Wood I (2002) The World of Gregory de Tours. Brill Leiden.

Morgan MJ (2004) The Origins of the New Terrorism. 34 Parameters: US Army War College 1:29–43.

Morrill DL (1974) Nicholas II and the Call for the First Hague Conference. Journal of Modern History 46:296-313.

Mueller KP et al. (2006) Striking First: Preemptive and Preventive Attack in US National Security Policy. RAND Project Air Force.

Mullerson R (1991) Self-Defence in the Contemporary World. In: Damrosch LF, Scheffer DJ (eds), Law and Force in the New International Order. Westview Press, Boulder, pp. 13–25.

Murphy JF (2009) Challenges of the New Terrorism. In: Armstrong D (ed), Routledge Handbook of International Law, Routledge, London, pp. 281–293.

Murphy SD (2002) Terrorism and the Concept of "Armed Attack" in Article 51 of the UN Charter. Harvard International Law Journal 43:41–51.

Murphy SD (2005) Self-Defence and the Israeli Wall Advisory Opinion: An Ipse Dixit from the ICJ? American Journal of International Law 99:62–76.

Myjer PJ, White ND (2002) The Twin Towers Attack: An Unlimited Right to Self-Defence? Journal of Conflict and Security Law 7:5–17.

Neff SC (2005) War and the Law of Nations: General History. Cambridge University Press, Cambrdige.

Nollkaemper A (2005) Attribution of Forcible Acts: connections between the Law on the Use of Force and the Law of State Responsibility. In: Blokker NM, Schrijver NJ (eds), The Security Council and the Use of Force: Theory and Reality, A Need for Change? Nijhoff, Leiden, pp. 133–171.

Nussbaum A (1947) A Concise History of the Law of Nations. Macmillan, New York.

Oppenheim L (1905) International Law: A Treatise, Vol. 1. Longmans, Green and Co., New York.

Oppenheim L (1906) International Law: A Treatise, Vol. 2. Longmans, Green and Co., New York.

Osiander A (2001) Sovereignty, International Relations and the Westphalian Myth. International Organization 55:251–287.

Phillimore R (1854) Commentaries upon International Law, Vol. 1. W. Benning, London.

Phillimore R (1857) Commentaries upon International Law, Vol. 3. W. Benning, London.

Phillipson C (1911) The International Law and Custom of Ancient Greece and Rome, Vol. 1–2. MacMillan, London.

Pierson C (2004) Preemptive Self-Defence in an Age of Weapons of Mass Destruction: Operation Iraqi Freedom. Denver Journal of International Law and Policy 33:150–178.

Plofchan TK (1992) Article 51: Limits on Self-Defence? Michigan Journal of International Law 13:336–373.

Pradelle AG de la (1950) Maîtres et doctrines du droit des gens. Editions internationales, Paris.

Printer NG Jr (2003) The Use of Force against Non-State Actors under International Law: An Analysis of the US Predator Strike in Yemen. UCLA Journal of International Law and Foreign Affairs 8:331–383.

Pufendorf S von (1934) De jure naturae et gentium libri octo, Vol. 2. Clarendon Press, Oxford.

Pufendorf S von (1991) On the Duty of Man and Citizen according to Natural Law. Cambridge University Press, Cambridge.

Ratner SR (2002) Jus ad Bellum and Jus in Bello after September 11. American Journal of International Law 96:905–921.

Redslob R (1923) Histoire des grands principes du droit des gens depuis l'antiquité jusqu'à la veille de la grande guerre. Rousseau, Paris.

Reichberg GM, Syse H. Begby E (eds) (2006) The Ethics of War: Classic and Contemporary Readings. Blackwell, Malden, Mass.

Reisman WM (2003) Self-Defence in an Age of Terrorism: Remarks. American Society of International Law Proceedings 97:142–143.

Roberts A (2008) The Equal Application of the Laws of War: A Principle under Pressure. International Review of the Red Cross 90(872):931–962.

Roelofsen CG (1990) Grotius and the International Politics of the Seventeenth Century. In: Bull H, Kingsbury B, Roberts A (eds), Hugo Grotius and International Relations. Clarendon, Oxford, pp. 96–131.

Roelofsen CG (1993–1994) History of the Law of Nations. A Few Remarks apropos Some Recent and Not So Recent Publications. Grotiana 13–14:52–58.

Röling BVA, Rüter CF (eds) (1977) The Tokyo Judgment: The International Military Tribunal for the Far East, 29 April 1946–12 November 1948. APA-University Press, Amsterdam.

Röling BVA (1993) The Tokyo Trial and Beyond: Reflections of a Peacemonger, ed. by Cassese A. Polity Press, Cambridge.

Rose G (1999) It Could Happen Here: Facing the New Terrorism. Foreign Affairs 78:131–137.

Rubin AP (1988) The Law of Piracy. Naval War College Press, Newport, RI.

Russell B (2009) History of Western Philosophy. Routledge, London.

Ruys T (2007) Crossing the Thin Blue Line: An Inquiry into Israel's Recourse to Self-Defence against Hezbollah. Stanford Journal of International Law 43:265–294.

Ruys T (2008) Quo Vadit Jus ad Bellum? A Legal Analysis of Turkey's Military Operations against the PKK in Northern Iraq. Melbourne Journal of International Law 9:334–364.

Ruys T (2010) 'Armed Attack' and Article 51 of the UN Charter. Evolutions in Customary Law and Practice. Cambridge University Press, Cambridge.

Sapiro M (2003) Iraq: The Shifting Sands of Preemptive Self-Defense. American Journal of International Law 97:599–607.

Sapiro M (2005) Preempting Prevention: Lessons Learned. NYU Journal of International Law and Politics 37:357–371.

Saul B (2006) Defining Terrorism in International Law. Oxford University Press, Oxford.

Schachter O (1985) The Lawful Resort to Unilateral Use of Force. Yale Journal of International Law 10:291–294.

Schachter O (1989) Entangled Treaty and Custom. In: Dinstein Y (ed), International Law at a Time of Perplexity. Essays in Honour of Shabtai Rosenne. Martinus Nijhoff, Dordrecht, pp. 717–738.

Schachter O (1991) International Law in Theory and Practice. Martinus Nijhoff, Dordrecht.
Schachter O (1992) Implementing Limitations on the Use of Force: The Doctrine of Proportionality and Necessity. American Society of International Law Proceedings 86:39–40.
Schick FB (1968) Some Reflections on the Legal Controversies concerning America's Involvement in Vietnam. International and Comparative Law Quarterly 17:953–995.
Schmitt C (1995) Staat, Grossraum, Nomos. Arbeiten aus den Jahren 1916–1969, Maschke G (ed), Duncker & Humblot, Berlin.
Schmitt MN (2003) Preemptive Strategies in International Law. Michigan Journal of International Law 24:513–548.
Schmitt MN (2008) "Change Direction" 2006: Israeli Operations in Lebanon and the International Law of Self-Defence. Michigan Journal of International Law 29:127–164.
Schmitt MN (2010) Targeting in Operational Law. In: Gill TD, Fleck D (eds), Handbook of the International Law of Military Operations. Oxford University Press, Oxford, pp. 245–275.
Schwebel SM (1970) What Weight to Conquest? American Journal of International Law 64:344–347.
Schwebel SM (1972) Aggression, Intervention and Self-Defence in Modern International Law. Recueil des Cours 136(1972-II): 411–497.
Shapira A (1971) The Six Day War and the Right of Self-Defence. Israel Law Review 6:65–80.
Shiryaev Y (2007–2008) The Right of Armed Self-Defense in International Law and Self-Defense Arguments Used in the Second Lebanon War. Acta Societatis Martensis 3:80–97.
Shotwell JT, Salvin M (1949) Lessons on Security and Disarmament. From the History of the League of Nations. King's Crown Press, New York.
Simma B (ed) (1995) The Charter of the United Nations, A Commentary. Oxford University Press, Oxford.
Singh MN (1956) The Right of Self-Defence in Relation to the Use of Nuclear Weapons. Indian Yearbook of International Affairs 5:3–26.
Slaughter AM (2004) The Use of Force in Iraq: Illegal and Illegitimate. American Society of International Law Proceedings 98:262–263.
Smith WS (2007) Augustine and the Limits of Preemptive and Preventive War. Journal of Religious Studies 35:141–162.
Sorenson DS (2008) An Introduction to the Modern Middle East. Westview Press, Boulder.
Spanier JW (1959) The Truman-MacArthur Controversy and the Korean War. Belknap Press of Harvard University Press, Cambridge, Mass.
Stanley GFG (1952) The Korean Dilemma. International Journal 7(4):278–282.
Steiger H (2001) From the International Law of Christianity to the International Law of the World Citizen: Reflections on the Formation of Epochs of the

History of International Law. Journal of the History of International Law 3:180–193.

Stueck W (1997) The Korean War: an International History. Princeton University Press, Princeton.

Strupp K (1934) Les règles générales du droit de la paix. Récueil des Cours 47:259–595.

Suárez F (1944) The Three Theological Virtues: On Charity. Reprinted in: Brown Scott J (ed), Selections from Three Works of Francisco Suárez, S.J., trans. by Williams GL et al. Clarendon Press, Oxford, pp. 799–865.

Swift LJ (1983) The Early Fathers on War and Military Service. Michael Glazier, Wilmington.

Taft WH (2004) Self-Defense and the Oil Platforms Decision. Yale Journal of International Law 29:295–306.

Taft WH, Buchwald TF (2003) Preemption, Iraq, and International Law. American Journal of International Law 97:557–563.

Tannenwald N (1999) The Nuclear Taboo: The United States and the Normative Basis of Nuclear Non-Use. International Organization 53:433–468.

Tesón FR (2005) Humanitarian Intervention: An Inquiry into Law and Morality. Transnational Ardsley, N.Y.

The Bryan Peace Treaties—Editorial Comment (1913). American Journal of International Law 7: 823–829.

The Chatham House Principles of International Law on the Use of Force in Self-Defence (2006) International Comparative Law Quarterly 55: 964.

Tucker D (2001) What is New about the New Terrorism and How Dangerous Is It? Terrorism and Political Violence 13(3):1–14.

Tunkin GI (1958) Co-existence and International Law. Recueil des Cours 95:1–81.

Tunkin GI (1961) Remarks on the Juridical Nature of Customary Norms of International Law. California Law Review 49:419–430.

Tute W (1989) The Reluctant Enemies: the Story of the Last War between Britain and France, 1940–1942. Collins, London.

Twiss T (1860) Law of Nations Considered as Independent Political Communities, Vol. 1. Oxford University Press, Oxford.

Twiss T (1863) Law of Nations Considered as Independent Political Communities, Vol. 2. Oxford University Press, Oxford.

Vandenberg AH Jr (1952) The Private Papers of Senator Vandenberg. Houghton Mifflin, Boston.

Vanderpol A (1919) La doctrine scolastique du droit de guerre. Pedone, Paris.

Vattel E de (1964) The Law of Nations or the Principles of Natural Law: Applied to the Conduct and to the Affairs of Nations and of Sovereigns. Oceana, New York.

Verhoeven S (2006) A Missed Opportunity to clarify the Modern Ius ad Bellum: Case Concerning Armed Activities on the Territory of the Congo. Military Law and the Law of War Review 45:355–368.

Villiger ME (1997) Customary International Law and Treaties. Kluwer Law International, The Hague.

Vitoria F de (1991a) De Indis. Reprinted in: Pagden A, Lawrance J (eds), Vitoria: Political Writings, Cambridge University Press, Cambridge.
Vitoria F de (1991b) De jure belli. Reprinted in: Pagden A, Lawrance J (eds), Vitoria: Political Writings, Cambridge University Press, Cambridge.
Waldock CHM (1952) The Regulation of the Use of Force by Individual States in International Law. Recueil Des Cours 81(1952-II):451–517.
Waldock CHM (1962) General Course on Public International Law. Recueil des Cours 106:1–251.
Walters FP (1965) A History of The League of Nations. Oxford University Press, London.
Waltz KN (1990) Nuclear Myths and Political Realities. American Political Science Review 84:731–745.
Walzer M (2006) Just and Unjust Wars. Basic Books, New York.
Watkins AC (1932) The Paris Pact. A Textbook for Schools and Colleges. Harcourt, Brace and Company, New York.
Watson A (1993) International Law in Archaic Rome: War and Religion. John Hopkins University Press, Baltimore.
Wedgwood R (1999) Responding to Terrorism: The Strikes against Bin Laden. Yale Journal of International Law 24:559–576.
Wedgwood R (2003) The Fall of Saddam Hussein: Security Council Mandates and Preemptive Self-Defense. American Journal of International Law 97:576–585.
Wedgwood R (2005) The ICJ Advisory Opinion on the Israeli Security Fence and the Limits of Self-Defense. American Journal of International Law 99:52–61.
Wehberg H (1931) The Outlawry of War. Carnegie Endowment for International Peace, Washington.
Weston BH (1997) Nuclear Weapons and the World Court: Ambiguity's Consensus. Transnational Law and Contemporary Problems 7:371–400.
Wolff C (1934) Jus gentium methodo scientifica pertractatum. Clarendon Press, Oxford.
Wolfke K (1993) Custom in Present International Law. Martinus Nijhoff, Dordrecht.
Wrachford JS (2007) The 2006 Israeli Invasion of Lebanon: Aggression, Self-Defence, or A Reprisal Gone Bad? Air Force Law Review 60:29–90.
Wright L (2006) The Looming Tower. Al-Qaeda and the Road to 9/11. Alfred Knopf, New York.
Wright Q (1957) Intervention 1956. American Journal of International Law 51:257–276.
Wright Q (1963) The Cuban Quarantine. American Journal of International Law 57:546–565.
Wright Q (1968) Legal Aspects of the Middle East Situation. Law and Contemporary Problems 33:5–31.
Yoo J (2003) International Law and the War in Iraq. American Journal of International Law 97:563–576.
Ziegler KH (1994) Völkerrechtsgeschichte: ein Studienbuch. Beck, Munich.
Zoller E (2004) The Law Applicable to the Preemption Doctrine. American Society of International Law Proceedings 98:333–337.

Table of Documents

United Nations

Ago R (1980) Addendum to the Eighth Report on State Responsibility. UN Doc. A/CN.4/318/Add.5-7 (1980)

Analytical Guide to the Work of the International Law Commission, 1949-1997 (1998). United Nations, New York

Repertoire of the Practice of the Security Council. http://www.un.org/en/sc/repertoire/

Report of the International Law Commission to the General Assembly on the Work of Its 32nd Session, 5 May-25 July 1980, UN Doc. A/35/10 (1980)

Report of the United Nations Fact Finding Mission on the Gaza Conflict, Human Rights in Palestine and Other Occupied Arab Territories (2009). UN Doc. A/HRC/12/48 (2009)

The Work of the International Law Commission, 5th edn. (1996). New York: United Nations

SCOR: Security Council Official Records. http://documents.un.org/simple.asp

UN High Level Panel: Report of the High-level Panel on Threats, Challenges and Change (2004). United Nations. http://www.un.org/secureworld/report2.pdf. Accessed 1 February 2011

UN travaux préparatoires: Documents of the United Nations Conference on International Organization, San Francisco, 1945 (1945-1955) United Nations Information Organizations, London

United Nations Monitoring, Verification and Inspection Commission (UNMOVIC)

Blix H, Executive Chairman UNMOVIC (27 January 2003) Briefing of the Security Council: An update on Inspections. http://www.un.org/Depts/unmovic/Bx27.htm. Accessed 11 January 2010

Blix H, Executive Chairman UNMOVIC (14 February 2003) Briefing of the Security Council: An update on Inspections. http://www.unmovic.org/. Accessed 11 January 2010

Blix H, Executive Chairman UNMOVIC (7 March 2003) Briefing of the Security Council: Oral Introduction of the 12th Quarterly Report of UNMOVIC. http://www.unmovic.org/. Accessed 11 January 2010

K. Tibori Szabó, *Anticipatory Action in Self-Defence,* DOI: 10.1007/978-90-6704-796-8,

International Atomic Energy Agency (IAEA)

ElBaradei M, Director General IAEA (27 January 2003) Statement to the United Nations Security Council: The Status of Nuclear Inspections in Iraq. http://www.un.org/News/dh/iraq/elbaradei27jan03.htm. Accessed 11 January 2010

ElBaradei M, Director General IAEA (14 February 2003) Statement to the United Nations Security Council: The Status of Nuclear Inspections in Iraq—An Update. http://www.un.org/News/dh/iraq/elbaradei-14feb03.pdf. Accessed 11 January 2010

ElBaradei M, Director General IAEA (7 March 2003) Statement to the United Nations Security Council: The Status of Nuclear Inspections in Iraq—An Update. http://www.un.org/News/dh/iraq/elbaradei-7mar03.pdf. Accessed 11 January 2010

Netherlands

Verhagen M (3 March 2008) Beantwoording vragen van het lid Van Bommel over een Turkse invasie in Noord-Irak. www.minbuza.nl/nl/Actueel/Kamerstukken/2008/03/Beantwoording_vragen_van_het_lid_Van_Bommel_over_een_Turkse_invasie_in_Noord_Irak. Accessed 5 June 2010

Rapport Commissie-Davids: Rapport Commissie van Onderzoek Besluitvorming Irak (Rapport Commissie-Davids), Conclusions (January 2010). http://www.rijksoverheid.nl/onderwerpen/irak/documenten-en-publicaties/rapporten/2010/01/12/rapport-commissie-davids-conclusions.html. Accessed 2 June 2010

United States

A Decade of Deception and Defiance: Saddam Hussein's Defiance of the United Nations (2002). The White House, Washington, D.C. www.gwu.edu/~nsarchiv/NSAEBB/NSAEBB80/wmd13.pdf. Accessed 15 February 2010

Albright M (9 September 1998) Address to the American Legion Convention New Orleans, Louisiana. http://avalon.law.yale.edu/20th_century/t_0025.asp. Accessed 29 November 2009

Bush GW (29 January 2002) State of the Union Address. http://georgewbush-whitehouse.archives.gov/news/releases/2002/01/20020129-11.html. Accessed 20 January 2010

Bush GW (1 June 2002) Graduation Speech at West Point. http://georgewbush-whitehouse.archives.gov/news/releases/2002/06/20020601-3.html. Accessed 21 January 2010

Bush GW (12 September 2002) Remarks at the United Nations General Assembly, New York. http://georgewbush-whitehouse.archives.gov/news/releases/2002/09/20020912-1.html. Accessed 26 January 2010

Bush GW (17 March 2003) Remarks by the President in Address to the Nation http://georgewbush-whitehouse.archives.gov/news/releases/2003/03/20030317-7.html. Accessed 26 January 2010

Clinton W (20 August 1998) Address to the Nation. www.state.gov/www/regions/africa/strike_clinton980820a.html. Accessed 29 November 2009

Comprehensive Report of the Special Advisor to the DCI on Iraq's WMD (September 2004). https://www.cia.gov/library/reports/general-reports-1/iraq_wmd_2004/index.html. Accessed 17 February 2010

Fact Sheet: U.S. Strike on Facilities in Afghanistan and Sudan (21 August 1998). US Department of State. www.state.gov/www/regions/africa/fs_binladin_facilities.html. Accessed 30 November 2009

FBI Headline Archives 1993 WTC bombing http://www2.fbi.gov/page2/feb08/tradebom_022608.html. Accessed 25 November 2009

FBI National Press Release (13 September 2001). http://www.fbi.gov/news/pressrel/press-releases/fbi-announces-list-of-19-hijackers Accessed 30 January 2010

Foreign Relations of the United States: Diplomatic Papers 1944, Vol. 1 (1966). US Government Printing Office, Washington, D.C

Foreign Relations of the United States: Diplomatic Papers 1945, Vol. 1: General (1967). US Government Printing Office, Washington, D.C

Jackson RH (1949) Report on the International Conference on Military Trials: London, 1945. US Government Printing Office, Washington, D.C. http://avalon.law.yale.edu/imt/jack_titlep.asp. Accessed 13 March 2009

Message from the President of the United States, Transmitting, in Answer to the Resolution of the Senate of the 12th instant, a Report from the Secretary of State, with Accompanying Correspondence, with regard to the Claim of Indemnity from Spain for the Execution at Santiago de Cuba of Persons who Were on Board the Virginius, US Senate Doc. No. 165 (54th Cong., 1st Sess. 1896)

Ninth Public Hearing, witness, Dr. Condoleezza Rice (8 April 2004) National Commission on Terrorist Attacks upon the United States. www.9-11commission.gov/archive/hearing9/9-11Commission_Hearing_2004-04-08.htm. Accessed 30 January 2010

Nairobi: Discussion and Findings: Report of the Accountability Review Boards on the Embassy Bombings in Nairobi, Kenya and Dar es Salaam, Tanzania on August 7, 1998 (1999). US Department of State, Washington, D.C. www.state.gov/www/regions/africa/board_ánairobi.html. Accessed 1 December 2009

Significant Terrorist Incidents, 1961–2003: A Brief Chronology (2004). US Department of State, Office of the Historian, Bureau of Public Affairs www.fas.org/irp/threat/terror_chron.html. Accessed 17 November 2009

Taft 2002: Taft WH (18 November 2002) The Legal Basis for Preemption. Council on Foreign Relations. www.cfr.org/publication/5250/legal_basis_for_preemption.html. Accessed 17 February 2010

Taft 2003: Taft WH (20 March 2003) Remarks to the National Association of Attorneys General, Washington. http://usinfo.org/wf-archive/2003/030321/epf516.htm. Accessed 17 February 2010

The 9/11 Commission Report: Final Report of the National Commission on Terrorist Attacks upon the United States (2004). National Commission on Terrorist Attacks upon the United States, Washington, D.C

The FBI Laboratory: US Department of Justice, Office of the Inspector General (1997) The FBI Laboratory: An Investigation into Laboratory Practices and Alleged Misconduct in Explosives-Related and Other Cases, Part 3, section D: The Bush Assassination Attempt. www.fas.org/irp/agency/doj/oig/fbilab1/05bush2.htm. Accessed 4 November 2008

The National Security Strategy of the United States of America Part V (2002). The White House. Washington, D.C

Webster 1841: Letter from Daniel Webster, US Secretary of State, to Henry Fox, British Minister in Washington, 24 April 1841, in British and Foreign State Papers, 1840–1841, Vol. 29 (1857). James Ridgway and Sons, London, pp. 1129–1139

Media

9/11 by numbers. New York Magazine. http://nymag.com/nymetro/news/sept11/features/n_7692/. 19 June 2010

Authorization of incursions into Iraq (2007) Keesing's Record of World Events 53: 48219–20

Beatty J (5 March 2003) In the name of God. Atlantic Online. www.theatlantic.com/magazine/archive/2003/03/in-the-name-of-god/3167. Accessed 20 February 2010

Bin Laden says he wasn't behind attacks (17 September 2001). CNN. http://archives.cnn.com/2001/US/09/16/inv.binladen.denial. Accessed 3 December 2010
Bin Laden claims responsibility for 9/11 (29 October 2004). CBC News. www.cbc.ca/world/story/2004/10/29/binladen_message041029.html. Accessed 30 January 2010
Clerics answer "no, no, no!" and invoke fates of past foes (22 September 2001). New York Times. www.nytimes.com/2001/09/22/world/nation-challenged-taliban-clerics-answer-no-no-no-invoke-fates-past-foes.html. Accessed 10 January 2010
Defiant Saddam accepts UN team (14 November 2002). Guardian. www.guardian.co.uk/world/2002/nov/14/iraq.ewenmacaskill
EU calls on Turkey to avoid "disproportionate" army action in Iraq (22 February 2008). EU Business. www.eubusiness.com/news-eu/1203683534.57/?searchterm=None. Accessed 3 June 2010
Gaza crisis: key maps and timeline (18 January 2009). BBC News. http://news.bbc.co.uk/2/hi/middle_east/7812290.stm. Accessed 12 June 2010
God knows it did not cross our minds to attack the towers (30 October 2004). Guardian. www.guardian.co.uk/world/2004/oct/30/alqaida.september11. Accessed 30 January 2010
Ground offensive against separatists (2008). Keesing's Record of World Events 54: 48427
Ignatieff M (23 March 2003) I am Iraq. New York Times. www.nytimes.com/2003/03/23/magazine/the-way-we-live-now-3-23-03-i-am-iraq.html. Accessed 13 March 2010
Interview with Jacques Chirac (9 September 2002), New York Times. http://www.nytimes.com/2002/09/09/international/europe/09CTEX.html. Accessed 26 January 2011
Iraq weapons inspectors find empty chemical warheads (17 January 2003). Guardian. www.guardian.co.uk/world/2003/jan/17/iraq.ewenmacaskill. Accessed 21 March 2010
Iraq's al-Samoud missile (3 March 2003). BBC World News. http://news.bbc.co.uk/1/hi/world/middle_east/2756987.stm. Accessed 21 March 2010
Israel knew attack was coming: Envoy to the US asserts (11 October 1973). New York Times, p. 1
Israeli jets fire on Lebanon (3 September 2003). BBC News. http://news.bbc.co.uk/2/hi/middle_east/3079072.stm. Accessed 4 April 2010
Offensive against PKK positions in Northern Iraq (2007) Keesing's Record of World Events 53:48316
Saddam risks war over arms dossier (8 December 2002). Guardian. www.guardian.co.uk/world/2002/dec/08/iraq. Accessed 21 March 2010
September 11: Chronology of terror (12 September 2001) CNN. http://articles.cnn.com/2001-09-11/us/chronology.attack_1_collapse-attacks-building?_s=PM:US. Accessed 8 January 2010
Special Report Iraq, Iraq timeline: July 16, 1979 to January 31, 2004. Guardian. www.guardian.co.uk/Iraq/page/0,12438,793802,00.html. Accessed 21 March 2010
Taliban won't turn over bin Laden (21 September 2001). CBS News. www.cbsnews.com/stories/2001/09/11/world/main310852.shtml. Accessed 8 January 2010
Timeline: Israeli-Hamas violence since truce ended (5 January 2009). Reuters. http://uk.reuters.com/article/idUKTRE50423320090105. Accessed 12 June 2010
Transcript of President Bush's address to a joint session of Congress on Thursday night, 20 September 2001 (21 September 2001). CNN. http://archives.cnn.com/2001/US/09/20/gen.bush.transcript. Accessed 8 January 2010
Turkey launches major land offensive into Northern Iraq (22 February 2008). Reuters. http://uk.reuters.com/article/idUKL22614485._CH_.242020080222. Accessed 3 June 2010
UN team finds Iraq has illegal missiles (13 February 2003). Guardian. www.guardian.co.uk/world/2003/feb/13/iraq.garyyounge. Accessed 21 March 2010
UN weapons inspectors arrive in Iraq (18 November 2002). Guardian. www.guardian.co.uk/world/2002/nov/18/iraq. Accessed 21 March 2010
US combat mission in Iraq ends (31 August 2010). CNN. http://articles.cnn.com/2010-08-31/politics/iraq.us_1_training-of-iraqi-security-iraqi-violence-united-states-and-iraq?_s=PM:POLITICS. Accessed 15 October 2010

US rejects Taliban offer to try bin Laden (7 October 2001). CNN. http://archives.cnn.com/2001/US/10/07/ret.us.taliban. Accessed 8 January 2010

Others

Battle Summary No. 1: Operations against the French Fleet at Mers-el-Kebir, 3–6 July 1940. HMS Hood Reference Materials, Doc. AIR 234/317. www.hmshood.org.uk/reference/official/adm234/adm234-317.htm. Accessed 5 June 2009

NATO Press Release (12 September 2001). http://www.nato.int/docu/pr/2001/p01-124e.htm. Accessed 10 January 2010

Report of the Independent International Fact-Finding Mission on the Conflict in Georgia, Vol. 2 (September 2009). http://www.ceiig.ch/Report.html. Accessed 2 June 2010

Table of Cases

International Court of Justice

Armed Activities on the Territory of the Congo (Democratic Republic of the Congo v. Uganda), Judgment of 19 December 2005, ICJ Rep. (2005)
Legal Consequences of the Construction of a Wall in the Occupied Palestinian Territory, Advisory Opinion of 9 July 2004, ICJ Rep. (2004)
Legality of the Threat or Use of Nuclear Weapons, Advisory Opinion of 8 July 1996, ICJ Rep. (1996)
Military and Paramilitary Activities in and Against Nicaragua (Nicaragua v. United States of America), Judgment of 27 June 1986, ICJ Rep. (1986)
Oil Platforms (Islamic Republic of Iran v. United States of America), Judgment of 6 November 2003, ICJ Rep. (2003)

International Criminal Tribunal for the Former Yugoslavia

Prosecutor v. Dusko Tadić, ICTY Case No. IT-94-1-A, Judgment, Appeals Chamber, 15 July 1999

International Military Tribunals

Nazi Conspiracy and Aggression: Opinion and Judgment (1947) Office of the United States Chief of Counsel for the Prosecution of Axis Criminality, Government Printing Office, Washington, D.C
Trial of Japanese War Criminals (1946) US Government Printing Office, Washington, D.C
Trial of the Major War Criminals before the International Military Tribunal: Proceedings, Vol. 3. http://avalon.law.yale.edu/imt/12-04-45.asp. Accessed 13 March 2009
Trial of the Major War Criminals before the International Military Tribunal: Proceedings, Vol. 14. http://avalon.law.yale.edu/imt/05-22-46.asp. Accessed 13 March 2009

K. Tibori Szabó, *Anticipatory Action in Self-Defence*, DOI: 10.1007/978-90-6704-796-8,

Index

MIX
Papier aus verantwortungsvollen Quellen
Paper from responsible sources
FSC® C105338

If you have any concerns about our products,
you can contact us on
ProductSafety@springernature.com

In case Publisher is established outside the EU,
the EU authorized representative is:
Springer Nature Customer Service Center GmbH
Europaplatz 3, 69115 Heidelberg, Germany

Printed by Libri Plureos GmbH
in Hamburg, Germany